DEFENDING DRINKING AND DRIVING CASES

2008

Alan D. Gold
Barrister

THOMSON
CARSWELL™

Canadian Cataloguing in Publication Data
Library and Archives Canada has catalogued this publication as follows:

Gold, Alan D.
Defending drinking and driving cases / Alan D. Gold.

Annual.
1993-
ISSN 1189-7473
ISBN 978-0-7798-1552-4 (2008 edition)

1. Drunk driving—Canada. 2. Defense (Criminal procedure)—Canada. I. Title.

KE2114.G65 345.71'0247 C94-300346-6
KF2231.G65

The acid-free paper used in this publication meets the minimum requirements of American National Standard for Information Sciences – Permanence of Paper for Printed Library Materials, ANSI Z39.48-1984.

Composition: Computer Composition of Canada Inc.
Content Editor: Amy Urquhart, B.A.

THOMSON
CARSWELL

One Corporate Plaza, 2075 Kennedy Road, Toronto, Ontario M1T 3V4
Customer Service:
Toronto 1-416-609-3800
Elsewhere in Canada/U.S. 1-800-387-5164
Fax 1-416-298-5094

Summary Table of Contents

For a detailed Table of Contents, see page v.

Introduction 1

Chapter 1: The Initial Telephone Call 3

Chapter 2: The Initial Interview 13

Chapter 3: Preparation 17

Chapter 4: Approved Screening Device Tests 23

Chapter 5: Breathalyzer Tests 49

Chapter 6: Blood Tests 75

Chapter 7: Proof of Impairment 83

Chapter 8: Proof of Excessive Blood Alcohol Level: "Over '80" 129

Chapter 9: Proof: Operation (Driving) 137

Chapter 10: Proof: Care or Control 139

Chapter 11: Causing Bodily Harm or Death 147

Chapter 12: Proof: Motor Vehicle, etc. 149

Chapter 13: The Defence 151

Chapter 14: Sentencing 165

Appendices 185

Index 315

Table of Contents

Table of Cases xi
Introduction 1

Chapter 1
THE INITIAL TELEPHONE CALL

1.1 STRUCTURING THE CALL 3
1.2 NOTES 3
1.3 PRIVACY 4
1.4 INITIAL INFORMATION 5
1.5 ADVICE 6
    1.5.1 Mandatory Testing/Right to Refuse 6
    1.5.2 Reasonable and Probable Grounds/Two Hour Limit 7
    1.5.3 Refusal to Blow 8
    1.5.4 Medical Samples 8
    1.5.5 Signs of Intoxication 9
    1.5.6 Release and After 9
    1.5.7 Client's Notes 10
1.6 CONVERSATION WITH THE POLICE 10

Chapter 2
THE INITIAL INTERVIEW

2.1 GENERAL 13
2.2 INFORMATION TO OBTAIN 13
2.3 DOCUMENTS 15
2.4 FUTURE OBLIGATIONS 15

Chapter 3
PREPARATION

3.1 EXAMINE DOCUMENTATION 17
3.2 INTERVIEW WITNESSES 17
3.3 INTERVIEW COUNSEL 17
3.4 TOXICOLOGIST'S REPORT 18
3.5 CHARGE(S) 18
3.6 DISCLOSURE 18
3.7 DRIVING RECORD 19
3.8 ACCIDENT REPORT 20
3.9 FURTHER PREPARATION 20
3.10 PROOF OF THE ELEMENTS OF THE OFFENCE 20

Chapter 4
APPROVED SCREENING DEVICE TESTS

4.1 REASONABLE SUSPICION ALCOHOL IN BODY 23
4.1.1 Roadside Questioning and Testing 26
4.2 FORTHWITH 29
4.3 RIGHT TO COUNSEL 34
4.4 REFUSAL 36
4.5 CONDUCTING TESTS 38
4.5.1 Proper Machine 38
4.5.2 Properly Calibrated 41
4.5.3 Properly Operated 42
4.6 OUTCOME OF TEST 45
4.6.1 Pass 45
4.6.2 Warn 45
4.6.3 Fail 45

Chapter 5
BREATHALYZER TESTS

5.1 REASONABLE GROUNDS 49
5.2 FORTHWITH OR AS SOON AS PRACTICABLE 51
5.3 RIGHT TO COUNSEL 52
5.3.1 Information Regarding Immediate, Free Duty Counsel Advice 57
5.3.2 Exclusion of Breathalyzer Evidence 59
5.3.3 'Holding Off' If Duty Counsel Unavailable 61
5.3.4 Waiver 63
5.3.5 Counsel of Choice 66
5.4 REFUSAL 70
5.5 CONDUCTING TESTS 72
5.6 BREATH TEMPERATURES 74

Chapter 6
BLOOD TESTS

6.1 REASONABLE GROUNDS 75
6.2 PROPER DEMAND 76
6.3 FORTHWITH OR AS SOON AS PRACTICABLE 76
6.4 RIGHT TO COUNSEL 77
6.5 REFUSAL 78
6.6 CONDUCTING TESTS 79
6.7 WARRANTS TO OBTAIN BLOOD SAMPLES 80

Chapter 7
PROOF OF IMPAIRMENT

7.1 ADMISSION 84
7.2 NATURE OF DRIVING 85
7.2.1 Accident 86
7.3 PHYSICAL SYMPTOMS 87
7.3.1 Bloodshot and/or Watery Eyes 88
7.3.2 Flushed Face 88
7.3.3 Odour of Alcohol 89
7.3.4 Unsteady on Feet 89
7.3.5 Slurred Speech 89
7.3.6 Police Evidence 90
7.4 PHYSICAL TESTS 91
7.5 OPINION OF POLICE OFFICER OR OTHERS 91
7.6 VIDEOTAPES 91
7.7 APPROVED SCREENING DEVICE "FAIL" RESULT 92
7.8 SPECIAL SECTION: THE NEW AMENDMENTS 92
7.8.1 Developments 114
7.9 BLOOD ALCOHOL READINGS 118
7.9.1 Breathalyzer Readings 118
(a) Breathalyzer Readings to Blood Alcohol Level at Material Time 121
(i) Method I: Breathalyzer Readings Plus Presumption Back 121
(ii) Method II: Breathalyzer Readings Plus Expert Testimony Relating Back 124
(b) Effect of Blood Alcohol Level at Material Time 124
7.9.2 Blood Test Readings 124
(a) Blood Test Results to Blood Alcohol Level at Material Time 126
(i) Method I: Blood Test Readings Plus Presumption Back 126
(ii) Method II: Blood Test Readings Plus Expert Testimony Relating Back 128
(b) Effect of Blood Alcohol Level at Material Time 128

Chapter 8
PROOF OF EXCESSIVE BLOOD ALCOHOL LEVEL: "OVER '80"

8.1 BREATHALYZER READINGS 129
8.1.1 Breathalyzer Readings to Blood Alcohol Level at Material Time 130

(a) Method I: Breathalyzer Readings Plus Presumption Back 131
(b) Method II: Breathalyzer Readings Plus Expert Testimony Relating Back 132
8.2 BLOOD TEST READINGS 132
8.2.1 Blood Test Results to Blood Alcohol Level at Material Time 134
(a) Method I: Blood Test Readings Plus Presumption Back 134
(b) Method II: Blood Test Readings Plus Expert Testimony Relating Back 136

Chapter 9
PROOF: OPERATION (DRIVING)

9.1 ADMISSIONS 137
9.2 OTHER WITNESSES 138
9.3 OWNERSHIP 138

Chapter 10
PROOF: CARE OR CONTROL

10.1 GENERAL 139
10.2 ADMISSIONS 144
10.3 OTHER WITNESSES 145
10.4 OWNERSHIP 146

Chapter 11
CAUSING BODILY HARM OR DEATH

11.1 CAUSATION 147

Chapter 12
PROOF: MOTOR VEHICLE, ETC.

12.1 GENERAL 149

Chapter 13
THE DEFENCE

13.1 GENERAL 151
13.1.1 Essential Elements of the Offence to be Established by the Prosecution 151
13.1.2 Defence Evidence Disproving an Element of the Offence 153
(a) "Last Drink" Defence 153

(b) "*Carter*" Defence 154
13.2 "EVIDENCE TO THE CONTRARY" 155
13.3 POST-DRIVING CONSUMPTION 157
13.4 INDEPENDENT BLOOD SAMPLE ANALYSIS 157
13.5 PRACTICE TIP: EXPERT EVIDENCE IN WRITING 158
13.6 VARIOUS CHARTER ISSUES 160
13.6.1 Disclosure 160
(a) Test Ampoule 160
(b) Video 160
(c) Machine Manuals and Records 161
13.6.2 Unlawful Arrests and Searches 161
13.6.3 Arbitrary Detention 162
13.6.4 Abuse of Process 162
13.6.5 Trial Procedures 162
13.6.6 Unconstitutional Sentences 163

Chapter 14
SENTENCING

14.1 FINES AND IMPRISONMENT 165
14.1.1 Sentencing Factors 166
14.1.2 Where Bodily Harm or Death is Caused 168
14.2 CURATIVE DISCHARGES 169
14.3 CONDITIONAL SENTENCES 171
14.4 LICENSE PROHIBITION ORDERS 175
14.4.1 Criminal Code Driving Prohibition Orders 175
14.4.2 Provincial License Suspensions 177
14.4.3 Ignition Interlock Device Program 179
14.5 PROBATION 179
14.6 FORFEITURE OF AUTOMOBILE 180
14.7 STAY PENDING APPEAL 181

APPENDICES

APPENDIX A: Record of Information from Initial Interview 185
APPENDIX B: Disclosure Request 187
APPENDIX C: Regulations 189
APPENDIX D: Provincial Licence Suspensions:
Alberta, *Traffic Safety Act*, R.S.A. 2000, c. T-6, sections 31, 64(r), 82-85, 87-90, 92-94, 96-100, 172-175, 179-181, 189, 190 and the Schedule 193
British Columbia, *Motor Vehicle Act*, R.S.B.C. 1996, c. 318, sections 1 (in part), 25.1, 89, 90.1–90.4, 93, 94.1–94.6, 95–104, 105.1–105.3, 105.5, 105.9, 215–215.4, 224–229, 232, 233, and 241–248 214

Ontario, *Highway Traffic Act*, R.S.O. 1990, c. H.8, sections 41, 41.1–41.3, 42–44, 46, 47(1), 47.1, 48, 48.1–48.3, 50.1–50.3, 55.1 and 198.5. 251
APPENDIX E: Notice and Certificates 291
APPENDIX F: Charges 295
APPENDIX G: Alcohol Influence Report 305
APPENDIX H: Blood Alcohol Content Report 307
APPENDIX I: Driver Record Search... 313
INDEX 315

Table of Cases

[All references are to section numbers of the Guide.]

Carpenter v. R. 14.2.2,14.7
Dennis v. British Columbia (Superintendent of Motor Vehicles) .... 7.9.1(a), 8.1.1
Horsefield v. Ontario (Registrar of Motor Vehicles) 14.4.2
R. v. A. (D.) 14.1
R. v. Abercrombie 13.3
R. v. Abraham 14.1.2
R. v. Adamson 14.6
R. v. Adustini 7.9.1
R. v. Aghaei 5.3.4
R. v. Ahenakew 14.2
R. v. Alton 14.2
R. v. Altseimer 5.2, 6.3
R. v. Amendt 10.1
R. v. Andrew 11.1
R. v. Andrews 7
R. v. Angel 11.1
R. v. Angell 5.1
R. v. Appapillai 10.1
R. v. Arrechea .... 13.1.2(b)
R. v. Arsenault 4.5.1
R. v. Arthurs 4.5.2
R. v. Ashberry 14.2
R. v. Bacon 4.3
R. v. Bailey 10.1
R. v. Baker 14.3
R. v. Balla 5.1
R. v. Ballem 13.1.2
R. v. Baradaran-Aghaei ..... 7.9.1(a)(i)
R. v. Barber 10.1
R. v. Barrick .... 7.9.1(a)(i)
R. v. Bartle 5.3
R. v. Bath 14.1.2
R. v. Baumber 10.1
R. v. Beaulieu 14.2
R. v. Beech 4.5.2, 4.5.3, 4.6.3
R. v. Beeching 4.5.2
R. v. Beierl 5.5
R. v. Benoit 10.1
R. v. Benson 4.3
R. v. Benincasa .... 13.6.1(b)
R. v. Berkach 14.7
R. v. Bernshaw 3.6, 4.2, 4.6.3, 7.7
R. v. Best 14.3
R. v. Beston 4.1.1
R. v. Bettridge 14.3
R. v. Biasiotto .... 13.6.1(b)
R. v. Beierl 5.5
R. v. Billette 4.2
R. v. Bird 10.1
R. v. Bishop 10.1
R. v. Bishop (2002) (N.S. Prov. Ct.) ... 4.1.1
R. v. Bissonnette 13.6.2
R. v. Black 4.6.2
R. v. Blackett 5.3.5
R. v. Blacklock .... 7.9.1(a)(i)
R. v. Bleau 10.1
R. v. Bloom 5.3.5
R .v. Bogdala 14.2
R. v. Bond (2006) (N.S. Prov. Ct.) 4.3
R. v. Bond (2008) (Man. Q.B.) ... 10.1
R. v. Boone .... 5.2, 6.3, 7.9.1(a)(i)
R. v. Boothby 14.1.1
R. v. Bormotko .... 13.6.1(b)
R. v. Borris .... 7.9.1(a)(i), 8.1.1(a)
R. v. Boucher .... 13.1.2(b)
R. v. Bouchey 5.3.1
R. v. Boudreau 10.1
R. v. Boulanger 4.2
R. v. Boutamine 4.2
R. v. Bowden 4.5.2
R. v. Bowie 4.1
R. v. Boyd 10.1, 14.3
R. v. Brala 10.1
R. v. Bray 13.2
R. v. Bridgeman 4.2, 4.5.3
R. v. Brouillette 5.3.5
R. v. Brown 14.1.1
R. v. Brydges 5.3, 5.3.1
R. v. Buchanan 4.5.1

R. v. Buckingham 10.1
R. v. Buckley 10.1
R. v. Budgell 5.3
R. v. Buffalo 5.3.5
R. v. Burbella 10.1
R. v. Buffi 14.3
R. v. Burley 1.3, 5.3
R. v. Burns (1993) (Sask. Prov. Ct.) 10.1
R. v. Burns (2002) (Alta. Q.B.) 4.2
R. v. Butler 1.3, 5.3
R. v. Byers 5.4
R. v. Callan 14.3
R. v. Cameron 4.4, 5.4, 7.3
R. v. Campbell (1988) (Ont. C.A.) 4.1
R. v. Campbell (1997) (Nfld. T.D.) 14.3
R. v. Campbell (2008) (Ont. S.C.J.) 4.4
R. v. Campbell (Sask. Prov. Ct.) 5.3.5
R. v. Caprarie-Melville 5.2, 6.3
R. v. Carey .... 5.2, 7.9.1(a)(i)
R. v. Carr 14.3
R. v. Carrie 7
R. v. Carroll 5.3
R. v. Carter .... 13.1.2(b)
R. v. Cassidy 5.3.4
R. v. Chance 4.4, 5.5, 6.6
R. v. Chapman 14.3
R. v. Charette 7.9.1
R. v. Chartrand 5.3.4, 10.1
R. v. Chekaluk 4.1
R. v. Chechel .... 13.6.1(b)
R. v. Checkley 14.1
R. v. Chisholm 14.1
R. v. Christie 10.1
R. v. Clark 5.3.5
R. v. Clarke (1997) 10.1
R. v. Clarke (2004) 4.3
R. v. Claus 14.7
R. v. Colak 5.3
R. v. Colbourne 4.5.2
R. v. Cobham 5.3
R. v. Cole 14.7
R. v. Colin 14.3
R. v. Cornelio 5.3.1
R. v. Cote 4.2, 4.3
R. v. Coulter 4.1.1
R. v. Court 7.3
R. v. Coutts .... 4.1.1, 4.6.3 ,7.7
R. v. Cove 4.3, 10.1
R. v. Crayne .... 13.1.2(b),13.2
R. v. Crawford 7, 7.9
R. v. Cresswell 4.1.1
R. v. Cromwell 14.3
R. v. Cunningham (1998) 14.1.2
R. v. Cunningham (2006) 14.7
R. v. Cutknife 5.3.5
R. v. Czorny 5.3
R. v. Daniels .... 7.9.1(a)(ii)
R. v. Danychuk 4.2
R. v. Davidson (1998) (N.S. S.C.) ...... 7.9.1(a)(ii), 8.2.1(b)
R. v. Davidson (2005) (Ont. S.C.J.) .... 7.9.1(a)(i)
R. v. Davison 14.3
R. v. Dearden 4.1
R. v. Decker 10.1
R. v. Deprez 11.1
R. v. Deruelle 5.1
R. v. Desrosiers 5.3.4
R. v. Dewald (*sub nom. R. v. Pierman*) 4.3
R. v. Dhaliwal 5.3.5
R. v. Dhillon 4.5.1
R. v. Dionne 7.9.1
R. v. Diotte 10.1
R. v. DiRuggiero (*sub nom. R. v. Diruggiero*) 4.3, 4.4
R. v. Dixon 5.3.1
R. v. Doell .... 13.1.2(b), 13.3
R. v. Doerksen 14.1.1
R. v. Dol 5.5
R. v. Dosa 10.1
R. v. Doust 14.3
R. v. Dubeau 5.3.1
R. v. Ducai 10.1
R. v. Dunham 4.5.1
R. v. Duplessis 7.9.1
R. v. Durnie .... 13.1.2(b)
R. v. Dyer 5.3.2
R. v. Earle 14.2
R. v. Eddingfield 13.3
R. v. Egger .... 7.9.2(a)(i), 8.2.1(a)

R. v. Einarson 4.2, 4.5.3
R. v. Ellinas 5.5
R. v. Ellsworth 14.2
R. v. Elvikis 7
R. v. Embry 5.1
R. v. Enright .... 13.1.2(b)
R. v. Enright 13.2
R. v. Euler 5.6
R. v. Evans 5.1
R. v. Ewart 11.1, 14.1
R. v. F. (D.L.) 14.1
R. v. Faulkner 13.6.4
R. v. Fehrenbach 4.5.3
R. v. Fetterley 4.1
R. v. Fisher (1992) (B.C. C.A.) 5.2, 6.3, 11.1, 14.1
R. v. Fisher (2000) (Ont. C.A.) ... 14.3
R. v. Fisher (2003) (Ont. S.C.J.) 14.3
R. v. Fisher (2006) (Ont. S.C.J.) ... 5.2
R. v. Fitzsimmons 1.6
R. v. Flores 4.1.1
R. v. Ford 10.1
R. v. Forsberg 5.1
R. c. Fortin 14.3
R. v. Forward 14.3
R. v. Franklin 5.1
R. v. Fraser 4.1
R. v. Froman 14.1.2
R. v. Furry 5.2, 6.3
R. v. Gaboury 14.1.2
R. v. Gairdner 7
R. v. Geerligs (1994) 7.3.6
R. v. Geerligs (1995) 7
R. v. Geoffroy 10.1
R. v. Gerrard 10.1
R. v. Gibson 13.3
R. v. Gilbert .... 1.3, 5.3, 13.1.2(b)
R. v. Gillis 4.5.1
R. v. Ginman 4.1, 5.3.3
R. v. Godfree 14.3
R. v. Gokul 4.6.3, 7.7
R. v. Gomes 14.1.2
R. v. Good 4.1
R. v. Goodline 5.3
R. v. Goulais 14.3
R. v. Graat 7.5
R. v. Graham 7.7
R. v. Grant 4.2, 4.3
R. v. Gratto 5.4, 6.5
R. v. Green (1989) (Alta. C.A.) .. 10.1
R. v. Green (1992) (S.C.C.) 6.2
R. v. Green (2005) (B.C. Prov. Ct.) 7.2.1
R. v. Greenan 10.1
R. v. Greene 1.3
R. v. Grimston 5.3.5
R. v. Grosse .. 7.9.1(a)(ii), 7.9.2(a)(ii), 8.1.1(b), 8.2.1(b)
R. v. Gundy 4.5.2, 7.9.1
R. v. Grover 10.1
R. v. Haas 5.1
R. v. Hadaway 7.3
R. v. Hakkarainen .... 13.6.1(b)
R. v. Hal 5.5
R. v. Halkett 11.1
R. v. Hall 7.9.1
R. v. Hannemann 10.1
R. v. Hanson 5.3.5
R. v. Harper 5.3
R. v. Hayward 14.1.2
R. v. Heimlick 4.1.1
R. v. Hendel 4.1
R. v. Hergott 7.9.1
R. v. Hesketh .... 5.2, 6.3, 7.9.1(a)(i)
R. v. Hey 4.1
R. v. Hibbs 10.1
R. v. Higgins 5.1
R. v. Hill 5.5
R. v. Hilton 4.4
R. v. Hines 4.4, 5.4, 6.6
R. v. Hisch 5.3
R. v. Hiscock 5.3.1
R. v. Hoffmer .... 7.9, 13.1.2(b)
R. v. Hogan .... 7.9.1(a)(i)
R. v. Holloway 14.7
R. v. Holman 7.3
R. v. Holt 4.4, 5.4
R. v. Howard 14.1.2
R. v. Hubbard 4.6.3
R. v. Huff 4.1.1
R. v. Hughes 13.3
R. v. Hurulak 4.2
R. v. I. (L.R.) 5.3.4
R. v. Iakouchev .... 13.6.1(b)
R. v. Ikuta 5.3
R. v. Ingram 10.1

R. v. J.J.A. 4.6.3
R. v. Jackson (1993) 14.2
R. v. Jackson (2005) 7.9.1, 14.3
R. v. Jalbert 4.2
R. v. Jauzen 4.3
R. v. Jay 14.7
R. v. Jedig 13.1
R. v. Jeerh 14.2
R. v. Jensen 4.3
R. v. Johal 10.1
R. v. Johnson 10.1
R. v. Jones 7
R. v. Kaczala 14.5
R. v. Kagayalingam 7.9.1
R. v. Kahlan 4.3
R. v. Kallu 4.5.3, 4.6.3
R. v. Kalyniak 14.2
R. v. Karnakov 5.3
R. v. Katwaru 5.2
R. v. Kawai 10.1
R. v. Keagan 5.3.5
R. v. Kearsey 4.6.2
R. v. Keeshig 5.3.4
R. v. Kelly 5.1
R. v. Khotar 4.1, 5.3.5
R. v. Kidson 10.1
R. v. King .... 7.9.1(a)(i)
R. v. Knott 5.3.4
R. v. Knox 6.1
R. v. Konyk .... 7.9.1(a)(i)
R. v. Kosa 4.5.1
R. v. Koszman 4.3
R. v. Kowalchuk 5.3.5
R. v. Koziolek 10.1
R. v. Kumarasamy 5.3.5
R. v. Kuokkanen 10.1
R. v. Kutash 5.2, 6.3
R. v. Kutsukake 14.3
R. v. Kyle 14.3
R. v. Lacey .... 4.5.1, 4.6.3, 7.7, 7.9.1(a)(ii), 7.9.2(a)(ii), 8.1.1(b), 8.2.1(b)
R. v. Lafleur 10.1
R. c. Laford 14.3
R. v. Landes 7, 7.3
R. v. Landolt 5.3
R. v. Larocque 11.1, 14.1
R. v. Latimer 5.3.1
R. v. Law 4.6.3
R. v. Lawrence 4.5.3
R. v. Laybourne 7.9.1, 7.9.2, 8.2
R. v. Laycock 14.2.1, 14.4.1
R. v. LeBrun 4.5.1
R. v. Legrove 10.1
R. v. Lesmeister 5.2, 6.3
R. v. Letestu 10.1
R. v. Letford .... 7, 7.9, 7.9.1(a)(i)
R. v. Leung 13.6.1
R. v. Lewis 13.6.3
R. v. Li .... 13.6.1(b)
R. v. Lieskovsky 4.1.1, 4.6.3, 7.7
R. v. Lilek .... 13.1.2(b)
R. v. Linstead 7
R. v. Litwin .... 5.2, 6.3, 7.9.1(a)(i)
R. v. Lockerby 10.1, 14.7
R. v. Logan 14.3
R. v. Loubier 10.1
R. v. Lui 5.5
R. v. Luong 5.3
R. v. M. (S.) 5.3.4
R. v. MacAulay 10.1
R. v. MacCormack (*sub nom. R. v. McCormick*) 14.4.2
R. v. MacCormack (2000) (N.B. C.A.) 14.2
R. v. MacDonald 13.3
R. v. MacDonald (1998) (N.S. S.C.) ... 7
R. v. MacDonald (1999) (Man. C.A.) .. 14.3
R. v. MacDonald (2006) (Alta. P.C.) ... 7.9.1(a)(i)
R. v. MacKay 5.3.5
R. v. Mackinnon 7.9.1, 7.9.2, 8.2
R. v. MacPherson 4.2
R. v. Madden 10.1
R. v. Maghdoori 13.6.1
R. v. Mahoney 5.3.5
R. v. Mallery 10.1
R. v. Malmholt 1.3, 5.3
R. v. Manyshots 14.2
R. v. Marcellus 5.5
R. v. Markovski 5.3.5
R. v. Maria 5.3.2
R. v. Martin 14.1.2
R. v. Martindale 10.1

R. v. Mastromartino (2003) 4.5.3
R. v. Mastromartino (2004) 4.2, 4.5.3
R. v. Matar 4.2
R. v. Matheson 5.3
R. v. Maynard 14.1.2, 14.3
R. v. Maxwell .... 13.6.1(b)
R. v. McClelland 5.1
R. v. McCue 10.1
R. v. McCullough 4.2
R. v. McDarby 4.1
R. v. McDougall 13.1.2
R. v. McGilvey 5.3.4
R. v. McGee 14.2.2
R. v. McKane 1.3, 5.3
R. v. McKelvey 1.4, 5.4
R. v. McKenzie 14.3, 5.3.2
R. v. McLinden 5.3.5
R. v. McMahon 14.1.2, 7.7
R. v. McNab 10.1
R. v. McPhee 14.2
R. v. McPherson 14.7
R. v. Meathrell 14.3
R. v. Mehta 4.5.1, 4.6.3
R. v. Mercer 14.3
R. v. Mercer (2006) 7.3.6
R. v. Merkley 10.1
R. v. Merrill 14.3
R. v. Meston 5.3.5
R. v. Middlebrook 13.6.6
R. v. Miller 7
R. v. Milne 4.1.1
R. v. Minter 5.4
R. v. Miron 10.1
R. v. Mischaud 14.3
R. v. Mitruk 4.1
R. v. Mittleholt 4.3
R. v. Moffatt 10.1
R. v. Moreau (1979) (S.C.C.) 13.2
R. v. Moreau (1998) (Sask. Q.B.) 10.1
R. v. Morey 10.1
R. v. Moric 7, 7.3
R. v. Morris 14.1
R. v. Moser 4.4, 5.4
R. v. Morton 5.5
R. v. Mould 14.3
R. v. Murji .... 7.9.1(a), 8.1.1(a), 8.2.1(b), 13.1
R. v. Murphy 14.7
R. v. Murtaugh 10.1
R. v. N. (B.A.) 14.1.2
R. v. Negridge 14.1
R. v. Neil Campbell .... 13.6.1(b)
R. v. Nicholson 14.1
R. v. Nielsen 10.1
R. v. Nolan 7
R. v. Noonan 7.3
R. v. Norwood 4.4, 5.4
R. v. Novais 7.5
R. v. O'Brien 14.2.2, 14.6
R. v. O'Flynn 7.9.1
R. v. Ogrodnick 10.1
R. v. Oldham 4.1.1
R. v. Orme 4.1
R. v. Parks 5.3.2
R. v. Parrill 1.3, 5.3
R. v. Patel 13.1
R. v. Pawluk .... 7.9.1(a), 8.1.1(b)
R. v. Paz 4.4, 5.4
R. v. Pec 11.1
R. v. Peill 10.1
R. v. Pendleton 13.1.2
R. v. Persichetti .... 13.6.1(b)
R. v. Peters 4.5.2
R. v. Peterson 5.3.1, 11.1
R. v. Petri 13.6.2
R. v. Petrie 5.1
R. v. Petrick 4.5.1
R. v. Petruk 4.6
R. v. Pharai 10.1
R. v. Phillip 13.6.1s
R. v. Phillips 5.2, 6.3
R. v. Phinney 4.4, 5.4
R. v. Phoenix 13.6.5
R. v. Pidwerbesky 5.3, 5.3.2
R. v. Pierman (*sub nom. R. v. Dewald*) 3.6, 4.1, 4.2
R. v. Pilon 10.1
R. v. Pineau 4.1.1
R. v. Pinske 11.1
R. v. Pittman 14.1.2
R. v. Place 14.3
R. v. Playford 1.3, 5.3
R. v. Polischuk 4.5.3

R. v. Ponte 4.5.2
R. v. Poulos 10.1
R. v. Powell 5.5
R. v. Pozniak 5.3
R. v. Prosper 5.3
R. v. Pruski .... 4.5.2, 7.9.1(a)(i)
R. v. Purdon 5.2, 6.3
R. v. Quiring ...... 7.9.1(a)(ii), 8.2.1(b)
R. v. Quong 4.3
R. v. Ralph 5.3
R. v. Randell 7, 7.9
R. v. Raven 7
R. v. Redding 4.3
R. v. Redondo 10.1
R. v. Reed 14.7
R. v. Richardson 4.5.3, 4.6.3, 5.4
R. v. Riley 7.9.1
R. v. Rishy-Mararaj 10.1
R. v. Ritson 5.3
R. v. Rhyason 5.1
R. v. Roasting 14.1.2
R. v. Robinson 4.6.3, 7.7
R. v. Rodriquez 4.1
R. v. Rohrich 5.1
R. v. Rooney 5.3.5
R. c. Rousseau 10.1
R. v. Roy 14.1.1
R. v. Rulli 4.4, 7.3
R. v. Russell 5.3.5
R. v. Ryland 5.3.5
R. v. Ryrak 5.3
R. v. Samuels 13.6.2
R. v. Sanghera 13.6.6
R. v. Santa Maria 5.3, 5.3.2
R. v. Sawatsky 5.3.4
R. v. Schmidt 4.1, 4.2
R. v. Schouten .... 7.9.1(a)(i)
R. v. Schroepfler 6.1, 6.4
R. v. Scott 7.3
R. v. Scurr 4.5.2, 13.6.2
R. v. Scurvey 5.1
R. v. Seabrook 5.1
R. v. Searle 5.1
R. v. Sears 7.3
R. v. Sedore 10.1
R. v. Seed 5.2, 6.3
R. v. Seo 4.6.3, 7.7
R. v. Sever 13.6.5
R. v. Sharun 10.1
R. v. Shave 14.3
R. v. Sheppard 14.4.1
R. v. Sherbrook 10.1
R. v. Sherlock 14.1.2
R. v. Shin .... 7.9.1(a)(i)
R. v. Shore 14.3
R. v. Shorter .... 13.6.1(b)
R. v. Shular 4.6.3
R. v. Shuparski 10.1
R. v. Sigiannis 7.9.1
R. v. Simmons 13.6.3
R. v. Singer 7.3
R. v. Singh (2000) 4.2, 4.3
R. v. Singh (2004) 14.3
R. v. Singh (2005) .... 13.6.1(b)
R. v. Singhal 11.1
R. v. Sisetsk 7.9.1
R. v. Skolnick 14.1
R. v. Skwara 4.1
R. v. Sleep .... 7.9.1(a)(i)
R. v. Sleno 10.1
R. v. Small 5.3.4
R. v. Smalridge 5.3.4
R. v. Smith (1992) (Alta. C.A.) 7
R. v. Smith (1993) (B.C. C.A.) 14.2.2, 14.7
R. v. Smith (1996) (Ont. C.A.) .. 4.1.1
R. v. Smith (1997) (Alta. Prov. Ct.) .... 7.9.1(a)(ii), 8.2.1(b)
R. v. Smith (1997) (Ont. Prov. Div.) ... 4.1
R. v. Smith (1998) (Ont. Gen. Div.) 14.3
R. v. Smith (2002) (O.C.J.) 4.1
R. v. Smith (Ont. Gen. Div.) 5.4
R. v. Snider .... 13.1.2(b)
R. v. Somers 14.1.2
R. v. Snow 10.1
R. v. Sousa .... 13.1.2(b)
R. v. Spanos 5.5
R. v. Springer 13.1.2
R. v. St. Pierre 13.2, 13.3
R. v. Steinhauser 5.3.5
R. v. Stellato 7
R. v. Stenset 1.6
R. v. Stephenson 10.1
R. v. Stevenson 4.1.1

R. v. Stewart 4.1
R. v. Storr 14.1.2, 14.2
R. v. Stubel 14.1.2
R. v. Sundquist 4.1.1
R. v. Suttie .... 13.1, 13.1.2(b)
R. v. Tavone 7.3.4
R. v. Taylor 5.4
R. v. Terrell 5.2, 6.3
R. v. Terzo .... 13.6.1(b)
R. v. Terzon .... 5.5, 13.6.1(b)
R. v. Tessier 4.5.1
R. v. Thibeault 5.5
R. v. Thompson (1998) 7
R. v. Thompson (2003) (Sask. Prov. Ct.) 4.1
R. v. Thomsen 4.3, 4.6.3, 7.7
R. v. Thulin 4.1
R. v. Toews 10.1
R. v. Toope 4.5.1, 4.6.3
R. v. Townsend 4.1.1
R. v. Tozer 14.1.1
R. v. Travers 14.3
R. v. Trecartin 7.2.1
R. v. Tremblay 4.1.1
R. v. Tricoteux 5.1
R. v. Trory 4.1
R. v. Truong 4.1
R. v. Ukrainetz 5.1
R. v. Valladares 14.3
R. v. Van Binnendyk 5.3.5
R. v. Vandale 5.3.5
R. v. Vanderbruggen .... 7.9.1(a)(i)
R. v. VanVliet 14.2
R. v. Vassie 4.5.3, 4.6.3
R. v. W. (D.) 4.1.1
R. v. Wackernagel 4.3
R. v. Waite 14.6
R. v. Walker .... 13.6.1(a)
R. v. Walkom 6.1
R. v. Wallace 14.1.2
R. v. Walton 10.1
R. v. Waterman 5.3.1
R. v. Watson 4.4, 5.4
R. v. Watson (2000) (Man. Prov. Ct.) .. 5.3
R. v. Webster 4.1
R. v. Weedon 5.3.4
R. v. Weir 5.4
R. v. Wentzell 7.3
R. v. Wheeler 10.1
R. v. White (1994) (N.S. C.A.) 7, 11.1
R. v. White (1997) (Ont. Prov. Div.) ... 7.9.1(a)
R. v. Whitesell 5.2, 6.3
R. v. Whitford 5.3
R. v. Whyte 10.1
R. v. Wilding 5.3.5
R. v. Williams .... 7.9.1(a)(i)
R. v. Wingerter 5.3.1
R. v. Wilson 4.2
R. v. Wilson (2006) 5.3.5
R. v. Wolowidnyk 4.3
R. v. Wong 7.6
R. v. Wood (2005) (Alta. Prov. Ct.) 14.3
R. v. Wood (2007) (Alta. Q.B.) 5.2
R. v. Woods 4.1, 4.1.1, 4.2, 4.6.3, 5.2, 7.8
R. v. Wren 4.4
R. v. Wydenes 5.3.1
R. v. Wynnychuk 13.1.2
R. v. Yakobchuk 10.1
R. v. Yerhoff 5.3.4
R. v. Yoshida 7.3
R. v. Young (1992) (Ont. C.A.) .. 5.3.4
R. v. Young (2005) (Alta. Prov. Ct.) ... 13.2
R. v. Yuen .... 7.9.1(a), 8.1.1(b)
R. v. Yuskow 4.3
R. v. Z. (C.W.) 4.4, 5.4
R. v. Zack 7.3.6
R. v. Zaidi 5.3.5
R. v. Zhu 13.6.1
R. v. Zoravkovic 4.1
Saunders v. R. 4.1.1, 10.1, 12.1
Woodhouse v. R. 13.1.2

Introduction

This manual is a basic guide to alert the reader to the relevant issues and authorities. Obviously, there is no substitute for exhaustive research in the caselaw reports.

Many of the cases cited below are found in *Drinking & Driving Law*. This monthly newsletter is written by Alan D. Gold and is published 10 times per year by Thomson Carswell. It is available by subscription.

The Appendices contain forms, statutory provisions and documents encountered when defending drinking and driving cases.

Legislative developments this year have resulted in a massive overhaul of the drinking and driving offence provisions. Bill C-2, *Tackling Violent Crime Act*, received Royal Assent on February 28, 2008 and the relevant provisions were proclaimed to come into force on July 2, 2008.

The major changes:

- Demand for screening and physical tests authorized for up to three hours after operation of a motor vehicle: s. 254(2).
- Physical tests for impairment by drugs and/or alcohol made compulsory for both. Screening demands: s. 254(2). Demands based on reasonable grounds that a person is impaired by alcohol and/or drugs and has operated a motor vehicle within three hours: s. 254(3.1).
- Evaluating officer (Drug Evaluation Officer) may make an approved instrument demand if there are reasonable grounds to suspect alcohol in person's body: s. 254(3.3).
- Bodily fluid demand to test for drugs upon failure of physical tests based on reasonable grounds: s. 254(3.4).
- Regulation making authority for qualifications and training for evaluating officers. Physical tests that may be conducted under s. 254(2)(a) and tests and procedures to be conducted during an evaluation under s. 254(3.1), s. 254.1.
- Minimum sentences increased. First offence—$1,000 minimum fine. Second offence—30 day minimum. Third offence—120 day minimum: s. 255(1)(a). Maximum sentence 18 months for summary conviction offence: s. 255(1)(c).
- New offences. Driving "over 80" causing bodily harm: s. 255(2.1) and

death: s. 255(3.2). Refusal to blow after causing accident resulting in bodily harm: s. 255(2.2).

Evidence:

- Evidence to the contrary defined as evidence of: Instrument malfunction or improper operation, to the extent that accurate reading would have shown accused's blood alcohol level was not over 80 at the time of the alleged offence: s. 258(1)(a) and (d). It is not to include evidence of alcohol consumption of accused, absorption and elimination rates of accused, or calculation based thereon of what accused's blood alcohol level would have been: s. 258(1)(d.01).
- Bolus and post offence drinking. Onus on accused to adduce evidence of drinking patterns such that would not have been over 80 at the time of the offence despite being over at the time of testing or sampling and drinking pattern must be consistent with blood alcohol level at the time of testing: s. 258(1)(d.1).
- Certified copy of print-out from approved instrument admissible as proof of the facts alleged in it: s. 258(1)(f.1).

This revision renders obsolete much of the decisional law in pursuit of making these offences easier for the Crown to prove. At the same time it renders obsolete the decisional case law that upheld the constitutionality of the various evidentiary provisions and presumption shortcuts available to the Crown. These issues will now all have to be re-litigated.

This year, new cases concerned sleeping drivers, the right to counsel of choice, the continuing debate as to the effect of the *Boucher* decision, the exclusion of breath test results under section 24(2) of the *Charter*, and the forfeiture of automobiles as offence related property upon conviction.

Cases available to June 30, 2008 are included.

1

THE INITIAL TELEPHONE CALL

When a client calls from the police station in circumstances where he or she requires advice concerning the offences that make up the subject matter of this Manual, or advice concerning matters such as breathalyzer breath tests or blood samples involved in the proof of such offences, it is often the middle of the night and a major inconvenience for counsel. Nevertheless, counsel's advice and actions during that initial and important telephone call may be crucial to an ultimately successful defence for the client.

1.1 STRUCTURING THE CALL

- Assume control of the conversation.

- Embark upon a carefully structured telephone interview to obtain the information that you need and to provide your client with the necessary professional advice to protect your client's rights and to preserve every benefit under the law to which he or she is entitled.

1.2 NOTES

- Make accurate notes concerning the entire conversation.

- Note the exact time the phone call commenced and was completed. *Do not overlook the fact that twice a year the time changes by one hour to and from daylight saving time.*

- Keep the original of the notes carefully secure.

- If the notes are transcribed, preserve the original contemporaneous notes and do not discard them.

- A small tape recorder can be kept handy to obviate note-taking as well as capture the client's actual voice and any relevant characteristics that might be demonstrated.

1.3 PRIVACY

- Make sure that your client is speaking in privacy.

- Find out the surrounding physical location from which the call is being placed and the whereabouts of any other persons, including police officers, who might be in a position to overhear the conversation.

- Ask about *any other persons*, not just police officers, so that civilian police employees are not overlooked by your client. *Clients will interpret all advice literally.*

- Advise your client of the right to privacy so that if anything changes during the course of your conversation your client will be alert to its significance and inform you accordingly.

- Ask your client to hand over the telephone to any officer violating the right to privacy so that you can request privacy directly if necessary.

- Ascertain the name and badge number of any officer spoken to and ask that a note of the request for privacy be made.

- Note any refusal of the right to converse in private and object that such constitutes a violation of the right to counsel, and therefore a reasonable excuse to refuse to provide breathalyzer breath test samples.

The accused must be afforded the right to consult counsel in private: *R. v. McKane* (1987), 49 M.V.R. 1, 58 C.R. (3d) 130, 35 C.C.C. (3d) 481 (Ont. C.A.). There is no requirement for the accused who is telephoning a lawyer while in police custody to request privacy: *R. v. Gilbert* (1988), 61 C.R. (3d) 149, 40 C.C.C. (3d) 423, 24 O.A.C. 150 (Ont. C.A.); *R. v. Playford* (1987), 61 C.R. (3d) 101, 40 C.C.C. (3d) 142, 63 O.R. (2d) 289 (Ont. C.A.). The failure of the detaining or arresting officer to advise a detained person that his right to retain and instruct counsel is a right to do so in privacy does not necessarily amount to a breach of the right of the detained person: *R. v. Butler* (1995), 104 C.C.C. (3d) 198, 68 B.C.A.C. 275, 112 W.A.C. 275 (B.C. C.A.), leave to appeal refused (1997), 105 C.C.C. (3d) vi (S.C.C.); *R. v. Parrill*, 38 M.V.R. (3d) 7, 169 Nfld. & P.E.I.R. 28, 58 C.R.R. (2d) 56, 1988 CarswellNfld 300.

The test to be applied in determining whether the accused was afforded privacy at the time of his arrest is a subjective one as to his belief as to whether or not he felt intimidated and therefore found it unwise as to whether or not he ought to freely discuss his problems with his lawyer; however, such belief should be based on reasonable grounds: *R. v. Malmholt* (1997), 29 M.V.R. (3d) 114, 32 O.T.C. 317, 1997 CarswellOnt 2367 (Ont. Gen. Div.). *R. v. Burley* (2004), 2004 CarswellOnt 523, [2004] O.J. No. 319, 49 M.V.R. (4th) 29, 181 C.C.C. (3d) 463, 182 O.A.C. 395, 115 C.R.R. (2d) 326 (Ont. C.A.) the right to privacy involved in s. 10(b) of the *Charter* was held not violated merely because accused had a "subjective and unreasonable belief that the call was not in private." In *R. v. Greene* (1999), 43 M.V.R. (3d) 13, 213 N.B.R. (2d) 68, 545 A.P.R. 68, 1999 CarswellNB 200 (N.B. C.A.), the accused's right to privately consult counsel was not infringed by the officer's ability to visually monitor the accused. Although the room was also equipped with an audio device, the switch was turned off.

1.4 INITIAL INFORMATION

- Obtain, and record accurately, the following information from the client:

    1. name
    2. address
    3. age and date of birth
    4. occupation
    5. telephone numbers at home and work
    6. family background (briefly)
    7. prior record, if any
    8. medical and physical condition
    9. if accident, any injuries
    10. mouth condition: dentures or other appliances
    11. consumption of alcohol: amount, time started, time finished
    12. consumption of food
    13. outline of events from initial police contact
    14. names and addresses of all witnesses to any or all of the relevant events
    15. language fluency

16. details of actions that may affect breath test results: burping, belching, vomiting, regurgitating, use of mouthwash, breath mints, smoking
17. any videotaping that has taken place
18. how the client is getting home and, in appropriate cases, invite the client to call again upon release.

1.5 ADVICE

If counsel does nothing else for a client or potential client who calls from the police station in this situation, the following advice alone may prove to be crucial.

Before giving advice consider an attempt to find out as much as possible from the arresting officer and/or the qualified technician. See section 1.6 ''Conversation With The Police'' below.

First and foremost advise your client that they are entitled to call you again if they wish to do so. There is no ''one phone call'' rule except on television. Thus, if they find they have questions about the advice given or are uncertain what to do or something unexpected or concerning arises they have the right to a second call for advice.

1.5.1 MANDATORY TESTING/RIGHT TO REFUSE

- Advise your client that all that is mandatory and required by law is the actual breath samples blown into the breathalyzer machine provided the officer had reasonable grounds for the demand. No questions need be answered and no physical tests need be performed. *This cannot be stressed enough to the client.*

- Advise if you can whether the officer did not have reasonable grounds, but advise a court may disagree and the decision to refuse is the client's.

- Warn your client and advise him or her about the right to refuse to answer or perform tests such as the following:

  - Questions that are an attempt to elicit incriminating admissions from him or her concerning the fact of driving, the timing and quantity of alcohol consumption and other matters. These questions may take place before and between the actual breathalyzer breath samples, thereby seeming to be part of the mandatory test requirements.

- Physical tests requested between the actual breathalyzer breath samples.

1.5.2 REASONABLE AND PROBABLE GROUNDS/ THREE HOUR LIMIT

- Consider whether the requirements to demand breathalyzer breath samples were present: reasonable and probable grounds to believe that the client was committing, or within the preceding three hours, committed an offence of impaired operation or “over ’80”.

- Try to speak to the arresting officer to ascertain the reasonable and probable grounds the officer claims. Try to get him to read the grounds from his notebook (assure him that “it’ll only take a minute”). If the grounds are not yet written up in the notebook, that is useful to know.

- If you are really ambitious, you could try speaking to the breathalyzer operator to ascertain the reasonable grounds as told to him/her. If the officer balks, explain that you need to know the reasonable grounds to advise the client properly.

- If the officer(s) cooperate(s), make careful notes of what you are told. If they refuse, it may affect their credibility at trial or lead to an argument that advice by counsel was impossible without the information.

- Determine if your client was pulled over while driving. If he or she was not pulled over, determine whether the time of last vehicular operation is known to the police, and whether they have overlooked the three hour limit.

- Advise your client where appropriate whether or not the requisite reasonable and probable grounds may be arguable, and that the lack of the requisite reasonable and probable grounds constitutes a reasonable excuse to refuse to provide the breathalyzer breath samples. But also advise a court may disagree and the decision to refuse is the client's.

1.5.3 REFUSAL TO BLOW

- Where grounds for a refusal to blow exist, stress that it is strictly your client's decision whether to blow or not and that it is inappropriate for you to expressly tell a client "not to blow". Stress that it is your client who suffers the consequences if he or she makes the wrong decision, and it is his or her responsibility therefore to make the decision.

- Where your client is inclined to refuse based upon a belief in the absence of reasonable and probable grounds, it would appear advisable for you as counsel to speak to the relevant police officer and try to persuade him or her of an absence of the requisite grounds. *For example, if a medical or physical condition such as weariness, a limp, etc. may be responsible for symptoms taken by the officer as indicative of intoxication, explain the innocent cause. Even if this attempt is unsuccessful, the conversation may well lay the foundation for a successful argument along the same lines later in court.*

1.5.4 MEDICAL SAMPLES

If the client is calling from an accident scene or a hospital it is important to advert to medical samples that have been already, or may yet be taken. Depending upon the circumstances the client may have to be advised to demand the destruction of any blood or other samples already taken and to make clear their lack of consent to any such taking. Otherwise, such samples could become evidence by means of a search warrant seizure.

1.5.5 SIGNS OF INTOXICATION

- During the conversation watch for signs of intoxication in your client, such as slurred speech or difficulty speaking.

- Note any such signs at the end of the conversation to avoid the allegation that a premature conclusion was reached.

- If you note any such symptom, ask your client about his or her normal speech so if a relevant condition exists that explains the apparent symptom, other than intoxication, two steps can be taken. First, the explanation can be noted and, second, counsel can notify the police officer of its existence and attempt to nullify any inculpatory inference that may have arisen in the officer's mind from the apparent symptom.

- If the effects of intoxication are making themselves apparent in your client's speech, advise your client to that effect, and remind him or her that there is no obligation to answer questions or engage in conversation. *With luck, your client will draw the obvious conclusion that he or she should speak as little as possible.*

1.5.6 RELEASE AND AFTER

- Advise your client to call you again upon release.

- When your client calls upon release, find out how he or she is getting home, if not done previously.

- Consider whether you can, by telephone calls or otherwise, assist your client in arranging for a credible witness to see him or her at the point of release. The witness can later give evidence negating any opinion of impairment.

- Arrange an appointment to see your client as soon as possible after release.

1.5.7 CLIENT'S NOTES

- Instruct your client to write up notes headed "Confidential - For My Lawyer" covering all of the relevant events in great detail. This should be done immediately after release, while matters are still fresh in mind.

- Instruct your client to bring the notes to the first interview.

1.6 CONVERSATION WITH THE POLICE

- In general, try to converse with the arresting police officer and/or the breathalyzer operator in order to get as much information from him or her concerning your client and the circumstances of the case.

One basis to do so is to explain to the officer that you are commencing to advise the client and cannot do so without some understanding of the case such as the grounds for any tests that have been demanded. A refusal of the police to provide any 'disclosure' before counsel commences to provide advice to the client may raise potential Charter issues at trial.

Furthermore, this is an opportunity to request videotaping of your client if facilities are available, or an interpreter if one is necessary.

In *R. v. Stenset*, 45 M.V.R. (3d) 153, 135 C.C.C. (3d) 112, 70 Alta. L.R. (3d) 45, 232 A.R. 284, 194 W.A.C. 284, [1999] 10 W.W.R. 350, 1999 CarswellAlta 290 (Alta. C.A.), at issue was whether a lawyer has the right to question the arresting police officer as to his reasonable grounds for the breath demand before he advises a driver whether to take a breath test. The Appeal Court held that the answer is "generally no, but sometimes maybe".

In *R. v. Fitzsimmons* (2006), [2006] O.J. No. 5079, 39 M.V.R. (5th) 111, 216 C.C.C. (3d) 141, 219 O.A.C. 200, 84 O.R. (3d) 266, 2006 CarswellOnt 8086 (Ont. C.A.), leave to appeal refused (2007), 370 N.R. 398 (note), 2007 CarswellOnt 2864, 2007 CarswellOnt 2863, [2007] S.C.C.A. No. 81 (S.C.C.), the Court held that the s. 10(b) right to counsel was not violated by the breathalyzer technician's refusal to answer defence counsel's questions where defence counsel did not first attempt to secure desired information from client. Thus, counsel should try to obtain the information from the client first and thereafter speak to the police.

- You may discuss with the arresting police officer, among other matters, any problem relating to the client's release upon completion of the legal requirements and formalities. In most cases, release is not an issue but occasionally it may be and the client may be held for a show-cause bail hearing in the morning.

2

THE INITIAL INTERVIEW

2.1 GENERAL

- Arrange to see your client as soon as possible after release to look after the formalities of retention and to ensure the case is brought under the lawyer's control while events are still relatively fresh.

- During the initial interview, review the information obtained during any earlier telephone conversation.

- If no earlier interview took place, proceed with a complete and exhaustive interview.

- Take from your client any notes he or she has made pursuant to instructions or otherwise and go through them to add any missing details.

2.2 INFORMATION TO OBTAIN

- Question your client thoroughly about the following. Make an accurate record of the information received: *(see Appendix A)*

  1. name
  2. address
  3. age and date of birth
  4. occupation
  5. telephone numbers at home and work
  6. height and weight
  7. family background (briefly)
  8. prior record, if any
  9. medical and physical condition, especially a medical

or physical condition such as weariness, a limp, etc., which may be responsible for symptoms taken by the officer as indicative of intoxication

10. mouth condition: dentures or other appliances which may trap mouth alcohol
11. if accident, any injuries
12. consumption of alcohol: amount, time started, time finished
13. consumption of food
14. any documentation such as restaurant bills or credit cards slips showing amount of consumption
15. outline of events from initial police contact
16. language fluency
17. details of actions that may affect breath test results: burping, belching, vomiting, regurgitating, use of mouthwash, breath mints, smoking
18. names and addresses of all witnesses to any or all of the relevant events, especially witnesses who saw accused immediately before, during, or immediately after police contact
19. name of any lawyer spoken to in exercise of right to counsel
20. if the right to counsel was waived, why and what the client was told or believed that led to the waiver
21. all the events from arrest to release in detail, including all comments, conversations, officers and other persons dealt with at police station, use of videotaping of booking and/or breath testing

- Trace your client's activities from the start of drinking, if not earlier, through to the end of the events and release by the police, in as much detail as possible. *This is very important and will form the foundation of your preparation, including locating of witnesses.*

- Observe your client's normal speech for any condition that might have been misinterpreted by the police as a sign of intoxication.

- If the client has spoken to legal aid duty counsel or any other lawyer any notes should be obtained from that source as well as duty counsel being interviewed to ascertain their recollection of the communication.

2.3 DOCUMENTS

- Take from your client copies of any documents served upon him or her in connection with the charge.
- Obtain a copy of your client's driving licence. *This is useful to have for reference.*
- Check all the documentation carefully for accuracy and note any inaccuracies.
- Send change of address notification to the appropriate provincial motor vehicles department if necessary.
- If the information is recorded on the driver's licence, make a comparison of the height recorded thereon with the client's stated height to ensure that there is no discrepancy.

2.4 FUTURE OBLIGATIONS

- Remind your client of any future obligation regarding fingerprinting or photographs to be taken in connection with the charge.
- Remind your client of the next court appearance, while emphasizing the importance of prompt court attendances.
- Emphasize to your client the importance of not having any further charge, especially of a similar nature, while the matter is pending.

3

PREPARATION

3.1 EXAMINE DOCUMENTATION

- Start by carefully examining all the documents served upon your client for errors.
- Examine the copy of your client's driving licence. Note any inaccuracy in address thereon.
- If necessary, send a change of address notification to the appropriate provincial motor vehicle department.
- If the information is recorded on the driver's licence, make a comparison of the height recorded thereon with the client's stated height to ensure that there is no discrepancy.

3.2 INTERVIEW WITNESSES

- Interview in detail all witnesses revealed or discovered from your client's detailed account of the events in question, or from other sources, such as disclosure materials.

Witnesses can include the client's friend or business associate who was with the client throughout, the person who saw the client last before the police contact and the witness who saw the client first after release by the police. A previously unknown person who was with the client at the police station by virtue of also being detained as a suspected impaired driver, who passed the breathalyzer test and was released, could in a rare case be an important defence witness.

3.3 INTERVIEW COUNSEL

- Interview any legal aid duty counsel or other lawyer spoken to by your client in the exercise of his or her right to counsel while in police custody.

- Obtain the originals of any notes or memoranda made by such counsel pertaining to the contact.

3.4 TOXICOLOGIST'S REPORT

- Where appropriate, send an outline based upon your client's evidence regarding the amount consumed and the timing of consumption to a toxicologist for an opinion as to blood alcohol level at material time. *(An example of such a request and report is found in Appendix G.)*

- The outline should include references to any medicines that the client was taking that impact on his condition.

  A toxicologist is also useful to examine any videotapes made to see if any issues are apparent regarding the testing procedures involved, or the client's apparent condition.

3.5 CHARGE(S)

- Obtain a complete copy of the charge document.

- Examine the charge document carefully for completeness and errors.

3.6 DISCLOSURE

- Ensure that full disclosure is obtained.

- Ensure that information regarding the anticipated testimony of all police witnesses, and a copy of their actual notes, is obtained.

- The alcohol influence report of the breathalyzer technician should be included.

- It is more and more common for videotape recordings to be made of the client at the police station, for example, as part of the normal "parade" procedure when an arrestee is brought into the station, their belongings checked, the right to counsel confirmed, etc. before the officer in charge of the station. A request for any such videotape or other recordings on which your client appears or even on which his voice appears should be requested.

- It is now becoming common to videotape the actual breath testing itself. It is essential to obtain a copy of any such videotape. It will show the timing of the breath tests and may contain times that conflict with those on the technician's certificate, or may show a failure by the technician to perform the tests according to proper procedure. A toxicologist or other expert should review the tape carefully.

The operator's manuals for any breath testing devices involved should be requested. The obligation on the Crown to provide copies or at least access to such documentation as part of disclosure would seem obvious. For example, in *R. v. Pierman* (1994), 92 C.C.C. (3d) 160, 19 O.R. (3d) 704 (Ont. C.A.), affirmed 26 O.R. (3d) 480, (*sub nom. R. v. Dewald*) 19 M.V.R. (3d) 1, [1996] 1 S.C.R. 68, 103 C.C.C. (3d) 382 (S.C.C.), a police officer's delay of 15 minutes in administering a roadside screening device was held to be acceptable because it was based upon the manufacturer's instructions in the operator's manual to wait at least 15 minutes from the cessation of drinking before administering such a test. This implicitly accepts that operation of devices must be in accordance with such manuals, and therefore an accused is entitled to disclosure of the manuals to assure each compliance. See also *R. v. Bernshaw* (1994), 8 M.V.R. (3d) 75, 35 C.R. (4th) 201, 95 C.C.C. (3d) 193, [1995] 1 S.C.R. 254 (S.C.C.).

- A request should be made for the calibration records of the particular approved screening device involved or the repair record of the particular breathalyzer machine.
- Review the contents of the disclosure with your client at a subsequent interview.

See 13.6.1, Diclosure and Appendix B, Comprehensive Disclosure Request.

3.7 DRIVING RECORD

- Order a copy of your client's driving record from the relevant government motor vehicles department. *(See Appendix H.)*

3.8 ACCIDENT REPORT

- Order a copy of the police accident report, if the incident involved an accident.

3.9 FURTHER PREPARATION

- Review the information regarding the client and the circumstances to see what further information may be required and what further questions or issues may arise that remain unanswered.

- Continually assess your client as a potential witness.

- Assist your client in understanding how to present himself or herself and the evidence in the most effective and credible manner.

3.10 PROOF OF THE ELEMENTS OF THE OFFENCE

- Consider the legal requirements regarding the elements of the offences as outlined below.

- Consider whether all elements are provable by credible evidence.

Some elements of the various offences are provable by statutory short-cuts made available to the prosecution in the form of presumptions or certificate evidence. However, the availability of these evidentiary short-cuts requires proof of certain conditions precedent imposed by statute. Counsel should consider the legal requirements for proof by means of any presumptions or by certificate evidence, as outlined below, that may be applicable, and consider whether all necessary conditions precedent are provable by credible evidence.

For example, consider whether the requirements to demand breathalyzer breath samples were present: reasonable and probable grounds to believe that the client was committing, or within the preceding three hours, committed an offence of impaired operation or "over '80".

If the client was not pulled over while driving, the time of last operation may be unknown to the police who may have overlooked the three hour limit.

- The legal requirements regarding the elements of the offences are outlined in the following chapters.

  If an approved screening device test, or refusal thereof, is involved in the case, see Chapter 4 below.

  If breathalyzer testing, or refusal thereof, is involved in the case, see Chapter 5 below.

  If blood tests, or refusal thereof, are involved in the case, see Chapter 6 below.

  If the charge is one of impaired ability requiring proof of impairment, see Chapter 7 below.

  If the charge is one of excessive blood alcohol level, or "over '80", see Chapter 8 below.

  If the charge is one involving an allegation of driving, see Chapter 9 below.

  If the charge is one involving an allegation of "care or control", see Chapter 10 below.

  If the charge involves an allegation of "causing bodily harm" or "causing death", see Chapter 11 below.

  All cases must involve an allegation of a motor vehicle or vessel or, more rarely, aircraft or railway equipment. See Chapter 12 below.

  Consider possible defence evidence from the client or another witness to refute an otherwise possibly successful prosecution. See Chapter 13 below.

4

APPROVED SCREENING DEVICE TESTS

4.1 REASONABLE SUSPICION ALCOHOL IN BODY

- Was the police officer's suspicion that there was alcohol in the body reasonable?

- Was the demand made while the driver was still operating, or in care or control of the car?

Where a peace officer ''reasonably suspects'' that a person who is operating or has the care or control of a vehicle has alcohol in his or her body, the peace officer may demand that the person provide ''forthwith'' a sample of breath for testing in an ''approved screening device'': section 254(2).

The absence of the requisite predicate belief that the officer ''reasonably suspects'' that the accused has alcohol in his body (e.g. he merely suspects the accused at some point had something to drink) negates a valid screening device test: *R. v. Hendel* (July 3, 1997), (Ont. Gen. Div.), Drinking & Driving Law Vol. XIII, no. 2, p. 9; *R. v. Smith* (September 2, 1997), Lampkin Prov. J. (Ont. Prov. Div.), Drinking & Driving Law Vol. XIII, no. 2 , p. 11; *R. v. Bowie* (March 3, 1999), Nicholas Prov. J. (Ont. Prov. Div.). In *R. v. Thompson*, [2003] S.J. No. 240, 2003 CarswellSask 255, 2003 SKPC 56 (Sask. Prov. Ct.), it was held that the Officer's determination that the accused motorist had "consumed alcohol" was not sufficient to allow a lawful screening device test. An officer's conclusion, "I had reasonable suspicion he had been consuming alcohol, and I therefore read the standard approved screening device" does not meet the legal standard required for a screening device test of a belief the accused has alcohol in his body: *R. v. Fetterley*, [2004] B.C.J. No. 1859, 2004 CarswellBC 2030, 2004 BCPC 321 (B.C. Prov. Ct.).

A lack of alcohol odour can negate ''reasonable suspicion'': *R. v. Zoravkovic* (March 10, 1997), Doc. Perth 2983/96 (Ont. Gen. Div.); affirmed (1998), 112 O.A.C. 119, 37 M.V.R. (3d) 93 (Ont. C.A.), Drinking & Driving Law Vol. XIII, no. 1, p. 1. The smell of alcohol on the body of the accused is not evidence of alcohol in the body. However, it is a reasonable inference that the smell of alcohol on a person's breath means that there is alcohol in the person's body: *R. v. McDarby* (1998), 1998

CarswellOnt 2404, [1998] O.J. No. 2443 (Ont. Gen. Div.); *R. v. Mitruk* (1998), 1998 CarswellOnt 2405, [1998] O.J. No. 2444 (Ont. Gen. Div.). The smell of alcohol on the breath does not necessarily lead to the conclusion that a person has alcohol in his body. The person may have washed the beverage around in his mouth and spat it out. However, where there is evidence that the accused admitted consuming alocohol plus evidence that the smell of alcohol was present on the accused's breath it is reasonable to conclude that the officer had a reasonable suspicion that the accused at the material time had alcohol in his body: *R. v. Trory* (1998), 1998 CarswellOnt 3359, [1998] O.J. No. 3297 (Ont. Gen. Div.). An odour of alcohol must be coming from the accused to provide the reasonable grounds for a screening device demand: *R. v. Hey*, 2008 CarswellAlta 383, [2008] A.J. No. 317, 2008 ABPC 74 (Alta. Prov. Ct.); *R. v. Truong*, [2008] B.C.J. No. 462, 2008 CarswellBC 527, 2008 BCPC 73 (B.C. Prov. Ct.). An odour of alcohol where it is not clear that the odour is not from a passenger is insufficient grounds: *R. v. Rodriques* (2005), [2005] O.J. No. 1551, 2005 CarswellOnt 4673 (Ont. C.J.).

An odour from the vehicle generally is insufficient: *R. v. Sood*, [2005] A.J. No. 1660, 2005 CarswellAlta 1765, 2005 ABPC 201, 389 A.R. 139 (Alta. Prov. Ct.). As is an odour "possibly" from the accused bar owner's clothes: *R. v. Thulin*, [2006] B.C.J. No. 1310, 2006 CarswellBC 1418, 2006 BCPC 261 (B.C. Prov. Ct.).

In *R. v. Webster*, 2004 CarswellBC 632, [2004] B.C.J. No. 631, 2004 BCPC 70 (B.C. Prov. Ct.) the screening device demand was held to have been made in the absence of the requisite "reasonable suspicion" where: "There was no admission of consumption, there was no smell of liquor apart from the general observation that she smelt liquor "on the driver". . .There was no other evidentiary basis for the approved screening device demand. Accordingly, I hold the demand to be invalid being without an evidentiary foundation."

R. v. Dearden, 2004 CarswellBC 439, [2004] B.C.J. No. 395, 2004 BCPC 40 (B.C. Prov. Ct.) the requirements of a proper ASD were considered (and found lacking).

"There are three parts to a proper ASD demand that must be conveyed to a motorist to comply with Section 254(2) of the *Criminal Code*. First the officer must tell the motorist that the officer reasonably suspects that the motorist has alcohol in his blood. Next, the officer must tell the motorist that he is required to provide forthwith a sample of his blood and finally the officer must tell him that the purpose of the sample is to enable a proper analysis of the breath by means of an approved instrument.

The officer never told the defendant why he was initially being stopped. The defendant was not told that the officer reasonably suspected that he had alcohol in his body while operating a motor vehicle. He was not told that the sample was to be used for a "proper analysis" of his breath. The demand, as given by the officer, may have been accurate to the extent that the defendant was told that he had to provide a sample of his breath "forthwith" but that was essentially the only element that was properly brought to the defendant's attention."

A demand is invalid that does not include requirement of immediate or 'forthwith' compliance in any way, and refusal thereof is not an offence: *R. v. Skwara*, [2005] M.J. No. 468, 2005 CarswellMan 483, 200 Man. R. (2d) 61 (Man. Prov. Ct.). "In this case, there is significant evidence that the police officer did not effectively ask Mr. Skwara to "please provide a sample of breath now". He had neither an ASD nor any clear plan to obtain one. On the evidence the only conclusion that can be drawn is that Constable Schell effectively asked Mr. Skwara to "please provide sample of breath if and when I can secure an ASD." Such a demand was not a lawful demand under s. 254(2). Given this finding Mr. Skwara committed no offence when he refused to do so." See also *R. v. Kwok*, [2005] O.J. No. 5713, 2005 CarswellOnt 7962, 2005 ONCJ 485 (Ont. C.J.).

The reasonable suspicion of a peace officer referred to in s. 254(2) of the Code applies only to the issue of whether an accused has alcohol in his body. In order to obtain a conviction under s. 254(5) for refusal to comply with a demand to provide a screening device breath sample, it must be proven as a fact, not as a matter of reasonable suspicion on the part of an officer that the accused was operating a motor vehicle or had the care or control of a motor vehicle. *R. v. Chekaluk*, [2004] B.C.J. No. 2555, 2004 CarswellBC 2880, 2004 BCPC 445 (B.C. Prov. Ct.). An approved screening device demand cannot be lawfully made where the police officer only has "a reasonable suspicion as to who the driver was." *Not* in fact being the operator of a motor vehicle constitutes a reasonable excuse for refusing to perform the screening device test: *R. v. Swietorzecki* (1995), 11 M.V.R. (3d) 30, 97 C.C.C. (3d) 285 (Ont. C.A.); *R. v. Hilton* (1998), 1998 CarswellOnt 756 (Ont. Prov. Div.).

The screening device demand must be made while the driver is still operating or in care or control of the vehicle. *R. v. Khotar* (2008), [2008] O.J. No. 721, 2008 CarswellOnt 729 (Ont. C.J.); *R. v. Ginman*, 2008 CarswellOnt 1409, 2008 ONCJ 111, [2008] O.J. No. 1009 (Ont. C.J.). It cannot be made after the driver has left the vehicle and accompanied the police officer to the police station: *R. v. Campbell* (1988), 9 M.V.R. (2d) 1, 66 C.R. (3d) 150, 44 C.C.C. (3d) 502 (Ont. C.A.), or even while he is sitting in the back seat of a police cruiser: *R. v. Pierman* (1994), 92 C.C.C. (3d) 160, 19 O.R. (3d) 704 (Ont. C.A.), affirmed 26 O.R. (3d) 480, (*sub nom. R. v. Dewald*) 19 M.V.R. (3d) 1, [1996] 1 S.C.R. 68, 103 C.C.C. (3d) 382 (S.C.C.), or if the accused has left his vehicle and entered licensed premises and is returning to the vehicle when detained by police: *R. v. Vassie* (2001), [2001] S.J. No. 312, 2001 CarswellSask 348, 209 Sask. R. 137 (Sask. Prov. Ct.) or is already under arrest on other matters (and is in fact in transit to a police station): *R. v. Good* (2007), [2007] A.J. No. 1256, 2007 CarswellAlta 1549, 57 M.V.R. (5th) 116, 85 Alta. L.R. (4th) 254, 2007 ABQB 696, [2008] 4 W.W.R. 748 (Alta. Q.B.). But see *R. v. Orme* (1998), 37 M.V.R. (3d) 179, 114 O.A.C. 321, 1998 CarswellOnt 4157 (Ont. C.A.), affirming (1998), 33 M.V.R. (3d) 224 (Ont. Gen. Div.) where a screening demand made in the police cruiser five minutes after the accused's car was stopped was a valid demand. The time lapse between the accused's actual care or control of his vehicle and the demand was no more than that which was reasonably necessary to enable the officer to discharge his duties.

A prosecution failed based upon a "failed" screening device test demanded during police investigation of accident after the accused's vehicle was immobilized and the accused was physically away from the vehicle, because the screening device demand held improper as the accused no longer "is" driving at the time of demand: *R. v. Stewart*, [2007] B.C.J. No. 235, 2007 CarswellBC 244, 2007 BCPC 26 (B.C. Prov. Ct.) (Doherty P.C.J.); *R. v. Schmidt* (2001), 2001 CarswellSask 525, 2001 SKQB 383, 211 Sask. R. 8, 17 M.V.R. (4th) 207, [2002] 3 W.W.R. 580, [2001] S.J. No. 493 (Sask. Q.B.). Similarly, a screening device demand cannot be made where the police arrive on the accident scene after the fact and the accused is no longer driving: *R. v. Fraser* (2002), 2002 CarswellAlta 491, 2002 ABPC 52, 23 M.V.R. (4th) 260, [2002] A.J. No. 462, 310 A.R. 228 (Alta. Prov. Ct.).

The roadside screening demand cannot be made to a driver who has been detained by the police for half an hour and is thus no longer "operating or in care or control of his vehicle": *R. v. Smith* (2002), 2002 CarswellOnt 807, [2002] O.J. No. 1115 (Ont. C.J.).

In *R. v. Woods*, 2005 CarswellMan 205, 2005 CarswellMan 206, 29 C.R. (6th) 240, 2005 SCC 42, [2005] S.C.J. No. 42, EYB 2005-92056, 197 C.C.C. (3d) 353, 254 D.L.R. (4th) 385, 19 M.V.R. (5th) 1, 336 N.R. 1, [2006] 1 W.W.R. 1, 132 C.R.R. (2d) 168, [2005] 2 S.C.R. 205, 195 Man. R. (2d) 131, 351 W.A.C. 131 (S.C.C.) the accused refused a demand for a screening device sample at roadside and was arrested, but subsequently at station agreed to provide a sample. His failure on that test provided the grounds for breathalyzer tests.

It was held that the screening device demand and test at station were impermissibly outside the terms of s. 254(2) of the *Criminal Code*, and thus were obtained in violation of *Charter*, and the breathalyzer readings should be excluded from evidence.

See also the cases in section 10.1: Care or control.

4.1.1 ROADSIDE QUESTIONING AND TESTING

Roadside questioning regarding ''what a driver has had to drink'' does not require the right to counsel reminder, although the driver is obviously detained, the Ontario Court of Appeal held in *R. v. Smith* (1996), 19 M.V.R. (3d) 262, 46 C.R. (4th) 229, 105 C.C.C. (3d) 58, 28 O.R. (3d) 75 (Ont. C.A.), relying on s. 48 of the Ontario *Highway Traffic Act* to provide the required ''reasonable limit prescribed by law'' to allow such a Charter violation. This was the same section the Court relied on in *Saunders v. R.* (1988), 4 M.V.R. (2d) 199, 63 C.R. (3d) 37, 41 C.C.C. (3d) 532 (Ont. C.A.) to allow roadside coordination tests in the same context. To the same effect is *R. v. Sundquist*, 145 C.C.C. (3d) 145, 189 Sask. R. 273, 216 W.A.C. 273, 2000 SKCA 50, [2000] 7 W.W.R. 411, 3 M.V.R. (4th) 218, 2000 CarswellSask 313 (Sask. C.A.). The Supreme Court of Canada authoritatively dealt with the issue in

R. v. Orbanski, [2005] S.C.J. No. 37, 2005 CarswellMan 190, 2005 CarswellMan 191, (*sub nom. R v. Elias*) 196 C.C.C. (3d) 481, (*sub nom. R. v. Elias*) 253 D.L.R. (4th) 385, 29 C.R. (6th) 205, 2005 SCC 37, 19 M.V.R. (5th) 23, [2005] 9 W.W.R. 203, 335 N.R. 342, 132 C.R.R. (2d) 117, [2005] 2 S.C.R. 3, 195 Man. R. (2d) 161, 351 W.A.C. 161, EYB 2005-91678 (S.C.C.).

However, such evidence is to be used by the police officer to decide whether reasonable grounds exist to demand the breathalyzer, and such evidence is not admissible at a subsequent trial to prove impairment by the accused, the Ontario Court of Appeal confirmed in *R. v. Milne* (1996), 18 M.V.R. (3d) 161, 48 C.R. (4th) 182, 107 C.C.C. (3d) 118 (Ont. C.A.), leave to appeal to S.C.C. refused (1996), 110 C.C.C. (3d) vi (note) (S.C.C.). *R. v. Pineau*, [2004] B.C.J. No. 1296, 2004 CarswellBC 1431, 2004 BCPC 183 (B.C. Prov. Ct.); *R. v. Lieskovsky*, 2004 CarswellAlta 1143, 9 M.V.R. (5th) 209, 2004 ABPC 153 (Alta. Prov. Ct.). The section would not survive as a valid section 1 limit on section 10(*b*)'s right to counsel if it were to be judged as a device to gather incriminating evidence for use at trial to incriminate the motorist. *R. v. Stevenson* (2004), 2004 CarswellOnt 1924, [2004] O.J. No. 2036 (Ont. S.C.J.) reiterated that it is reversible error to use an accused's roadside statements made pre-*Charter* warning as evidence in the trial:

". . .[T]hat question and answer session was inadmissible for either the truth of its contents, or as a legally permissible basis upon which to cross-examine. It was only admissible to substantiate the legality of the roadside test, which was not attacked. It is obvious that the appellant was detained at the time of the questioning by the arresting officer, and it is equally obvious that she had not been given her rights to counsel."

"A roadside statement given by a detained accused who has not been given her right to counsel should not be admitted at trial (other than to support the legality of a roadside demand if challenged) and it is an error to permit the use of such inadmissible statement to assess the accused's credibility. . ."

In *R. v. Heimlick* (1997), 161 Sask. R. 70 (Sask. Q.B.), a new trial was ordered where the accused's statement to the arresting police officer regarding her alcohol consumption was used as evidence at trial and not merely as part of the basis for the breath test demand.

In *R. v. Huff* (1999), 1999 CarswellOnt 4791, [1999] O.J. No. 5153 (Ont. S.C.J.), affirmed (2000), 2000 CarswellOnt 3404, [2000] O.J. No. 3487 (Ont. C.A.), leave to appeal refused (2001), 2001 CarswellOnt 864, 2001 CarswellOnt 865, [2000] S.C.C.A. No. 562, 271 N.R. 191 (note), 149 O.A.C. 392 (note) (S.C.C.), a new trial was ordered in a drinking and driving case where the trial judge used the accused's initial statement to police regarding consumption to reject the accused's trial evidence regarding consumption in support of the "*Carter*" defence. Affirmed by the Ontario Court of Appeal: *R. v. Huff* (2000), 2000 CarswellOnt 3404, [2000] O.J. No. 3487 (Ont. C.A.), leave to appeal refused (2001), 2001 CarswellOnt 864, 2001 CarswellOnt 865, [2000] S.C.C.A. No. 562, 271 N.R. 191 (note), 149 O.A.C. 392 (note) (S.C.C.). See also *R. v. Coulter* (2001), 2001 CarswellOnt 4889, 24 M.V.R.

(4th) 61, [2001] O.J. No. 5608 (Ont. S.C.J.), *R. v. Boothby* (2001), 2001 CarswellOnt 4470, [2001] O.J. No. 5078 (Ont. C.A.), *R. v. Cresswell* (2002), 2002 CarswellOnt 2025, [2002] O.J. No. 2492, 161 O.A.C. 45 (Ont. C.A.).

The same principle applies to the screening device test result: *R. v. Coutts* (1999), 43 M.V.R. (3d) 28, 25 C.R. (5th) 362, 121 O.A.C. 342, 64 C.R.R. (2d) 34, 136 C.C.C. (3d) 225, 45 O.R. (3d) 288, 1999 CarswellOnt 1773, [1999] O.J. No. 2013 (Ont. C.A.) and even to observations. In *R. v. Flores*, [2007] A.J. No. 951, 2007 CarswellAlta 1133, 2007 ABQB 528 (Alta. Q.B.) it was held that the Trial Judge erred in relying on inadmissible evidence to convict when she took into account evidence of observations of the Appellant made by a police officer during the Appellant's compelled participation in a roadside screening procedure at a time prior to his being advised of his right to counsel. This limitation has no application to observations of speech and condition made lawfully in the course of a valid stop for a traffic offence: *R. v. Townsend*, 58 M.V.R. (5th) 10, 2008 ABCA 44, [2008] A.J. No. 270, 2008 CarswellAlta 333 (Alta. C.A.).

In Saskatchewan the result on the Approved Screening Device can be used to assess the credibility of the accused's claimed consumption: *R. v. Beston*, [2006] S.J. No. 717, 2006 SKCA 131, 2006 CarswellSask 744, 214 C.C.C. (3d) 509, 40 M.V.R. (5th) 235, 382 W.A.C. 165, 289 Sask. R. 165 (Sask. C.A.).

The situation may vary as between provinces because the valid section 1 limit depends on provincial legislation.

In *R. v. Bishop*, [2002] N.S.J. No. 219, 2002 CarswellNS 191, 2002 NSPC 2, 26 M.V.R. (4th) 133, 205 N.S.R. (2d) 275, 643 A.P.R. 275 (N.S. Prov. Ct.), affirmed 2003 CarswellNS 381, [2003] N.S.J. No. 413, 2003 NSSC 213, 44 M.V.R. (4th) 127 (N.S. S.C.), it was held that in Nova Scotia the questioning of a detained driver prior to giving the s. 10(b) rights resulting in self-criminating statements given by the detainee, then used to make a demand for tests under s. 254 of the *Criminal Code* results in a breach of the s. 7 rights of the detained driver.

Physical roadside co-ordination tests required from a motorist before the right to counsel is given under section 10(*b*) of the Charter are a permissible section 1 limit on that right, authorized under section 636.1 of the *Highway Safety Code* (Que.), it was held in *R. v. Tremblay* (1995), 105 C.C.C. (3d) 91 (Que. C.A.). Note that that section is expressly limited to "reasonable physical co-ordination tests" and would not include oral utterances.

Where there is no provincial legislation, the roadside tests are impermissible absent the right to counsel: *R. v. Oldham* (1996), 21 M.V.R. (3d) 1, 49 C.R. (4th) 251, 109 C.C.C. (3d) 392, 181 N.B.R. (2d) 321, 460 A.P.R. 321 (N.B. C.A.).

The admissibility of Drug Recognition Examination evidence was considered in *R. v. Wood*, [2007] A.J. No. 895, [2007] 11 W.W.R. 330, 79 Alta. L.R. (4th) 358, 51 M.V.R. (5th) 93, 2007 CarswellAlta 1048, 2007 ABQB 503 (Alta. Q.B.), and rejected. It was held on appeal that the Trial judge erred in admitting as expert evidence a police officer's drug recognition examination ("DRE") and opinion that accused's ability was impaired by cannabis because insufficient reliability was shown.

4.2 FORTHWITH

- Was the demand made forthwith?
- Was the approved screening device accessible forthwith?
- If the demand did not fall within these requirements, was the right to counsel given?

The section (while it does not explicitly so state) *implicitly* requires that the screening device demand be made by a peace officer forthwith after the requisite suspicion arises: *R. v. Woods* (2005), 2005 CarswellMan 205, 2005 CarswellMan 206, 29 C.R. (6th) 240, 2005 SCC 42, [2005] S.C.J. No. 42, EYB 2005-92056, 197 C.C.C. (3d) 353, 254 D.L.R. (4th) 385, 19 M.V.R. (5th) 1, 336 N.R. 1, [2006] 1 W.W.R. 1, 132 C.R.R. (2d) 168, [2005] 2 S.C.R. 205, 195 Man. R. (2d) 131, 351 W.A.C. 131 (S.C.C.); *R. v. Pierman* (1994), 92 C.C.C. (3d) 160, 19 O.R. (3d) 704 (Ont. C.A.), affirmed 26 O.R. (3d) 480, (*sub nom. R. v. Dewald*) 19 M.V.R. (2d) 1, [1996] 1 S.C.R. 68, 103 C.C.C. (3d) 382 (S.C.C.), *R. v. Billette*, [2001] S.J. No. 227, 2001 SKQB 150, 2001 CarswellSask 258, 205 Sask. R. 79, 13 M.V.R. (4th) 192 (Sask. Q.B.), and it explicitly thereafter requires that the motorist forthwith comply. A delay in making the screening device demand means a *Charter* violation in the obtaining of breath samples: *R. v. McCullough*, [2007] A.J. No. 885, 2007 CarswellAlta 1089, 2007 ABQB 423, 51 M.V.R. (5th) 142, 79 Alta. L.R. (4th) 317, [2007] 11 W.W.R. 301 (Alta. Q.B.).

In *R. v. Jalbert*, [2006] A.J. No. 1028, 2006 CarswellAlta 1066, 2006 ABPC 218 (Alta. Prov. Ct.) (LeGrandeur P.C.J.) the accused was acquitted of refusing to provide a roadside screening device test where the demand was not made "forthwith". The accused in *R. v. Husulak*, [2006] S.J. No. 480, [2006] 9 W.W.R. 259, 283 Sask. R. 31, 2006 SKQB 284, 2006 CarswellSask 465, 35 M.V.R. (5th) 1 (Sask. Q.B.) (Kleber J.) was successful on appeal for the same reason. A similar result obtained in *R. v. Schmidt* (2000), 2000 CarswellOnt 1213, [2000] O.J. No. 1227, 31 M.V.R. (4th) 261 (Ont. S.C.J.); *R. v. Billette*, [2001] S.J. No. 227, 2001 SKQB 150, 2001 CarswellSask 258, 205 Sask. R. 79, 13 M.V.R. (4th) 192 (Sask. Q.B.) and *R. v. Boutamine*, 2004 CarswellOnt 4561, 10 M.V.R. (5th) 224, 2004 ONCJ 264, [2004] O.J. No. 4527 (Ont. C.J.) (8 minute delay); *R. v. Boulanger*, [2008] Y.J. No. 10, 2008 CarswellYukon 12, 2008 YKTC 22 (Y.T. Terr. Ct.).

In *R. v. McMahon* (2002), [2002] S.J. No. 765, 2002 CarswellSask 818, 228 Sask. R. 217, 34 M.V.R. (4th) 254, 2002 SKPC 139 (Sask. Prov. Ct.), a s. 9 *Charter* violation was found to have been occasioned by the officer's failure to demand the approved screening device test ''forthwith'' pursuant to s. 254(2) of the *Criminal Code*, failing which the accused was arbitrarily detained within the meaning of s. 9 of the *Charter*.

Regarding the second requirement, a delay of 15 minutes in administering a roadside screening device was held to be acceptable in *R. v. Pierman* (1994), 92 C.C.C. (3d) 160, 19 O.R. (3d) 704 (Ont. C.A.), affirmed 26 O.R. (3d) 480, (*sub nom. R. v. Dewald*) 19 M.V.R. (3d) 1, [1996] 1 S.C.R. 68, 103 C.C.C. (3d) 283 (S.C.C.), because it was based upon the manufacturer's instructions in the operator's manual to wait at least 15 minutes from the cessation of drinking before administering such a test. This implicitly accepts that operation of devices must be in accordance with such manuals.

The Supreme Court of Canada dealt with this issue in *R. v. Bernshaw* (1994), 8 M.V.R. (3d) 75, 35 C.R. (4th) 201, 95 C.C.C. (3d) 193 (S.C.C.). In that case, the police training course advised officers to ascertain when the last drink was consumed and, if unable to do so, to wait 15 minutes before administering the test in order to allow mouth alcohol to dissipate. The manufacturer's manual recommended waiting 20 minutes where the subject had recently had a drink, or vomited or regurgitated, to allow any mouth alcohol to be dispersed. In *Bernshaw* the officer did not wait the 15 minutes but administered the test immediately without checking when the accused had completed consumption. The Supreme Court ruled that the tests were valid, notwithstanding the failure to wait the 15 minutes, and the accused was convicted (based upon the breathalyzer test results that flowed from his ''fail'' on the screening device test). The Court held that a 15-minute delay before administering an approved screening device test *in circumstances where the delay is warranted* is proper and does not violate the requirement that such test be administered ''forthwith.'' However, *where there is no evidence that warrants the delay* then the test can be validly administered without waiting the 15 minutes and such would be a proper test. The crucial determinant, the majority of the Court said, was whether there was evidence of one of the circumstances that mandate the delay, such as recent consumption, vomiting, regurgitation or any other factor that requires the wait.

R. v. Burns, 2002 CarswellAlta 218, 2002 ABQB 135, [2002] A.J. No. 219, 26 M.V.R. (4th) 158, 311 A.R. 187 (Alta. Q.B.) considered when the 15-minute wait for a screening device test is required, holding: ". . .[W]hen an officer has reason to believe or suspect that alcohol has been consumed within 15 minutes, the officer should delay administering the [screening device] test to ensure that the ASD results are reliable. However, where there is no credible evidence that the suspect was drinking within 15 minutes, then the screening analysis should be administered as soon as reasonably possible."

R. v. Mastromartino (2004), 2004 CarswellOnt 1412, [2004] O.J. No. 1435, 4 M.V.R. (5th) 198, 70 O.R. (3d) 540 (Ont. S.C.J.) considered ". . . [w]hen must officers delay obtaining an ASD sample because of concerns for residual mouth alcohol?"

"In summary, I take Bernshaw, and Einarson to establish the following:

1. Officers making ASD demands must address their minds to whether or not they would be obtaining a reliable reading by administering the test without a brief delay.

2. If officers do not, or reasonably could not, rely on the accuracy of the test results, the results cannot assist in determining whether there are reasonable and probable grounds to arrest.

3. Officers making ASD demands may briefly delay administering the test if, in their opinion, there is credible evidence which causes them to doubt the accuracy of the test result unless the test was briefly delayed.

4. Officers are not required to wait before administering the test in every case where a driver may have been in a bar shortly before being stopped. The mere possibility that a driver has consumed alcohol within 15 minutes before taking the test does not preclude an officer from relying on the accuracy of the screening device.

5. Whether or not officers are required to wait before administering the screening test is determined on a case-by-case analysis, focusing on the officer's belief as to the accuracy of the test results if the tests were administered without delay, and the reasonableness of that belief.

6. The fact the driver is observed leaving a bar is a relevant circumstance in determining whether it was reasonable for the officer to delay the taking of the test in order to obtain an accurate sample. However, officers are not required to ask drivers when they last consumed alcohol.

7. If the officer decides to delay taking the sample and that delay is challenged at trial, the court must decide whether the officer honestly and reasonably felt that an appropriately short delay was necessary to obtain a reliable reading.

8. If the officer decides not to delay taking the sample and that decision is challenged at trial, the court must decide whether the officer honestly and reasonably believed that he could rely on the test result if the sample was taken without delay.

See also *R. v. Bridgeman* (2005), [2005] O.J. No. 5334, 2005 CarswellOnt 7233, 28 M.V.R. (5th) 61 (Ont. S.C.J.).

In *R. v. Einarson* (2003), 2003 CarswellOnt 5718, [2003] O.J. No. 5702, 48 M.V.R. (4th) 74 (Ont. S.C.J.), reversed (2004), 2004 CarswellOnt 903, [2004] O.J. No. 852, 184 O.A.C. 176, 48 M.V.R. (4th) 85, 183 C.C.C. (3d) 19, 70 O.R. (3d) 286, 21 C.R. (6th) 185 (Ont. C.A.) the drinking and driving conviction was set aside on appeal where the arresting officer failed to wait 15 minutes before taking a sample of the accused's breath for testing in an approved screening device, to eliminate the possibility of the presence of mouth alcohol.

"In the case at bar it is not disputed that Officer Williams knew that the presence of mouth alcohol would render the result of the approved screening device unreliable.

He also knew that the appellant had driven off the parking lot of Arizona's bar within a couple of minutes of being stopped and he admitted that this raised the red flag of consumption of alcohol by the appellant within fifteen minutes. The officer attempted to address that issue by asking the two questions referred to in the evidence. It is not disputed that he clearly did not believe the answer to the first question. The trial judge characterized the appellant's response to the second question as meaning that not only had she not been drinking at all but that she had just come to Arizona's to pick up her boyfriend. I'm not prepared to disagree with that finding, however, the evidence is quite clear and the trial judge found that the officer was not willing to accept that answer as truthful but that the officer wasn't willing at that point to reject it. . .

In these circumstances it is my opinion that the officer could not have a sufficient basis for believing that the results of the approved screening device test were reliable and therefore could not have had the requisite subjective belief that grounds existed for the making of the demand under s. 254(3). . ."

R. v. Mastromartino (2004), 2004 CarswellOnt 1412, [2004] O.J. No. 1435, 4 M.V.R. (5th) 198, 70 O.R. (3d) 540 (Ont. S.C.J.) considered whether ". . .the accused [is] required to call expert evidence regarding the effects of residual mouth alcohol on the reliability of the ASD results and held "no".

. . .I am not persuaded that expert evidence is required in the determination of whether the officer had reasonable and probable grounds to arrest. First, dealing with the officer's subjective belief, the fact officers receive training in regards to the 15 minute period is relevant to their belief in the reliability of the ASD test. Their opinion as to the reliability of the ASD result impacts on their reasonable and probable grounds to make an Intoxilyzer demand. No expert evidence is required when the training goes to the officer's subjective belief.

Second, as regards the objective criteria, the "reasonable person" standing in the shoes of the officer must possess the same information as the officer. That knowledge includes that residual mouth alcohol may affect the reliability of the test. If it is part of the officer's knowledge, it is also part of the reasonable person's knowledge.

Further, even if I am in error with respect to these conclusions, the effects of residual mouth alcohol on the ASD are so well known that expert evidence is not required. It appears beyond dispute that the presence of mouth alcohol can affect the reliability of ASD tests. The Alcohol Test Committee of Canada, the manufacturer's manual, the RCMP, and other police services' training cautioned against taking ASD samples within 15 minutes of alcohol consumption. Indeed in *Einarson, supra* Doherty J.A. acknowledged, "it is well known by police officers that where a driver has consumed alcohol in the 15 to 20 minutes before the test is administered, the results of the test may be unreliable." I have not been directed to any case in which evidence was called bringing into question the need to delay tests when there is evidence of consumption within 15 minutes of the test."

To be a valid demand for an approved screening device breath sample, the demand must be made with the approved screening device machine accessible forthwith. A demand made but not capable of such fulfillment (because no approved screening device machine is forthwith available) is not a proper demand for an approved screening device sample: *R. v. Grant* (1991), 31 M.V.R. (2d) 309, 7 C.R. (4th) 388, 67 C.C.C. (3d) 268 (S.C.C.); *R. v. Cote* (1992), 39 M.V.R. (2d) 124, 11 C.R. (4th) 214, 70 C.C.C. (3d) 280 (Ont. C.A.). Some caselaw has focused on actual outcome: if the machine arrives in time (notwithstanding the officer did not know when it would arrive), the demand is within the section. If it had arrived later, the demand would not have been within the section. In *R. v. Wilson* (1999), 41 M.V.R. (3d) 1, 121 B.C.A.C. 111, 198 W.A.C. 111, 1999 CarswellBC 406 (B.C. C.A.), affirming (1997), 29 M.V.R. (3d) 189 (B.C. S.C.), the B.C. Court of Appeal held that *Grant* did not add to the ingredients of the offence under s. 254(2) the requirement that the Crown prove in every case that an approved screening device was in the possession of the police or immediately available. In *Grant*, it was not the absence of the device that was fundamental to the acquittal, but the 30-minute delay.

A charge of refusing a screening device demand was dismissed where the demanding officer was not equipped with a screening device, which was delivered some six to eight minutes later: *R. v. MacPherson* (November 9, 1998), Cain Prov. J. (N.B. Prov. Ct.), Drinking & Driving Law, Vol. XIV, no. 2, p. 16. In *R. v. Matar* (1999), 1999 CarswellOnt 3550 (Ont. S.C.J.), an appeal by the accused from a refusal of a demand for a screening device sample was allowed and an acquittal entered where the accused was convicted based upon a refusal before the screening device was in fact on the scene.

In *R. v. Singh* (2000), [2000] O.J. No. 4992, 2000 CarswellOnt 5028, 79 C.R.R. (2d) 166, 9 M.V.R. (4th) 292 (Ont. S.C.J.), section 10(b) of the *Charter* was held violated in circumstances where demand for screening device test was 'stalled' by the officer because he was unsure when the device would be available. Demand thus not within s. 254(2) of *Criminal Code* and no s. 1 limit dispensing with right to counsel warning applied.

In *R. v. Danychuk* (2003), [2003] O.J. No. 1286, 2003 CarswellOnt 1133, 36 M.V.R. (4th) 101 (Ont. S.C.J.), reversed (2004), 2004 CarswellOnt 632, 184 O.A.C. 131, 183 C.C.C. (3d) 337, 47 M.V.R. (4th) 25, [2004] O.J. No. 615, 70 O.R. (3d) 215 (Ont. C.A.), a conviction under s. 254(5) of the *Criminal Code* for failing or refusing to comply with a demand to provide forthwith a sample of breath for analysis by an Approved Screening Device was set aside on appeal and an acquittal entered. A refusal is not illegal where screening device not at hand and available for test.

To conclude: refusing or failing to comply with a demand outside the section is not an offence. Further, a right to counsel must be given before requiring compliance with a demand outside those provisions, since only a valid demand within those provisions is effective to limit the right to counsel.

4.3 RIGHT TO COUNSEL

- Was your client given the right to counsel?

- If not, were all the requirements of a valid demand for an approved screening device test met? (*See below 4.5.1 Proper Machine*)

Before an approved screening device test required pursuant to a valid demand, there is no right to consult counsel, as guaranteed by section 10(*b*) of the *Charter of Rights and Freedoms*, as those provisions have been held by the courts to constitute a valid section 1 limitation on the *Charter* right: *R. v. Thomsen* (1988), 4 M.V.R. (2d) 185, 63 C.R. (3d) 1, 40 C.C.C. (3d) 411 (S.C.C.); *R. v. Redding* (1988), 8 M.V.R. (2d) 132 (N.S. C.A.); *R. v. Yuskow* (1989), 18 M.V.R. (2d) 121, 73 C.R. (3d) 159, 52 C.C.C. (3d) 382 (Alta. C.A.); *R. v. Bacon* (1990), 26 M.V.R. (2d) 165, 60 C.C.C. (3d) 446 (Sask. C.A.); *R. v. Benson*, (June 12, 1990), Brooke, Houlden, Galligan JJ.A. (Ont. C.A.); *R. v. Grant* (1991), 31 M.V.R. (2d) 309, 7 C.R. (4th) 388, 67 C.C.C. (3d) 268 (S.C.C.).

However, a right to counsel must be given before requiring compliance with a demand outside those provisions, since only a valid demand within those provisions is effective to limit the right to counsel: *R. v. Grant* (1991), 31 M.V.R. (2d) 309, 7 C.R. (4th) 388, 67 C.C.C. (3d) 268 (S.C.C.); *R. v. Cote* (1992), 39 M.V.R. (2d) 124, 11 C.R. (4th) 214, 70 C.C.C. (3d) 280, (Ont. C.A.); *R. v. Dewald*, 19 M.V.R. (3d) 1, 103 C.C.C. (3d) 382, [1996] 1 S.C.R. 68, (*sub nom. R. v. Pierman*) 26 O.R. (3d) 480. *R. v. Clarke*, 2004 CarswellNS 254, 224 N.S.R. (2d) 78, 2004 NSPC 39 (N.S. Prov. Ct.). As was said in *R. v. George* (2004), [2004] O.J. No. 3287, 2004 CarswellOnt 3243, 121 C.R.R. (2d) 172, 3 M.V.R. (5th) 159, 187 C.C.C. (3d) 289, 189 O.A.C. 161, 23 C.R. (6th) 181 (Ont. C.A.), a screening device demand and sample is not within the authorizing provisions and s. 10(b) right to counsel is violated where "...the police officer is not in a position to require that a breath sample be provided by the accused before any realistic opportunity to consult counsel [because] then the officer's demand is not a demand made under s. 238(2). In *R. v. Wackernagel* (2004), 2004 CarswellOnt 5795, 16 M.V.R. (5th) 297, 2005 CarswellOnt 4673 (Ont. S.C.J.), additional reasons at (2005), 2005 CarswellOnt 390, 16 M.V.R. (5th) 310 (Ont. S.C.J.) there was a detailed consideration of the temporal requirements concerning the approved screening device test. See also *R. v. Quong*, [2006] A.J. No. 423, 2006 CarswellAlta 468, 2006 ABPC 111, 32 M.V.R. (5th) 287, 399 A.R. 55 (Alta. Prov. Ct.). A failure to afford the defendant his Section 10(b) rights in such circumstances operates to exclude both the results of the approved screening device and the intoxilyzer following a Section 24(2) analysis: *R. v. Kahlon*, 2004 CarswellOnt 5633, 2004 ONCJ 359, 15 M.V.R. (5th) 128 (Ont. C.J.); *R. v. Clarke*, [2004] N.S.J. No. 245, 2004 CarswellNS 254, 224 N.S.R. (2d) 78, 2004 NSPC 39 (N.S. Prov. Ct.). In *R. v. DiRuggiero* (1998), (*sub nom. R. v. Diruggiero*) 52 C.R.R. (2d) 132 (B.C. S.C.), Drinking & Driving Law, Vol. XIII, no. 4, p. 29, the accused was entitled to be informed of his right to counsel before the approved screening demand was made. The officer already had reasonable and probable grounds for a charge of impaired driving and had made an arrest on that charge. As the accused was detained, he was entitled to be informed of his right to counsel before he was required to submit to the screening demand.

In *R. v. Cove*, 2006 CarswellAlta 436, 2006 ABQB 264, 57 Alta. L.R. (4th) 117, [2006] A.J. No. 399, 32 M.V.R. (5th) 63 (Alta. Q.B.); *R. v. Bond*, [2006] N.S.J. No. 142, 2006 CarswellNS 145, 2006 NSPC 17, 244 N.S.R. (2d) 48, 774 A.P.R. 48 (N.S. Prov. Ct.) a thirteen minute delay between the screening device demand and the arrival of the device so the accused could provide the sample resulted in the demand not being made "forthwith". Accordingly the demand was not legal under s. 254(4) of the *Criminal Code* and the defendant was found not guilty of the charge of refusal under s. 254(4).

In *R. v. Koszman*, [2001] S.J. No. 295, 2001 SKQB 201, 2001 CarswellSask 335, 206 Sask. R. 292, 18 M.V.R. (4th) 178 (Sask. Q.B.) it was held that the thirteen-minute delay while awaiting the arrival of the roadside screening device meant that section 10(*b*) of the *Charter* was violated because the accused was detained without being given the right to counsel warning, but the demand was outside the *Criminal Code* screening device provisions due to the delay and thus not within that section 1 limit.

In *R. v. Singh* (2000), [2000] O.J. No. 4992, 79 C.R.R. (2d) 166, 9 M.V.R. (4th) 292, 2000 CarswellOnt 5028 (Ont. S.C.J.) section 10(*b*) was held violated in circumstances where the demand for the screening device test was 'stalled' by the police officer because he was unsure when the device would be available. The demand was thus not within s. 254(2) of the *Criminal Code* and there was thus no section 1 limit dispensing with right to counsel *Charter* compliance.

Where a peace officer arrests a citizen for a drinking and driving offence, and the circumstances are such that: (a) the officer knows there is no approved screening device immediately available, and (b) the citizen has a cell phone, or there is a police station or a telephone facility close at hand, and (c) there are no urgent or serious security problems, the police officer cannot ignore or prevent the citizen from exercising his constitutional right to retain and instruct counsel without delay by accessing a telephone facility pending the arrival of the screening device: *R. v. Wolowidnyk* (1998), 233 A.R. 353, 58 C.R.R. (2d) 101, 1998 CarswellAlta 939, [1998] A.J. No. 1249 (Alta. Prov. Ct.), Drinking & Driving Law, Vol. XIV, no. 3, p. 22.

In *R. v. Quong*, [2006] A.J. No. 423, 2006 CarswellAlta 468, 2006 ABPC 111, 32 M.V.R. (5th) 287, 399 A.R. 55 (Alta. Prov. Ct.) the law was summarized as follows:

> Whether there is a realistic opportunity for the detained person to consult with legal counsel will depend upon both (a) the anticipated delay between the time when the demand is made and the time when the sample can be received by the officer, and (b) the availability of a telephone which the detained person can use to consult with legal counsel with privacy.

> The police officer is obligated to enquire of the detained person whether he or she has an operational cellular telephone only if (a) the presence of such a telephone would, in the circumstances (including any security concerns giving rise to a need to restrict the movements of the detained person), be capable of permitting the detained person to consult with legal counsel with privacy, and (b) the anticipated delay between the time when the demand is made and the time when the sample can be received by the officer is such that it would realistically facilitate such contact.
>
> The facts of the case before me do not require me to rule on what duty, if any, is imposed on the police officer to provide information such as telephone books if it is determined that there is a realistic opportunity for the detained person to consult with legal counsel. However, since the detained person's section 10(b) rights have not been suspended in such a situation (i.e., a situation in which there has not been a valid section 254(2) breath demand), it may be that the entirety of those rights would apply.

In *R. v. Mittleholt* (2005), [2005] O.J. No. 5800, 2005 CarswellOnt 7756 (Ont. C.J.) a screening device refusal charge was dismissed where the accused had a cell phone with him and should have been allowed to contact counsel.

4.4 REFUSAL

- Was there a valid demand, properly made?

See above 4.1 Reasonable Suspicion Alcohol in Body
4.2 Forthwith
See below 4.5.1 Proper Machine

- If so, did your client fail or refuse to comply with that demand?

- If so, did your client have a reasonable excuse for the failure or refusal?

- Was there a demand for any samples of bodily substance other than breath or blood?

A person commits an offence who fails or refuses "without reasonable excuse" to comply with a demand made by a peace officer under this provision: section 254(5). This presumes a "valid" demand, so any basis upon which the demand failed to comply with the provision or otherwise was not properly made and provides a defence to such a charge. Furthermore, the failure or refusal must be "without reasonable excuse". In *R. v. DiRuggiero* (1998), (*sub nom. R. v. Diruggiero*) 52 C.R.R. (2d) 132 (B.C. S.C.), Drinking & Driving Law, Vol. XIII, no. 4 p. 29, the accused's conviction for roadside refusal was set aside on appeal where the demand was made after the accused was already arrested for impaired driving. The *mens rea* was considered in *R. v. Campbell* (2008), [2008] O.J. No. 47, 2008 CarswellOnt

69 (Ont. S.C.J.) where the accused was acquitted where he had run away from officers to avoid an illegal search after the screening device demand was made.

There is no all-inclusive definition of reasonable excuse. For example, an accused's honest belief that the machine was not functioning properly afforded a reasonable excuse because it was based on objective evidence that there may have been a problem with the machine: *R. v. Phinney* (1979), 3 M.V.R. 38, 49 C.C.C. (2d) 81 (N.S. C.A.); *R. v. Rulli* (1998), 1998 CarswellOnt 736 (Ont. Prov. Div.); a medical condition such as a cleft palate: *R. v. Holt* (1996), 11 M.V.R. (3d) 75; an injury making it impossible or dangerous for the accused to blow into a breathalyzer machine also afforded a reasonable excuse: *R. v. Moser* (1992), 36 M.V.R. (2d) 207, 13 C.R. (4th) 96, 71 C.C.C. (3d) 165 (Ont. C.A.). Other ''reasonable excuses'' have related to police mistreatment: *R. v. Paz* (1996), 183 A.R. 161 (Alta. Prov. Ct.); or physical injury: *R. v. Watson* (1997), 26 M.V.R. (3d) 194 (Alta. Prov. Ct.), Drinking & Driving Law Vol. XIII, no. 7, p. 55, and lack of an unequivocal refusal: *R. v. McKelvey*, [1996] A.W.L.D. 507 (Alta. Prov. Ct.), Drinking & Driving Law Vol. XIII, no. 2, p. 14. In *R. v. Cameron* (1999), 245 A.R. 383 (Alta. Prov. Ct.), a charge of "refuse breathalyzer" was dismissed where the accused had a "reasonable excuse" for failure to blow because she had asthma and reasonably believed that if she expelled from her lungs all the air present she might suffer an asthma attack. In *R. v. Fantham* (2000), 2000 CarswellOnt 2759, [2000] O.J. No. 1179 (Ont. C.J.), the accused was acquitted of refusing a roadside test where a reasonable doubt made out that he could not comply with the demand because of a shortness of breath condition.

In *R. v. Norwood* (2002), [2002] O.J. No. 5218 (Ont. C.J.), the accused was found not guilty of impaired and refusal of breathalyzer demand where his impairment and inability to understand the demand were due to the unforeseen effects of the combination of alcohol consumption, accused's diabetes and a missed lunch meal.

The accused should be afforded a ''last chance'' to provide a breath sample after being charged if he or she volunteers to do so within a reasonable period of time after making the unsuccessful attempts or refusal: *R. v. Chance* (1997), 32 M.V.R. (3d) 70 (Ont. Prov. Div.); *R. v. Buckley*, 2002 CarswellSask 439, 2002 SKQB 281, [2002] S.J. No. 409, 221 Sask. R. 152 (Sask. Q.B.), leave to appeal refused (2003), 2003 CarswellSask 416, 2003 CarswellSask 417, 326 N.R. 400 (note), 257 Sask. R. 160 (note), 342 W.A.C. 160 (note) (S.C.C.).

A "refusal" by an accused is not absolute and irrevocable the instant uttered. In *R. v. Hines* (1998), [1998] O.J. No. 5831 (Ont. S.C.J.), a conviction for refusing the screening device demand was set aside on appeal and an acquittal entered where the accused refused but then within eight minutes of arrest changed his mind and agreed to provide the sample. However, eleven minutes was held too long: *R. v. Jensen*, [2007] A.J. No. 38, 2007 ABPC 15, 2007 CarswellAlta 46 (Alta. Prov. Ct.) (Ogle P.C.J.).

In *R. v. Z. (C.W.)*, [2003] N.S.J. No. 98, 2003 CarswellNS 101, 2003 NSPC 6, 214 N.S.R. (2d) 328 (N.S. Prov. Ct.), it was held that in a case of failing to provide suitable breath samples for analysis, it is essential that the Crown prove beyond a reasonable doubt that the person whose opinion is the determinative trigger is, in fact and in law, a qualified technician designated by the Attorney General. Also considered was the level of acceptable proof.

Not in fact being the operator of a motor vehicle constitutes a reasonable excuse for refusing to perform the screening device test: *R. v. Swietorzecki* (1995), 11 M.V.R. (3d) 30, 97 C.C.C. (3d) 285 (Ont. C.A.). The court must be satisfied beyond a reasonable doubt that the accused was operating the motor vehicle before it can convict him of refusing to comply with a demand. Even if the demanding officer believed on reasonable and probable grounds that the accused was operating the motor vehicle in question, the court must give the benefit of the doubt to the accused: *R. v. Hilton* (1998), 1998 CarswellOnt 756 (Ont. Prov. Div.).

No person is required to provide a sample of any bodily substance for analysis except samples of breath or blood as required under these provisions. Evidence of a failure or refusal to give such other samples is not admissible nor to be the subject of comment in any proceedings: section 258(2). On the other hand, evidence of a failure or refusal to give any samples of breath or blood as required under these provisions is admissible and can lead to an adverse inference against the accused: section 258(3).

4.5 CONDUCTING TESTS

The approved screening devices test for the presence of alcohol in a person's blood, not the precise level thereof, and generally produce one of three readings reflected by different coloured lights: green equals ''pass''; yellow equals ''warn''; and red equals ''fail''. The approved screening devices are generally calibrated so that ''pass'' is below the legal limit of 80 milligrams of alcohol in 100 millilitres of blood; ''warn'' is between 80 and 100; and ''fail'' is over 100.

4.5.1 PROPER MACHINE

- Was the proper screening device used?
- If the Crown cannot prove that the police officer used, or had available to use, a "proper" machine (an approved screening device) was there a violation of the accused's right to counsel? (*See 4.3 Right to Counsel above*)
- If the Crown cannot prove that the accused blew into an approved screening device, consider whether other *Charter* violations occurred:

- violation of section 8 of the *Charter*: Search and seizure
- violation of section 9 of the *Charter*: Arbitrary detention
- see also section 4.6.3 Fail below

These devices are presently approved by order-in-council as approved screening devices: the Alcolmeter S-L2, the Alco-sur, the Alcotest 7410 PA3, the Alcotest 7410 GLC, the Alco-Sensor IV DWF, the Alco-Sensor IV PWF and the Intoxilyzer 400D; see Appendix B.

If an "improper" machine was used or going to be used by the peace officer, who had one of these machines at hand, then such would seem to be a demand outside the provisions in section 254(2) of the Code, which require an approved screening device. A section 10(b) right to counsel violation is thus brought about.

On a charge involving failure or refusal to provide an approved screening device, it would appear obvious that the Crown must prove, if the matter is raised as a live issue, that the accused was in fact being requested to blow into an approved instrument: *R. v. Kosa* (1992), 42 M.V.R. (2d) 290 (Ont. C.A.); *R. v. Petrick* (1996), 22 M.V.R. (3d) 113 (Ont. Gen. Div.), Drinking & Driving Law, Vol. XII, no. 3 p. 21. Therefore, if the police officer making the demand used or intended to use, an "improper" machine then the demand would seem to be outside the provisions which require an approved screening device. A charge of failure or refusal must, therefore, be dismissed.

Similarly in *R. v. Dhillon*, [2006] A.J. No. 156, 2006 CarswellAlta 168, 2006 ABQB 109, 394 A.R. 269 (Alta. Q.B.) it was held that the accused was properly acquitted of failure or refusal to comply with a demand to provide a breath sample contrary to s. 254(2) of the *Criminal Code* on the basis that the police officer who testified for the Crown failed to adequately identify the approved screening device (ASD) which had been used. Accord *R. v. Tessier*, [2006] A.J. No. 1266, 2006 ABPC 267, 2006 CarswellAlta 1305, 408 A.R. 305 (Alta. Prov. Ct.) (Daniel J.) and *R. v. Gillis*, [2006] A.J. No. 1445, 2006 CarswellAlta 1505, 2006 ABPC 323 (Alta. Prov. Ct.), (Le Grandeur P.C.J.).

In *R. v. Toope*, [2002] N.S.J. No. 398, 2002 CarswellNS 375, 2002 NSPC 30, 208 N.S.R. (2d) 129, 652 A.P.R. 129 (N.S. Prov. Ct.), a charge of 'over 80' was dismissed where the breathalyzer tests were demanded and taken based upon the accused's failure on a screening device but the Crown failed to adduce evidence that the device used was "approved screening device". Accord *R. v. Mehta*, [2007] O.J. No. 2749, 2007 CarswellOnt 4402, 2007 ONCJ 305 (Ont. C.J.).

Where an accused blows into a device that cannot be proved to be an approved screening device because of the manufacturer modifications, then in addition to the section 10(b) violation as indicated above, it would also appear that the breath sample into the unauthorized machine amounts to additional *Charter* violations as follows: a section 8 (search or seizure) violation in demanding the breath sample, because breath samples are a form of search and seizure and only samples into an approved screening device are authorized by law; section 9 arbitrary detention violation because the accused is detained for a purpose not authorized by law, to blow into an unapproved machine. It would also appear that any resulting "fail" on an unapproved machine would not constitute the reasonable and probable grounds to demand a breathalyzer test. Thus, if a breathalyzer machine demand was made and breathalyzer samples given, a further section 8 violation resulted in the demanding and taking of breathalyzer test samples without the requisite grounds in law: *R. v. LeBrun* (1999), 46 M.V.R. (3d) 100, 178 N.S.R. (2d) 388, 549 A.P.R. 388 (N.S. S.C.).

Recent authorities to the same effect are: *R. v. Buchan*, (2006), [2006] O.J. No. 3085, 2006 CarswellOnt 4698, 36 M.V.R. (5th) 274 (Ont. S.C.J.) (A. Heeney J.). *R. v. Dunham*, [2005] N.B.J. No. 482, 2005 CarswellNB 660, 2005 NBQB 386, 25 M.V.R. (5th) 260, 290 N.B.R. (2d) 218, 755 A.P.R. 218 (N.B. Q.B.): "Fail on screening device cannot provide grounds where evidence failed to prove device was approved device"; and especially *R. v. Arsenault*, [2005] N.B.J. No. 529, 2005 CarswellNB 716, 2005 CarswellNB 717, 2005 NBCA 110, 24 M.V.R. (5th) 168, 204 C.C.C. (3d) 75, 295 N.B.R. (2d) 123, 766 A.P.R. 123 (N.B. C.A.): "In the absence of evidence the roadside test was administered using an approved device, the court was not entitled to assume the device was approved. That evidence is necessary to establish the statutory authority under which the breath sample is obtained. Peace officers are only entitled to require drivers to provide samples for testing on an approved screening device and the approved screening device is the only one that in fact can be used to collect the sample."

The judge was correct to conclude the roadside screening test result could not be taken into account in the determination of whether or not the officer had reasonable and probable grounds for making a breathalyzer demand. Only a "fail" reading on an "approved screening device", as defined by the *Code*, can provide the necessary reasonable and probable grounds. The officer did not have statutory authority to make a breath sample demand . . .

> Considering that the presence of reasonable and probable grounds is both a statutory and constitutional pre-condition for a lawful breathalyzer demand, my view is that when an accused properly challenges the admissibility of breathalyzer results by reason of the absence of an honest belief to make the breathalyzer demand, *Rilling* looses its significance and, if a violation of a *Charter* right is found, the matter must be disposed of on the basis of a s. 24(2) analysis. In this case, the samples were admittedly collected following a demand and without a warrant. Thus, the onus was on the Crown to prove the reasonableness of the seizure. As the Crown failed to establish an honest belief to make the demand it was therefore unlawful and unauthorized. In such circumstances, because the search and seizure was not authorized by law, it cannot be regarded as reasonable. In my view, the Crown had failed to discharge the onus of establishing reasonableness and the appeal judge was correct in agreeing with the trial judge that Mr. Arsenault's right under s. 8 to be secure against unreasonable seizure was violated in the course of obtaining the breathalyzer results.

However the test for an officer to prove the device used was an ASD is not very high: *R. v. Gundy*, [2008] O.J. No. 1410, 2008 CarswellOnt 2091, 2008 ONCA 284

(Ont. C.A.). ". . . [I]f the officer testifies that he or she used an approved screening device, or agrees with the suggestion that it is an approved screening device, such testimony is direct evidence upon which the trial judge can rely. . . . In the absence of some credible evidence to the contrary, it is not reasonable to infer that an officer who says that he or she used an approved screening device actually used an unapproved device. . . ."

4.5.2 PROPERLY CALIBRATED

- When was the screening device last calibrated?

- Is there proof of proper calibration?

The screening devices do not show readings, but must be calibrated for the lights or readouts on the machine to have any significance relevant to the level of alcohol in the driver's blood. The screening device should be calibrated according to the frequency set out in the owner's manual, usually weekly or every two weeks. Proof of the proper calibration of the device is required for its results to have any significance: *R. v. Pruski*, [2006] O.J. No. 5256, 2006 CarswellOnt 8462, 2006 ONCJ 506, 44 M.V.R. (5th) 106 (Ont. C.J.) (Green J.); *R. v. Ponte* (November 25, 1995), Lenz Prov. J. (Ont. Prov. Ct.), Drinking & Driving Law, Vol. XII, no. 2, p. 14; *R. v. Peters* (November 2, 1989), Earle-Renton P.C.J. (Ont. Prov. Ct.); *R. v. Bowden* (Sept. 6, 1995), Doc. Ottawa 95-60127 (Ont. Prov. Div.), Drinking & Driving Law, Vol. XI, no. 9, p. 49. The manufacturer's manual for the particular machine involved in a given case should be carefully examined to ensure that it was properly calibrated. However, there is no need for the Crown to adduce evidence that the approved screening device was properly calibrated as long as the officer had reasonable grounds to believe the approved screening device was functioning properly: *R. v. Arthurs* (1981), 25 C.R. (3d) 83, 63 C.C.C. (2d) 572 (Sask. C.A.), and *R. v. Beech* (1993), 44 M.V.R. (2d) 273 (Ont. C.A.); *R. v. Beeching* (1999), 40 M.V.R. (3d) 98 (Ont. Gen. Div.). Disclosure of calibration records was considered in *R. v. Scurr*, [2008] A.J. No. 203, 2008 CarswellAlta 269, 2008 ABQB 127 (Alta. Q.B.).

R. v. Colbourne (1999), [1999] O.J. No. 4729, 1999 CarswellOnt 4808 (Ont. C.J.), the accused was acquitted of a drinking and driving offence where breathalyzer test results were excluded for a section 8 violation where the demand was based upon a failure on an improperly calibrated screening device test.

In *R. v. Fehrenbach* (2001), 2001 CarswellOnt 6052, [2001] O.J. No. 4552 (Ont. C.J.) it was held that evidence that a roadside device was not tested every 14 days in accordance with manufacturer's recommendations and expert evidence regarding the necessity for such testing meant that s. 8 of *Charter* was violated by reliance on such device.

4.5.3 PROPERLY OPERATED

- Did your client have a drink within fifteen minutes before taking the test?

- Was your client smoking within three minutes before taking the test?

In *R. v. Kallu* (2000), [2000] B.C.J. No. 936 (B.C. Prov. Ct.), breathalyzer test results were excluded under section 24(2) of the *Charter* where the tests were obtained based upon the accused's "fail" on a roadside screening device where the evidence showed the screening device was not properly operated by the police officer.

According to the owner's manual, proper operation of some screening devices requires 15 minutes to pass after the cessation of drinking and 3 minutes to pass after the cessation of smoking. Failure to follow these directions may cast doubt on the probative value of a negative test result: *R. v. Richardson* (1990) (Ont. Prov. Div.) Drinking & Driving Law, Vol. VI, no. 9, pp. 71-72; though if the trial judge rejects that argument, he may find there was no credible evidence to the contrary: *R. v. Beech* (1993), 44 M.V.R. (2d) 273 (Ont. C.A.).

Similarly it was held that where cessation of drinking could have occurred within 15 minutes of the screening device test, or could have occurred recently, the test result "fail" was invalid and could not be relied upon to provide proper grounds for a valid breathalyzer demand: *R. v. Vassie* (2001), [2001] S.J. No. 312, 2001 CarswellSask 348, 209 Sask. R. 137 (Sask. Prov. Ct.); *R. v. Lawrence* (2000), [2000] O.J. No. 4021 (Ont. C.J.).

In *R. v. Mastromartino* (2003), [2003] O.J. No. 127, 2003 CarswellOnt 147 (Ont. C.J.), recent consumption was held to invalidate the screening device result, such that, the resulting breath tests became an unlawful search and seizure leading to acquittal.

In *R. v. Polischuk*, [2003] B.C.J. No. 669, 2003 CarswellBC 612, 2003 BCPC 76 (B.C. Prov. Ct.), breath tests were ruled inadmissable where the demand therefore was based upon screening device test which was taken where accused could have been drinking within previous 15 minutes and said to officer he ''just had a couple of drinks''.

R. v. Mastromartino (2004), 2004 CarswellOnt 1412, [2004] O.J. No. 1435, 4 M.V.R. (5th) 198, 70 O.R. (3d) 540 (Ont. S.C.J.) considered ". . . [w]hen must officers delay obtaining an ASD sample because of concerns for residual mouth alcohol?"

"In summary, I take Bernshaw, and Einarson to establish the following:

1. Officers making ASD demands must address their minds to whether or not they would be obtaining a reliable reading by administering the test without a brief delay.

2. If officers do not, or reasonably could not, rely on the accuracy of the test results, the results cannot assist in determining whether there are reasonable and probable grounds to arrest.

3. Officers making ASD demands may briefly delay administering the test if, in their opinion, there is credible evidence which causes them to doubt the accuracy of the test result unless the test was briefly delayed.

4. Officers are not required to wait before administering the test in every case where a driver may have been in a bar shortly before being stopped. The mere possibility that a driver has consumed alcohol within 15 minutes before taking the test does not preclude an officer from relying on the accuracy of the screening device.

5. Whether or not officers are required to wait before administering the screening test is determined on a case-by-case analysis, focusing on the officer's belief as to the accuracy of the test results if the tests were administered without delay, and the reasonableness of that belief.

6. The fact the driver is observed leaving a bar is a relevant circumstance in determining whether it was reasonable for the officer to delay the taking of the test in order to obtain an accurate sample. However, officers are not required to ask drivers when they last consumed alcohol.

7. If the officer decides to delay taking the sample and that delay is challenged at trial, the court must decide whether the officer honestly and reasonably felt that an appropriately short delay was necessary to obtain a reliable reading.

8. If the officer decides not to delay taking the sample and that decision is challenged at trial, the court must decide whether the officer honestly and reasonably believed that he could rely on the test result if the sample was taken without delay."

See also *R. v. Bridgeman* (2005), [2005] O.J. No. 5334, 2005 CarswellOnt 7233, 28 M.V.R. (5th) 61 (Ont. S.C.J.).

In *R. v. Einarson* (2003), 2003 CarswellOnt 5718, [2003] O.J. No. 5702, 48 M.V.R. (4th) 74 (Ont. S.C.J.), reversed (2004), 2004 CarswellOnt 903, [2004] O.J. No. 852, 184 O.A.C. 176, 48 M.V.R. (4th) 85, 183 C.C.C. (3d) 19, 70 O.R. (3d) 286, 21 C.R. (6th) 185 (Ont. C.A.) Ontario Superior Court of Justice, Spiegel J., August 6, 2003 the drinking and driving conviction was set aside on appeal where the arresting officer failed to wait 15 minutes before taking a sample of the accused's breath for testing in an approved screening device, to eliminate the possibility of the presence of mouth alcohol.

"In the case at bar it is not disputed that Officer Williams knew that the presence of mouth alcohol would render the result of the approved screening device unreliable.

He also knew that the appellant had driven off the parking lot of Arizona's bar within a couple of minutes of being stopped and he admitted that this raised the red flag of consumption of alcohol by the appellant within fifteen minutes. The officer attempted to address that issue by asking the two questions referred to in the evidence. It is not disputed that he clearly did not believe the answer to the first question. The trial judge characterized the appellant's response to the second question as meaning that not only had she not been drinking at all but that she had just come to Arizona's to pick up her boyfriend. I'm not prepared to disagree with that finding, however, the evidence is quite clear and the trial judge found that the officer was not willing to accept that answer as truthful but that the officer wasn't willing at that point to reject it. . .

In these circumstances it is my opinion that the officer could not have a sufficient basis for believing that the results of the approved screening device test were reliable and therefore could not have had the requisite subjective belief that grounds existed for the making of the demand under s. 254(3). . ."

R. v. Mastromartino (2004), 2004 CarswellOnt 1412, [2004] O.J. No. 1435, 4 M.V.R. (5th) 198, 70 O.R. (3d) 540 (Ont. S.C.J.) considered whether ". . .the accused [is] required to call expert evidence regarding the effects of residual mouth alcohol on the reliability of the ASD results and held "no".

. . .I am not persuaded that expert evidence is required in the determination of whether the officer had reasonable and probable grounds to arrest. First, dealing with the officer's subjective belief, the fact officers receive training in regards to the 15 minute period is relevant to their belief in the reliability of the ASD test. Their opinion as to the reliability of the ASD result impacts on their reasonable and probable grounds to make an Intoxilyzer demand. No expert evidence is required when the training goes to the officer's subjective belief.

Second, as regards the objective criteria, the "reasonable person" standing in the shoes of the officer must possess the same information as the officer. That knowledge includes that residual mouth alcohol may affect the reliability of the test. If it is part of the officer's knowledge, it is also part of the reasonable person's knowledge.

Further, even if I am in error with respect to these conclusions, the effects of residual mouth alcohol on the ASD are so well known that expert evidence is not required. It appears beyond dispute that the presence of mouth alcohol can affect the reliability of ASD tests. The Alcohol Test Committee of Canada, the manufacturer's manual, the RCMP, and other police services' training cautioned against taking ASD samples within 15 minutes of alcohol consumption. Indeed in *Einarson, supra* Doherty J.A. acknowledged, "it is well known by police officers that where a driver has consumed alcohol in the 15 to 20 minutes before the test is administered, the results of the test may be unreliable." I have not been directed to any case in which evidence was called bringing into question the need to delay tests when there is evidence of consumption within 15 minutes of the test."

The manufacturer's manual for the particular machine involved in a given case should be carefully examined to ensure that it was properly operated on the relevant occasion in accordance with the manufacturer's instructions. Recommended temperature ranges for accurate operation should be especially noted regarding cases arising in extremely cold or hot weather. See 13.6.1, Disclosure, (c) Machine Manuals and Records.

4.6 OUTCOME OF TEST

4.6.1 PASS

The approved screening devices are generally calibrated so that "pass" is below the legal limit of 80 milligrams of alcohol in 100 millilitres of blood.

4.6.2 WARN

The approved screening devices are generally calibrated so that "warn" is between the legal limit of 80 milligrams of alcohol in 100 millilitres of blood and a level of 100 milligrams in 100 millilitres of blood.

A "warn" result on a test on an approved screening device does not provide the reasonable and probable grounds required for a breathalyzer demand: *R. v. Kearsey* (1992), 98 Nfld. & P.E.I.R. 310 (Nfld. T.D.), reversed (1994), 2 M.V.R. (3d) 123 (Nfld. C.A.); *R. v. Black* (1994), 4 M.V.R. (3d) 301 (N.S. S.C.).

4.6.3 FAIL

The approved screening devices are generally calibrated so that "fail" is not just above the legal limit of 80 milligrams of alcohol in 100 millilitres of blood, but in fact represents a level of 100 milligrams in 100 millilitres of blood.

Failure of a test on an approved screening device properly calibrated (see 4.5.2 above) and properly operated (see 4.5.3 above), amounts to the reasonable and probable grounds required for a breathalyzer demand, provided that the approved screening device test is carried out in accordance with proper procedures as set out in the machine manual: *R. v. Richardson* (1990), (Ont. Prov. Div.), Drinking & Driving Law, Vol. VI, no. 9, pp. 71-72; *R. v. Beech* (1993), 44 M.V.R. (2d) 273 (Ont. C.A.); *R. v. Bernshaw* (1994), 8 M.V.R. (3d) 75, 35 C.R. (4th) 201, 95 C.C.C. (3d) 193 (S.C.C.); *R. v. Kallu* (2000), [2000] B.C.J. No. 936 (B.C. Prov. Ct.). A police officer cannot properly and reasonably rely on a flawed screening device test: *R. v. Shular*, 2004 CarswellAlta 743, 2004 ABQB 434 (Alta. Q.B.); *R. v. Hubbard*, 2005 CarswellYukon 28, 2005 YKSC 9, 21 M.V.R. (5th) 85 (Y.T. S.C.).

In *R. v. Toope*, [2002] N.S.J. No. 398, 2002 CarswellNS 375, 2002 NSPC 30, 208 N.S.R. (2d) 129, 652 A.P.R. 129 (N.S. Prov. Ct.), a charge of 'over 80' was dismissed where the breathalyzer tests were demanded and taken based upon the accused's failure on a screening device but the Crown failed to adduce evidence that the device used was ''approved screening device''. Failure of the Crown to prove the screening device used was an approved screening device was also fatal to the prosecution in *R. v. Mehta*, [2007] O.J. No. 2749, 2007 CarswellOnt 4402, 2007 ONCJ 305 (Ont. C.J.). *R. v. Low*, 2005 CarswellSask 425, 2005 SKPC 63, [2005] S.J. No. 416, 266 Sask. R. 284 (Sask. Prov. Ct.) and *R. v. A. (J.J.)*, [2005] A.J. No. 775, 2005 CarswellAlta 884, 2005 ABPC 168, 18 M.V.R. (5th) 307, 383 A.R. 179 (Alta. Prov. Ct.).

In *R. v. Arsenault*, 2004 CarswellNB 257, [2004] N.B.J. No. 209, 2004 NBQB 181, 7 M.V.R. (5th) 176, 277 N.B.R. (2d) 117, 727 A.P.R. 117 (N.B. Q.B.), affirmed 2005 CarswellNB 716, 2005 CarswellNB 717, [2005] N.B.J. No. 529, 2005 NBCA 110, 24 M.V.R. (5th) 168, 204 C.C.C. (3d) 75, 295 N.B.R. (2d) 123, 766 A.P.R. 123 (N.B. C.A.), a Crown appeal in a drinking and driving case was dismissed, the issue being whether the trial judge erred in having a reasonable doubt that the screening device used was an approved device where the officer had described it as an "approved screening device, a Draeger".

A fail result on the screening device where the test was taken pursuant to an improper or invalid demand cannot provide proper grounds for a valid breathalyzer demand, meaning the breathalyzer tests were taken without proper grounds in violation of the Charter: *R. v. Woods* (2005), 2005 CarswellMan 205, 2005 CarswellMan 206, 29 C.R. (6th) 240, 2005 SCC 42, [2005] S.C.J. No. 42, EYB 2005-92056, 197 C.C.C. (3d) 353, 254 D.L.R. (4th) 385, 19 M.V.R. (5th) 1, 336 N.R. 1, [2006] 1 W.W.R. 1, 132 C.R.R. (2d) 168, [2005] 2 S.C.R. 205, 195 Man. R. (2d) 131, 351 W.A.C. 131 (S.C.C.). The Court there held: "The admissibility of the breathalyzer readings was dependent upon the validity of the ASD result, which was the sole basis for the "reasonable and probable grounds" required for the breathalyzer demand and tests. Accordingly, the only issue in the case is whether the ASD breath sample was legally obtained. If it was, the breathalyzer evidence was properly admitted and the respondent's conviction was sound. If not, the conviction cannot stand."

An ASD breath sample is legally obtained where it is either provided forthwith, pursuant to a lawful demand under s. 254(2), or provided voluntarily.

"The second demand for a breath sample made at the police station did not fall within s. 254(2), as it failed the "immediacy" criterion implicit in that provision. Thus the sample provided was not provided validly pursuant to the section and it was not admissible at trial to provide reasonable and probably grounds for a breathalyzer demand under s. 254(3) of the Criminal Code." See also *R. v. Vassie* (2001), [2001] S.J. No. 312, 2001 CarswellSask 348, 209 Sask. R. 137 (Sask. Prov. Ct.).

A ''fail'' result on an approved screening device has no evidentiary value beyond providing grounds for a breathalyzer demand, is no evidence showing that the accused's blood alcohol level was above the legal limit of .08 and is not admissible at trial as evidence: *R. v. Lieskovsky*, 2004 CarswellAlta 1143, 9 M.V.R. (5th) 209,

2004 ABPC 153 (Alta. Prov. Ct.). *R. v. Gokul* (1998), 1998 CarswellOnt 844, [1998] O.J. No. 921 (Ont. Gen. Div.); *R. v. Seo* (1986), 25 C.C.C. (3d) 385, 51 C.R. (3d) 1, 38 M.V.R. 161 (Ont. C.A.); *R. v. Thomsen* (1988), 4 M.V.R. (2d) 185, 63 C.R. (3d) 1, 40 C.C.C. (3d) 411 (S.C.C.); *R. v. McMahon* (1989) (Ont. Dist. Ct.), Drinking & Driving Law, Vol. V, no. 1, pp. 3-5; *R. v. Robinson* (1990) (Ont. Dist. Ct.), Drinking & Driving Law, Vol. V, no. 10, p. 78; *R. v. Lacey* (1992), 113 N.S.R. (2d) 348 (N.S. Co. Ct.); *R. v. Coutts* (1999), 43 M.V.R. (3d) 28, 121 O.A.C. 342, 64 C.R.R. (2d) 34, 25 C.R. (5th) 362, 136 C.C.C. (3d) 225, 45 O.R. (3d) 288, 1999 CarswellOnt 1773, [1999] O.J. No. 2013 (Ont. C.A.). See also section 4.1.1 Road-side Questioning and Testing above.

5

BREATHALYZER TESTS

5.1 REASONABLE GROUNDS

- Did the police officer have reasonable and probable grounds for believing that your client was driving or had control of the car while impaired or "over '80"?
- Did your client fail an approved screening device test?
- Was the breathalyzer demand based on the belief that an offence was or had been committed within the three previous hours? (increased from two hours by S.C. 1999, c. 32, s. 2 proclaimed in force July 1, 1999.)

Where a peace officer believes on reasonable and probable grounds that a person is committing, or has committed within the preceding three hours (increased from two hours by S.C. 1999, c. 32, s. 2, proclaimed in force July 1, 1999), an offence of impaired operation or ''over '80'', the peace officer may by demand made ''forthwith or as soon as practicable'' require that person to provide ''then or as soon as practicable'' breath samples as are necessary to determine the concentration of alcohol in the person's blood: section 254(3)(*a*).

For a valid demand within this section, the requisite reasonable grounds and resulting belief that an offence was being committed within the preceding three hours (or two hours as previously required), must be present: *R. v. Rhyason*, 2007 CarswellAlta 1001, 2007 CarswellAlta 1002, [2007] S.C.J. No. 39, [2007] 9 W.W.R. 581, 48 C.R. (6th) 74, 221 C.C.C. (3d) 1, 49 M.V.R. (5th) 1, 404 W.A.C. 282, 2007 SCC 39, 78 Alta. L.R. (4th) 1, 281 D.L.R. (4th) 577, 365 N.R. 200, [2007] 3 S.C.R. 108, 412 A.R. 282 (S.C.C.); *R. v. Searle*, [2006] N.B.J. No. 533, 797 A.P.R. 216, 308 N.B.R. (2d) 216, 215 C.C.C. (3d) 374, 2006 CarswellNB 684, 2006 CarswellNB 685, 2006 NBCA 118, 40 M.V.R. (5th) 207 (N.B. C.A.); *R. v. Deruelle* (1992), 38 M.V.R. (2d) 1, 15 C.R. (4th) 215, 75 C.C.C. (3d) 118 (S.C.C.); *R. v. Balla* (1992), 36 M.V.R. (2d) 259 (Alta. Prov. Ct.); *R. v. Seabrook* (1991), 33 M.V.R. (2d) 260 (B.C. C.A.); *R. v. Angell*, [2005] A.J. No. 1884, 2005 CarswellAlta 2027, 2005 ABPC 287, 395 A.R. 6 (Alta. Prov. Ct.). In *R. v. Evans*, 2004 CarswellOnt 2333, [2004] O.J. No. 2437, 2004 ONCJ 70 (Ont. C.J.), the breath demand was held to be improper in breach of s. 8 of the *Charter*, and the breath readings inadmissible under

s. 24(2), because the arresting officer lacked the subjective belief necessary under *Code* s. 254(3) that the offence had occurred in the previous 3 hours.

Failure of a test on an approved screening device (see 4.5.1 above) properly calibrated (see 4.5.2 above) and properly operated (see 4.5.3 above) amounts to the reasonable and probable grounds required for a breathalyzer demand. See 4.6.3, above. It is especially important to ensure the possibility of recent consumption within 15 minutes was considered: see 4.5.3 above.

In *R. v. Tricoteux*, 2004 CarswellNWT 60, 2004 NWTSC 71, 6 M.V.R. (5th) 275 (N.W.T. S.C.) an acquittal for refusing a breathalyzer demand was entered on appeal where Crown failed to prove the demand was made by an officer who formed the requisite belief on reasonable grounds required for a valid demand. "There was no evidence that Constable Leckie believed that the Appellant had committed a s. 253 offence. Indeed, the evidence is that he was acting on instructions from Constable Kosmenko and that is what led to the demand rather than his own judgment. The law permits his judgment to be based on information he receives from another officer but it has to be his own judgment."

The important issue of onus of proof was considered in *R. v. Haas* (2005), 2005 CarswellOnt 3316, [2005] O.J. No. 3160, 20 M.V.R. (5th) 32, 201 O.A.C. 52, 200 C.C.C. (3d) 81, 76 O.R. (3d) 737, 138 C.R.R. (2d) 29 (Ont. C.A.), leave to appeal refused (2005), 2005 CarswellOnt 7401, 2005 CarswellOnt 7402, [2005] S.C.C.A. No. 423, 349 N.R. 397 (note), 215 O.A.C. 395 (note) (S.C.C.). The Court held that breathalyzer samples are a warrantless search and seizure, and therefore the onus is on the Crown to establish the requisite reasonable grounds to legalize the warrantless seizure under the relevant *Criminal Code* provisions. The onus is not on the defence to establish the absence of reasonable grounds. In the s. 8 context, the onus to prove a *Charter* breach requires the accused simply to prove a warrantless search. ". . .[T]he fundamental proposition [is] that an accused bears the burden of persuading the court on a balance of probabilities that his or her Charter rights have been infringed, but. . .in the s. 8 context, once the accused has demonstrated that the search or seizure was a warrantless one, the burden of persuasion shifts to the Crown to show that on a balance of probabilities the search or a seizure was reasonable. . ."

In *R. v. Forsberg* (2000), 2000 CarswellSask 150, [2000] S.J. No. 154 (Sask. Prov. Ct.), it was held that the factors of the accused admitting to drinking, and the presence of a strong smell of alcohol, are not in of themselves sufficient to constitute reasonable and probable grounds to demand breathalyzer samples. Accord *R. v. Petrie*, [2006] N.S.J. No. 437, 248 N.S.R. (2d) 353, 789 A.P.R. 353, 2006 NSPC 53, 2006 CarswellNS 625 (N.S. Prov. Ct.) (Gibson A.C.J.).

An odour of alcohol, glassy eyes and minor erratic driving while using a cell phone did not constitute reasonable grounds for the breathalyzer demand: *R. v. Embry* (2000), [2000] O.J. No. 4020 (Ont. C.J.)

The slurring of speech and the odour of alcohol are not sufficient to establish a reasonable and probably grounds: *R. v. Franklin* (1997), [1997] A.J. No. 760, 221

A.R. 356, 1997 CarswellAlta 1248 (Alta. Q.B.). The existence of a strong odour of alcohol, erratic driving, and watery eyes, are not sufficient to establish reasonable and probable grounds for the demand: *R. v. McClelland* (1995), 98 C.C.C. (3d) 509, 1995 CarswellAlta 176, 29 Alta. L.R. (3d) 351, 165 A.R. 332, 89 W.A.C. 332, 12 M.V.R. (3d) 288, [1995] A.J. No. 539 (Alta. C.A.); even when some weaving while standing with the officer is added in: *R. v. Ukrainetz*, [2006] S.J. No. 770, 2006 CarswellSask 779, 2006 SKPC 102, 288 Sask. R. 42 (Sask. Prov. Ct.) (Green P.C.J.). Nor is a strong odour of alcohol on his breath, glossy eyes and slightly slurred speech: *R. v. Kelly*, [2006] A.J. No. 1060, 2006 CarswellAlta 1098, 2006 ABPC 226, 407 A.R. 140 (Alta. Prov. Ct.) (Malin P.C.J.).

In *R. v. Rohrich*, [2006] O.J. No. 1697, 2006 CarswellOnt 2617, 2006 ONCJ 150, 141 C.R.R. (2d) 52 (Ont. C.J.) insufficient grounds (and hence a s. 8 and 9 *Charter* violation) was found where an arrest for impaired driving was based upon "... an odour...bloodshot eyes and...the suspicious factor of the accused trying to avoid the police. None of these speak directly to his ability to drive impaired..."

A single vehicle accident combined with the smell of alcohol on the accused is not sufficient for reasonable grounds to demand blood alcohol level tests under section 254(3) of the *Criminal Code*: *R. v. Higgins*, [2001] M.J. No. 97, 2001 MBQB 65, 154 Man. R. (2d) 255, 2001 CarswellMan 98, 12 M.V.R. (4th) 45 (Man. Q.B.).

R. v. Scurvey, [2002] Y.J. No. 97, 2002 CarswellYukon 103, 2002 YKTC 87, 31 M.V.R. (4th) 274 (Y.T. Terr. Ct.) considered whether the horizontal astigmas test could provide the requisite grounds for a breathalyzer test.

The admissibility of Drug Recognition Examination evidence was considered in *R. v. Wood*, [2007] A.J. No. 895, [2007] 11 W.W.R. 330, 79 Alta. L.R. (4th) 358, 51 M.V.R. (5th) 93, 2007 CarswellAlta 1048, 2007 ABQB 503 (Alta. Q.B.) and rejected. It was held on appeal that the Trial judge erred in admitting as expert evidence a police officer's Drug Recognition Examination ("DRE") and opinion that accused's ability was impaired by cannabis because insufficient reliability was shown.

5.2 FORTHWITH OR AS SOON AS PRACTICABLE

- At what time did the officer form the belief that the offence had been committed?
- At what time did the officer make the demand?
- Was there a substantial delay between the time of forming the belief and making the demand?

For a valid demand within this section, the peace officer must make the demand "forthwith or as soon as practicable" after forming the requisite belief on reasonable and probable grounds. Any substantial delay between forming the requisite belief and the making of the demand will mean that the demand was not made in compliance with these provisions: *R. v. Carey* (2006), [2006] O.J. No. 3821, 2006 CarswellOnt 5780, 215 O.A.C. 151, 36 M.V.R. (5th) 35, 83 O.R. (3d) 49 (Ont. C.A.); *R. v. Fisher*, [2006] O.J. No. 5277, 2006 ONCJ 517, 2006 CarswellOnt 8501 (Ont. C.J.) (G. Campbell J.). *R. v. Furry* (August 17, 1990), Doc. New Westminster X027522 (B.C. S.C.), Drinking & Driving Law, Vol. VI, no. 3, p. 20; *R. v. Fisher* (October 6, 1995), Doc. Calgary 50303502P10101, 0102 (Alta. Prov. Ct.); *R. v. Terrell* (August 28, 1987), Doc. 08807413 (Ont. Prov. Ct.). The fact that the police officer was waiting for a tow truck was not a reasonable explanation for a delay of 26 minutes between the formation of the opinion that the accused was impaired and the demand for a breath sample: *R. v. Katwaru* (2006), [2006] O.J. No. 5721, 2006 CarswellOnt 8407 (Ont. C.J.) (C. Brewer J.). See also *R. v. Budgell*, [2007] A.J. No. 602, 2007 CarswellAlta 740, 2007 ABPC 138 (Alta. Prov. Ct.) (wait for tow truck not reasonable in circumstances) and *R. v. Ritson*, [2008] B.C.J. No. 273, 2008 CarswellBC 304, 2008 BCPC 26 (B.C. Prov. Ct.) (wait for tow truck was reasonable). *R. v. Whitesell* (1998), 32 M.V.R. (3d) 318 (B.C. S.C.), Drinking & Driving Law, Vol. XIII, no. 4, p. 27.

The phrase "as soon as practicable" does not mean "as soon as possible": *R. v. Seed* (1998), 38 M.V.R. (3d) 44, 114 O.A.C. 326, 1998 CarswellOnt 4176, [1998] O.J. No. 4362 (Ont. C.A.); *R. v. Caprarie-Melville* (1998), 1998 CarswellYukon 101 (Y.T. S.C.); *R. v. Kutash* (1991), 31 M.V.R. (2d) 76, 92 Sask. R. 52 (Sask. Q.B.); *R. v. Purdon* (1989), 19 M.V.R. (2d) 129, 52 C.C.C. (3d) 270, 100 A.R. 313 (Alta. C.A.); *R. v. Phillips* (1988), 4 M.V.R. (2d) 239, 64 C.R. (3d) 154, 42 C.C.C.(3d) 150 (Ont. C.A.); *R.v. Altseimer* (1982), 17 M.V.R. 8, 29 C.R. (3d) 276, 1 C.C.C. (3d) 7, 38 O.R. (2d) 783, 142 D.L.R. (3d) 246 (Ont. C.A.); *R. v. Lesmeister* (1985), 41 Sask. R. 260 (Sask. Q.B.).

It does not negate the breathalyzer presumption requirement that the breath tests be taken "as soon as practicable" that there was a one hour delay between the 911 call to report the accused's motor vehicle accident and the time the police arrived to investigate where during the 911 call, the caller did not mention that alcohol might have been involved: *R. v. Carey* (2006), [2006] O.J. No. 3821, 2006 CarswellOnt 5780, 215 O.A.C. 151, 36 M.V.R. (5th) 35, 83 O.R. (3d) 49 (Ont. C.A.).

"As soon as practicable" is also a condition precedent to the breathalyzer presumption applying. See s. 7.9.1(a)(i).

5.3 RIGHT TO COUNSEL

- Did the police inform your client when he or she was arrested or detained that he or she had a right to counsel?

- Are there any language issues?

- Was there any delay in telling your client about those rights?

- Was the information given before the actual testing took place?

- Did your client have a reasonable opportunity to exercise the right to retain and instruct counsel?

- Did the police question your client or attempt in any other way to get evidence from him or her before that reasonable opportunity had been given.

- Was your client able to consult with his or her counsel in private?

- If a waiver of the right to counsel is alleged, was the waiver valid? If the right to counsel was initially requested and then a change of mind occurred, was the client given the additional information required by the Supreme Court of Canada for a valid waiver in such a situation?

A person's right to counsel as guaranteed by section 10(*b*) of the *Charter of Rights and Freedoms* must be respected before breathalyzer testing actually takes place. Besides requiring the peace officer to inform an accused upon arrest or detention of his or her right to consult counsel without delay, section 10(*b*) of the *Charter* requires two additional correlative duties: the accused must be afforded a reasonable opportunity to exercise the right to retain and instruct counsel, and the peace officer must cease questioning the accused or otherwise eliciting evidence until such reasonable opportunity has been provided: *R. v. Brydges* (1990), 74 C.R. (3d) 129, 53 C.C.C. (3d) 330 (S.C.C.). The police's implementation obligations were fully considered in *R. v. Landolt*, [2007] S.J. No. 208, 2007 CarswellSask 219, 295 Sask. R. 99, 2007 SKPC 32 (Sask. Prov. Ct.).

An impartial interpreter may be necessary for section 10(*b*) to be satisfied: *R. v. Karnakov* (1996), 3 O.T.C. 212 (Ont. Gen. Div.). *R. v. Ryrak*, [2007] O.J. No. 3006, 2007 CarswellOnt 4912, 2007 ONCJ 350 (Ont. C.J.).

Section 10(*b*) of the *Charter* was held violated where the Japanese accused with some knowledge of English asked for a Japanese-speaking lawyer and was told none was available, with the possibility of a Japanese-interpreter never being suggested by the police officer: *R. v. Ikuta* (2000), 38 C.R. (5th) 123, 2000 CarswellOnt 2635, [2000] O.J. No. 2764 (Ont. C.J.). The same result was reached for a Turkish accused in *R. v. Colak*, [2006] O.J. No. 4953, 2006 CarswellOnt 7978, 2006 ONCJ

481 (Ont. C.J.) (M. Green J.), when the police failed to respect the need for an interpreter.

R. v. Hisch, 2004 CarswellBC 665, [2004] B.C.J. No. 610, 2004 BCSC 410, (*sub nom. R. v. H. (S.L.)*) 118 C.R.R. (2d) 14 (B.C. S.C.) held that the test for whether an accused understands his or her right to obtain counsel under s. 10(b) of the *Charter* appears to be a "modified" objective one, notwithstanding some authority that the test is subjective.

"Thus, there may be special circumstances requiring the police to make inquiries as to whether an accused understands his or her s. 10(b) rights that arise without the police being aware of them. There is no allegation in this case of reduced intellectual capacity, language issues or that Ms. S.L.H. was too intoxicated to comprehend her legal rights. However . . . emotional distress may qualify as such special circumstances, whether or not the distress is overt and whether or not the accused explains his or her mental state. . .

Although Ms. S.L.H. did not articulate her emotional upset to Cpl. Maze, this upset nonetheless existed and impacted on her capacity to understand what was being said to her. While no criticism can be levelled at Cpl. Maze in these circumstances, the reality was such that Ms. S.L.H. did not understand her rights.

. . .If an accused truly does not understand his or her right to counsel, for whatever reason, that right has been breached. That will be so even when, as here, the accused has communicated to the police officer that he or she did understand."

The accused must be afforded a right to consult with counsel in private: *R. v. McKane* (1987), 49 M.V.R. 1, 58 C.R. (3d) 130, 35 C.C.C. (3d) 481 (Ont. C.A.). There is no requirement for the accused who is telephoning a lawyer while in police custody to request privacy: *R. v. Gilbert* (1988), 61 C.R. (3d) 149, 40 C.C.C. (3d) 423, 24 O.A.C. 150 (Ont. C.A.); *R. v. Playford* (1987), 61 C.R. (3d) 101, 40 C.C.C. (3d) 142, 63 O.R. (2d) 289 (Ont. C.A.). The test to be applied in determining whether the accused was afforded privacy at the time of his arrest is a subjective one as to his belief as to whether or not he felt intimidated and therefore found it unwise as to whether or not he ought to freely discuss his problems with his lawyer; however, such belief should be based on reasonable grounds: *R. v. Malmholt* (1997), 29 M.V.R. (3d) 114 (Ont. Gen. Div.); *R. v. Watson* (2000), 2000 CarswellMan 320 (Man. Prov. Ct.). The failure of the detaining or arresting officer to advise a detained person that his right to retain and instruct counsel is a right to do so in privacy does not necessarily amount to a breach of the right of the detained person: *R. v. Butler* (1995), 104 C.C.C. (3d) 198, 68 B.C.A.C. 275, 112 W.A.C. 275 (B.C. C.A.), leave to appeal refused (1997), 105 C.C.C. (3d) vi (S.C.C.); *R. v. Parrill* (1998), 38 M.V.R. (3d) 7, 169 Nfld. & P.E.I.R. 28, 521 A.P.R. 28, 58 C.R.R. (2d) 56 (Nfld. C.A.).

Another case finding a violation of the privacy aspect of the right to counsel is *R. v. Carroll* (2002), 2002 CarswellOnt 987, 24 M.V.R. (4th) 248, [2002] O.J. No. 1215 (Ont. C.J.).

R. v. Burley (2004), 2004 CarswellOnt 523, [2004] O.J. No. 319, 49 M.V.R. (4th) 29, 181 C.C.C. (3d) 463, 182 O.A.C. 395, 115 C.R.R. (2d) 326 (Ont. C.A.) the right to privacy involved in s. 10(b) of the *Charter* was held not violated merely because accused had a "subjective and unreasonable belief that the call was not in private."

In *R. v. Pidwerbesky* (September 18, 1997), Doc. Blaine Lake 2039532 (Sask. Prov. Ct.), Drinking & Driving Law, Vol. XIII no. 7, p. 54, the right to counsel was violated where the police officer cut short the accused's conversation with counsel because he thought it had gone on long enough.

Even successive consultations with counsel may be required to satisfy the *Charter*. *R. v. Whitford* (1997), 115 C.C.C. (3d) 52, 141 W.A.C. 97, 196 A.R. 97, 1997 CarswellAlta 232, [1997] A.J. No. 309, 43 C.R.R. (2d) 363 (Alta. C.A.), leave to appeal refused, 117 C.C.C. (3d) vi, [1997] 3 S.C.R. xiii, 168 W.A.C. 395 (note), 212 A.R. 395 (note), 46 C.R.R. (2d) 376 (note), 224 N.R. 160 (note) (S.C.C.); *R. v. Goodine* (1989), [1989] A.J. No. 220, 1989 CarswellAlta 49, 97 A.R. 102, 13 M.V.R. (2d) 330, 66 Alta. L.R. (2d) 69 (Alta. C.A.). But see *R. v. Ferstl* (2007), 2007 CarswellAlta 1835, [2007] A.J. No. 1507, 2008 ABQB 3 (Alta. Q.B.) (one call may be enough to satisfy police implementation obligation). In *R. v. Ralph* (1999), 46 M.V.R. (3d) 119 (Ont. C.J.), breathalyzer readings were excluded under section 24(2) of the *Charter* because of a section 10(b) violation where the police failed to comply with the accused's successive and further requests to speak to counsel even though he spoke to one counsel previously. To similar effect is *R. v. Santa Maria* (1998), 58 C.R.R. (2d) 129 (Ont. Prov. Div.) where the accused, after speaking to duty counsel, indicated his wish to speak to a different counsel because of dissatisfaction with the advice received and difficulty in communication.

Inadequate legal aid duty counsel advice may found a section 10(b) violation: *R. v. Czorny* (1996), 1996 CarswellOnt 3218, 39 C.R.R. (2d) 302, 15 O.T.C. 111 (Gen. Div.), Drinking & Driving Law, Vol. XII, no. 1, p. 6.

The Supreme Court of Canada stated some important principles in five drinking and driving cases that were argued together: *R. v. Bartle* (1994), 33 C.R. (4th) 1, 92 C.C.C. (3d) 289, 19 O.R. (3d) 802 (note) (S.C.C.), *R. v. Pozniak* (1994), 33 C.R. (4th) 49, 92 C.C.C. (3d) 472, 19 O.R. (3d) 802 (note) (S.C.C.), *R. v. Cobham* (1994), 6 M.V.R. (3d) 89, 33 C.R. (4th) 73, 92 C.C.C. (3d) 333 (S.C.C.), *R. v. Prosper* (1994), 6 M.V.R. (3d) 181, 33 C.R. (4th) 85, 92 C.C.C. (3d) 353 (S.C.C.), and *R. v. Matheson* (1994), 6 M.V.R. (3d) 161, 33 C.R. (4th) 136, 92 C.C.C. (3d) 434 (S.C.C.). A sixth decision *R. v. Harper* (1994), 33 C.R. (4th) 61, 92 C.C.C. (3d) 423 (S.C.C.) was not a drinking and driving case and did not add anything to the analysis in the other cases.

The court held that as part of the announcement right or informational component in section 10(*b*) of the *Charter* the police must tell a detainee how to access any provincial 24-hour duty counsel system, including any toll-free number to call.

The court considered the elements of a valid waiver of the right to counsel.

The court also affirmed in not uncertain terms the availability of the exclusion of breathalyzer samples under section 24(2) of the *Charter* and made some important statements regarding what the Crown must prove under section 24(2) to resist exclusion of evidence.

A useful summary is found in *R. v. Luong*, [2000] A.J. No. 1310, 2000 ABCA 301, 6 M.V.R. (4th) 183, 149 C.C.C. (3d) 571, 85 Alta. L.R. (3d) 217, 271 A.R. 368, 234 W.A.C. 368, 2000 CarswellAlta 1238 (Alta. C.A.). The applicable principles were summarized as follows:

1. The onus is upon the person asserting a violation of his or her Charter right to establish that the right as guaranteed by the Charter has been infringed or denied.

2. Section 10(*b*) imposes both informational and implementational duties on state authorities who arrest or detain a person.

3. The informational duty is to inform the detainee of his or her right to retain and instruct counsel without delay and of the existence and availability of Legal Aid and duty counsel.

4. The implementational duties are two-fold and arise upon the detainee indicating a desire to exercise his or her right to counsel.

5. The first implementational duty is "to provide the detainee with a reasonable opportunity to exercise the right (except in urgent and dangerous circumstances . . .".

6. The second implementational duty is "to refrain from eliciting evidence from the detainee until he or she has had that reasonable opportunity (again, except in cases of urgency or danger) . . .".

7. A trial judge must first determine whether or not, in all of the circumstances, the police provided the detainee with a reasonable opportunity to exercise the right to counsel; the Crown has the burden of establishing that the detainee who invoked the right to counsel was provided with a reasonable opportunity to exercise the right.

8. If the trial judge concludes that the first implementation duty was breached, an infringement is made out.

9. If the trial judge is persuaded that the first implementation duty has been satisfied, only then will the trial judge consider whether the detainee, who has invoked the right to counsel, has been reasonably diligent in exercising it; the detainee has the burden of establishing that he was reasonably diligent in the exercise of his rights.

10. If the detainee, who has invoked the right to counsel, is found not to have been reasonably diligent in exercising it, the implementation duties either do not arise in the first place or will be suspended.

11. Once a detainee asserts his or her right to counsel and is duly diligent in exercising it, (having been afforded a reasonable opportunity to exercise it), if the detainee indicates that he or she has changed his or her mind and no longer wants legal advice, the Crown is required to prove a valid waiver of the right to counsel. In such a case, state authorities have an additional informational obligation to "tell the detainee of his or her right to a reasonable opportunity to contact a lawyer and of the obligation on the part of the police during this time not to take any statements or require the detainee to participate in any potentially incriminating process until he or she has had that reasonable opportunity" (sometimes referred to as a "Prosper warning") . . . Absent such a warning, an infringement is made out.

5.3.1 INFORMATION REGARDING IMMEDIATE, FREE DUTY COUNSEL ADVICE

The famous decision in *R. v. Brydges* (1990), 74 C.R. (3d) 129, 53 C.C.C. (3d) 330 (S.C.C.) expanded the information component of section 10(*b*) beyond its express words: 'you have the right to retain and instruct counsel without delay,' to apparently require that police authorities inform detainees about Legal Aid and duty counsel services in existence and available at the time of detention. *Bartle* expressly emphasized that a detainee is entitled, under the informational component of section 10(*b*), to be advised of whatever system for free, preliminary legal advice exists in the jurisdiction. In *R. v. Peterson* (1998), 220 A.R. 30 (Alta. Prov. Ct.), it was held that once the police provide a *prima facie* reasonable caution they are entitled to conclude that the detainee understands his or her rights unless the detainee reveals otherwise. The police need not explain the meaning of duty counsel unless the detainee shows he does not understand.

Further, so there be no doubt, *Bartle* held that the police are also expressly required to provide basic information about how to access available duty counsel or other services which provide free, preliminary legal advice. This is to be done, for example, by telling a detainee in plain language of any phone number available to contact a lawyer right away, e.g., a 1-800 number, or by providing a list of telephone numbers for lawyers acting as duty counsel.

Failure to provide all the information required as part of the informational component constitutes a breach of section 10(*b*). Therefore, once the informational component under section 10(*b*) has not been properly complied with, questions about whether a detainee wanted to exercise the right to counsel or was reasonably diligent with respect to such exercise or whether the detainee waived their facilitation rights do not properly arise for consideration. They are simply not relevant under section 10(*b*), because the breach of section 10(*b*) is complete upon the failure by the state authorities to properly inform the detainee in accordance with section 10(*b*), *Bartle* held.

The failure to repeat the information regarding the availability of duty counsel on the toll-free line after arriving at the police station did not amount to a breach of the accused's rights under s. 10(b): *R. v. Bouchey* (1998), 39 M.V.R. (3d) 125 (Ont. Gen. Div.). The requisite informational component of s. 10(b) of the Charter does not mandate that, in all cases, the detainee be informed of the toll-free Legal Aid telephone number. Neither does such a requirement exist in all instances where an arrest occurs outside regular office hours. The day and hour of the arrest of the accused as well as the non-disclosure of the specific toll-free telephone number are facts which must be considered in conjunction with all other circumstances. These circumstances would include a review of the specific information provided to the accused by the officer, a determination of whether the accused understood the information provided in the officer's caution, and whether, expressly or impliedly, the accused indicated that he wished to contact counsel: *R. v. Waterman*, 128 Man. R. (2d) 310, 56 C.R.R. (2d) 341, 1998 CarswellMan 366 (Man. Q.B.).

In *R. v. Latimer* 4 C.R. (5th) 1, 112 C.C.C. (3d) 193, [1997] 1 S.C.R. 217, 142 D.L.R. (4th) 577, [1997] 2 W.W.R. 525, 207 N.R. 215, 41 C.R.R. (2d) 281, 152 Sask. R. 1, 140 W.A.C. 1 (S.C.C.), the toll-free number for access to immediate free legal advice by Legal Aid duty counsel was not in operation at the time of day that the accused was arrested. The Supreme Court of Canada held that it was therefore not necessary to inform him of that number. The accused was made aware of the duty counsel service that was offered by the local Legal Aid office, which could be reached by a local phone call at no cost to him. The rights of the accused under s. 10(b) of the Charter were therefore not violated. See also *R. v. Wingerter* (1998), 38 M.V.R. (3d) 284, 174 Sask. R. 48, 1998 CarswellSask 703, [1998] S.J. No. 768 (Sask. Q.B.).

R. v. Dixon (2002), [2002] N.J. No. 277, 2002 CarswellNfld 290, 217 Nfld. & P.E.I.R. 348, 651 A.P.R. 348, 31 M.V.R. (4th) 143 (Nfld. T.D.), considered – and found wanting – the standard s. 10(b) right to counsel warning.

Where the accused's rights are violated by a police failure to provide all the information required for the informational component, the Crown must show that the accused would not have acted differently had the right to counsel been properly administered: *R. v. Wydenes* (1999), 123 B.C.A.C. 236, 201 W.A.C. 236, 1999 CarswellBC 738, [1999] B.C.J. No. 794 (B.C. C.A.). Police are also obliged to advise the accused that the right to counsel means the right to effective counsel, but only if they have reason to believe on a balance of probabilities that the accused's current counsel is incompetent: *R. v. Dubeau* (1998), 213 A.R. 346, 58 Alta. L.R. (3d) 393 (Alta. Prov. Ct.).

The accused was not sufficiently advised of his right to counsel where the officer did not address the matter of who counsel was or how the accused might be able to "retain and instruct" counsel if he was inclined to do so: *R. v. Hiscock* (1998), 162 Nfld. & P.E.I.R. 84, 500 A.P.R. 84 (Nfld. Prov. Ct.); The Spanish-speaking accused's right to counsel was breached where the paraphrased Spanish translations of the primary and secondary cautions provided to him by a police officer did not include mention of his right to the services of a free legal aid duty counsel: *R. v. Cornelio* (1998), 58 C.R.R. (2d) 43 (Ont. Gen. Div.).

5.3.2 EXCLUSION OF BREATHALYZER EVIDENCE

Bartle reiterated that there are two requirements for exclusion of evidence under section 24(2): first, there has to have been a *Charter* violation in the course of obtaining the evidence, and second, it must be found that having regard to all the circumstances, admission of the evidence would bring the administration of justice into disrepute.

Under the first threshold requirement, there must be some connection or relationship between the infringement of the right or freedom in question and the obtaining of the evidence which is sought to be excluded. However, a strict causal link between the *Charter* infringement and the discovery of the evidence is not required. Generally speaking, so long as it is not too remotely connected with the violation, all the evidence obtained as part of the "chain of event" involving the *Charter* breach will fall within the scope of section 24(2). This means that in the initial inquiry under section 24(2) as to whether evidence has been "obtained in a manner that infringed or denied" *Charter* rights, courts should take a *generous* approach.

The analysis must then proceed to the second stage of inquiry under section 24(2), where it must be determined whether, in all of the circumstances, admission of the evidence would tend to bring the admission of justice into disrepute. In order to make this determination, a court must balance factors relating to the effect of admission on the fairness of the trial, the seriousness of the breach, and the effect of exclusion on the repute of the administration of justice.

Bartle reminded that the overall burden of persuasion under section 24(2) rests on the party seeking exclusion of the evidence. That is, it is the applicant for exclusion under section 24(2) who must ultimately satisfy the court on a balance of probabilities that admission of the evidence could bring the administration of justice into disrepute.

However, the important point was added that just because the applicant bears the ultimate burden of persuasion under section 24(2) it does not mean that he or she will bear this burden on every issue relevant to the inquiry. As a practical matter, the onus on any issue will tend to shift back and forth between the applicant and the Crown, depending on what the particular contested issue is, which party is seeking to rely on it and, of course, the nature of the *Charter* right which has been violated.

The court held that the burden of establishing a violation of the *Charter* which always falls on the applicant, does *not* mean that the applicant must formally prove every single fact upon which his or her claim of a violation is based, including one which is not in dispute between the parties and is (or should be) common knowledge amongst members of the criminal bar and those on the bench. The existence of duty counsel services, for example, was not a matter which required independent proof by the accused. Duty counsel and legal aid services are an intrinsic part of the practice of criminal law in this country and, as such, courts are entitled to take judicial notice of the broad parameters of these services, such as their existence and how they are generally accessed.

If there were, for some unusual reason, no duty counsel system available at the time of detention in a jurisdiction known to have such a system, perhaps because the bar had just gone on strike, then it is up to the party alleging the exceptional circumstances, be it the Crown or the applicant, to prove that the service that was routinely available was in fact not operational at the relevant time and place, *Bartle* held.

Bartle noted that one of the issues that tends to arise in cases where there has been a breach of section 10(*b*) of the *Charter* is whether the accused would have acted any differently had there been no violation of his or her right to counsel. The court held that the Crown should bear the legal burden (the burden of persuasion) of establishing, on the evidence, that the section 24(2) applicant would not have acted differently had his or her section 10(*b*) rights been fully respected, and that, as a consequence, the evidence would have been obtained irrespective of the section 10(*b*) breach.

Bartle reiterated that the second of the two requirements for exclusion of evidence under section 24(2) is that it must be found that having regard to all the circumstances, admission of the evidence would bring the administration of justice into disrepute. In order to make this determination, a court must balance factors relating to:

- the effect of admission on the fairness of the trial,
- the seriousness of the breach, and
- the effect of exclusion on the repute of the administration of justice.

In *Bartle*, the evidence being challenged under section 24(2) included not only a statement by the accused about having five to six beers, which was clearly self-incriminatory, but also the result of the breathalyzer tests, and these too were self-incriminatory, the court held. The breath sample provided by the accused emanated from his body and, unlike real evidence, could not have been obtained but for the accused's participation in their construction. The conscriptive character of breathalyzer evidence in the impaired driving context warrants further discussion, the court said, in light of a line of argument which seeks to downplay or even deny the self-incriminatory nature of breath samples. The argument can be summarized as follows: because the breathalyzer evidence was statutorily compellable whether or not the accused spoke to counsel, it could not have affected the fairness of the trial and, therefore, should be admitted under section 24(2) of the *Charter*. The court rejected this argument.

Although the scope of available legal advice in the impaired driving context is necessarily limited, the court noted that it had clearly stated in the past that, where the right to counsel has been infringed, it is improper to speculate about the nature of the advice that a detainee would have received and whether the evidence would have been obtained had the right not been infringed.

The court in *Bartle* thus specifically held that it was satisfied that there is sufficient scope for legal advice to a detainee who has received a breathalyzer demand pursuant to section 254(3)(*a*) of the *Code* to say that courts must not speculate about the nature of that advice and whether it would have made any difference to the outcome of the case. In *R. v. Pidwerbesky* (September 18, 1997), Doc. Blaine Lake 2039532 (Sask. Prov. Ct.), Drinking & Driving Law, Vol. XIII no. 7, p. 54, breathalyzer readings were excluded from evidence as a result of s. 10(b) violation. The police officer cut short the accused's conversation with counsel because he thought it had gone on long enough. The accused's breath tests were also excluded in *R. v. Santa Maria* (1998), 58 C.R.R. (2d) 129 (Ont. Prov. Div.), Drinking & Driving Law, Vol. XIV no. 3, p. 19, where the accused, after speaking to duty counsel, indicated that he wanted to speak to different counsel because of dissatisfaction with the advice received and the difficulty in communication.

R. v. McKenzie (1999), 48 M.V.R. (3d) 61, 28 C.R. (5th) 394, 68 C.R.R. (2d) 155 (Ont. S.C.J.), an appeal by the accused from his conviction where breathalyzer test results were admitted into evidence under section 24(2) of the *Charter* after a section 10(*b*) violation was found, has affirmed the general rule that breath tests results are inadmissible after a section 10(*b*) violation. The issue was considered in detail in *R. v. Dyer*, [2007] A.J. No. 487, 2007 ABPC 116, 2007 CarswellAlta 564, 419 A.R. 296, 74 Alta. L.R. (4th) 383 (Alta. Prov. Ct.) (A.A. Fradsham Prov. Ct. J.) and *R. v. Parkes*, [2007] O.J. No. 502, 2007 ONCJ 43, 2007 CarswellOnt 675 (Ont. C.J.) (D.A. Fairgrieve J.) and both cases held that breath test results obtained by a *Charter* violation constitute self-incriminatory evidence that is presumptively prejudicial to a fair trial, and hence such evidence is presumptively inadmissible under s. 24(2). See also *R. v. Brown*, [2007] B.C.J. No. 1086, 2007 BCPC 152, 2007 CarswellBC 1196 (B.C. Prov. Ct.). But *R. v. Ginman*, [2008] O.J. No. 1009, 2008 CarswellOnt 1409, 2008 ONCJ 111 (Ont. C.J.) (not s. 10(b) breach).

5.3.3 'HOLDING OFF' IF DUTY COUNSEL UNAVAILABLE

Two of the cases dealt with the situation where no 24-hour duty counsel system was in fact in existence. *Prosper* and *Matheson* both noted that the information referred to in *Brydges* was the "applicable system of duty counsel and Legal Aid in the jurisdiction," and so if there is no such system in existence then the police need not advise regarding any right to duty counsel. These cases also held that;

> s. 10(b) of the Charter does not create a positive constitutional obligation on governments to ensure that free and immediate, preliminary legal advice is available to all detainees.

However, the court noted as follows concerning the implications if a government chooses to not set up such a system: that the detainee's right to a reasonable opportunity to obtain legal advice may require the police to "hold off" demanding the breath samples, even to the point of passing the two-hour presumption time limit. This important holding will also obviously apply where a duty counsel system exists but for some reason accessing duty counsel is difficult.

Section 10(*b*) imposes both informational and implementational duties on state authorities who arrest or detain a person. Once a detainee has indicated a desire to exercise his or her right to counsel, the state is required:

- to provide him or her with a reasonable opportunity in which to do so, and
- state agents must refrain from eliciting incriminatory evidence from the detainee until he or she has had a reasonable opportunity to reach counsel.

Once a detainee asserts his or her right to counsel, the police cannot in any way compel him or her to make a decision or participate in a process which could ultimately have an adverse effect in the conduct of an eventual trial until that person has had a reasonable opportunity to exercise that right. In other words, the police are obliged to "*hold off*" from attempting to elicit incriminatory evidence from the detainee until he or she has had a reasonable opportunity to reach counsel.

The court held that what constitutes a "reasonable opportunity" will depend on all the surrounding circumstances. These circumstances will include the availability of duty counsel services in the jurisdiction where the detention takes place. As the majority in *Brydges* suggested, the existence of duty counsel services may affect what constitutes "reasonable diligence" of a detainee in pursuing the right to counsel, which will in turn affect the length of the period during which the state authorities' section 10(*b*) implementational duties will require them to "hold off" from trying to elicit incriminatory evidence from the detainee. The non-existence of such services will also affect the determination of what, under the circumstances, is a "reasonable opportunity" to consult counsel. The absence of duty counsel in a jurisdiction does not give persons detained the more rights under section 10(*b*) than those who are detained in jurisdictions which have duty counsel. It does, however, serve to extend the period in which a detainee will have been found to have been duly diligent in exercising his or her right to counsel. Similarly, if duty counsel exists but is simply unavailable at the time of detention, the "reasonable opportunity" given to detainees to contact counsel will have to reflect this fact.

In a situation such as in *Prosper*, where duty counsel services are available during regular office hours (although only to those eligible for legal aid) and a detainee expresses a desire to contact counsel and is duly diligent in exercising that right, but is prevented from doing so due to institutional factors beyond his or her control, section 10(*b*) requires that the police hold off from trying to elicit incriminatory evidence from the detainee until he or she has had a reasonable opportunity to reach counsel. Similarly, the "reasonable opportunity" provided to detainees in jurisdictions lacking duty counsel might extend to when the local Legal Aid office opens, when a private lawyer willing to provide free summary advice can be reached, or when the detainee is brought before a justice of the peace for bail purposes and his or her needs can be properly assessed and accommodated. In determining what is a reasonable opportunity, the fact that the evidence may cease to be available as a result of a long delay is a factor to be considered.

In *Prosper*, the court below had accepted the argument that the two-hour evidentiary presumption under section 258(1)(*d*) of the *Criminal Code* created a situation of "urgency" which served to override the accused's section 10(*b*) rights. The Supreme Court disagreed, holding that where the accused had clearly asserted his right to counsel but was prevented from exercising it because of institutional conditions entirely beyond his control, it would be inappropriate to allow a statutory provision benefiting the prosecution to trump the accused's *Charter* rights.

In the context of impaired driving cases, the court said that the existence of the two-hour evidentiary presumption available to the Crown under section 258(1)(*c*)(ii) of the *Code* does not, by itself, constitute a compelling or urgent circumstance. A detainee's *Charter* guaranteed right to counsel must take precedence over the statutory right afforded to the Crown which allows it to rely on an evidentiary presumption about what a breathalyzer reading would have been at the time of care and control of a vehicle. Loss of the benefit of this presumption is simply one of the prices which has to be paid by governments which refuse to ensure that a system of "Brydges duty counsel" is available to give detainees free, preliminary legal advice on an on-call, 24-hour basis.

5.3.4 WAIVER

Waiver of the substantive right in its various aspects is also addressed in *Bartle* and *Prosper* in what are clearly important and significant holdings.

It is hard to see how, if ever, the informational component of section 10(*b*) can be waived, since a knowing, valid, effective waiver requires a communication containing the very information that satisfies this aspect of section 10(*b*).

A valid waiver is described in *Bartle* as "a rarity," and when the requirements as laid out in *Bartle* are examined, that statement appears to be clearly an accurate prophecy. First, unless there is complete and proper compliance with the informational component, a detainee's conduct cannot amount to a waiver. The standard for waiver of a *Charter* right is high. It is a precondition for a valid waiver that a person know what they are waiving. Unless the detainee has complete information, including any telephone number that will allow immediate and free legal advice, they are not in a position to give a valid and effective waiver.

Thus, compliance with the informational component under section 10(*b*) is itself a condition precedent for a valid and effective waiver under the substantive right under section 10(*b*).

This issue is in theory separate and distinct from waiver of the other aspects of section 10(*b*): the substantive right to counsel and its corollaries, a reasonable opportunity to exercise the right and the right to cessation of police interrogative activity pending such exercise.

Even if the informational component is complied with, *Prosper* goes on to set out a further *informational component* required for a valid and effective waiver by a detainee of the substantive right to consult counsel under section 10(*b*). *Prosper* held that in circumstances where a detainee has asserted his or her right to counsel and has been reasonably diligent in exercising it, yet has been unable to reach a lawyer because duty counsel is unavailable at the time of detention, courts must ensure that the *Charter*-protected right to counsel is not too easily waived. Therefore, there is *an additional informational obligation* on police that is triggered once a detainee, who has previously asserted the right to counsel, indicates that he or she has changed his or her mind and no longer wants legal advice. At this point, police will be required to tell the detainee of:

- his or her right to a reasonable opportunity to contact a lawyer, and
- of the obligation on the part of the police during this time not to take any statements or require the detainee to participate in any potentially incriminating process until he or she has had that reasonable opportunity.

This additional informational requirement on police ensures that a detainee who persists in wanting to waive the right to counsel will know what it is that he or she is actually giving up.

Given the importance of the right to counsel, the court went on to say with respect to waiver that once a detainee asserts the right there must be a clear indication that he or she has changed his or her mind, and the burden of establishing an unequivocal waiver will be on the Crown. Further, the waiver must be free and voluntary and it must not be the product of either direct or indirect compulsion. The standard required for an effective waiver of the right to counsel is very high.

In *R. v. Knott* (1998), 213 A.R. 71, 50 C.R.R. (2d) 183 (Alta. Q.B.), *Prosper* was explained as establishing that the Crown must prove that the accused knew what he was giving up when he declined to contact counsel. In effect, the court must be satisfied that the accused knew what he was doing or was in a position to make an informed judgment; that is that he had an adequate knowledge of his right to counsel and had been informed of the duty of the police to hold off obtaining evidence until he had exercised his or her right to counsel.

In *R. v. Cassidy*, 40 M.V.R. (4th) 145, 106 C.R.R. (2d) 97, [2003] B.C.J. No. 1000, 2003 CarswellBC 1015, 2003 BCSC 669 (B.C. S.C.) s. 10(b) of the *Charter* was held violated where the accused was not provided with a "supplementary warning" following failed attempts to contact counsel and subsequent waiver of his s. 10(b) rights. ". . .Prosper did determine that a supplementary warning is required."

"The supplementary warning applies where the accused indicates that he or she wishes to contact counsel and then proceeds to change their mind. Paraphrased, the warning reads, "You have the right to a reasonable period of time to contact counsel. I am obliged to refrain from eliciting incriminatory evidence from you until you have had that reasonable opportunity. Do you understand?"

R. v. Desrosiers, 2005 CarswellOnt 2655, 2005 ONCJ 212 (Ont. C.J.) s. 10(b) of the *Charter* was held violated where duty counsel was called for accused drinking driver but then the tests were taken before duty counsel called back because, due to the delay, the accused "decided" he did not want to wait any longer. The accused's "change of mind" about waiting to speak to duty counsel required an additional Prosper warning to be valid. A change of mind without a Prosper warning was not a valid waiver of the right to counsel, the court said.

In *R. v. Turney* breathalyzer readings excluded for a violation of s. 10(b) of the *Charter* where the Crown failed to establish a valid waiver of the right to counsel.

The accused changed his mind about wanting to consult counsel when the particular lawyer was unable to be reached.

It was held that the police did not make clear to accused his right to a reasonable opportunity to contact a lawyer and of the obligation on the part of the police during this time not to take any statements or require the detainee to participate in any potentially incriminating process until he or she had that reasonable opportunity.

If there is any equivocation in the waiver by the detained individual of his right to counsel, either by speech or body language, it is incumbent upon the police to ensure that such a waiver is both informed and unequivocal before proceeding: *R. v. Keeshig* (1999), 1999 CarswellOnt 997 (Ont. Gen. Div.). The accused's statement in response to the Charter warning that "he wished to see his counsel but would do so after he was released from hospital" was not a valid waiver of right to counsel: *R. v. Smalridge* (2000), [2000] A.J. No. 1073, 272 A.R. 59, 2000 CarswellAlta 977 (Alta. Q.B.).

Where an accused denies that he or she waived the right to counsel, the Crown has the burden of establishing that the accused did so. The standard for establishing waiver is high. Waiver of the right to counsel cannot be effectively given in the abstract. A detained person cannot be expected to make an informed choice to either retain counsel or waive the right unless he or she is given or is possessed of information about the matter under investigation sufficient to identify the circumstances and alert the detainee to the scope of his or her jeopardy: *R. v. Small* (1998), 15 C.R. (5th) 345, 123 C.C.C. (3d) 560, 212 A.R. 356, 168 W.A.C. 356, 52 C.R.R. (2d) 315, 1998 CarswellAlta 222 (Alta. C.A.).

Where the focus of the questioning of the accused changes to a matter different than the incident giving rise to the charge, the police are not entitled to continue their investigation on the assumption that the accused's waiver of the right to counsel is still operative. The accused must again be given his right to counsel: *R. v. McGilvey* (February 22, 1999), Beaulieu J. (Ont. Gen. Div.) See also *R. v. Young* (1992), 73 C.C.C. (3d) 289, 9 O.R. (3d) 23 (Ont. C.A.), leave to appeal refused (1993), 78 C.C.C. (3d) vi (note), 11 O.R. (3d) xiv (S.C.C.); *R. v. Chartrand* (1992), 15 C.R. (4th) 231, 74 C.C.C. (3d) 409 (Man. C.A.). In *R. v. Hodgson*, 230 A.R. 18, [1998] 8 W.W.R. 204, 59 Alta. L.R. (3d) 383, 1998 ABQB 71, 1998 CarswellAlta 130, [1998] A.J. No. 175 (Alta. Q.B.), the court stated, "While the police do not have to reiterate the right to counsel every time an investigation touches on a different offence, police must restate the accused's right to counsel when there is a fundamental and discreet change in the purpose of the investigation, one involving a different and unrelated offence or significantly more serious offence than that contemplated at the time of the warning''. For a discussion of the factors to be considered in determining whether a detainee should be re-cautioned, see *R. v. Sawatsky* (1997), 9 C.R. (5th) 23, 118 C.C.C. (3d) 17, 35 O.R. (3d) 767, 150 D.L.R. (4th) 750 (Ont. C.A.).

In *R. v. Yerhoff* (1998), 37 M.V.R. (3d) 293, 171 Sask. R. 245, 1998 CarswellSask 597 (Sask. Q.B.), the accused stated at the police station that he wished to make a telephone call. When asked if he wanted to call counsel, the accused said he wished to call his sister, who would take care of things by calling the accused's mother. That statement was considered an implicit waiver of the accused's right to consult legal counsel.

The determination of whether a young person has waived his right to counsel depends not upon the explanation of the right but upon the young person's actual awareness of the consequences of his actions: *R. v. I. (L.R.)*, 26 C.R. (4th) 119, (*sub nom. R. v. T. (E.)*) 86 C.C.C. (3d) 289, [1993] 4 S.C.R. 504, 109 D.L.R. (4th) 140 (S.C.C.); *R. v. M. (S.)* (1996), 106 C.C.C. (3d) 289, 28 O.R. (3d) 776 (Ont. C.A.).

R. v. Weedon (1990), 24 M.V.R. (2d) 312 (Ont. Prov. Ct.), is the authority for the proposition that after a section 10(*b*) violation not only the breathalyzer test results but also evidence of any physical observations made following the violation are to be excluded.

5.3.5 COUNSEL OF CHOICE

There is a right to a reasonable opportunity to contact counsel of one's choice: *R. v. Brouillette*, [2007] S.J. No. 288, 50 M.V.R. (5th) 242, 297 Sask. R. 113, 2007 CarswellSask 295, 2007 SKPC 67 (Sask. Prov. Ct.); *R. v. Zaidi* (2007), [2007] O.J. No. 4105, 2007 CarswellOnt 6841 (Ont. S.C.J.); *R. v. Khotar* (2008), [2008] O.J. No. 721, 2008 CarswellOnt 729 (Ont. C.J.); *R. v. Carter* (2008), [2008] O.J. No. 1373, 2008 CarswellOnt 2032 (Ont. C.J.); *R. v. Wilding* (2006), [2006] O.J. No. 4784, 2006 CarswellOnt 7603, 149 C.R.R. (2d) 90 (Ont. S.C.J.) (Trafford J.), reversed (2007), 88 O.R. (3d) 680, 2007 ONCA 853, 2007 CarswellOnt 7887, 55 M.V.R. (5th) 10, [2007] O.J. No. 4776 (Ont. C.A.); *R. v. Blackett* (2006), [2006] O.J. No. 2999, 2006 CarswellOnt 4585, 36 M.V.R. (5th) 223 (Ont. S.C.J.) (D.S. Ferguson J.); *R. v. Wilson*, [2006] O.J. No. 3222, 2006 CarswellOnt 4738, 2006 ONCJ 284, 36 M.V.R. (5th) 99 (Ont. C.J.) (Pugsley J.); *R. v. Mahoney*, [2007] O.J. No. 122, 2007 CarswellOnt 130, 2007 ONCJ 19, 149 C.R.R. (2d) 369, 44 M.V.R. (5th) 268 (Ont. C.J.) (K.J. Caldwell J.); *R. v. Meston* (1995), 16 M.V.R. (3d) 275, 175 A.R. 161 (Alta. Prov. Ct.); *R. v. Rooney* (1996), 2 O.T.C. 270 (Ont. Gen. Div.); *R. v. Grimston* (February 20, 1998), Casey Prov. J. (Ont. Prov. Div.), Drinking & Driving Law, Vol. XIII, no. 5, p. 35; *R. v. Kowalchuk* (1999), 179 Sask. R. 31, 67 C.R.R. (2d) 307, 1999 CarswellSask 2, [1999] S.J. No. 1 (Sask. Q.B.). In *R. v.*

MacKay, 2000 CarswellAlta 451, 2000 ABPC 65, 76 C.R.R. (2d) 72, 265 A.R. 170 (Alta. Prov. Ct.), the accused was acquitted of refusing a breathalyzer demand because of the denial of his right to counsel of choice.

R. v. Campbell, [2003] S.J. No. 355, 2003 CarswellSask 356, 2003 SKPC 82, 235 Sask. R. 127 (Sask. Prov. Ct.), also held that the Accused's right to counsel was violated by the lack of police effort to assist in contacting counsel of choice and breathalyzer test results were excluded.

"The problem in this case stems from the perfunctory fashion in which police dealt with the defendant and the physical arrangements for contacting counsel. The implementational duties on the police to allow a person, when they wish to speak to a certain named lawyer, to pursue that may require access to a working phone, telephone directories or directory assistance. If this equipment is not available for use by a detained individual, then the arresting officer or detention staff must make every effort that the detained person would to speak to their lawyer of choice. This did not happen here."

That right is not absolute. If the lawyer chosen is not available within a reasonable amount of time, the accused person will be expected to exercise the right to counsel by calling a different lawyer: *R. v. Van Binnendyk*, (sub nom. *R. v. Binnendyk (D.V.)*) 227 O.A.C. 24, 49 M.V.R. (5th) 178, 2007 CarswellOnt 4723, 2007 ONCA 537, 160 C.R.R. (2d) 159, [2007] O.J. No. 2899 (Ont. C.A.).

Cases dealing with this principle have also made it clear that accessing duty counsel in lieu is not a valid waiver. In *R. v. Wilding* (2006), [2006] O.J. No. 4784, 2006 CarswellOnt 7603, 149 C.R.R. (2d) 90 (Ont. S.C.J.) (W.B.Trafford J.), reversed (2007), 88 O.R. (3d) 680, 2007 ONCA 853, 2007 CarswellOnt 7887, 55 M.V.R. (5th) 10, [2007] O.J. No. 4776 (Ont. C.A.) 10(b) was held violated by the constable's perfunctory two phone calls in an effort to contact the defendant's counsel of choice. "He did not check any Yellow Pages. He did not use Canada 411 on a computer. Nor did he dial 411 for Directory Assistance. . .Where, as here, the arresting officer relied on the Ontario Lawyers Phone Book of 2003 when he investigated the alleged offence in March 2005 and did not complement that effort with a call to 411 Directory Assistance or accessing a website like the one I have mentioned, he was not reasonably diligent. In my view, the limited availability of resources at a police station does not reduce, or otherwise alter, the concept of reasonable diligence under s. 10(b) of the *Charter*. . .[T]he decision by the appellant to use the duty counsel was not, in the circumstances of the case, a waiver of his right to counsel of choice." See also *R. v. Bloom*, [2006] B.C.J. No. 3165, 42 M.V.R. (5th) 186, 2006 CarswellBC 2998, 2006 BCSC 1823 (B.C. S.C.) (Masuhara J.).

R. v. Dhaliwal, [2003] A.J. No. 600, 2003 CarswellAlta 733, 2003 ABPC 57, 345 A.R. 118 (Alta. Prov. Ct.) held that an Accused's right to counsel was violated by lack of police effort to assist accused in contacting counsel of choice and breathalyzer test results were excluded.

"At a minimum, the police must provide the accused with a telephone and telephone directory. . . .[T]he police also have a duty to facilitate an accused by assisting him to obtain a telephone number through directory assistance when that is the only way to obtain it.

In *R. v. Vandale* (2005), [2005] M.J. No. 365, 2005 CarswellMan 379, 198 Man. R. (2d) 314 (Man. Prov. Ct.) the right to counsel in s. 10(b) was held to be violated and breath test results excluded where the officer simply dialed legal aid duty counsel because she "didn't want to wait all night" until the accused found his lawyer. In *R. v. Ryland*, [2006] S.J. No. 119, 2006 CarswellSask 108, 2006 SKPC 22, 140 C.R.R. (2d) 338, 277 Sask. R. 7 (Sask. Prov. Ct.) the violation was found by the policy of the R.C.M.P. in not allowing the accused to place his own calls to counsel, as well as asking directly if he wished to call legal aid following an unsuccessful attempt to reach counsel of choice, in effect streaming him away from any other alternative.

In *R. v. Keagan*, [2003] N.J. No. 89, 2003 CarswellNfld 87, 2003 NLSCTD 48, 106 C.R.R. (2d) 54, 225 Nfld. & P.E.I.R. 150, 672 A.P.R. 150, 36 M.V.R. (4th) 284 (N.L. T.D.) the duty on a police officer to facilitate contact with counsel was considered in detail.

In *R. v. McLinden*, 2004 CarswellAlta 166, [2004] A.J. No. 200, 2004 ABPC 7, 4 M.V.R. (5th) 96, 116 C.R.R. (2d) 219 (Alta. Prov. Ct.), s. 10(b) of the *Charter* was held to have been breached by (1) the failure of the arresting officer to provide to the accused the white and yellow pages of the telephone directory; and by (2) the police's placing the call to the lawyer chosen by the accused from a list provided by the police, rather than allowing the accused to place the call himself.

R. v. Webster, 2004 CarswellBC 238, [2004] B.C.J. No. 208, 2004 BCPC 19 (B.C. Prov. Ct.) s. 10(b)'s right to counsel was held violated where the accused, who was "from out of town," was ostensibly limited by police to a choice of "a local lawyer" or "Legal Aid".

". . .I agree with the defence that it should have become clear to Constable Wielgosz that the Defendant did not understand the full extent of his right to counsel as soon as the Defendant, who was known to be from out of town, stated that he did not know any local lawyers. The clear implication of that statement, in the context in which it was given, could only be that the Defendant believed his choice of counsel to be limited to those lawyers practising in the local Quesnel area. That was a faulty assumption on the Defendant's part, but a predictable one, and one which the police officer could easily have corrected, as was his duty.

Unfortunately, the police officer's response, asking if Legal Aid would be satisfactory, by implication confirmed the Defendant's misunderstanding, rather than correcting it. There is no evidence that the error was ever corrected."

Section 10(b) of the *Charter* was held violated by the police failure to provide means for the accused to place a long distance call to his counsel of choice in *R. v. Hanson*, 2005 CarswellAlta 697, 2005 ABPC 111, [2005] A.J. No. 603, 378 A.R. 371 (Alta. Prov. Ct.).

Section 10(*b*) of the *Charter* was violated where an accused was unable to reach counsel of choice and gave up without being informed of the "holding off" obligation: *R. v. Cutknife* (2000), [2000] A.J. No. 1105, 272 A.R. 172, 2000 CarswellAlta 1033 (Alta. Q.B.), or where the accused changed his mind about contacting counsel without the requisite information being provided by police: *R. v. Russell*, [2000] N.B.J. No. 461, 2000 NBCA 53, 150 C.C.C. (3d) 243, 8 M.V.R. (4th) 188, 232 N.B.R. (2d) 297, 598 A.P.R. 297, 2000 CarswellNB 474 (N.B.C.A.).

The standard required for an effective, informed waiver is not diminished because a detainee has requested an opportunity to consult with specific counsel. Coerced participation in a consultation with duty counsel cannot meet the standard of waiver required under s. 10(b): *R. v. Wilson*, [2006] O.J. No. 3222, 2006 CarswellOnt 4738, 2006 ONCJ 284, 36 M.V.R. (5th) 99 (Ont. C.J.) (Pugsley J.); *R. v. Steinhauser* (1999), 40 M.V.R. (3d) 212, 60 C.R.R. (2d) 337, 1999 CarswellOnt 501, [1999] O.J. No. 522 (Ont. Gen. Div.). The accused does not necessarily waive the right to counsel of his choice when he consults duty counsel. In *R. v. Markovski* (1998), 55 C.R.R. (2d) 139 (Ont. Prov. Div.), Drinking & Driving Law, Vol. XIV, no. 2, p. 9, the arresting officer called the accused's lawyer but did not leave a message for him as the voice mail instructed. The police officer simply told the accused that the lawyer was unavailable. The accused consulted duty counsel and then provided samples of his breath. In these circumstances, the accused did not waive the right to counsel of his choice as his consent to consult duty counsel was not informed.

In *R. v. Clark* (1998), 38 M.V.R. (3d) 120 (Ont. Prov. Div.), Drinking & Driving Law, Vol. XIV, no. 3, p. 17, the accused was informed of his right to counsel at roadside only. His s. 10(b) *Charter* rights were not repeated upon his arrival at the detachment. Instead, the arresting officer decided on her own to telephone duty counsel on the accused's behalf. Following his conversation with duty counsel, the accused clearly indicated that he wished to speak to a different lawyer, but the officer discouraged him from doing so. The court held that the officer's conversation with the accused, whether intentional or not, had the effect of making him abandon his intention to pursue his s.10(b) rights and resulted in a violation of the accused's right to counsel.

Denial of right to counsel of choice leads to drinking and driving acquittal on appeal: *R. v. Kumarasamy* (2002), 2002 CarswellOnt 368, [2002] O.J. No. 303, 22 M.V.R. (4th) 234 (Ont. S.C.J.). The court said: "The availability of duty counsel 24 hours a day cannot be used to trump a detainee's right to counsel of choice."

In *R. v. Buffalo*, [2003] A.J. No. 186, 2003 CarswellAlta 165, 2003 ABQB 124, 35 M.V.R. (4th) 159, 337 A.R. 120 (Alta. Q.B.), the Accused's s. 7 and 10(b) rights were held violated because she was not provided a reasonable opportunity to contact her lawyer of choice after she had been placed under arrest for impaired driving.

In *R. v. Diep*, [2002] O.J. No. 3070, 2002 CarswellOnt 2628, 98 C.R.R. (2d) 182, 30 M.V.R. (4th) 89 (Ont. C.J.), a denial of the right to counsel of choice was found to defeat a drinking and driving charge notwithstanding that duty counsel had in fact been consulted by the accused.

5.4 REFUSAL

- Did your client fail or refuse to comply with the demand to provide a breath sample?
- Was a valid demand properly made?
- Did the requisite grounds and belief exist?
- Did your client have a reasonable excuse for not complying?
- Did your client honestly believe that the machine was not functioning properly?
- Did your client have an injury that would make it dangerous for him or her to provide a breath sample?
- Did your client have any other excuse?
- Was your client requested to give any samples of bodily substances other than blood or breath?

A person commits an offence who fails or refuses "without reasonable excuse" to comply with a demand made by a peace officer under this provision: section 254(5). This presumes a "valid" demand. Any basis upon which the demand failed to comply with the provision or otherwise was not properly made provides a defence to such a charge. For example, if the demand was not made forthwith: *R. v. Gratto*, [2006] N.S.J. No. 79, 2006 CarswellNS 84, 2006 NSSC 65, 31 M.V.R. (5th) 104, 241 N.S.R. (2d) 288, 767 A.P.R. 288 (N.S. S.C.). See section 5.2. Furthermore, the failure or refusal must be "without reasonable excuse".

No person is required to provide a sample of any bodily substance for analysis except samples of breath or blood as required under these provisions. Evidence of a failure or refusal to give such other samples is not admissible nor to be the subject of comment in any proceedings: section 258(2). On the other hand, evidence of a failure or refusal to give any samples of breath or blood as required under these provisions is admissible and can lead to an adverse inference against the accused: section 258(3).

An offer to provide a blood sample in response to a proper demand for breathalyzer samples is not a "reasonable excuse" for failing to provide the breathalyzer samples: *R. v. Weir* (1993), 42 M.V.R. (2d) 1, 79 C.C.C. (3d) 538 (N.S. C.A.); *R. v. Richardson*

(1993), 42 M.V.R. (2d) 261, 80 C.C.C. (3d) 287 (Ont. C.A.); *R. v. Taylor* (1993), 43 M.V.R. (2d) 240 (B.C. C.A.).

There is no all-inclusive definition of reasonable excuse. For example, an accused's honest belief that the machine was not functioning properly afforded a reasonable excuse because it was based on objective evidence that there may have been a problem with the machine: *R. v. Phinney* (1979), 3 M.V.R. 38, 49 C.C.C. (2d) 81 (N.S. C.A.); also a medical condition, such as a cleft palate *R. v. Holt* (1996), 11 M.V.R. (3d) 75 (B.C. S.C.), or an injury may make it impossible or dangerous for the accused to blow into a breathalyzer machine: *R. v. Moser* (1992), 36 M.V.R. (2d) 207, 13 C.R. (4th) 96 (Ont. C.A.). Other ''reasonable excuses'' have related to police mistreatment: *R. v. Paz* (1996) 183 A.R. 161 (Alta. Prov. Ct.); or physical injury: *R. v. Watson* (1997), 26 M.V.R. (3d) 194 (Alta. Prov. Ct.), Drinking & Driving Law Vol. XIII, no. 7, p. 55, and lack of an unequivocal refusal: *R. v. McKelvey*, [1996] A.W.L.D. 507 (Alta. Prov. Ct.), Drinking & Driving Law Vol. XIII, no. 2, p. 14. In *R. v. Cameron* (1999), 245 A.R. 383 (Alta. Prov. Ct.), a charge of "refuse breathalyzer" was dismissed where the accused had a "reasonable excuse" for failure to blow because she had asthma and reasonably believed that if she expelled from her lungs all the air present she might suffer an asthma attack. In *R. v. Fantham* (2000), 2000 CarswellOnt 2759, [2000] O.J. No. 1179 (Ont. C.J.), the accused was acquitted of refusing a roadside test where a reasonable doubt made out that he could not comply with the demand because of a shortness of breath condition.

It is a reasonable excuse for refusing to comply with the breathalyzer demand where the accused has a concern of sanitation when the officer gave her an unwrapped mouthpiece. "A mouthpiece that falls to the floor certainly raises an even greater concern about sanitation, and therefore I find that the. . .accused has a reasonable excuse for refusing to provide a sample": *R. v. Byers*, 2005 CarswellAlta 474, 2005 ABPC 75, 378 A.R. 131 (Alta. Prov. Ct.).

In *R. v. Norwood* (2002), [2002] O.J. No. 5218 (Ont. C.J.), the accused was found not guilty of impaired and refusal of breathalyzer demand where his impairment and inability to understand the demand were due to the unforeseen effects of the combination of alcohol consumption, accused's diabetes and a missed lunch meal.

An accused's own evidence is sufficient to make out a medical condition constituting a "reasonable excuse" to refuse the request for a blood alcohol level blood sample. *R. v. Smith* (2000), [2000] N.S.J. No. 406, 189 N.S.R. (2d) 88, 590 A.P.R. 88, 2000 CarswellNS 394 (N.S. S.C.).

It is not a "reasonable excuse" or an excusable "officially-induced error" to a charge of refusing to provide breath samples that the accused was told by legal aid duty counsel "not to blow": *R. v. Beierl*, [2007] O.J. No. 2389, 159 C.R.R. (2d) 254, 48 C.R. (6th) 382, 2007 CarswellOnt 3871, 2007 ONCJ 267 (Ont. C.J.).

A "refusal" by an accused is not absolute and irrevocable the instant uttered. In *R. v. Hines* (1999), [1998] O.J. No. 5831 (Ont. S.C.J.), a conviction for refusing the screening device demand was set aside on appeal and an acquittal entered where the accused refused but then within eight minutes of arrest changed his mind and agreed to provide the sample.

The accused should be afforded a "last chance" to provide a breath sample after being charged if he or she volunteers to do so within a reasonable period of time after making the unsuccessful attempts or refusal: *R. v. Chance* (1997), 32 M.V.R. (3d) 70, 1997 CarswellOnt 4766 (Ont. Prov. Div.).

In *R. v. Minter*, 2004 CarswellAlta 1397, 2004 ABQB 748, 373 A.R. 396 (Alta. Q.B.) the accused was acquitted on appeal of refusing to provide a breath sample where there was no evidence that a qualified technician opined that the accused's samples were inadequate. "On the facts of the case before me, there was no evidence that the Apellant refused to blow into the Intoxilyzer. On the contrary, his evidence and that of the two constables, was that he made a number of attempts to do so. . .Where. . .an accused person blows into the instrument and adequacy or sufficiency is an issue, the opinion of a qualified technician is necessary."

In *R. v. Z. (C.W.)*, [2003] N.S.J. No. 98, 2003 CarswellNS 101, 2003 NSPC 6, 214 N.S.R. (2d) 328 (N.S. Prov. Ct.), it was held that in a case of failing to provide suitable breath samples for analysis, it is essential that the Crown prove beyond a reasonable doubt that the person whose opinion is the determinative trigger is, in fact and in law, a qualified technician designated by the Attorney General. Also considered was the level of acceptable proof.

R. v. Gratto, [2006] N.S.J. No. 79, 2006 CarswellNS 84, 2006 NSSC 65, 31 M.V.R. (5th) 104, 241 N.S.R. (2d) 288, 767 A.P.R. 288 (N.S. S.C.) held that a refusal to a breathalyzer demand made where the accused has not yet been given his right to counsel under s. 10(b) of the *Charter* is inadmissible pursuant to s. 24(2) of the *Charter* since the accused has not been given his rights before being put in the position of providing self-incriminatory evidence.

5.5 CONDUCTING TESTS

- Did the technician that carried out the tests have the proper qualifications?
- Was the person designated as a "qualified technician" by the Attorney General of the province?
- Was the device used in the test an "approved instrument"?
- Was it a device approved as suitable by order of the Attorney General of Canada?

- Was the machine operated properly in accordance with the operator's manual and the manufacturer's instructions?
- Were the tests conducted "pursuant to a demand" made under subsection 154(3)?

The breathalyzer tests must be carried out by a ''qualified technician'' as defined in the *Criminal Code*, which means a person designated as such by the Attorney General of a province. A designation by the Minister of Public Safety pursuant to a delegation of authority from the Attorney General was valid: *R. v. Spanos*, 44 M.V.R. (5th) 84, [2007] O.J. No. 1197, 2007 CarswellOnt 1857, 2007 ONCA 241 (Ont. C.A.) and by means of an ''approved instrument'', which means a device approved as suitable by order of the Attorney General of Canada. Approved instruments are the Breathalyzer, Models 800, 900, 900A, and 900B; Intoximeter Mark IV; Alcolmeter AE-D1; Intoxilyzer 4011AS; Alcotest 7110; Intoxilyzer 5000C; Intoxilyzer 8000C; Intoxilyzer 1400; BAC Datamaster C, Alco-Sensor IV-RBT IV; Breathalyzer 7410-CD with Printer; Alco-Sensor IV/RBT IV-K and Alcotest 7110 MKIII Dual C: section 254(1). See Appendix C for a list of breath testing devices.

In *R. c. Thibeault*, 2007 CarswellNB 469, 2007 CarswellNB 470, [2007] N.B.J. No. 360, 2007 NBCA 67, (sub nom. *R. v. Thibeault*) 823 A.P.R. 334, 287 D.L.R. (4th) 128, 226 C.C.C. (3d) 334, 52 M.V.R. (5th) 99, 319 N.B.R. (2d) 334 (N.B. C.A.), an appeal by the accused from a conviction for "over 80" was allowed and an acquittal entered because the customs officer who administered the breath tests was not a designated peace officer for the purposes of the *Criminal Code*.

In *R. v. Dol* (1999), 1999 CarswellOnt 1503 (Ont. C.J.), a reasonable doubt whether the breath tests purportedly taken with a 16 minute gap between the finish of the first and the start of the second were in fact taken with at least 15 minutes in between meant that they failed to meet the requirements of section 258(1)(c)(ii) of the *Criminal Code*. *R. v. Marcellus* (1999), 2 M.V.R. (4th) 129, 214 N.B.R. (2d) 72, 547 A.P.R. 72 (N.B. C.A.), leave to appeal to S.C.C. refused (1999), 252 N.R. 195 (note), 221 N.B.R. (2d) 200 (note), 567 A.P.R. 200 (note) (S.C.C.), also considered the interpretation to be given to the phrase in section 258(1)(*c*)(ii) of the *Criminal Code* dealing with the breathalyzer presumption that requires "an interval of at least 15 minutes between the times when the samples were taken".

In *R. v. Hill* (1999), [1999] N.S.J. No. 276, 1999 CarswellNS 469 (N.S. Prov. Ct.), the accused was acquitted of drinking and driving offences when the Crown failed to establish that the police officer witness was a qualified technician.

The manufacturer's manual for the particular machine involved in a given case should be carefully examined to ensure that it was properly operated on the relevant occasion in accordance with the manufacturer's instructions. See 13.6.1, Disclosure, (c) Machine Manuals and Records.

It is now becoming common to videotape the actual breath testing itself. It is essential to obtain a copy of any such videotape. It will show the timing of the breath tests and may contain times that conflict with those on the technician's certificate, or may show a failure by the technician to perform the tests according to proper procedure. A toxicologist or other expert should review the tape carefully. See 13.6.1 Disclosure, (b) Video.

In *R. v. Ellinas* (2003), 2003 CarswellOnt 4504, [2003] O.J. No. 4260, 48 M.V.R. (4th) 289 (Ont. C.J.), drinking and driving charges were dismissed where the officer took three intoxilyzer samples but discarded the record of the second one. The second was allegedly unsatisfactory and justified the third sample except that the officer kept no records and discarded the intoxilyzer record of second sample.

A failure to follow proper procedures or the protocol regarding breath testing can occasion a reasonable doubt regarding the validity of the test results: *R. v. Powell* (2006), [2006] O.J. No. 2555, 2006 CarswellOnt 9569 (Ont. C.J.) (R.J. Richards J.). Examples include failure to prove the time limitations regarding the alcohol standard solution were respected: *R. v. Euler* (2007), [2007] O.J. No. 4046, 2007 CarswellOnt 6743 (Ont. S.C.J.) (failure to follow protocol that alcohol standard test solution be charged every 7 days renders test results invalid); *R. v. Morton* (2003), [2003] O.J. No. 279, 2003 CarswellOnt 206 (Ont. S.C.J.) (Howden J.); *R. v. Lui* (June 30, 2004), Doc. Newmarket 03-06658, [2004] O.J. No. 4043 (Ont. C.J.) (O. Tetley J., Newmarket); *R. v. Terzo* (2004), [2004] O.J. No. 5529, 2004 CarswellOnt 6899 (Ont. C.J.) (A. Shaw J., Newmarket).

5.6 BREATH TEMPERATURES

Body temperature is considered to be 37°C. Because air loses its heat as it passes through and out of the respiratory system, end-expiratory breath temperatures can vary from 32.4–35.7°C. Since all breath testing instruments assume a breath temperature of 34.0°C, a lower body temperature would result in less alcohol per given volume of breath and a higher temperature would result in more alcohol for the same volume of breath. It has been shown that a breath-testing instrument will overestimate the true BAC by about 8.6% per °C increase in body temperature.

6

BLOOD TESTS

6.1 REASONABLE GROUNDS

- Was a demand made for a blood sample?
- Did the police officer have reasonable and probable grounds for believing that your client was driving or had control of the car while impaired or "over '80"?
- Was there any reason, by reason of his or her physical condition or otherwise, that your client was not capable of giving a breath sample?
- Was there any reason that made it impractical for the police to obtain a breath sample?
- Did the police officer have reasonable and probable grounds for believing that your client was not capable of giving a breath sample?
- Did the police officer have reasonable and probable grounds for believing that obtaining a breath sample would be impractical?
- Did a qualified medical practitioner take the blood samples, or direct another person in taking them?
- Was that medical practitioner satisfied that taking the blood samples would not endanger the life or health of your client?

Where a peace officer believes on reasonable and probable grounds that a person is committing, or has committed within the preceding three hours (increased from two hours by S.C. 1999, c. 32, s. 2 proclaimed in force July 1, 1999), an offence of impaired operation or ''over '80'', the peace officer may by demand made ''forthwith or as soon as practicable'' require that person to provide ''then or as soon as practicable'' blood samples as are necessary to determine the concentration of alcohol in the person's blood. Blood, rather than breath samples, may only be demanded where the peace officer has reasonable and probable grounds to believe that the person, by reason of his or her physical condition, either may be incapable of providing a breath sample or it would be impractical to obtain a breath sample: section 254(3)(*b*). Furthermore, the blood samples must be taken by or under the direction of a qualified medical practitioner and the qualified medical practitioner must be satisfied that the taking of the samples will not endanger the life or health of the person: section 254(4); *R. v. Knox* (1996), 1 C.R. (5th) 254, 109 C.C.C. (3d) 481, 23 M.V.R. (3d) 93 (S.C.C.).

In *R. v. Schroepfler*, [2006] A.J. No. 990, 35 M.V.R. (5th) 284, 2006 CarswellAlta 1038, 2006 ABPC 179 (Alta. Prov. Ct.) (Mandamin Prov. Ct. J.) the "impracticality" requirement was held not to be demonstrated on the evidence.

In *R. v. Walkom* (1998), [1998] A.J. No. 1568, 221 A.R. 21 (Alta. Prov. Ct.), the accused was acquitted of a drinking and driving charge where the police officer lacked requisite grounds to demand a blood sample. The inability to get an accused to a breathalyzer machine on time is not a "physical condition" of an accused that leads to an "impracticability" as envisaged by the *Criminal Code* to justify blood samples.

6.2 PROPER DEMAND

- Did the demand inform the person that the blood samples would be taken by or under the direction of a qualified medical practitioner and that the qualified medical practitioner must be satisfied that the taking of the samples will not endanger the life or health of the person?

For a valid demand within this section, the requisite reasonable grounds must be present. Furthermore, the demand must inform the person that the blood samples will be taken by or under the direction of a qualified medical practitioner and the qualified medical practitioner must be satisfied that the taking of the samples will not endanger the life or health of the person: *R. v. Green* (1992), 34 M.V.R. (2d) 129, 11 C.R. (4th) 196, 70 C.C.C. (3d) 285 (S.C.C.).

6.3 FORTHWITH OR AS SOON AS PRACTICABLE

- At what time did the police officer form the belief that there were reasonable and probable grounds for taking blood samples?

- At what time did the police officer make the demand that the sample be given?

- Was there any substantial delay between these two times?

For a valid demand within this section, the peace officer must make the demand "forthwith or as soon as practicable" after forming the requisite belief on reasonable and probable grounds. Any substantial delay between forming the requisite belief and the making of the demand will mean that the demand was not made in compliance with these provisions: *R. v. Furry* (August 17, 1990), Doc. New Westminster X027522 (B.C. S.C.), Drinking & Driving Law, Vol. VI, no. 3, p. 20; *R. v. Fisher* (October 6, 1995), Doc. Calgary 50303502P10101, 0102 (Alta. Prov. Ct.); *R. v. Terrell* (August 28, 1987), Doc. 08807413 (Ont. Prov. Ct.). The fact that the police officer was waiting for a tow truck was not a reasonable explanation for a delay of 26 minutes between the formation of the opinion that the accused was impaired and the demand for a breath sample: *R. v. Whitesell* (1998), 32 M.V.R. (3d) 318 (B.C. S.C.), Drinking & Driving Law, Vol. XIII, no. 4, p. 27.

The phrase "as soon as practicable" does not mean "as soon as possible": *R. v. Seed* (1998), 38 M.V.R. (3d) 44, 114 O.A.C. 326, 1998 CarswellOnt 4176, [1998] O.J. No. 4362 (Ont. C.A.); *R. v. Caprarie-Melville* (1998), 1998 CarswellYukon 101 (Y.T. S.C.); *R. v. Kutash* (1991), 31 M.V.R. (2d) 76, 92 Sask. R. 52 (Sask. Q.B.); *R. v. Purdon* (1989), 19 M.V.R. (2d) 129, 52 C.C.C. (3d) 270, 100 A.R. 313 (Alta. C.A.); *R. v. Phillips* (1988), 4 M.V.R. (2d) 239, 64 C.R. (3d) 154, 42 C.C.C.(3d) 150 (Ont. C.A.); *R.v. Altseimer* (1982), 17 M.V.R. 8, 29 C.R. (3d) 276, 1 C.C.C. (3d) 7, 38 O.R. (2d) 783, 142 D.L.R. (3d) 246 (Ont. C.A.); *R. v. Lesmeister* (1985), 41 Sask. R. 260 (Sask. Q.B.).

"As soon as practicable" is also a condition precedent to the breathalyzer presumption applying. See s. 7.9.1(a)(i).

6.4 RIGHT TO COUNSEL

- Did the police inform your client when he or she was arrested or detained that he or she had a right to counsel?

- Was there any delay in telling your client about those rights?

- Was the information given before the actual testing took place?

- Did your client have a reasonable opportunity to exercise the right to retain and instruct counsel?

- Did the police question your client or attempt in any other way to get evidence from him or her before that reasonable opportunity had been given?

- Was your client able to consult with his or her counsel in private?

- If a waiver of the right to counsel is alleged, was the waiver valid? If the right to counsel was initially requested and then a change of mind occurred, was the client given the additional information required by the Supreme Court of Canada for a valid waiver in such a situation?

In *R. v. Schroepfler*, [2006] A.J. No. 990, 35 M.V.R. (5th) 284, 2006 CarswellAlta 1038, 2006 ABPC 179 (Alta. Prov. Ct.) (Mandamin Prov. Ct. J.), it was held that when the officer switches from a breath demand to a blood demand the accused must again be given his right to counsel reminder under s. 10(b) of the *Charter*: ". . .The accused is faced with a different type of legal jeopardy. . .An accused may want to pose different questions to legal counsel upon being presented with a blood sample demand and legal counsel may provide different legal advice."

See section 5.3 Right to Counsel above for a detailed discussion of the right to counsel under section 10(*b*), issues around waiving the right and the exclusion of evidence under section 24(2) consequent upon a breach.

6.5 REFUSAL

- Did your client fail or refuse to comply with the demand to provide blood samples?

- Was a valid demand properly made?

- Did the requisite grounds and belief exist?

- Did your client have a reasonable excuse for not complying?

- Was your client requested to give any samples of bodily substances other than blood or breath?

A person commits an offence who fails or refuses ''without reasonable excuse'' to comply with a demand made by a peace officer under this provision: section 254(5).

This presumes a ''valid'' demand. Any basis upon which the demand failed to comply with the provision or otherwise was not properly made provides a defence to such a charge. Furthermore, the failure or refusal must be ''without reasonable excuse''.

See 5.4 Refusal re: ''reasonable excuse'' above.

No person is required to provide a sample of any bodily substance for analysis except samples of breath or blood as required under these provisions. Evidence of a failure or refusal to give such other samples is not admissible nor to be the subject of comment in any proceedings: section 258(2). On the other hand, evidence of a failure or refusal to give any samples of breath or blood as required under these provisions is admissible and can lead to an adverse inference against the accused: section 258(3).

The following cases involve breath samples, but it is arguable the same principles should apply.

The accused should be afforded a "last chance" to provide a breath sample after being charged if he or she volunteers to do so within a reasonable period of time after making the unsuccessful attempts or refusal: *R. v. Chance* (1997), 32 M.V.R. (3d) 70, 1997 CarswellOnt 4766 (Ont. Prov. Div.).

A "refusal" by an accused is not absolute and irrevocable the instant uttered. In *R. v. Hines* (1998), [1998] O.J. No. 5831 (Ont. S.C.J.), a conviction for refusing the screening device demand was set aside on appeal and an acquittal entered where the accused refused but then within eight minutes of arrest changed his mind and agreed to provide the sample.

R. v. Gratto, [2006] N.S.J. No. 79, 2006 CarswellNS 84, 2006 NSSC 65, 31 M.V.R. (5th) 104, 241 N.S.R. (2d) 288, 767 A.P.R. 288 (N.S. S.C.) held that a refusal to a breathalyzer demand made where the accused has not yet been given his right to counsel under s. 10(b) of the *Charter* is inadmissible pursuant to s. 24(2) of the *Charter* since the accused has not been given his rights before being put in the position of providing self-incriminatory evidence.

6.6 CONDUCTING TESTS

- Was the medical practitioner who conducted or directed the test qualified to do so as defined in the *Criminal Code*?

- Was the technician who conducted the test under the direction of the medical practitioner qualified as designated by the Attorney General of the province?

- Did the blood samples go into an approved blood sample container, i.e., approved as suitable by order of the Attorney General of Canada?

The blood samples must be obtained by a ''qualified medical practitioner'' or by a ''qualified technician'' under the direction of a ''qualified medical practitioner'' as defined in the *Criminal Code*, which means, in respect of ''qualified technician'', a person designated as such by the Attorney General of a province: section 254(1). The samples must go into an ''approved blood sample container'', which means a container approved as suitable by order of the Attorney General of Canada. Approved containers include the Vacutainer XF947; BD Vacutainer 367001; Vacutainer 367001 and Tri-Tech Inc. TUG1O. See Appendix B.

6.7 WARRANTS TO OBTAIN BLOOD SAMPLES

- If blood samples were obtained from your client pursuant to a warrant, did the requisite grounds exist?

- Were there grounds for believing that your client committed within four hours preceding, an offence of impaired operation or "over '80"?

- Was your client involved in an accident resulting in death or bodily harm to anyone?

- Was a qualified medical practitioner of the opinion that by reason of what took place, your client was unable to consent to the taking of blood samples?

- Did that practitioner believe that the taking of the blood samples would not endanger the life or health of your client?

- If the requisite grounds are shown, were the blood samples taken by a qualified medical practitioner or by a qualified technician acting under the direction of the practitioner?

- Were the samples placed in an approved blood sample container?

The *Criminal Code* authorizes the issuance and execution of warrants to take blood samples: section 256. Like any search warrant, it issues upon an information on oath establishing the requisite reasonable grounds of belief. It can be a regular warrant obtained in person before the issuing justice of the peace or can be a telewarrant obtained by telephone or other means of telecommunication.

The requisite grounds shown above are contained in section 256(1) of the *Criminal Code*. Section 254 defines a qualified medical practitioner and technician. The latter is a person designated as such by the Attorney General of the province. An ''approved blood sample container'' means a container approved as suitable by order of the Attorney General of Canada. Approved containers include the Vacutainer XF947; BD Vacutainer 367001; Vacutainer 367001 and Tri-Tech Inc. TUG1O. See Appendix B.

7

PROOF OF IMPAIRMENT

With regard to proof of impairment, reference is often made to a test: "a marked departure from the norm", as expressing what the Crown evidence must show for conviction: see, e.g., *R. v. Smith* (1992), 37 M.V.R. (2d) 9, 13 C.R. (4th) 125, 73 C.C.C. (3d) 285 (Alta. C.A.).

In *R. v. Stellato* (1993), 43 M.V.R. (2d) 120, 78 C.C.C. (3d) 380, 18 C.R. (4th) 127 (Ont. C.A.) the court said it was rejecting the "marked departure" test, pointing out that the *Criminal Code* only requires proof of impairment and does not require "marked impairment".

This was upheld by the Supreme Court of Canada: (1994), 3 M.V.R. (3d) 1, 31 C.R. (4th) 60, 90 C.C.C. (3d) 160 (S.C.C.). To the same effect is *R. v. White* (1994), 3 M.V.R. (3d) 283, 28 C.R. (4th) 160, 89 C.C.C. (3d) 336 (N.S. C.A.). It is suggested, however, that these courts are clearly confusing proof of a legal element with the evidence that goes to prove it. The "marked departure" test was not a test defining the legal element of impairment; those cases never required "marked impairment". What was being discussed was the evidence to prove impairment of driving, and the point was being made that normal driving is never perfect and encompasses an entire range of conduct from the good to the bad or worse. The marked departure test was simply cautioning that not all bad driving reasonably gives rise to an inference of impairment. A driver can drive badly on occasion not because of impaired ability, but because that is their normal ability. Thus, the requirement of a marked departure from normal driving was simply a statement as to when an inference of impaired driving ability could reasonably be drawn. Unless there was a marked departure from the norm, an inference of impaired driving ability was unreasonable and simply assumed that all less than perfect driving was to be blamed on alcohol consumption, the logical fallacy called *post hoc, ergo propter hoc*.

An authority making this point is *R. v. Geerligs* (1995) (Alta. Prov. Ct.), Drinking & Driving Law, Vol. 10, no. 1, p. 6. Most importantly, in an extensive consideration of the issue, the Alberta Court of Appeal in *R. v. Andrews* (1996), 20 M.V.R. (3d) 140, 46 C.R. (4th) 74, 104 C.C.C. (3d) 392 (Alta. C.A.), leave to appeal to S.C.C. refused (1996), 106 C.C.C. (3d) vi (note) (S.C.C.) has now held to the same effect.

The refinement of the *Stellato* test provided by the court in *Andrews* has been adopted in other provinces: *R. v. Gairdner* (1999), 40 M.V.R. (3d) 133 (B.C. S.C.); *R. v. Miller* (1999), 1999 CarswellBC 353 (B.C. S.C.); *R. v. MacDonald* (1998), 37 M.V.R. (3d) 316, 167 N.S.R. (2d) 318, 520 A.P.R. 318 (N.S. S.C. [In Chambers]).

But see the Saskatchewan case of *R. v. MacDonald* (1996), 146 Sask. R. 306 (Sask. Q.B.) where the court did not think that *Andrews* interpreted the *Stellato* decision in a manner that was inconsistent with the reasons given by the Ontario Court of Appeal, reasons that were specifically adopted by the Supreme Court when it dismissed the appeal. In this case, the "marked departure" of conduct was not accepted as the threshold for a conviction for impaired driving. Support for the proposition that *Andrews* does not apply in Saskatchewan is also found in *R. v. Landes* (1997), 161 Sask. R. 305 (Sask. Q.B.), Drinking & Driving Law Vol. XIII, no. 7, p. 49; and *R. v. Thompson* (1998), 1998 CarswellSask 649 (Sask. Q.B.).

The courts in Ontario, however, have followed the analysis in *Andrews*. As observed in *R. v. Raven* (1999), 1999 CarswellOnt 76, [1999] O.J. No. 48 (Ont. Gen. Div.), "[i]t appears that no Ontario court has rejected the *Andrews* interpretation of *Stellato*." See *R. v. Linstead* (1998), [1998] O.J. No. 2950, 1998 CarswellOnt 3008 (Ont. Gen. Div.); *R. v. Moric* (1998), 1998 CarswellOnt 1240, [1998] O.J. No. 1271 (Ont. Gen. Div.); *R. v. Elvikis* (1997), 25 M.V.R. (3d) 256 (Ont. Gen. Div.); *R. v. Jones* (February 13, 1996), Doc. Thunder Bay 119-95 (Ont. Gen. Div.); *R. v. Nolan* (1997), 27 M.V.R. (3d) 241 (Ont. Gen. Div.); *R. v. Carrie* (1997), 32 M.V.R. (3d) 53, 10 C.R. (5th) 356 (Ont. Prov. Div.).

In the absence of expert testimony, the court is not, in considering the quantity of alcohol consumed, empowered by the judicial notice principle to conclude that "the amount that he admits having had to drink is sufficient to impair a person.": *R. v. Letford* (2000), [2000] O.J. No. 4841, 150 C.C.C. (3d) 225, 51 O.R. (3d) 737, 8 M.V.R. (4th) 6, 139 O.A.C. 387, 2000 CarswellOnt 5034 (Ont. C.A.); *R. v. Crawford* (2000), [2000] O.J. No. 3616, 2000 CarswellOnt 3490 (Ont. S.C.J.); and *R. v. Randell* (1994), 118 Sask. R. 48, 1994 CarswellSask 124 (Sask. Q.B.). Drinking & Driving Law, Vol. XIII, no. 7, p. 65.

7.1 ADMISSION

- Did your client expressly admit that he or she was impaired?
- Did your client make any other comments that may be considered as an indirect admission of impairment?

A client's admission of impaired ability is one damaging kind of evidence tending to prove this element of this offence. However, it seems rare for there to be such an express admission. Less explicit comments, such as "perhaps I should not have been driving", can be explained as merely the accused's natural conclusion resulting from the police apprehension and subsequent breathalyzer testing, but adding nothing to the probative value of the prosecution's case.

7.2 NATURE OF DRIVING

- Does police evidence contain references to instances of improper or abnormal driving by your client?
  - weaving
  - traffic infractions
  - poor parking
  - failure to respond to flashing lights or siren
  - other abnormal driving behaviour
- Can the behaviour be explained as being within the range of the driving behaviour of a sober driver. *Instances of abnormal driving may well be in the range of a sober, but less than perfect driver.*
- Can your client explain his or her behaviour? *Weaving from side to side and speeding up and slowing down can be a driver checking street signs for a particular street.*
- Did the client's behaviour result from nervousness at being followed, etc., by a police car? *If your client was followed by a marked police car over some distance, it can be argued that any weaving, etc., was natural and understandable nervous driving on his or her part due to this fact.*
- Was poor parking by your client upon being pulled over by the police caused by nervousness, rather than impairment? *A few carefully crafted questions to emphasize how intimidating a police pull-over is, with lights flashing and siren screaming, will serve to remind the court how even the most innocent driver can be intimidated and nervous as a result. Nervousness would be compounded on the part of an innocent driver who has had one or two drinks and is worried about the odour of alcohol, notwithstanding that his ability is not impaired and his blood alcohol level is below the legal limit.*
- Did your client fail to pull over in response to the flashing lights or siren due to factors other than a consciousness of guilt or of an impaired ability shown by a failure to see or hear the lights or siren?

- Was your client's visibility hampered? Consider:
  - the time of day
  - the location of bright sun
  - other bright lights ahead that may have attracted the driver's attention
- Was your client's ability to hear the police siren hampered? Consider:
  - whether client's radio was on
  - whether the car windows were closed
  - whether the car air conditioning was on
  - other interferences with the ability to hear external sources of sound
- Had your client driven a long distance and for a long time before encountering the police? *If so, how impaired could he or she have been, and perhaps eventual fatigue, rather than alcohol, is the operative factor.*
- Can police evidence be used to assist your client? *If your client were followed by the police for any substantial length of time or distance, it can be argued from that fact that he or she could not have been driving obviously improperly or the police would have halted your client sooner.*
- What was done correctly by your client during the period of police observation? Emphasize the following if possible:
  - the distance over which your client drove apparently properly
  - the number of intersections, stop signs and stop lights navigated by your client without note or comment by the police following behind
  - the absence of visible infractions while the police were observing if such is the case

7.2.1 ACCIDENT

The cause of any accident must be explored to negate the evidentiary value of the fact of the accident as proof of impaired ability.

- Investigate the road conditions and weather conditions.
- What was the immediate explanation for the accident:
  - the client dropping a cigarette?
  - putting a cassette in the tape player?
  - changing radio stations?
  - talking on the telephone?
- Were the circumstances of the accident such that it was unavoidable for *any* driver?
- If so, does the fact of the accident tend to prove anything about your client's ability to drive having been impaired?

R. v. Green, [2005] B.C.J. No. 3011, 2005 BCPC 678, 2005 CarswellBC 3500 (B.C. Prov. Ct.) held that impaired driving was not proved by evidence of a police officer's opinion based on watery bloodshot eyes, slight sway, the strong odour of alcohol and the fact of a motor-vehicle accident where there is not evidence that the accused was to blame for the accident.

> I am careful to note that there is no onus on an accused person to provide an explanation for an accident such as this. I find that I must take into consideration only the evidence of Cpl. Neuman, Cst. Jardine, to a lesser extent the evidence of Cst. Scott, and the evidence of Mr. Morgan, the ambulance driver. I find that on the basis of all that evidence the Crown has not proven beyond a reasonable doubt that Mr. Green's ability to operate a motor vehicle was impaired by alcohol to the level of the test as set out in *R. v. Stellato*; accordingly, Mr. Green must be acquitted on Count 1. However, if I am wrong and I ought to have taken into consideration the fact of the evidence [sic; accident?] then I would have arrived at the opposite conclusion...

The evidentiary value of an accident was also described as follows in *R. v. Trecartin*, [2006] N.B.J. No. 388, 2006 NBPC 26, 2006 CarswellNB 513, 784 A.P.R. 107, 302 N.B.R. (2d) 107, 36 M.V.R. (5th) 250 (N.B. Prov. Ct.), where it was said:

> What evidence do we have here of an impairment of the accused's ability to drive: There is no evidence of anything when he was observed driving by Ms. St. Peter, Ms. Webb or even Mr. Donovan. True we have an accident that occurred but in my view I may not reason backwards that because an accident occurred in daylight hours without apparent reason the accused must have been impaired. Accidents happen all too often and even when the drivers are not consuming alcohol. Undue speed, momentary inattention, fatigue or other factors can and do cause accidents of the sort that claimed the life of Mr. Clark.

7.3 PHYSICAL SYMPTOMS

Judges appropriately attach little significance to the standard litany of observations by police officers. Aside from their lack of any scientific relationship to impaired driving ability caused by alcohol, these factors can arise from such a multitude of causes that they lack any significant probative weight in proving anything on the issue of guilt or innocence. They function mainly as matters tending to provide to a police officer reasonable and probable grounds for a breathalyzer demand or an arrest.

A useful summary regarding physical symptoms is found in *R. v. Landes* (1997), [1997] S.J. No. 785, 161 Sask. R. 305, 1997 CarswellSask 701 (Sask. Q.B.). And *R. v. Wentzell*, [2006] N.S.J. No. 423, 789 A.P.R. 383, 248 N.S.R. (2d) 383, 2006 CarswellNS 472, 2006 NSPC 47 (N.S. Prov. Ct.) (A.G. Crawford P.C.J.).

For cases in which the observation of physical symptoms of intoxication by a police officer was insufficient for a finding of impairment see the following: odour of alcohol, bloodshot eyes and clumsiness: *R. v. Scott* (1999), 1999 CarswellAlta 76 (Alta. Prov. Ct.); odour of alcohol, bloodshot eyes and slurred speech: *R. v. Court* (1999), 1999 CarswellOnt 243, [1999] O.J. No. 270 (Ont. Gen. Div.); *R. v. Hadaway* (1998), 1998 CarswellOnt 873 (Ont. Prov. Div.); *R. v. Landes* (1997), 161 Sask. R. 305 (Sask. Q.B.), Drinking & Driving Law Vol. XIII, no. 7, p. 49; odour of alcohol and bloodshot eyes: *R. v. Singer* (1999), 43 M.V.R. (3d) 160, 1999 CarswellSask 209 (Sask. Q.B.); *R. v. Rulli* (1998), 1998 CarswellOnt 736 (Ont. Prov. Div.); *R. v. Sears* (August 1, 1997), Doc. CR SY 4805/97 (N.S. S.C.), Drinking & Driving Law, Vol. XIII, no. 7, p. 52; odour of alcohol, glassy eyes and unsteadiness: *R. v. Noonan* (1998), 1998 CarswellOnt 2592 (Ont. Prov. Div.); *R. v. Yoshida* (October 29, 1997), Rice Prov. J. (Ont. Prov. Div.), Drinking & Driving Law Vol. XIII, no. 3, p. 17; slightly slurred speech and dry mouth: *R. v. Moric* (1998), 1998 CarswellOnt 1240, [1998] O.J. No. 1271 (Ont. Gen. Div.); difficulty walking: *R. v. Cameron* (1999), 245 A.R. 383 (Alta. Prov. Ct.); odour of alcohol, slurred speech and red and watery eyes: *R. v. Holman* (1998), 173 Sask. R. 214 (Sask. Q.B.).

7.3.1 BLOODSHOT AND/OR WATERY EYES

- Can these matters be related to fatigue, especially late in the day or night?
- Can they be related to the wearing of contact lenses, or other innocent causes such as colds or allergies?

7.3.2 FLUSHED FACE

- Can the flushed face be explained from some condition other than alcohol consumption?
- Does your client suffer from any medical conditions such as diabetes?

- Is sunburn a factor?

7.3.3 ODOUR OF ALCOHOL

It is generally recognized that odour has no relationship to amount consumed, and is probative of little beyond the fact of some consumption of an alcoholic beverage. A strong odour tends to show recent consumption. Ironically, alcohol itself is odourless and the odour arises from the non-alcoholic content of the drink consumed.

Undue reliance on odour as evidence led to reversal of a conviction in *R. v. Tavone* (2007), [2007] O.J. No. 3073, 2007 CarswellOnt 5763, 54 M.V.R. (5th) 278 (Ont. S.C.J.).

7.3.4 UNSTEADY ON FEET

- Is the unsteadiness related to fatigue, especially late in the day or night?
- Is it related to some physical problem or injury in the leg?
- Was your client unsteady because of nervousness in the presence of uniformed police officers?
- If the police officer said that your client stumbled on exiting his or her vehicle, note the surface on which the vehicle stopped upon being signalled by the police.
- Was the stop, from a desire to comply immediately, made on non-level portions of the road shoulder or in any other location where cars would not normally stop except for an emergency?
- Can it be said that your client, like most drivers was not used to exiting his or her vehicle in such a location?

7.3.5 SLURRED SPEECH

- Has the police officer concluded that your client's speech was abnormally slurred based upon an erroneous assumption that he or she talks differently when "normal"?

- Does your client always talk in a manner that the officer would characterize as slurred if it were accompanied by an odour of alcohol?

- Has the police officer ever encountered your client on any other occasion where the officer would have heard him or her speak?

- Did the speech that took place in fact contain letters capable of being slurred?

7.3.6 POLICE EVIDENCE

A useful caution regarding disparate police evidence appears in *R. v. Geerligs* (1994), [1994] A.J. No. 871, 1994 CarswellAlta 645, 159 A.R. 254 (Alta. Prov. Ct.), per Fradsham P.C.J. at para. 27:

> Where two police officers are asked about the physical condition of an accused person, and assuming that one of them does not qualify his or her answers by indicating that he or she did not pay particular attention for some reason (e.g., a division of duties between the two officers which gave one and not the other the task of noting the physical condition and actions of the accused), a significant difference between the two officer's descriptions of the accused's condition will often result in a reasonable doubt arising about the reliability of the descriptive evidence which disfavours the accused. If two police officers, sharing like testimonial factors (e.g., attention paid to the matter, vantage point to observe, etc.), give conflicting evidence about the presence of a physical condition unfavourable to the accused, then the trier of fact may well have a doubt as to the existence of that fact.

Several cases have commented on the lack of credibility of police evidence of symptoms "recalled" by the officer but not entered into the contemporaneous notes: *R. v. Mercer* (2006), [2006] O.J. No. 5522, 2006 CarswellOnt 8994 (Ont. C.J.) (T.A. Culver J.); Justice Duncan in *R. v. Zack* (May 26, 1999), [1999] O.J. No. 5747 (Ont. C.J.) (B. Duncan J.). In Mercer it was said:

> . . .[I]t cannot be an acceptable explanation for a police officer to say, I did not note it because I would remember it. It is necessary for the officer to at least somewhere, maybe not necessarily in his notebook, put the significant observations that he made.
>
> In my view, the absence of the questions, observations in his notebook, lead to the conclusion that those observations were not in fact made at the time, but are perhaps something that over the course of time the officer had come to believe what he saw. I cannot accept on the balance of probabilities that those observations were made.

7.4 PHYSICAL TESTS

There is a complete lack of any scientifically demonstrated relationship between impaired driving ability caused by alcohol and performance on these standard tests. Nevertheless, the assumption continues to be made routinely that any imperfect performance reflects a lessened ability to drive a motor vehicle. In fact, depending precisely on how the tests are defined to the accused driver, they may be difficult to perform at the best of times by the average person even when fully sober.

7.5 OPINION OF POLICE OFFICER OR OTHERS

Intoxication or impairment by alcohol is one of those matters on which non-expert opinion evidence is admissible: *R. v. Graat* (1982), 18 M.V.R. 287, 31 C.R. (3d) 289, 2 C.C.C. (3d) 365 (S.C.C.). The Supreme Court of Canada has held that these are matters not requiring medical expertise to recognize and most people have had sufficient personal experience to be able to express an opinion on these matters. Police officers can give such opinion evidence under this category of permissible evidence. However, the important point is that in giving such evidence, police officers are testifying simply as non-expert laypersons and their opinion evidence is entitled to no greater weight by virtue of their being police officers. Similarly, it was held to be reversible error in an impaired driving case where trial judge's main reason for not accepting the defence witnesses' testimony regarding the appellant's state of sobriety was that they were not experts trained to observe signs of impairment: *R. v. Novais* (2006), [2006] O.J. No. 3152, 2006 CarswellOnt 4778 (Ont. S.C.J.) (N.E. Garton J.).

7.6 VIDEOTAPES

As mentioned earlier, it is now becoming common to videotape the client at the police station, including the actual breath testing itself. This can be used to assist the defence as earlier discussed, but it may also prove useful in this context: the accused may appear in normal condition on the tape and while performing any tests. If the accused appears normal but it is alleged that he failed coordination tests, which happened not to be videotaped, the failure to videotape may be used to draw a negative inference against the claimed deficiencies.

Even more importantly, if the Crown wishes to use the videotapes because they are inculpatory, there is an argument available that such videotapes can only be used with the consent of the defence, because they otherwise constitute a violation of s. 8 (and s. 7) of the *Charter*. Videotaping *per se* is a form of search and seizure that must be "reasonable" under s. 8: *R. v. Wong* (1990), 1 C.R. (4th) 1, 60 C.C.C. (3d) 460 (S.C.C.). Surreptitious videotaping is a s. 8 violation: *R. v. Wong*. While this videotaping is not surreptitious, the only other basis for its being lawful is as a "consent" search and seizure. But the driver does not consent; the driver only submits. The driver is not asked whether or not the videotaping should be turned off. This issue has not been considered in any cases as yet.

See 13.6.1 Disclosure, (b) Videos.

7.7 APPROVED SCREENING DEVICE "FAIL" RESULT

A "fail" result on an approved screening device has no evidentiary value beyond providing grounds for a breathalyzer demand, is no evidence showing that the accused's blood alcohol level was above the legal limit of .08 and is not admissible at trial as evidence etc. *R. v. Lieskovsky*, 2004 CarswellAlta 1143, 9 M.V.R. (5th) 209, 2004 ABPC 153 (Alta. Prov. Ct.). *R. v. Gokul* (1998), 1998 CarswellOnt 844, [1998] O.J. No. 921 (Ont. Gen. Div.); *R. v. Seo* (1986), 25 C.C.C. (3d) 385, 51 C.R. (3d) 1, 38 M.V.R. 161 (Ont. C.A.); *R. v. Thomsen* (1988), 4 M.V.R. (2d) 185, 63 C.R. (3d) 1, 40 C.C.C. (3d) 411 (S.C.C.); *R. v. McMahon* (1989) (Ont. Dist. Ct.), Drinking & Driving Law, Vol. V, no. 1, pp. 3-5; *R. v. Robinson* (1990) (Ont. Dist. Ct.), Drinking & Driving Law, Vol. V, no. 10, p. 78; *R. v. Lacey* (1992), 113 N.S.R. (2d) 348 (Co. Ct.); *R. v. Bernshaw* (1994), 8 M.V.R. (3d) 75, 35 C.R. (4th) 201, 95 C.C.C. (3d) 193 (S.C.C.); *R. v. Coutts* (1999), 43 M.V.R. (3d) 28, 121 O.A.C. 342, 64 C.R.R. (2d) 34, 25 C.R. (5th) 362, 136 C.C.C. (3d) 225, 45 O.R. (3d) 288, 1999 CarswellOnt 1773, [1999] O.J. No. 2013 (Ont. C.A.); *R. v. Graham* (1998), 40 M.V.R. (3d) 59, 59 C.R.R. (2d) 87, 1998 CarswellOnt 4868 (Ont. Prov. Div.).

7.8 SPECIAL SECTION: THE NEW AMENDMENTS

Section 7.9.1(a)(i), 7.9.2(a)(i), 8.1.1(a), 8.2.1(a) dealing with the presumptions, section 13.1.2(b) "Carter" Defence and 13.2 "Evidence to the Contrary" must be read subject to the amendments to sections 254 to 261 of the *Criminal Code*, in force July 2, 2008. As of that date these provisions will read as follows (new provisions are in italics):

Definitions

254. *(1) In this section and sections 254.1 to 258.1,*

"analyst" means a person designated by the Attorney General as an analyst for the purposes of section 258;

"approved container" means

(a) in respect of breath samples, a container of a kind that is designed to receive a sample of the breath of a person for analysis and is approved as suitable for the purposes of section 258 by order of the Attorney General of Canada, and

(b) in respect of blood samples, a container of a kind that is designed to receive a sample of the blood of a person for analysis and is approved as suitable for the purposes of section 258 by order of the Attorney General of Canada;

"approved instrument" means an instrument of a kind that is designed to receive and make an analysis of a sample of the breath of a person in order to measure the concentration of alcohol in the blood of that person and is approved as suitable for the purposes of section 258 by order of the Attorney General of Canada;

"approved screening device" means a device of a kind that is designed to ascertain the presence of alcohol in the blood of a person and that is approved for the purposes of this section by order of the Attorney General of Canada;

__"evaluating officer"__ means a peace officer who is qualified under the regulations to conduct evaluations under subsection (3.1);

"qualified medical practitioner" means a person duly qualified by provincial law to practise medicine;

"qualified technician" means,

(a) in respect of breath samples, a person designated by the Attorney General as being qualified to operate an approved instrument, and

(b) in respect of blood samples, any person or person of a class of persons designated by the Attorney General as being qualified to take samples of blood for the purposes of this section and sections 256 and 258.

Testing for presence of alcohol or a drug

(2) If a peace officer has reasonable grounds to suspect that a person has alcohol or a drug in their body and that the person has, within the preceding three hours, operated a motor vehicle or vessel, operated or assisted in the operation of an aircraft or railway equipment or had the care or control of a motor vehicle, a vessel, an aircraft or railway equipment, whether it was in motion or not, the peace officer may, by demand, require the person to comply with paragraph (a), in the case of a drug, or with either or both of paragraphs (a) and (b), in the case of alcohol:

(a) to perform forthwith physical coordination tests prescribed by regulation to enable the peace officer to determine whether a demand may be made under subsection (3) or (3.1) and, if necessary, to accompany the peace officer for that purpose; and

(b) to provide forthwith a sample of breath that, in the peace officer's opinion, will enable a proper analysis to be made by means of an approved screening device and, if necessary, to accompany the peace officer for that purpose.

Video recording

(2.1) For greater certainty, a peace officer may make a video recording of a performance of the physical coordination tests referred to in paragraph (2)(a).

Samples of breath or blood

(3) If a peace officer has reasonable grounds to believe that a person is committing, or at any time within the preceding three hours has committed, an offence under section 253 as a result of the consumption of alcohol, the peace officer may, by demand made as soon as practicable, require the person

(a) to provide, as soon as practicable,

(i) samples of breath that, in a qualified technician's opinion, will enable a proper analysis to be made to determine the concentration, if any, of alcohol in the person's blood, or

(ii) if the peace officer has reasonable grounds to believe that, because of their physical condition, the person may be incapable of providing a sample of breath or it would be impracticable to obtain a sample of breath, samples of blood that, in the opinion of the qualified medical practitioner or qualified technician taking the samples, will enable a proper analysis to be made to determine the concentration, if any, of alcohol in the person's blood; and

(b) if necessary, to accompany the peace officer for that purpose.

Evaluation

(3.1) If a peace officer has reasonable grounds to believe that a person is committing, or at any time within the preceding three hours has committed, an offence under paragraph 253(1)(a) as a result of the consumption of a drug or of a combination of alcohol and a drug, the peace officer may, by demand made as soon as practicable, require the person to submit, as soon as practicable, to an evaluation conducted by an evaluating officer to determine whether the person's ability to operate a motor vehicle, a vessel, an aircraft or railway equipment is impaired by a drug or by a combination of alcohol and a drug, and to accompany the peace officer for that purpose.

Video recording

(3.2) For greater certainty, a peace officer may make a video recording of an evaluation referred to in subsection (3.1).

Testing for presence of alcohol

(3.3) If the evaluating officer has reasonable grounds to suspect that the person has alcohol in their body and if a demand was not made under paragraph (2)(b) or subsection (3), the evaluating officer may, by demand made as soon as practicable, require the person to provide, as soon as practicable, a sample of breath that, in the evaluating officer's opinion, will enable a proper analysis to be made by means of an approved instrument.

Samples of bodily substances

(3.4) If, on completion of the evaluation, the evaluating officer has reasonable grounds to believe, based on the evaluation, that the person's ability to operate a motor vehicle, a vessel, an aircraft or railway equipment is impaired by a drug or by a combination of alcohol and a drug, the evaluating officer may, by demand made as soon as practicable, require the person to provide, as soon as practicable,

(a) a sample of either oral fluid or urine that, in the evaluating officer's opinion, will enable a proper analysis to be made to determine whether the person has a drug in their body; or

(b) samples of blood that, in the opinion of the qualified medical practitioner or qualified technician taking the samples, will enable a proper analysis to be made to determine whether the person has a drug in their body.

Condition

(4) Samples of blood may be taken from a person under subsection (3) or (3.4) only by or under the direction of a qualified medical practitioner who is satisfied that taking the samples would not endanger the person's life or health.

Failure or refusal to comply with demand

(5) Everyone commits an offence who, without reasonable excuse, fails or refuses to comply with a demand made under this section.

Only one determination of guilt

(6) A person who is convicted of an offence under subsection (5) for a failure or refusal to comply with a demand may not be convicted of another offence under that subsection in respect of the same transaction.

R.S.C. 1985, c. 27 (1st Supp.), s. 36; R.S.C. 1985, c. 1 (4th Supp.), s. 14; R.S.C. 1985, c. 32 (4th Supp.), s. 60; 1999, c. 32, s. 2; 2008, c. 6, s. 19

Regulations

254.1 *(1) The Governor in Council may make regulations*

(a) respecting the qualifications and training of evaluating officers;

(b) prescribing the physical coordination tests to be conducted under paragraph 254(2)(a); and

(c) prescribing the tests to be conducted and procedures to be followed during an evaluation under subsection 254(3.1).

Incorporated material

(2) A regulation may incorporate any material by reference either as it exists on a specified date or as amended from time to time.

Incorporated material is not a regulation

(3) For greater certainty, material does not become a regulation for the purposes of the Statutory Instruments Act because it is incorporated by reference.

2008, c. 6, s. 20

[Note: The *Evaluation of Impaired Operation (Drugs and Alcohol) Regulations*, SOR/2008-196, made under s. 254.1 are reproduced in Appendix C.]

Punishment

255. (1) Every one who commits an offence under section 253 or 254 is guilty of an indictable offence or an offence punishable on summary conviction and is liable,

(a) whether the offence is prosecuted by indictment or punishable on summary conviction, to the following minimum punishment, namely,

(i) for a first offence, to a fine of not less than $1,000,

(ii) for a second offence, to imprisonment for not less than 30 days, and

(iii) for each subsequent offence, to imprisonment for not less than 120 days;

(b) where the offence is prosecuted by indictment, to imprisonment for a term not exceeding five years; and

(c) if the offence is punishable on summary conviction, to imprisonment for a term of not more than 18 months.

[Note: Section 3 of S.C. 1999, c. 32 increased the minimum fine prescribed by s. 255(1)(a)(i) for a first offence under s. 253 or 254 from three hundred to six hundred dollars. Section 7 of S.C. 1999, c. 32 provides, however, that where any penalty or punishment provided by the *Criminal Code* is varied by 1999, c. 32, the lesser penalty or punishment applies in respect to any offence that was committed before the coming into force of section 7 (i.e. before July 1, 1999). The three hundred dollar minimum would thus continue to apply to first offences committed before that date.]

Impaired driving causing bodily harm

(2) Everyone who commits an offence under paragraph 253(1)(a) and causes bodily harm to another person as a result is guilty of an indictable offence and liable to imprisonment for a term of not more than 10 years.

Blood alcohol level over legal limit — bodily harm

(2.1) Everyone who, while committing an offence under paragraph 253(1)(b), causes an accident resulting in bodily harm to another person is guilty of an indictable offence and liable to imprisonment for a term of not more than 10 years.

Failure or refusal to provide sample — bodily harm

(2.2) Everyone who commits an offence under subsection 254(5) and, at the time of committing the offence, knows or ought to know that their operation of the motor vehicle, vessel, aircraft or railway equipment, their assistance in the operation of the aircraft or railway equipment or their care or control of the motor vehicle, vessel, aircraft or railway equipment caused an accident resulting in bodily harm to another person is guilty of an indictable offence and liable to imprisonment for a term of not more than 10 years.

Impaired driving causing death

(3) Everyone who commits an offence under paragraph 253(1)(a) and causes the death of another person as a result is guilty of an indictable offence and liable to imprisonment for life.

Blood alcohol level over legal limit — death

(3.1) Everyone who, while committing an offence under paragraph 253(1)(b), causes an accident resulting in the death of another person is guilty of an indictable offence and liable to imprisonment for life.

Failure or refusal to provide sample — death

(3.2) Everyone who commits an offence under subsection 254(5) and, at the time of committing the offence, knows or ought to know that their operation of the motor vehicle, vessel, aircraft or railway equipment, their assistance in the operation of the aircraft or railway equipment or their care or control of the motor vehicle, vessel, aircraft or railway equipment caused an accident resulting in the death of another person, or in bodily harm to another person whose death ensues, is guilty of an indictable offence and liable to imprisonment for life.

Proposed Addition — 255(3.3)

Interpretation

(3.3) For greater certainty, everyone who is liable to the punishment described in any of subsections (2) to (3.2) is also liable to the minimum punishment described in paragraph (1)(a).

2008, c. 18, s. 7 [To come into force October 1, 2008. Amended 2008, c. 18, s. 45.2(2).]

Previous convictions

(4) A person who is convicted of an offence committed under section 253 or subsection 254(5) is, for the purposes of this Act, deemed to be convicted for a second

or subsequent offence, as the case may be, if they have previously been convicted of

(a) an offence committed under either of those provisions;

(b) an offence under subsection (2) or (3); or

(c) an offence under section 250, 251, 252, 253, 259 or 260 or subsection 258(4) of this Act as this Act read immediately before the coming into force of this subsection.

Conditional discharge

(5) Notwithstanding subsection 730(1), a court may, instead of convicting a person of an offence committed under section 253, after hearing medical or other evidence, if it considers that the person is in need of curative treatment in relation to his consumption of alcohol or drugs and that it would not be contrary to the public interest, by order direct that the person be discharged under section 730 on the conditions prescribed in a probation order, including a condition respecting the person's attendance for curative treatment in relation to that consumption of alcohol or drugs.

[Note: s. 255(5) has been proclaimed in force in the provinces of Alberta, Manitoba, New Brunswick, Nova Scotia, Prince Edward Island, Saskatchewan and in Yukon and the Northwest Territories.]

R.S.C. 1985, c. 27 (1st Supp.), s. 36; 1995, c. 22, s. 18 (Sched. IV, item 26); 1999, c. 32, s. 3; 2000, c. 25, s. 2; 2008, c. 6, s. 21

Aggravating circumstances for sentencing purposes

255.1 Without limiting the generality of section 718.2, where a court imposes a sentence for an offence committed under this Act by means of a motor vehicle, vessel or aircraft or of railway equipment, evidence that the concentration of alcohol in the blood of the offender at the time when the offence was committed exceeded one hundred and sixty milligrams of alcohol in one hundred millilitres of blood shall be deemed to be aggravating circumstances relating to the offence that the court shall consider under paragraph 718.2(a).

1999, c. 32, s. 4

Warrants to obtain blood samples

256. (1) Subject to subsection (2), if a justice is satisfied, on an information on oath in Form 1 or on an information on oath submitted to the justice under section 487.1 by telephone or other means of telecommunication, that there are reasonable grounds to believe that

(a) a person has, within the preceding four hours, committed, as a result of the consumption of alcohol or a drug, an offence under section 253 and the person was involved in an accident resulting in the death of another person or in bodily harm to himself or herself or to any other person, and

(b) a qualified medical practitioner is of the opinion that

(i) by reason of any physical or mental condition of the person that resulted from the consumption of alcohol or a drug, the accident or any other occurrence related to or resulting from the accident, the person is unable to consent to the taking of samples of his or her blood, and

(ii) the taking of samples of blood from the person would not endanger the life or health of the person,

the justice may issue a warrant authorizing a peace officer to require a qualified medical practitioner to take, or to cause to be taken by a qualified technician under the direction of the qualified medical practitioner, the samples of the blood of the person that in the opinion of the person taking the samples are necessary to enable a proper analysis to be made in order to determine the concentration, if any, of alcohol or drugs in the person's blood.

Form

(2) A warrant issued pursuant to subsection (1) may be in Form 5 or 5.1 varied to suit the case.

Information on oath

(3) Notwithstanding paragraphs 487.1(4)(*b*) and (*c*), an information on oath submitted by telephone or other means of telecommunication for the purposes of this section shall include, instead of the statements referred to in those paragraphs, a statement setting out the offence alleged to have been committed and identifying the person from whom blood samples are to be taken.

Duration of warrant

(4) Samples of blood may be taken from a person pursuant to a warrant issued pursuant to subsection (1) only during such time as a qualified medical practitioner is satisfied that the conditions referred to in subparagraphs (1)(*b*)(i) and (ii) continue to exist in respect of that person.

Copy or facsimile to person

(5) When a warrant issued under subsection (1) is executed, the peace officer shall, as soon as practicable, give a copy of it — or, in the case of a warrant issued by telephone or other means of telecommunication, a facsimile — to the person from whom the blood samples are taken.

R.S.C. 1985, c. 27 (1st Supp.), s. 36; 1992, c. 1, s. 58(1) (Sched. I, item 5); 1994, c. 44, s. 13; 2000, c. 25, s. 3; 2008, c. 6, s. 22

No offence committed

257. (1) No qualified medical practitioner or qualified technician is guilty of an offence only by reason of his refusal to take a sample of blood from a person for the purposes of section 254 or 256 and no qualified medical practitioner is guilty of an offence only by reason of his refusal to cause to be taken by a qualified technician under his direction a sample of blood from a person for such purposes.

No criminal or civil liability

(2) No qualified medical practitioner by whom or under whose direction a sample of blood is taken from a person under subsection 254(3) or (3.4) or section 256, and no qualified technician acting under the direction of a qualified medical practitioner, incurs any criminal or civil liability for anything necessarily done with reasonable care and skill when taking the sample.

R.S.C. 1985, c. 27 (1st Supp.), s. 36; 2008, c. 6, s. 23

Proceedings under section 255

***258.** (1) In any proceedings under subsection 255(1) in respect of an offence committed under section 253 or subsection 254(5) or in any proceedings under any of subsections 255(2) to (3.2),*

(a) where it is proved that the accused occupied the seat or position ordinarily occupied by a person who operates a motor vehicle, vessel, or aircraft or any railway equipment or who assists in the operation of an aircraft or of railway equipment, the accused shall be deemed to have had the care or control of the vehicle, vessel, aircraft or railway equipment, as the case may be, unless the accused establishes that the accused did not occupy that seat or position for the purpose of setting the vehicle, vessel, aircraft or railway equipment in motion or assisting in the operation of the aircraft or railway equipment, as the case may be;

(b) the result of an analysis of a sample of the accused's breath, blood, urine or other bodily substance — other than a sample taken under subsection 254(3), (3.3) or (3.4) — may be admitted in evidence even if the accused was not warned before they gave the sample that they need not give the sample or that the result of the analysis of the sample might be used in evidence;

(c) where samples of the breath of the accused have been taken pursuant to a demand made under subsection 254(3), if

Proposed Addition — 258(1)(c)(i)

(i) at the time each sample was taken, the person taking the sample offered to provide to the accused a specimen of the breath of the accused in an approved container for his own use, and, at the request of the accused made at that time, such a specimen was thereupon provided to the accused,

R.S.C. 1985, c. 27 (1st Supp.), s. 36 [Not in force at date of publication.]

(ii) each sample was taken as soon as practicable after the time when the offence was alleged to have been committed and, in the case of the first sample, not later than two hours after that time, with an interval of at least fifteen minutes between the times when the samples were taken,

(iii) each sample was received from the accused directly into an approved container or into an approved instrument operated by a qualified technician, and

(iv) an analysis of each sample was made by means of an approved instrument operated by a qualified technician,

evidence of the results of the analyses so made is conclusive proof that the concentration of alcohol in the accused's blood both at the time when the analyses were made and at the time when the offence was alleged to have been committed was, if the results of the analyses are the same, the concentration determined by the analyses and, if the results of the analyses are different, the lowest of the concentrations determined by the analyses, in the absence of evidence tending to show all of the following three things — that the approved instrument was malfunctioning or was operated improperly, that the malfunction or improper operation resulted in the determination that the concentration of alcohol in the accused's blood exceeded 80 mg of alcohol in 100 mL of blood, and that the concentration of alcohol in the accused's blood would not in fact have exceeded 80 mg of alcohol in 100 mL of blood at the time when the offence was alleged to have been committed;

(d) if a sample of the accused's blood has been taken under subsection 254(3) or section 256 or with the accused's consent and if

(i) at the time the sample was taken, the person taking the sample took an additional sample of the blood of the accused and one of the samples was retained to permit an analysis of it to be made by or on behalf of the accused and, in the case where the accused makes a request within six months from the taking of the samples, one of the samples was ordered to be released under subsection (4),

(ii) both samples referred to in subparagraph (i) were taken as soon as practicable and in any event not later than two hours after the time when the offence was alleged to have been committed,

(iii) both samples referred to in subparagraph (i) were taken by a qualified medical practitioner or a qualified technician under the direction of a qualified medical practitioner,

(iv) both samples referred to in subparagraph (i) were received from the accused directly into, or placed directly into, approved containers that were subsequently sealed, and

(v) an analysis was made by an analyst of at least one of the samples,

evidence of the result of the analysis is conclusive proof that the concentration of alcohol in the accused's blood both at the time when the samples were taken and at the time when the offence was alleged to have been committed was the concentration determined by the analysis or, if more than one sample was analyzed and the results of the analyses are the same, the concentration determined by the analyses and, if the results of the analyses are different, the lowest of the concentrations determined by the analyses, in the absence of evidence tending to show all of the following three things — that the analysis was performed improperly, that the improper performance resulted in the determination that the concentration of alcohol in the accused's blood exceeded 80 mg of alcohol in 100 mL of blood, and that the concentration of alcohol in the accused's blood would not in fact have exceeded 80 mg of alcohol in 100 mL of blood at the time when the offence was alleged to have been committed;

(d.01) for greater certainty, evidence tending to show that an approved instrument was malfunctioning or was operated improperly, or that an analysis of a sample of the accused's blood was performed improperly, does not include evidence of

(i) the amount of alcohol that the accused consumed,

(ii) the rate at which the alcohol that the accused consumed would have been absorbed and eliminated by the accused's body, or

(iii) a calculation based on that evidence of what the concentration of alcohol in the accused's blood would have been at the time when the offence was alleged to have been committed;

(d.1) if samples of the accused's breath or a sample of the accused's blood have been taken as described in paragraph (c) or (d) under the conditions described in that paragraph and the results of the analyses show a concentration of alcohol in blood exceeding 80 mg of alcohol in 100 mL of blood, evidence of the results of the analyses is proof that the concentration of alcohol in the accused's blood at the time when the offence was alleged to have been committed exceeded 80 mg of alcohol in 100 mL of blood, in the absence of evidence tending to show that the accused's consumption of alcohol was consistent with both

(i) a concentration of alcohol in the accused's blood that did not exceed 80 mg of alcohol in 100 mL of blood at the time when the offence was alleged to have been committed, and

(ii) the concentration of alcohol in the accused's blood as determined under paragraph (c) or (d), as the case may be, at the time when the sample or samples were taken;

(e) a certificate of an analyst stating that the analyst has made an analysis of a sample of the blood, urine, breath or other bodily substance of the accused and stating the result of that analysis is evidence of the facts alleged in the certificate without proof of the signature or the official character of the person appearing to have signed the certificate;

(f) a certificate of an analyst stating that the analyst has made an analysis of a sample of an alcohol standard that is identified in the certificate and intended for use with an approved instrument and that the sample of the standard analyzed by the analyst was found to be suitable for use with an approved instrument, is evidence that the alcohol standard so identified is suitable for use with an approved instrument without proof of the signature or the official character of the person appearing to have signed the certificate;

(f.1) the document printed out from an approved instrument and signed by a qualified technician who certifies it to be the printout produced by the approved instrument when it made the analysis of a sample of the accused's breath is evidence of the facts alleged in the document without proof of the signature or official character of the person appearing to have signed it;

(g) where samples of the breath of the accused have been taken pursuant to a demand made under subsection 254(3), a certificate of a qualified technician stating

(i) that the analysis of each of the samples has been made by means of an approved instrument operated by the technician and ascertained by the technician to be in proper working order by means of an alcohol standard, identified in the certificate, that is suitable for use with an approved instrument,

(ii) the results of the analyses so made, and

(iii) if the samples were taken by the technician,

Proposed Addition — 258(1)(g)(iii)(A)

(A) that at the time each sample was taken the technician offered to provide the accused with a specimen of the breath of the accused in an approved container for his own use and, at the request of the accused made at that time, the accused was thereupon provided with such a specimen,

R.S.C. 1985, c. 27 (1st Supp.), s. 36 [Not in force at date of publication.]

(B) the time when and place where each sample and any specimen described in clause (A) was taken, and

(C) that each sample was received from the accused directly into an approved container or into an approved instrument operated by the technician,

is evidence of the facts alleged in the certificate without proof of the signature or the official character of the person appearing to have signed the certificate;

[Note: Paragraphs 258(1)(f) and (g) [incorrectly noted in R.S.C. 1985, c. 27 (1st Supp.), s. 204 as paragraphs 255(1)(f) and (g)] of the Code, as they read immediately before the coming into force of the amendments to those paragraphs, as enacted by s. 36 of the *Criminal Law Amendment Act, 1985*, R.S.C. 1985, c. 27 (1st Supp.), continue to apply to any proceedings in respect of which a certificate referred to in those paragraphs was issued prior to the coming into force of the amendments to those paragraphs.]

(h) if a sample of the accused's blood has been taken under subsection 254(3) or (3.4) or section 256 or with the accused's consent,

(i) a certificate of a qualified medical practitioner stating that

(A) they took the sample and before the sample was taken they were of the opinion that taking it would not endanger the accused's life or health and, in the case of a demand made under section 256, that by reason of any physical or mental condition of the accused that resulted from the consumption of alcohol or a drug, the accident or any other occurrence related to or resulting from the accident, the accused was unable to consent to the taking of the sample,

(B) at the time the sample was taken, an additional sample of the blood of the accused was taken to permit analysis of one of the samples to be made by or on behalf of the accused,

(C) the time when and place where both samples referred to in clause (B) were taken, and

(D) both samples referred to in clause (B) were received from the accused directly into, or placed directly into, approved containers that were subsequently sealed and that are identified in the certificate,

(ii) a certificate of a qualified medical practitioner stating that the medical practitioner caused the sample to be taken by a qualified technician under his direction and that before the sample was taken the qualified medical practitioner was of the opinion referred to in clause (i)(A), or

(iii) a certificate of a qualified technician stating that the technician took the sample and the facts referred to in clauses (i)(B) to (D)

is evidence of the facts alleged in the certificate without proof of the signature or official character of the person appearing to have signed the certificate; and

(i) a certificate of an analyst stating that the analyst has made an analysis of a sample of the blood of the accused that was contained in a sealed approved container identified in the certificate, the date on which and place where the sample was analyzed and the result of that analysis is evidence of the facts alleged in the certificate without proof of the signature or official character of the person appearing to have signed it.

Evidence of failure to give sample

(2) Unless a person is required to give a sample of a bodily substance under paragraph 254(2)(b) or subsection 254(3), (3.3) or (3.4), evidence that they failed or refused to give a sample for analysis for the purposes of this section or that a sample was not taken is not admissible and the failure, refusal or fact that a sample was not taken shall not be the subject of comment by any person in the proceedings.

Evidence of failure to comply with demand

(3) In any proceedings under subsection 255(1) in respect of an offence committed under paragraph 253(1)(a) or in any proceedings under subsection 255(2) or (3), evidence that the accused, without reasonable excuse, failed or refused to comply with a demand made under section 254 is admissible and the court may draw an inference adverse to the accused from that evidence.

Release of sample for analysis

(4) If, at the time a sample of an accused's blood is taken, an additional sample is taken and retained, a judge of a superior court of criminal jurisdiction or a court of criminal jurisdiction shall, on the summary application of the accused made within six months after the day on which the samples were taken, order the release of one of the samples for the purpose of examination or analysis, subject to any terms that appear to be necessary or desirable to ensure that the sample is safeguarded and preserved for use in any proceedings in respect of which it was taken.

Testing of blood for concentration of a drug

(5) A sample of an accused's blood taken under subsection 254(3) or section 256 or with the accused's consent for the purpose of analysis to determine the concentration, if any, of alcohol in the blood may be tested to determine the concentration, if any, of a drug in the blood.

Attendance and right to cross-examine

(6) A party against whom a certificate described in paragraph (1)(e), (f), (f.1), (g), (h) or (i) is produced may, with leave of the court, require the attendance of the qualified medical practitioner, analyst or qualified technician, as the case may be, for the purposes of cross-examination.

Notice of intention to produce certificate

(7) No certificate shall be received in evidence pursuant to paragraph (1)(*e*), (*f*), (*g*), (*h*) or (*i*) unless the party intending to produce it has, before the trial, given to the other party reasonable notice of his intention and a copy of the certificate.

R.S.C. 1985, c. 27 (1st Supp.), s. 36; R.S.C. 1985, c. 32 (4th Supp.), s. 61; 1994, c. 44, s. 14; 1997, c. 18, s. 10; 2008, c. 6, s. 24(1), (2), (4)-(9)

Unauthorized use of bodily substance

258.1 *(1) Subject to subsections 258(4) and (5) and subsection (3), no person shall use a bodily substance taken under paragraph 254(2)(b), subsection 254(3), (3.3) or (3.4) or section 256 or with the consent of the person from whom it was taken after a request by a peace officer or medical samples that are provided by consent* *and subsequently seized under a warrant, except for the purpose of an analysis that is referred to in that provision or for which the consent is given.*

Unauthorized use or disclosure of results

(2) Subject to subsections (3) and (4), no person shall use, disclose or allow the disclosure of the results of physical coordination tests under paragraph 254(2)(a), the results of an evaluation under subsection 254(3.1), the results of the analysis of a bodily substance taken under paragraph 254(2)(b), subsection 254(3), (3.3) or (3.4) or section 256 or with the consent of the person from whom it was taken after a request by a peace officer, or the results of the analysis of medical samples that are provided by consent and subsequently seized under a warrant, except

(a) in the course of an investigation of, or in a proceeding for, an offence under any of sections 220, 221, 236 and 249 to 255, an offence under Part I of the Aeronautics Act, or an offence under the Railway Safety Act in respect of a contravention of a rule or regulation made under that Act respecting the use of alcohol or a drug; or

(b) for the purpose of the administration or enforcement of the law of a province.

Exception

(3) Subsections (1) and (2) do not apply to persons who for medical purposes use samples or use or disclose the results of tests, taken for medical purposes, that are subsequently seized under a warrant.

Exception

(4) The results of physical coordination tests, an evaluation or an analysis referred to in subsection (2) may be disclosed to the person to whom they relate, and may be disclosed to any other person if the results are made anonymous and the disclosure is made for statistical or other research purposes.

Offence

(5) Every person who contravenes subsection (1) or (2) is guilty of an offence punishable on summary conviction.

2008, c. 6, s. 25

Mandatory order of prohibition

259. *(1) When an offender is convicted of an offence committed under section 253 or 254 or this section or discharged under section 730 of an offence committed under section 253 and, at the time the offence was committed or, in the case of an offence committed under section 254, within the three hours preceding that time, was operating or had the care or control of a motor vehicle, vessel or aircraft or of railway equipment or was assisting in the operation of an aircraft or of railway* *equipment, the court that sentences the offender shall, in addition to any other punishment that may be imposed for that offence, make an order prohibiting the offender from operating a motor vehicle on any street, road, highway or other public place, or from operating a vessel or an aircraft or railway equipment, as the case may be,*

(a) for a first offence, during a period of not more than three years plus any period to which the offender is sentenced to imprisonment, and not less than one year;

(b) for a second offence, during a period of not more than five years plus any period to which the offender is sentenced to imprisonment, and not less than two years; and

(c) for each subsequent offence, during a period of not less than three years plus any period to which the offender is sentenced to imprisonment.

[Note: Section 5 of S.C. 1999, c. 32 increased the mandatory minimum driving prohibition to be imposed in the circumstances prescribed by s. 259 from three months to one year for a first offence (except where an offender participates in an alcohol interlock program for a specified period), from six months to two years for a second, and from one to three years on a subsequent offence, and increased the maximum prohibitions from three to five years for a second offence, and from three years to life for a subsequent offence. That section also changed the relevant operation/care/control period for the offence under s. 254 from two to three hours. Section 7 of S.C. 1999, c. 32 provides, however, that where any penalty or punishment provided by the *Criminal Code* is varied by 1999, c. 32, the lesser penalty or punishment applies in respect to any offence that was committed before the coming into force of section 7 (i.e. before July 1, 1999).]

Alcohol ignition interlock device program

(1.1) In making the order, the court may authorize the offender to operate a motor vehicle equipped with an alcohol ignition interlock device during the prohibition period if the offender registers in an alcohol ignition interlock device program established under the law of the province in which the offender resides.

Proposed Amendment — 259(1.1)

Alcohol ignition interlock device program

(1.1) If the offender is registered in an alcohol ignition interlock device program established under the law of the province in which the offender resides and complies with the conditions of the program, the offender may, subject to subsection (1.2), operate a motor vehicle equipped with an alcohol ignition interlock device during the prohibition period, unless the court orders otherwise.

2008, c. 18, s. 8(1) [To come into force October 1, 2008.]

Minimum absolute prohibition period

(1.2) The authorization has no effect until the expiry of a period fixed by the court

(a) of at least 3 months, for a first offence;

(b) of at least 6 months, for a second offence; and

(c) of at least 12 months, for each subsequent offence.

Proposed Amendment — 259(1.2)

Minimum absolute prohibition period

(1.2) An offender who is registered in a program referred to in subsection (1.1) may not operate a motor vehicle equipped with an alcohol ignition interlock device until

(a) the expiry of a period of

(i) for a first offence, 3 months after the day on which sentence is imposed,

(ii) for a second offence, 6 months after the day on which sentence is imposed, and

(iii) for each subsequent offence, 12 months after the day on which sentence is imposed; or

(b) the expiry of any period that may be fixed by order of the court that is greater than a period referred to in paragraph (a).

2008, c. 18, s. 8(1) [To come into force October 1, 2008.]

Change of province of residence

(1.3) The authorization applies to an offender who becomes resident in another province and registers in a program referred to in subsection (1.1) in that province.

Proposed Repeal — 259(1.3)

(1.3) [Repealed 2008, c. 18, s. 8(1). To come into force October 1, 2008.]

Authorization suspended

(1.4) The authorization has no effect during any period that the offender is not registered in a program referred to in subsection (1.1).

Proposed Repeal — 259(1.4)

(1.4) [Repealed 2008, c. 18, s. 8(1). To come into force October 1, 2008.]

Discretionary order of prohibition

(2) If an offender is convicted or discharged under section 730 of an offence under section 220, 221, 236, 249, 249.1, 250, 251 or 252 or any of subsections 255(2) to (3.2) committed by means of a motor vehicle, a vessel, an aircraft or railway equipment, the court that sentences the offender may, in addition to any other punishment that may be imposed for that offence, make an order prohibiting the offender from operating a motor vehicle on any street, road, highway or other public place, or from operating a vessel, an aircraft or railway equipment, as the case may be,

(a) during any period that the court considers proper, if the offender is liable to imprisonment for life in respect of that offence;

Proposed Amendment — 259(2)(a)

(a) during any period that the court considers proper, if the offender is sentenced to imprisonment for life in respect of that offence;

2008, c. 18, s. 8(2) [To come into force October 1, 2008.]

Proposed Addition — 259(2)(a.1)

(a.1) during any period that the court considers proper, plus any period to which the offender is sentenced to imprisonment, if the offender is liable to imprisonment for life in respect of that offence and if the sentence imposed is other than imprisonment for life;

2008, c. 18, s. 8(2) [To come into force October 1, 2008.]

(b) during any period not exceeding ten years plus any period to which the offender is sentenced to imprisonment, if the offender is liable to imprisonment for more than five years but less than life in respect of that offence; and

(c) during any period not exceeding three years plus any period to which the offender is sentenced to imprisonment, in any other case.

Proposed Addition — 259(2.1)

Consecutive prohibition periods

(2.1) The court may, when it makes an order under this section prohibiting the operation of a motor vehicle, a vessel, an aircraft or railway equipment, as the case may be, order that the time served under that order be served consecutively to the time served under any other order made under this section that prohibits the operation of the same means of transport and that is in force.

2008, c. 18, s. 8(3) [To come into force October 1, 2008.]

Saving

(3) No order made under subsection (1) or (2) shall operate to prevent any person from acting as master, mate or engineer of a vessel that is required to carry officers holding certificates as master, mate or engineer.

Mandatory order of prohibition — street racing

(3.1) When an offender is convicted or discharged under section 730 of an offence committed under subsection 249.4(1), the court that sentences the offender shall, in addition to any other punishment that may be imposed for that offence, make an order prohibiting the offender from operating a motor vehicle on any street, road, highway or other public place

(a) for a first offence, during a period of not more than three years plus any period to which the offender is sentenced to imprisonment, and not less than one year;

(b) for a second offence, during a period of not more than five years plus any period to which the offender is sentenced to imprisonment, and not less than two years; and

(c) for each subsequent offence, during a period of not less than three years plus any period to which the offender is sentenced to imprisonment.

Mandatory order of prohibition — bodily harm

(3.2) When an offender is convicted or discharged under section 730 of an offence committed under section 249.3 or subsection 249.4(3), the court that sentences the offender shall, in addition to any other punishment that may be imposed for that offence, make an order prohibiting the offender from operating a motor vehicle on any street, road, highway or other public place

(a) for a first offence, during a period of not more than ten years plus any period to which the offender is sentenced to imprisonment, and not less than one year;

(b) for a second offence, during a period of not more than ten years plus any period to which the offender is sentenced to imprisonment, and not less than two years; and

(c) for each subsequent offence, during a period of not less than three years plus any period to which the offender is sentenced to imprisonment.

Mandatory order of prohibition — death

(3.3) When an offender is convicted or discharged under section 730 of a first offence committed under section 249.2 or subsection 249.4(4), the court that sentences the offender shall, in addition to any other punishment that may be imposed for that offence, make an order prohibiting the offender from operating a motor vehicle on any street, road, highway or other public place

(a) for an offence under section 249.2, during a period of not less than one year plus any period to which the offender is sentenced to imprisonment; and

(b) for an offence under subsection 249.4(4), during a period of not more than ten years plus any period to which the offender is sentenced to imprisonment, and not less than one year.

Mandatory life prohibition

(3.4) When an offender is convicted or discharged under section 730 of an offence committed under section 249.2 or 249.3 or subsection 249.4(3) or (4), the offender has previously been convicted or discharged under section 730 of one of those offences and at least one of the convictions or discharges is under section 249.2 or subsection 249.4(4), the court that sentences the offender shall make an order prohibiting the offender from operating a motor vehicle on any street, road, highway or other public place for life.

Operation while disqualified

(4) Every one who operates a motor vehicle, vessel, aircraft or railway equipment in Canada while disqualified from doing so

Proposed Amendment — 259(4) opening words

Operation while disqualified

(4) Every offender who operates a motor vehicle, vessel or aircraft or any railway equipment in Canada while disqualified from doing so, other than an offender who is registered in an alcohol ignition interlock device program established under the law of the province in which the offender resides and who complies with the conditions of the program,

2008, c. 18, s. 8(4) [To come into force October 1, 2008.]

(a) is guilty of an indictable offence and liable to imprisonment for a term not exceeding five years; or

(b) is guilty of an offence punishable on summary conviction.

[Note: Subsection 5(2) of S.C. 1999, c. 32 increased the maximum sentence available in indictable proceedings for the offence under s. 259(4) from two to five years. Section 7 of S.C. 1999, c. 32 provides, however, that where any penalty or punishment provided by the *Criminal Code* is varied by 1999, c. 32, the lesser penalty or punishment applies in respect to any offence that was committed before the coming into force of section 7 (i.e. before July 1, 1999). The two year maximum would thus continue to apply for offences committed before that date.]

Definition of "disqualification"

(5) For the purposes of this section, **"disqualification"** means

(a) a prohibition from operating a motor vehicle, vessel or aircraft or any railway equipment ordered pursuant to any of subsections (1), (2) and (3.1) to (3.4); or

(b) a disqualification or any other form of legal restriction of the right or privilege to operate a motor vehicle, vessel or aircraft imposed

(i) in the case of a motor vehicle, under the law of a province, or

(ii) in the case of a vessel or an aircraft, under an Act of Parliament,

in respect of a conviction or discharge under section 730 of any offence referred to in any of subsections (1), (2) and (3.1) to (3.4).

R.S.C. 1985, c. 27 (1st Supp.), s. 36; R.S.C. 1985, c. 32 (4th Supp.), s. 62; 1995, c. 22, ss. 10, 18; 1997, c. 18, s. 11; 1999, c. 32, s. 5; 2000, c. 2, s. 2; 2001, c. 37, s. 1; 2006, c. 14, s. 3(2), (3); 2008, c. 6, s. 26

Proceedings on making of prohibition order

260. (1) If a court makes a prohibition order under section 259 in relation to an offender, it shall cause

(a) the order to be read by or to the offender;

(b) a copy of the order to be given to the offender; and

(c) the offender to be informed of subsection 259(4).

Endorsement by offender

(2) After subsection (1) has been complied with in relation to an offender who is bound by an order referred to in that subsection, the offender shall endorse the order, acknowledging receipt of a copy thereof and that the order has been explained to him.

Validity of order not affected

(3) The failure of an offender to endorse an order pursuant to subsection (2) does not affect the validity of the order.

Onus

(4) In the absence of evidence to the contrary, where it is proved that a disqualification referred to in paragraph 259(5)(*b*) has been imposed on a person and that notice of the disqualification has been mailed by registered or certified mail to that person, that person shall, after five days following the mailing of the notice, be deemed to have received the notice and to have knowledge of the disqualification, of the date of its commencement and of its duration.

Certificate admissible in evidence

(5) In proceedings under section 259, a certificate setting out with reasonable particularity that a person is disqualified from

(a) driving a motor vehicle in a province, purporting to be signed by the registrar of motor vehicles for that province, or

(b) operating a vessel or aircraft, purporting to be signed by the Minister of Transport or any person authorized by the Minister of Transport for that purpose

is evidence of the facts alleged therein without proof of the signature or official character of the person by whom it purports to be signed.

Notice to accused

(6) Subsection (5) does not apply in any proceedings unless at least seven days notice in writing is given to the accused that it is intended to tender the certificate in evidence.

Definition of "registrar of motor vehicles"

(7) In subsection (5), **"registrar of motor vehicles"** includes the deputy of that registrar and any other person or body, by whatever name or title designated, that from time to time performs the duties of superintending the registration of motor vehicles in the province.

R.S.C. 1985, c. 27 (1st Supp.), s. 36; 2006, c. 14, s. 4

Stay of order pending appeal

261. *(1) Subject to subsection (1.1), if an appeal is taken against a conviction or discharge under section 730 for an offence committed under any of sections 220, 221, 236, 249 to 255 and 259, a judge of the court being appealed to may direct that any prohibition order under section 259 arising out of the conviction or discharge shall, on any conditions that the judge or court imposes, be stayed pending the final disposition of the appeal or until otherwise ordered by that court.*

Appeals to Supreme Court of Canada

(1.1) In the case of an appeal to the Supreme Court of Canada, the direction referred to in subsection (1) may be made only by a judge of the court being appealed from and not by a judge of the Supreme Court of Canada.

Effect of conditions

(2) If conditions are imposed under a direction made under subsection (1) or (1.1) that a prohibition order be stayed, the direction shall not operate to decrease the period of prohibition provided in the order.

R.S.C. 1985, c. 27 (1st Supp.), s. 36; 1994, c. 44, ss. 15, 103; 1997, c. 18, ss. 12, 141(a); 2006, c. 14, s. 5; 2008, c. 6, s. 27

7.8.1 DEVELOPMENTS

1. Under section 254(2) the contemporaneity requirement is abolished and screening demands can be made up to three hours after driving just like breath demands.

2. Drug evaluation officers can, under section 254(3.1), on reasonable grounds demand a drug evaluation examination.

In *R. v. Wood*, [2007] A.J. No. 895, [2007] 11 W.W.R. 330, 79 Alta. L.R. (4th) 358, 51 M.V.R. (5th) 93, 2007 CarswellAlta 1048, 2007 ABQB 503 (Alta. Q.B.) Mr. Justice Topolniski excluded drug recognition evidence in allowing an accused's appeal from his conviction for impaired driving. He held that insufficient reliability was shown to admit as expert evidence an officer's drug recognition examination ("DRE") and opinion that accused's ability was impaired by cannabis.

> DRE accuracy rates between 44 and 76 percent fall far below the acceptable paradigm of reliability on issues of critical importance in criminal proceedings. The DRE is not sufficiently reliable to meet the standard of relevance. As such, it was of no benefit to the trial judge. Further, be benefits of receiving the expert opinion evidence were outweighed by the associated costs. To paraphrase the words of Sopinka J. in Mohan, the DRE was misleading in the sense that its effect on the trier of fact was out of proportion with its reliability.

3. Drug evaluation officers can, under section 254(3.3), demand breath samples based merely on reasonable suspicion, though it appears these are simply screening tests albeit performed with approved instruments.

4. The presumption under section 258(1)(c) that subsequent breath sample test results are the same as the accused's blood alcohol level at the time the samples were taken and also the material time of the alleged offence is made "conclusive proof".

It is refuted only by evidence that

> **(a) the approved instrument was malfunctioning or was operated improperly,**
>
> **(b) that the malfunction or improper operation resulted in the determination that the concentration of alcohol in the accused's blood exceeded 80 mg of alcohol in 100 mL of blood, and**
>
> **(c) that the concentration of alcohol in the accused's blood would not in fact have exceeded 80 mg of alcohol in 100 mL of blood at the time when the offence was alleged to have been committed.**

(The situation regarding blood samples is analogous, with evidence of an improper analysis substituted for machine malfunction.)

Furthermore, by section 258(1)(d.01) evidence of malfunctioning or impropriety requires more than merely proof of a lower expected reading based upon the accused's evidence of consumption.

5. The presumption under section 258(1)(d.1) which requires, to refute test results showing a blood alcohol level greater than .08, evidence that the accused's actual blood alcohol level was under .08 at the material time, also now requires evidence that is at the same time consistent with the test readings obtained.

6. The impact on the Crown's disclosure obligation of the fact that it is now made a relevant issue whether the approved instrument was "malfunctioning" or "operated properly" would appear to be substantial. Access to the approved instrument by the defence, its examination by a defence expert, review of its operating software, its history of operation and maintenance all would seem to be inevitably required.

7. An important issue will be the application of the new versions of the presumptions to cases arising prior to July 2, 2008.

Previous amendments to the breathalyzer presumption were considered in *R. v. Cvitkovic* (1998), 31 M.V.R. (3d) 271, 1998 CarswellOnt 16, [1998] O.J. No. 50, 49 C.R.R. (2d) 73 (Ont. Prov. Div.) (then new s. 258(1)(d.1) of the *Criminal Code* does apply retrospectively) and *R. v. Ali* (1979), 1979 CarswellNfld 4, 2 M.V.R. 75, 10 C.R. (3d) 136, 108 D.L.R. (3d) 41, 51 C.C.C. (2d) 282, 27 N.R. 243, 56 A.P.R. 361, 21 Nfld. & P.E.I.R. 361, 14 C.R. (3d) 117, 1979 CarswellNfld 8, [1980] 1 S.C.R. 221 (S.C.C.) (new requirement for two smaples rather than merely one does not apply retrospectively).

> In *Ali* the Supreme Court majority referenced its eralier decisions and said as follows on this issue: "In the present case, as in the case of Howard Smith, *supra*, the amendment has created "no offence, it takes away no defence, it does not render criminal any course of conduct which was not already so declared before its enactment" and I am satisfied that the only charge effected by the amendment was a change in the mode of proof so that the rebuttable presumption created by the production of a technician's certificate did not arise unless more than one sample had been analysed, whereas before the amendment a technician's certificate based on only one sample was sufficient to raise a presumption as to proof of its contents.

If an applicable principle is whether the amendment "render[s] criminal any course of conduct which was not already so declared before its enactment" then this amendment is penal — and hence not retrospective — in nature. The new presumtpions apply, as do the predecssor versions, to all those arrestees who become accused persons because they produce blood alcohol test results by breath or blood that is greater than the legal limit. But the new presumptions subdivide that group of previously acquitted persons. The category of accused persons who are found not guilty at present — those who are able to leave the court with a reasonable doubt that their blood alcohol level was below the legal limit — becomes divided into two groups, one of whom will now stand convicted. Not guilty will no longer be the verdict for all those accused who at present are found not guilty, but only for those who in addition can show one of machine malfunction or improper operation and also can show their innocent blood alcohol level under the legal limit is consistent with the instrument test readings. Previously acquitted accused who cannot show both one of malfunction or impropriety and test consistency must be convicted. Presumptions that move a group of previously-acquitted accused into the category of presumptively-convicted accused would seem, it is submitted, to be more than merely evidentiary and procedural changes and rather to be penal in nature and not retrospective in operation.

As to the second issue, a major difficulty in applying the presumtpions at on-going trials will be the accused's access to the instruments involved in order to show malfunction or impropriety. Until the legsilation is in force, there is no legal basis for the accsued to take the necessary dislcosure and production steps. Once the legislation is in force the accused's breath testing event is long in the past and the state of the machine cannot be reconstructed.

8. Another important issue is the constitutional validity of the new versions of the presumptions.

The new presumptions, which have been changed from mere "proof" to "conclusive proof," have the effect of convicting accused whose blood alcohol level was in fact under .08 at the material time but who are unable to adduce evidence of both machine malfunction or improper operation and consistency of their innocent blood alcohol level with the instrument test readings.

The presumptions as they previous read were upheld: *R. v. Phillips* (1988), [1988] O.J. No. 415, 44 C.R.R. 244, 42 C.C.C. (3d) 150, 64 C.R. (3d) 154, 27 O.A.C. 380, 1988 CarswellOnt 65, 4 M.V.R. (2d) 239 (Ont. C.A.); *R. v. Cvitkovic* (1998), 31 M.V.R. (3d) 271, 1998 CarswellOnt 16, [1998] O.J. No. 50, 49 C.R.R. (2d) 73 (Ont. Prov. Div.) (though one court held otherwise: *R. v. Ballem* (September 7, 1988), Fitzgerald Prov. J., [1988] P.E.I.J. No. 150 (P.E.I. Prov. Ct.), reversed (1989), 1989 CarswellPEI 141, 246 A.P.R. 137, 79 Nfld. & P.E.I.R. 137, 44 C.R.R. 270 (P.E.I. T.D.), affirmed (1990), 1990 CarswellPEI 1, 49 C.R.R. 169, 262 A.P.R. 125, 84 Nfld. & P.E.I.R. 125, 58 C.C.C. (3d) 46, 22 M.V.R. (2d) 14 (P.E.I. C.A.). They were violations of s.11(d) of the Charter because they permitted conviction notwithstanding a reasonable doubt of an element of the criminal offence: *R. v. Downey*, 1992 CarswellAlta 467, 1992 CarswellAlta 56, [1992] S.C.J. No. 48, 72 C.C.C. (3d) 1, 9 C.R.R. (2d) 1, 13 C.R. (4th) 129, [1992] 2 S.C.R. 10, 90 D.L.R. (4th) 449, 14 W.A.C. 342, 125 A.R. 342, 136 N.R. 266, 2 Alta. L.R. (3d) 193, EYB 1992-66871 (S.C.C.) (re constitutionality of presumptions generally). But the presumptions were held justifiable under s.1.

The section 1 analysis has been cleraly established since *R. v. Oakes*, 1986 CarswellOnt 1001, 1986 CarswellOnt 95, 53 O.R. (2d) 719, 19 C.R.R. 308, 50 C.R.

(3d) 1, 24 C.C.C. (3d) 321, 14 O.A.C. 335, 65 N.R. 87, 26 D.L.R. (4th) 200, [1986] 1 S.C.R. 103, EYB 1986-67556, [1986] S.C.J. No. 7 (S.C.C.). "[S]. 1 that requires two things be established: the impugned state action must have an objective of pressing and substantial concern in a tree and democratic society; and there must be proportionality between the objective and the impugned measure. The second part of the s. 1 analysis, the "proportionality test" involves three determinations: that the measure adopted is rationally connected to the objective (rational connection); that the measure impair as little as possible the right or freedom in question (minimal impairment); and that there be proportionality between the effects of the measure and the objective."

It is in the latter elements of the proportionality test that the new presumptions run aground on unconstitutionality. In *Phillips* in upholding the predecessor presumption the Court's response to the argument that innocents would be convicted (thereby negating minimal impairment and proportionality) was: "It is, of course, open to an accessed to give evidence of drinking shortly before the breathalyser test together with appropriate scientific evidence and thus establish that the BAC shown by the breathalyser test was higher than at the time of the alleged driving offence. This would be "evidence to the contrary" which could rebut the presumtpion under s. 241(1)(c)." The fact is that under the new presumptions this will be insufficient and such innocent accused will be convicted without further evidence.

Another way to view the matter is to recognize that the present wording of the presumptions go a long way to proving the unconstitutionality of the new provisions. The present provisions are less violative of *Charter* rights, so the new provisions to be upheld require proof that the present provisions are insufficient to secure the public interest. This means it must be demonstrated that the present provisions are resulting in an unacceptable number of 'unjust acquittals,' acquittals of guilty drinking drivers. There has been no demonstration of such a fact. There is simply the government's presumption that the breath machines are always right and the accused's evidence of consumption always wrong.

It can also be said that the amendments to the presumption provisions in para. (c)and (d.1) and new (d.01) in their essence assume the inevitable accuracy of the breath testing machinery. Under (c) evidence of machine malfunction or improper operation is made an express requirement in order to rebut the machine readings as "conclusive proof". Under (d.01) evidence establishing the machine readings could not be right based upon consumption evidence, no matter how credible, is by law made insufficient to allow an inference the machine was wrong. Under (d.1) the Carter-type evidence to the contrary must not only be below the legal limit but must be consistent with the machine readings. However couched, these provisions set up a presumption that results in conviction. To survive under s. 1 of the *Charter*, the validity must meet the constitutional proportionality requirements of rationality, minimal impairment and proportional effects. This requires proof that the machine is invariably correct absent evidence that will be accessible and available to an accused of malfunction or improper operation. Again, this would seem to be an unconstitutional presumption. (d.01) would appear especially vulnerable.

7.9 BLOOD ALCOHOL READINGS

In this offence the element of impairment of ability to drive is required; simple proof of blood alcohol level at the material time of operation or care or control is not probative of this issue. Thus, there is required the additional step of relating proved blood alcohol level at the material time of operation or care or control to the element of impairment.

A breathalyzer reading or blood test result without expert evidence interpreting the reading, with respect to its meaning with regard to the ability to drive a motor vehicle, is arguably meaningless, and even irrelevant, except perhaps to confirm that there was alcohol consumption. Nevertheless, it is sometimes assumed that a reading, for example, double the legal limit of .08, has probative value with respect to impairment without any additional evidence. It is suggested that a court cannot take judicial notice on the issue since the matter is not notorious, but properly the subject of expert opinion evidence. This view was confirmed in *R. v. Letford* (2000), [2000] O.J. No. 4841, 150 C.C.C. (3d) 225, 51 O.R. (3d) 737, 8 M.V.R. (4th) 6, 139 O.A.C. 387, 2000 CarswellOnt 5034 (Ont. C.A.); *R. v. Crawford* (2000), [2000] O.J. No. 361, 2000 CarswellOnt 3490 (Ont. S.C.J.); *R. v. Randell* (1994), 118 Sask. R. 48, 1994 CarswellSask 124 (Sask. Q.B.); *R. v. Hoffner* (2005), [2005] O.J. No. 3862, 2005 CarswellOnt 4347, 24 M.V.R. (5th) 280 (Ont. S.C.J.).

The following sections deal with the evidentiary issues regarding breathalyzer breath test results and blood test results on a charge of this nature.

7.9.1 BREATHALYZER READINGS

- Breathalyzer test results may be proved by the oral testimony of the breathalyzer operator, the qualified technician.
- The *Criminal Code* also provides for proof of breathalyzer test results by documentary evidence, in the form of a breathalyzer certificate. Under section 258(1)(*g*), a certificate by the qualified technician (breathalyzer operator) is evidence of its contents (without proof of the signature thereon) where:
  - samples of an accused's breath have been taken pursuant to a breathalyzer demand as described above (pursuant to section 254(3)) and
  - where the certificate states the following:

  - that the analysis of each sample was made using an approved instrument operated by the qualified technician
  - that the qualified technician ascertained the approved instrument to be in proper working order by means of a suitable alcohol standard
  - the alcohol standard used
  - the results of the analyses so made
  - the time when each sample was taken
  - the place where each sample was taken
  - that each sample was received from the accused directly into the approved instrument operated by the qualified technician

- For the certificate to be adduced into evidence, the accused must, before the trial:

  - receive notice that the prosecution intends to use the certificate in evidence (section 258(7))
  - receive a copy of the certificate (section 258(7))

- With reference to the certificate evidence, the accused can ask the court for leave to require the attendance of the qualified technician for the purposes of cross-examination: section 258(6).

See 5.5 Conducting Tests.

Both the presumption of blood alcohol level in s. 258(1)(c) and the provision for the admissibility of a qualified technician's certificate in s. 258(1)(g) depend as the first condition precedent that the samples of breath be taken "pursuant to a demand made under subsection 254(3)." Consequently test results have been held inadmissible in those rare cases where there was absent proof they were taken pursuant to the appropriate statutory demand: *R. v. Kagayalingam*, 36 M.V.R. (5th) 80, [2006] O.J. No. 2201, 2006 CarswellOnt 3359, 2006 ONCJ 196 (Ont. C.J.); *R. v. Hall*, 2003 CarswellAlta 1039, 2003 ABPC 124, 19 Alta. L.R. (4th) 324, [2003] A.J. No. 921, 341 A.R. 33 (Alta. Prov. Ct.); *R. v. Riley* (1978), 1 M.V.R. 84, [1978] O.J. No. 266, 1978 CarswellOnt 5 (Ont. Co. Ct.); *R. v. O'Flynn*, 2006 CarswellBC 374, 2006 BCPC 56, [2006] B.C.J. No. 371 (B.C. Prov. Ct.); *R. v. Dionne* (April 18, 2005), J.N. Wilson J., [2005] O.J. No. 3433 (Ont. C.J.); *R. v. Hergott* (1999), 1 M.V.R. (4th) 165, 1999 CarswellOnt 4655, [1999] O.J. No. 5314 (Ont. S.C.J.); *R. v. Sigiannis* (January 21, 2000), Weinper J., [2000] O.J. No. 5412 (Ont. C.J.); *R. v. Adustini*, [2005] A.J. No. 374, 2005 ABPC 69, 2005 CarswellAlta 441 (Alta. Prov. Ct.).

Courts have also held this requirement not made out where the officer lacked the required reasonable grounds for the demand, it then not being a demand "... under subsection 254(3)": *R. v. Charette* (2008), 2008 CarswellOnt 1431, [2008] O.J. No. 1016 (Ont. S.C.J.); *R. v. Jackson*, 381 A.R. 294, [2005] A.J. No. 496, 2005 CarswellAlta 586, 2005 ABQB 268 (Alta. Q.B.).

However in *R. v. Gundy*, [2008] O.J. No. 1410, 2008 CarswellOnt 2091, 2008 ONCA 284 (Ont. C.A.), the appeal court held that aside from being raised by the accused as a *Charter* issue to prove that the investigating officer made a valid Intoxilizer demand under s. 254(3) of the *Criminal Code*, the Crown need not prove reasonable and probable grounds as an element of its case or to rely on the breathalyser presumption. The absence of such grounds is an issue to e raised by the accused on a *Charter* application.

Certificate Evidence and Service

In *R. v. Mackinnon* (2003), [2003] O.J. No. 323, 2003 CarswellOnt 228 (Ont. S.C.J.), reversed (2003), 2003 CarswellOnt 3827, 42 M.V.R. (4th) 205, 177 O.A.C. 188 (Ont. C.A.), the principles governing proof that accused was served with a 'true copy' of breathalyzer certificate were considered as an acquittal was entered on appeal for lack of sufficient proof. The fact that a copy of the certificate was provided in the crown disclosure to the defence does not satisfy the notice requirement: *R. v. Sisetski*, 2004 CarswellSask 715, 255 Sask. R. 53, 2004 SKPC 129 (Sask. Prov. Ct.).

In a case where the officer testified he "may have slid" document over to the accused across the table of "may have" handed it to him, but he lacked any recollection, an acquittal was upheld based upon lack of proof of proper service: *R. v. Duplessis* (March 9, 2006), Doc. Edmonton 020805776S1, [2006] A.J. No. 660 (Alta. Q.B.) (Murray J.).

> One might reasonably conclude that, at that point, our law contemplates the accused's judgment is impaired to the extent he or she ought not to be allowed to operate a motor vehicle. Therefore, in my view, it is particularly important to ensure that the accused is properly given a Certificate, and that he understands it. This takes compliance with all elements of s. 258(7) out of the realm of "mere technicality". . .[S]imply placing the Certificate in front of the accused, after it has been explained to him, [does not] satisfie[. . .] the requirement. . .[I]t is necessary for the officer to physically hand over the Certificate and Notice to the accused and to indicate that the document is for him to take with him when he leaves.

The admissibility of breath test results by way of a certificate requires evidence of a proper demand for a breathalyzer test as one of the two conditions precedent: *R. v. Jackson*, 2005 CarswellAlta 586, 2005 ABQB 268, 381 A.R. 294, [2005] A.J. No. 496 (Alta. Q.B.).

Evidence is required that the alcohol standard solution is suitable for use with the approved instrument: *R. v. Laybourne*, [2002] A.J. No. 392, 2002 CarswellAlta 412, 2002 ABPC 46, 318 A.R. 80 (Alta. Prov. Ct.).

(a) Breathalyzer Readings to Blood Alcohol Level at Material Time

Note that this form of evidence, just like oral testimony from the breathalyzer technician, proves only the breathalyzer test results at the time of the tests. Without any further evidentiary link, those test results would completely fail to prove anything about the accused's blood alcohol level or his or her condition at the material time, the earlier time when the accused was operating or had the care or control of the vehicle.

Judicial notice is not permitted of blood alcohol extrapolation: *Dennis v. British Columbia (Superintendent of Motor Vehicles)*, [2000] B.C.J. No. 2447, 2000 BCCA 653, 82 B.C.L.R. (3d) 313, 7 M.V.R. (4th) 23, 150 C.C.C. (3d) 544, 146 B.C.A.C. 73, 239 W.A.C. 73, 2000 CarswellBC 2449 (B.C. C.A.).

There are two methods by which the breathalyzer machine test results at the later time can be related back to show the corresponding values at the earlier material time, when the accused was operating or had the care or control of the vehicle. The first method is by the statutory presumption in section 258(1)(*c*). The second is by expert testimony.

(i) Method I: Breathalyzer Readings Plus Presumption Back

- If the prosecutor is relying on this presumption, has he or she provided proof of the following factual matters as condition precedent to the application of the statutory presumption as to the blood alcohol level at the time of the alleged offence:
  - that breath samples were taken pursuant to a breathalzyer demand made in accordance with section 254(3)
  - that each sample was taken "as soon as practicable" after the time when the offence was alleged to have been committed
  - that the first sample was taken not more than two hours after the time when the offence was alleged to have been committed
  - that an interval, of at least fifteen minutes between the samples, passed
  - that each sample was received from the accused directly into an approved instrument operated by a qualified technician

- that an analysis of each sample was made using an approved instrument operated by a qualified technician
- that there is an "absence of evidence to the contrary"

- These matters may be proved by oral testimony or by breathalyzer certificate evidence or by a combination thereof.

- If any of the above factual requirements to the application of the presumption is not proved by the prosecution, then the statutory presumption fails to apply and the breathalyzer machine test results fail to prove anything relevant to the material time of operation or care or control of the vehicle.

See 5.5 Conducting Tests.

See 7.9.1 Samples "pursuant to a demand..."

Regarding the 2 hour limit on the first breath, in *R. v. King* (March 3, 2008), Doc. 1307A00552, [2008] N.J. No. 99 (N.L. Prov. Ct.) the accused was acquitted of drinking and driving offence where crown unable to prove case by reliance on presumption for inability to prove case by reliance on presumption for inability to prove beyond reasonable doubt that the first breath sample was taken "not later than two hours" after the time at which it is alleged that the offence was committed.

The "as soon as practicable" requirement for breathalyzer tests was considered in *R. v. Letford* (2000), [2000] O.J. No. 4841, 150 C.C.C. (3d) 225, 51 O.R. (3d) 737, 8 M.V.R. (4th) 6, 139 O.A.C. 387, 2000 CarswellOnt 5034 (Ont. C.A.). It was held that a 25-minute unexplained delay meant breathalyzer tests were not taken as soon as practicable in *R. v. Williams* (2000), 2000 CarswellOnt 4788, [2000] O.J. No. 4740 (Ont. S.C.J.).

In *R. v. Murji* (1998), [1998] O.J. No. 6001 (Ont. Prov. Div.), the accused was acquitted of drinking and driving charges because the delay between the demand and the taking of breathalyzer tests defeated the breathalyzer presumption where the accused was delayed because he was waiting for two other drivers to take tests.

In *R. v. Schouten* (2002), [2002] O.J. No. 4777, 2002 CarswellOnt 4528 (Ont. S.C.J.), the Accused's appeal from a drinking and driving conviction was allowed and an acquittal entered where the breathalyzer tests were not proved to have been taken "as soon as practicable" where "there was an 18 minute period when it is uncertain what the arresting officer and the appellant were doing. . . ."

In *R. v. Konyk* (2006), 2006 CarswellOnt 9199, [2006] O.J. No. 1844 (Ont. C.J.) (B.E. Pugsley J.) an unexplained 38 minute delay between the taking of the two breath tests "does not allow the court to find that the second breath sample was taken as soon as practicable". Accord *R. v. Blacklock* (2008), [2008] O.J. No. 1472, 2008 CarswellOnt 2163 (Ont. S.C.J.) (32-minute gap between tests).

In *R. v. Boone* (September 1997), Duncan Prov. J. (Ont. Prov. Div.), Drinking & Driving Law, Vol. XIII, no. 7, p. 4, a delay of one hour while waiting for duty counsel to call back offended the ''as soon as practicable'' requirement. In fact, calling duty counsel when the accused does not wish to speak to duty counsel can negate the "as soon as practicable" requirement: *R. v. Shin*, [2007] O.J. No. 125, 2007 ONCJ 20, 2007 CarswellOnt 141 (Ont. C.J.) (J.W. Bovard J.); *R. v. MacDonald*, [2006] A.J. No. 1714, 2006 CarswellAlta 1819, 2006 ABPC 329, 69 Alta. L.R. (4th) 330, 411 A.R. 342 (Alta. Prov. Ct.) (Fradsham Prov. Ct. J.); *R. v. Pruski*, [2006] O.J. No. 5256, 2006 CarswellOnt 8462, 2006 ONCJ 506, 44 M.V.R. (5th) 106 (Ont. C.J.) (M. Green J.). *R. v. Davidson* (2005), [2005] O.J. No. 3474, 2005 CarswellOnt 3708, 23 M.V.R. (5th) 77 (Ont. S.C.J.); *R. v. Hogan*, [2006] O.J. No. 150, 2006 CarswellOnt 194, 2006 ONCJ 9 (Ont. C.J.); *R. v. Litwin* (1998), 1998 CarswellOnt 3291 (Ont. Gen. Div.), affirming (1997), 30 M.V.R. (3d) 152, 1997 CarswellOnt 3925, [1997] O.J. No. 4242 (Ont. Prov. Div.); *R. v. Barrick* (1998), 36 M.V.R. (3d) 258, 55 C.R.R. (2d) 327, 1998 CarswellOnt 3193, [1998] O.J. No. 3252 (Ont. Gen. Div.); *R. v. Hesketh*, [2003] B.C.J. No. 1242, 2003 CarswellBC 1357, 2003 BCPC 173 (B.C. Prov. Ct.); *R. v. Sleep*, 2004 CarswellOnt 3675, 2004 ONCJ 179, [2004] O.J. No. 3681 (Ont. C.J.).

This should be contrasted with the situation in *R. v. Baradaran-Aghaei* (1998), 1998 CarswellOnt 15, [1998] O.J. No. 47 (Ont. Prov. Div.) where the 55-minute delay between entering the police station and administering the breathalyzer test was caused by the police officer's decision to wait for the accused to speak to duty counsel. Here, the accused had not waived his right to confer with counsel and the officer was obliged to ensure the accused had an opportunity to exercise that right.

In the most recent authority *R. v. Vanderbruggen* (2006), [2006] O.J. No. 1138, 2006 CarswellOnt 1759, 29 M.V.R. (5th) 260, 206 C.C.C. (3d) 489, 208 O.A.C. 379 (Ont. C.A.) the Ontario Court of Appeal said: "In deciding whether the tests were taken as soon as practicable, the trial judge should look at the whole chain of events bearing in mind that the *Criminal Code* permits an outside limit of two hours from the time of the offence to the taking of the first test. The "as soon as practicable" requirement must be applied with reason. In particular, while the Crown is obligated to demonstrate that—in all the circumstances—the breath samples were taken within a reasonably prompt time, there is no requirement that the Crown provide a detailed explanation of what occurred during every minute that the accused is in custody..." See also *R. v. Carey* (2006), [2006] O.J. No. 3821, 2006 CarswellOnt 5780, 215 O.A.C. 151, 36 M.V.R. (5th) 35, 83 O.R. (3d) 49 (Ont. C.A.).

For "evidence to the contrary" caselaw see 13.1.2 (b) and 13.2.

(ii) Method II: Breathalyzer Readings Plus Expert Testimony Relating Back

A toxicologist or other expert witness can, based on certain assumptions, calculate backwards from a known blood alcohol level at a certain point in time to calculate the individual's blood alcohol level at an earlier point in time. However, the evidence must establish all of the factual assumptions and hypothetical facts that the expert is using to draw his or her conclusions. A crucial area is often the exact temporal pattern of the accused's drinking and especially the time of the last consumption: see *R. v. Grosse* (1996), 19 M.V.R. (3d) 197, 107 C.C.C. (3d) 97 (Ont. C.A.); leave to appeal refused (1997), 99 O.A.C. 239 (note) (S.C.C.) *R v. Lacey* (1992), 113 N.S.R. (2d) 348 (N.S. Co. Ct.); *R. v. Pawluk* (April 1, 1997), Doc. Wynyard Q.B. 47/95 (Sask. Q.B.), Drinking & Driving Law Vol. XII, no. 7, p. 54. *R. v. Smith* (1997), 30 M.V.R. (3d) 217, 207 A.R. 339 (Alta. Prov. Ct.); *R. v. Daniels* (1997), 156 Nfld. & P.E.I.R. 324, 483 A.P.R. 324 (Nfld. T.D.); *R. v. Smith* (1998), 36 M.V.R. (3d) 301 (Ont. Gen. Div.); *R. v. Quiring* (1998), 38 M.V.R. (3d) 195 (B.C. S.C.); *R. v. Davidson* (1998), 39 M.V.R. (3d) 33, 171 N.S.R. (2d) 312, 519 A.P.R. 312 (N.S. S.C.).

An "Over 80" charge was dismissed where the toxicologist's extrapolation of blood alcohol level back to the time of driving depended upon an unsupported assumption that there would be no unabsorbed alcohol in the accused's system at the time of driving, meaning there had been no consumption of alcohol within the previous one half hour of driving: *R. v. Yuen*, [2001] B.C.J. No. 780, 2001 BCPC 45, 2001 CarswellBC 540 (B.C. Prov. Ct.).

Note that evidence to this point proves the accused's blood alcohol level at the material time as deduced from the breathalyzer machine test results. This is sufficient on a charge of "over '80". However, with regard to a charge involving the element of impaired ability, there must be some evidence relating the relationship between the proved blood alcohol level and the issue of impairment. The following section deals with this further step.

(b) Effect of Blood Alcohol Level at Material Time

Expert opinion evidence may be given that a given blood alcohol level established by the evidence at the material time may have effect upon a person's ability to drive a motor vehicle. Such evidence would then tend to prove the issue of impaired ability required upon those charges.

7.9.2 BLOOD TEST READINGS

- Blood sample test results may be proved by the oral testimony of a relevant witness or witnesses according to the ordinary rules of evidence.

- The *Criminal Code* also provides for proof of blood sample test results by documentary evidence, in the form of a certificate of a qualified medical practitioner or qualified technician. Under section 258(1)(*h*), a certificate by the qualified medical practitioner or a qualified technician is evidence of its contents (without proof of the signature thereon or offical character of the person appearing to have signed the certificate) where:

  - samples of an accused's blood have been taken pursuant to a demand as described above (pursuant to section 254(3)), or otherwise with the consent of the accused, or pursuant to a blood sample warrant (section 256) and

  - where the certificate states the following:

    - that a medical practitioner took the sample or a certificate by a qualified medical practitioner stating that he or she had caused the sample to be taken by a qualified technician under his or her direction, or the certificate of a qualified technician stating that he or she took the sample
    - that before taking the sample, the medical practitioner was of the opinion that the taking of blood samples from the accused would not endanger his or her life
    - that in the case of a blood sample taken pursuant to a warrant, the accused was unable to consent to the taking of his or her blood, by reason of any physical or mental condition of the accused that resulted from the consumption of alcohol, the accident or any other occurrence related to or resulting from the accident
    - that the medical practitioner or the technician took an additional sample of the blood at the time the sample was taken to permit an analysis of one of the samples to be made by or on behalf of the accused
    - that the time and the place of the taking of the sample
    - that both samples were received from the accused and placed directly into approved containers that were subsequently sealed and that are identified in the certificate

- Section 258(1)(*i*) goes on to provide for certificate evidence from an analyst as to the results of the analysis of such blood samples.
- For the certificate to be adduced into evidence, the accused must, before the trial:
  - receive a copy of the certificate (section 258(7))
  - have been given reasonable notice of the intention to introduce the certificate into evidence (section 258(7))
- The accused can ask the court for leave to require the attendance of the qualified medical practitioner, qualified technician or analyst, as the case may be, for the purposes of cross-examination: section 258(6).

In *R. v. Mackinnon* (2003), [2003] O.J. No. 323, 2003 CarswellOnt 228 (Ont. S.C.J.), reversed (2003), 2003 CarswellOnt 3827, 42 M.V.R. (4th) 205, 177 O.A.C. 188 (Ont. C.A.), the principles governing proof that accused was served with a 'true copy' of breathalyzer certificate were considered as an acquittal was entered on appeal for lack of sufficient proof.

(a) Blood Test Results to Blood Alcohol Level at Material Time

Proof of blood sample test results, whether by certificate or by oral testimony, proves only the blood sample test results at the time of the taking of the samples. Without any further evidence or evidentiary link, those test results would completely fail to prove anything about the accused's blood alcohol level or his or her condition at the material time, the earlier time when the accused was operating or had the care or control of the vehicle.

There are two methods by which the blood sample test results at the later time can be related back to show the corresponding values at the earlier material time, when the accused was operating or had the care or control of the vehicle. The first method is by the statutory presumption in section 258(1)(*d*). The second is by expert testimony.

(i) Method I: Blood Test Readings Plus Presumption Back

- If the prosecutor is relying on this presumption, has he or she provided proof of the following factual matters as a condition precedent to the application of the statutory presumption of blood alcohol level, that is:

- that the blood samples were taken pursuant to a demand made in accordance with section 254(3), or with the consent of the accused, or pursuant to a blood sample warrant (section 256)
- that an additional sample was taken and retained to permit an analysis on behalf of the accused upon request made within six months from the taking of the samples
- that both samples were taken "as soon as practicable" after the time when the offence was alleged to have been committed
- that the samples were taken not more than two hours after the time when the offence was alleged to have been committed
- that both samples were taken by a qualified medical practitioner or by a qualified technician under the direction of a qualified medical practitioner
- that both samples were received from the accused directly into approved containers and sealed
- that an analyst made an analysis of a sample which had been contained in a sealed approved container
- and there is an absence of "evidence to the contrary"

- These matters may be proved by oral testimony or by certificate evidence or by a combination thereof.

- If any of the above factual requirements to the application of the presumption is not proved by the prosecution, then the statutory presumption fails to apply and the blood sample test results fail to prove anything relevant to the material time of operation or care or control of the vehicle.

- Because of the requirement of a sample for the accused to be released upon application within six months, it has been held that the statutory presumption is not available where the accused is not made aware within that time frame that a second sample is available for testing and there is reason (criminal jeopardy) to obtain it: *R. v. Egger* (1993), 21 C.R. (4th) 186, 82 C.C.C. (3d) 193 (S.C.C.).

- Section 258(4) provides for the application by the accused for release of the extra blood sample taken for independent analysis within six months of the day the samples were taken.

See 5.5 Conducting Tests.

See 7.9.1(a)(i) at p. 70 re "as soon as practicable".

For "evidence to the contrary" caselaw see 13.1.2 (b) and 13.2.

(ii) Method II: Blood Test Readings Plus Expert Testimony Relating Back

A toxicologist or other expert witness can, based on certain assumptions, calculate backwards from a known blood alcohol level at a certain point in time to calculate the individual's blood alcohol level at an earlier point in time. However, the evidence must establish all of the factual assumptions and hypothetical facts that the expert is using to draw his or her conclusions. A crucial area is often the exact temporal pattern of the accused's drinking and especially the time of the last consumption: see *R. v. Grosse* (1996), 19 M.V.R. (3d) 197, 107 C.C.C. (3d) 97 (Ont. C.A.); *R. v. Lacey* (1992), 113 N.S.R. (2d) 348 (N.S. Co. Ct.).

Note that evidence to this point proves the accused's blood alcohol level at the material time as deduced from the blood sample test results. This is sufficient on a charge of "over '80". However, with regard to a charge involving the element of impaired ability, there must be some evidence relating the relationship between the proved blood alcohol level and the issue of impairment. The following section deals with this further step.

(b) Effect of Blood Alcohol Level at Material Time

Expert opinion evidence may be given that a given blood alcohol level established by the evidence at the material time may have effect upon a person's ability to drive a motor vehicle. Such evidence would then tend to prove the issue of impaired ability required upon those charges.

8

PROOF OF EXCESSIVE BLOOD ALCOHOL LEVEL: "OVER '80"

In this offence the element of impairment of ability to drive is not required, but simply proof of blood alcohol level at the material time of operation or care or control. Thus, the relevant considerations are the same as the preceding section except that the additional step of relating proved blood alcohol level to the element of impairment need not be taken.

8.1 BREATHALYZER READINGS

- Breathalyzer test results may be proved by the oral testimony of the breathalyzer operator, the qualified technician.

- The *Criminal Code* also provides for proof of breathalyzer test results by documentary evidence, in the form of a breathalyzer certificate. Under section 258(1)(*g*), a certificate by the qualified technician (breathalyzer operator) is evidence of its contents (without proof of the signature thereon) where:

  - samples of an accused's breath have been taken pursuant to a breathalyzer demand as described above (pursuant to section 254(3)) and

  - the certificate states the following:

    - that the analysis of each sample was made using an approved instrument operated by the qualified technician
    - that the qualified technician ascertained the approved instrument to be in proper working order by means of a suitable alcohol standard
    - the alcohol standard used

- the results of the analyses so made
- the time when each sample was taken
- the place where each sample was taken
- that each sample was received from the accused directly into the approved instrument operated by the qualified technician

- For the certificate to be adduced into evidence, the accused must, before the trial:

  - receive notice that the prosecution intends to use the certificate in evidence (section 258(7))
  - receive a copy of the certificate (section 258(7))

- With reference to the certificate evidence, the accused can ask the court for leave to require the attendance of the qualified technician for the purposes of cross-examination: section 258(6).

See 5.5 Conducting Tests.

See 7.9.1 Breathalyzer Readings

8.1.1 BREATHALYZER READINGS TO BLOOD ALCOHOL LEVEL AT MATERIAL TIME

Note that this form of evidence, just like oral testimony from the breathalyzer technician, proves only the breathalyzer test results at the time of the tests. Without any further evidentiary link, those test results would completely fail to prove anything about the accused's blood alcohol level or his or her condition at the material time, the earlier time when the accused was operating or had the care or control of the vehicle.

There are two methods by which the breathalyzer machine test results at the later time can be related back to show the corresponding values at the earlier material time, when the accused was operating or had the care or control of the vehicle. Judicial notice is not permitted of blood alcohol extrapolation: *Dennis v. British Columbia (Superintendent of Motor Vehicles)*, [2000] B.C.J. No. 2447, 2000 BCCA 653, 82 B.C.L.R. (3d) 313, 7 M.V.R. (4th) 23, 150 C.C.C. (3d) 544, 146 B.C.A.C. 73, 239 W.A.C. 73, 2000 CarswellBC 2449 (B.C. C.A.) The first method is by the statutory presumption in section 258(1)(*c*). The second is by expert testimony.

(a) Method I: Breathalyzer Readings Plus Presumption Back

- If the prosecutor is relying on this presumption, has he or she provided proof of the following factual matters as condition precedent to the application of the statutory presumption as to the blood alcohol level at the time of the alleged offence:

  - that the breath samples were taken pursuant to a breathalzyer demand made in accordance with section 254(3)
  - that each sample was taken "as soon as practicable" after the time when the offence was alleged to have been committed
  - that the first sample was taken not more than two hours after the time when the offence was alleged to have been committed
  - that an interval, of at least fifteen minutes between the samples, passed
  - that each sample was received from the accused directly into an approved instrument operated by a qualified technician
  - that an analysis of each sample was made using an approved instrument operated by a qualified technician
  - that there is an absence of "evidence to the contrary"

- These matters may be proved by oral testimony or by breathalyzer certificate evidence or by a combination thereof.

- If any of the above factual requirements to the application of the presumption is not proved by the prosecution, then the statutory presumption fails to apply and the breathalyzer machine test results fail to prove anything relevant to the material time of operation or care or control of the vehicle.

See 5.5 Conducting Tests.

See 7.9.1 Breathalyzer Readings

For "evidence to the contrary" caselaw see 13.1.2 (b) and 13.2.

(b) Method II: Breathalyzer Readings Plus Expert Testimony Relating Back

A toxicologist or other expert witness can, based on certain assumptions, calculate backwards from a known blood alcohol level at a certain point in time to calculate the individual's blood alcohol level at an earlier point in time. However, the evidence must establish all of the factual assumptions and hypothetical facts that the expert is using to draw his or her conclusions. A crucial area is often the exact temporal pattern of the accused's drinking and especially the time of the last consumption: see *R. v. Grosse* (1996), 19 M.V.R. (3d) 197, 107 C.C.C. (3d) 97 (Ont. C.A.); *R. v. Lacey* (1992), 113 N.S.R. (2d) 348 (N.S. Co. Ct.); *R. v. Pawluk* (April 1, 1997), Doc. Wynyard Q.B. 47/95 (Sask. Q.B.), Drinking & Driving Law Vol. XII, no. 7, p. 54.

An "Over 80" charge was dismissed where the toxicologist's extrapolation of blood alcohol level back to the time of driving depended upon an unsupported assumption that there would be no unabsorbed alcohol in the accused's system at the time of driving, meaning there had been no consumption of alcohol within the previous one half hour of driving: *R. v. Yuen*, [2001] B.C.J. No. 780, 2001 BCPC 45, 2001 CarswellBC 540 (B.C. Prov. Ct.).

Note that evidence to this point proves the accused blood alcohol level at the material time as deduced from the breathalyzer machine test results. This is sufficient on a charge of "over '80".

8.2 BLOOD TEST READINGS

- Blood sample test results may be proved by the oral testimony of a relevant witness or witnesses according to the ordinary rules of evidence.

- The *Criminal Code* also provides for proof of blood sample test results by documentary evidence, in the form of a certificate of a qualified medical practitioner or qualified technician. Under section 258(1)(*h*), a certificate by the qualified medical practitioner or a qualified technician is evidence of its contents (without proof of the signature thereon or official character of the person appearing to have signed the certificate) where:

- samples of an accused's blood have been taken pursuant to a demand as described above (pursuant to section 254(3)), or otherwise with the consent of the accused, or pursuant to a blood sample warrant (section 256) and

- where the certificate states the following:

  - that a medical practitioner took the sample or a certificate by a qualified medical practitioner stating that he or she had caused the sample to be taken by a qualified technician under his or her direction, or the certificate of a qualified technician stating that he or she took the sample
  - that before taking the sample, the medical practitioner was of the opinion that the taking of blood samples from the accused would not endanger his or her life
  - that in the case of a blood sample taken pursuant to a warrant, the accused was unable to consent to the taking of his or her blood, by reason of any physical or mental condition of the accused that resulted from the consumption of alcohol, the accident or any other occurrence related to or resulting from the accident
  - that the medical practitioner or the technician took an additional sample of the blood at the time the sample was taken to permit an analysis of one of the samples to be made by or on behalf of the accused
  - the time and the place of the taking of the sample
  - that both samples were received from the accused and placed directly into approved containers that were subsequently sealed and that are identified in the certificate

- Section 258(1)(*i*) goes on to provide for certificate evidence from an analyst as to the results of the analysis of such blood samples.

- For the certificate to be adduced into evidence, the accused must, before the trial:

  - be given a copy of the certificate: section 258(7)

- be given reasonable notice, of the intention to introduce the certificate into evidence: section 258(7)

- The accused can ask the court for leave to require the attendance of the qualified medical practitioner, qualified technician or analyst, as the case may be, for the purposes of cross-examination: section 258(6).

In *R. v. Mackinnon* (2003), [2003] O.J. No. 323, 2003 CarswellOnt 228 (Ont. S.C.J.), reversed (2003), 2003 CarswellOnt 3827, 42 M.V.R. (4th) 205, 177 O.A.C. 188 (Ont. C.A.), the principles governing proof that accused was served with a 'true copy' of breathalyzer certificate were considered as an acquittal was entered on appeal for lack of sufficient proof. The fact that a copy of the certificate was provided in the crown disclosure to the defence does not satisfy the notice requirement: *R. v. Sisetski*, 2004 CarswellSask 715, 255 Sask. R. 53, 2004 SKPC 129 (Sask. Prov. Ct.).

Evidence is required that the alcohol standard solution is suitable for use with the approved instrument: *R. v. Laybourne*, [2002] A.J. No. 392, 2002 CarswellAlta 412, 2002 ABPC 46, 318 A.R. 80 (Alta. Prov. Ct.).

8.2.1 BLOOD TEST RESULTS TO BLOOD ALCOHOL LEVEL AT MATERIAL TIME

Proof of blood sample test results, whether by certificate or by oral testimony, proves only the blood sample test results at the time of the taking of the samples. Without any further evidence or evidentiary link, those test results would completely fail to prove anything about the accused's blood alcohol level or his or her condition at the material time, the earlier time when the accused was operating or had the care or control of the vehicle.

There are two methods by which the blood sample test results at the later time can be related back to show the corresponding values at the earlier material time, when the accused was operating or had the care or control of the vehicle. The first method is by the statutory presumption in section 258(1)(*d*). The second is by expert testimony.

(a) Method I: Blood Test Readings Plus Presumption Back

- If the prosecutor is relying on this presumption, has he or she provided proof of the following factual matters as a condition precedent to the application of the statutory presumption of blood alcohol level, that is:

- that the blood samples were taken pursuant to a demand made in accordance with section 254(3), or with the consent of the accused, or pursuant to a blood sample warrant (section 256)
- that an additional sample was taken and retained to permit an analysis on behalf of the accused upon request made within six months from the taking of the samples
- that both samples were taken "as soon as practicable" after the time when the offence was alleged to have been committed
- that the samples were taken not more than two hours after the time when the offence was alleged to have been committed
- that both samples were taken by a qualified medical practitioner or by a qualified technician under the direction of a qualified medical practitioner
- that both samples were received from the accused directly into approved containers and sealed
- that an analyst made an analysis of a sample which had been contained in a sealed approved container
- and there is an absence of "evidence to the contrary"

- These matters may be proved by oral testimony or by certificate evidence or by a combination thereof.

- If any of the above factual requirements to the application of the presumption is not proved by the prosecution, then the statutory presumption fails to apply and the blood sample test results fail to prove anything relevant to the material time of operation or care or control of the vehicle.

- Because of the requirement of a sample for the accused to be released upon application within six months, it has been held that the statutory presumption is not available, where the accused is not made aware within that time frame that a second sample is available for testing and there is reason (criminal jeopardy) to obtain it: *R. v. Egger*

(1993), 45 M.V.R. (2d) 161, 21 C.R. (4th) 186, 82 C.C.C. (3d) 193 (S.C.C.).

- Section 258(4) provides for the application by the accused for release of the extra blood sample taken for independent analysis

See 5.5 Conducting Tests.

See 7.9.1(a)(i) re "as soon as practicable".

For "evidence to the contrary" caselaw see 13.1.2 (b) and 13.2.

(b) Method II: Blood Test Readings Plus Expert Testimony Relating Back

A toxicologist or other expert witness can, based on certain assumptions, calculate backwards from a known blood alcohol level at a certain point in time to calculate the individual's blood alcohol level at an earlier point in time. However, the evidence must establish all of the factual assumptions and hypothetical facts that the expert is using to draw his or her conclusions. A crucial area is often the exact temporal pattern of the accused's drinking and especially the time of the last consumption: see *R. v. Grosse* (1996), 19 M.V.R. (3d) 197, 107 C.C.C. (3d) 97 (Ont. C.A.), leave to appeal refused (1997), 99 O.A.C. 239 (note) (S.C.C.); *R. v. Lacey* (1992), 113 N.S.R. (2d) 348 (N.S. Co. Ct.); *R. v. Smith* (1997), 30 M.V.R. (3d) 217, 207 A.R. 339 (Alta. Prov. Ct.); *R. v. Daniels* (1997), 156 Nfld. & P.E.I.R. 324, 483 A.P.R. 324 (Nfld. T.D.); *R. v. Smith* (1998), 36 M.V.R. (3d) 301 (Ont. Gen. Div.); *R. v. Quiring* (1998), 38 M.V.R. (3d) 195 (B.C. S.C.); *R. v. Davidson* (1998), 39 M.V.R. 33, 171 N.S.R. (2d) 312, 519 A.P.R. 312 (N.S. S.C.).

Note that evidence to this point proves the accused's blood alcohol level at the material time as deduced from the blood sample test results. This is sufficient on a charge of "over '80".

9

PROOF: OPERATION (DRIVING)

9.1 ADMISSIONS

- Did your client admit to being the driver of the motor vehicle?
- If the admission was made to a person in authority, was the admission "voluntary"?
- Was the admission made after your client was arrested or "detained"?
- If so, did the admission comply with the section 10(*b*) requirements that provide for the accused's right to retain and instruct counsel without delay? *Without compliance with section 10(b) of the Charter, the statement may be excluded from evidence.*
- Did police questioning of your client cease until he or she had a reasonable opportunity to consult counsel?
- Did your client have the opportunity to consult counsel in private?

To "operate" in respect of a motor vehicle means to drive the vehicle: *Criminal Code* s. 214.

The client's admission of being the driver of the motor vehicle at the material time is a common type of evidence establishing that fact.

Any such admission constitutes a statement by an accused and, if made to a person in authority such as a police officer, must be "voluntary" within the rules of evidence in that regard.

Any such admission made after an accused has been arrested or, as is more often the case, has been "detained" by a police officer must comply with the requirements of section 10(*b*) of the *Charter of Rights and Freedoms*. That is, it must be preceeded by the section 10(*b*) reminder given to the accused upon arrest or detention that he or she has the right to retain and instruct counsel without delay. Without compliance with section 10(b) the statement may be excluded from evidence under section 24(2) of the *Charter*.

See section 5.3 above for a detailed discussion of the right to counsel under section 10(*b*), issues around waiving the right and the exclusion of evidence under section 24(2) consequent upon a breach.

9.2 OTHER WITNESSES

- Is the identity of the driver in issue?
- Are there eyewitnesses identifying your client as the driver?
- What are the limits of this eyewitness evidence? *Consult evidence texts on the eyewitness evidence caselaw in an appropriate case.*

The fact of the accused's identity as the driver of the motor vehicle at the material time may also be established by witnesses who identify the client as the driver. In many cases this is not in dispute because one or more police officers may identify the accused as the driver at the time they stopped the vehicle.

Where the identity of the driver is in issue, evidence of witnesses identifying the accused constitutes a form of eyewitness identification and should be treated as such by counsel. The law of evidence views eyewitness identification with well justified suspicion and there are numerous evidence cases outlining the proper approach to the reliability of eyewitness identification. Counsel should consult evidence texts for that body of case law in an appropriate case.

9.3 OWNERSHIP

- Ownership does not identify the driver and has no probative value.

The mere fact of vehicle ownership in and of itself has no probative value with regard to the identity of the driver where such is disputed. There is no presumption that an owner is the driver for the purposes of criminal guilt which must be proved beyond a reasonable doubt.

10

PROOF: CARE OR CONTROL

10.1 GENERAL

- Care or control can be proved by:
  - showing actual care or control which involves some use of the vehicle or some course of conduct associated with the vehicle which involves a risk of putting the vehicle in motion so that it could become dangerous
  - showing the accused occupied the driver's seat for the purpose of putting the vehicle in motion.

Care or control can be proved by showing actual care or control or by relying on the presumption created by the *Criminal Code*. Where an accused is proved to have occupied the driver's seat, the accused is presumed to have had care or control of the vehicle unless the accused establishes that he or she did not occupy that seat for the purpose of putting the vehicle in motion: section 258(1)(*a*). The accused to rebut the presumption must do so on a balance of probabilities: *R. v. Whyte* (1988), 6 M.V.R. (2d) 138, 64 C.R. (3d) 123, 42 C.C.C. (3d) 97 (S.C.C.).

Proof of actual care or control of a motor vehicle without the benefit of the statutory presumption involves some use of the vehicle or some course of conduct associated with the vehicle which involves a risk of putting the vehicle in motion so that it could become dangerous: *R. v. Toews* (1985), 36 M.V.R. 1, 47 C.R. (3d) 213, 21 C.C.C. (3d) 24 (S.C.C.); *R. v. Ford* (1982), 13 M.V.R. 237, 65 C.C.C. (2d) 392 (S.C.C.). 'Danger' is an essential component of the offence: *R. v. Mallery*, 2008 CarswellNB 110, 2008 CarswellNB 111, [2008] N.B.J. No. 72, 2008 NBCA 18, 57 M.V.R. (5th) 172 (N.B. C.A.); *R. v. Kidson*, 2007 CarswellNS 612, [2007] N.S.J. No. 546, 2007 NSPC 68, 261 N.S.R. (2d) 45, 835 A.P.R. 45 (N.S. Prov. Ct.). In *R. v. Lafleur* (1998), 39 M.V.R. (3d) 213 (Ont. Prov. Div.) the court concluded after a review of these two S.C.C. cases that the risk of movement of the vehicle and the danger to the public are not an essential element for the Crown to prove. The accused's starting the engine on its own was sufficient to amount to care and control of the motor vehicle. See also *R. c. Loubier* (28 Avril 1994), n° C.A. Québec 200-10-000041-926 (C.A. Qué.) and *R. v. Green* (1989), 19 M.V.R. (2d) 58, 52 C.C.C. (3d) 93, 100 A.R. 131 (Alta. C.A.).

In *R. v. Ogrodnick*, 2006 CarswellAlta 368, [2006] A.J. No. 340, 2006 ABQB 91, 393 A.R. 6, 58 Alta. L.R. (4th) 154, [2006] 8 W.W.R. 267 (Alta. Q.B.), reversed 2007 CarswellAlta 619, 2007 ABCA 161, 409 A.R. 56, 402 W.A.C. 56, [2007] A.J. No. 514, 76 Alta. L.R. (4th) 45, [2007] 9 W.W.R. 596 (Alta. C.A.), leave to appeal refused (2007), 2007 CarswellAlta 1292, 2007 CarswellAlta 1291 (S.C.C.) the accused's appeal from conviction for impaired care and control allowed because *de facto* care or control was held not proved.

This requires the possible use of a vehicle or its fittings which creates a risk of dangerously setting it in motion.

> The Alberta and Supreme Court jurisprudence that binds me determines care or control with reference to the gravity of danger presented by the accused's actual course of conduct...
>
> ...Speculation and conjecture about future conduct is no basis for a criminal conviction. It is one thing to convict a person of impaired care or control because the level of intoxication demonstrates unpredictability or a risky pattern of behaviour. It is an entirely different matter to apprehend an impaired person, accept that the person does not intend to drive, yet convict solely because that person might change his or her mind, without anything else to establish risk. To do so allows for the potential of absurd results, and ignores that the accused might be sober once the change of mind occurs.
>
> To ground a conviction, the inquiry into the risk of changing one's mind must establish a concrete and tangible risk of deliberately setting the vehicle in motion. It is trivial to say that "anything can happen" and "everything has risk". Convictions based upon trivial speculation offend the notion of justice,,,[C]onjecture or speculation has no place in the criminal law. That cannot be how the phrase "care or control" should be construed...
>
> ...
>
> Therefore, I conclude that, for the purpose of s. 253, absent a risk of unintentionally setting the vehicle in motion. Care or control is established where the circumstances demonstrate a tangible risk that the accused will change his or her mind to put the vehicle in motion.

A determination of whether the accused was in care or control will depend upon a careful consideration of the particular facts of the case. A driver found by the police changing his tire was found to be in care or control in *R. v. Madden*, 2001 ABPC 58, 2001 CarswellAlta 367 [2001] A.J. No. 366, 288 A.R. 34 (Alta. Prov. Ct.).

However in *R. v. Buckley*, 2002 CarswellSask 439, 2002 SKQB 281, [2002] S.J. No. 409, 221 Sask. R. 152 (Sask. Q.B.), leave to appeal refused (2003), 2003 CarswellSask 416, 2003 CarswellSask 417 (S.C.C.) care and control was held not made out for a car with three flat tires. Accord, *R. v. Annable*, 2004 CarswellSask 272, [2004] S.J. No. 256, 2004 SKQB 107, 250 Sask. R. 1 (Sask. Q.B.). *R. v. Pharai*, [2007] O.J. No. 4137, 2007 CarswellOnt 6919, 2007 ONCJ 486 (Ont. C.J.) (vehicle immobilized after accident).

In *R. v. Burbella* (2002), [2002] M.J. No. 355, 2002 CarswellMan 382, 2002 MBCA 106, 28 M.V.R. (4th) 126, 217 D.L.R. (4th) 604, 167 C.C.C. (3d) 495, 5 C.R. (6th) 174, [2003] 1 W.W.R. 613, 166 Man. R. (2d) 198, 278 W.A.C. 198 (Man. C.A.), an appeal by the accused from his conviction for care or control of a motor vehicle while impaired contrary to s. 253 of the *Criminal Code* was allowed and an acquittal entered where the accused's motor vehicle was immobilized in a snow bank. Accord *R. v. Bond*, [2008] M.J. No. 124, 2008 CarswellMan 221, 2008 MBQB 100 (Man. Q.B.) (accused waiting with vehicle stuck in snow for return of driver): "The element of dangerousness should not be established by speculation or possibility."

Accused was held not to be in care or control of his vehicle where car keys were removed from possession of accused by third party prior to arrival of police: *R. v. MacAulay*, 2002 CarswellPEI 21, 2002 PESCTD 18, 210 Nfld. & P.E.I.R. 234, 630 A.P.R. 234, [2002] P.E.I.J. No. 23 (P.E.I. T.D.), reversed 2002 CarswellPEI 107, 2002 PESCAD 24, 169 C.C.C. (3d) 321, 30 M.V.R. (4th) 263, 218 Nfld. & P.E.I.R. 312, 653 A.P.R. 312, 8 C.R. (6th) 109 (P.E.I. C.A.).

In *R. v. Wren* (2000), 2 M.V.R. (4th) 188, 144 C.C.C. (3d) 374, 47 O.R. (3d) 544, 130 O.A.C. 302, 34 C.R. (5th) 81, 2000 CarswellOnt 685, [2000] O.J. No. 756 (Ont. C.A.), leave to appeal refused (2000), 147 C.C.C. (3d) vi (note), 264 N.R. 198 (note), 2000 CarswellOnt 4192, 2000 CarswellOnt 4193, [2000] S.C.C.A. No. 235, 145 O.A.C. 199 (note) (S.C.C.), an appeal by the Crown form the accused's acquittal for care and control of a motor vehicle based upon his sitting in his inoperable car to keep warm was dismissed as the Court considered in detail the contradictory caselaw in this area:

> [para. 29] In my view, the cases from the Supreme Court of Canada and from this court can be reconciled on the issue of the *actus reus* of care or control. The issue to be determined on the facts of each case is whether any acts by the accused could cause the vehicle to become a danger whether by putting it in motion or in some other way.
>
> [para. 30] In the case as presented below, the only potential danger was of putting the vehicle in motion. It was therefore open to the trial judge to conclude, at the point in time when the respondent was in the vehicle waiting for the tow truck, that he was not in care or control within the meaning of those terms as defined in the caselaw to which I have referred.

See also *R. v. Ducai* (2002), 2002 CarswellOnt 1224, 24 M.V.R. (4th) 264, [2002] O.J. No. 1411 (Ont. S.C.J.) where a similar result was resolved in respect of an inoperable vehicle. A car out of gas meant the accused was acquitted in *R. v. Sleno*, 2003 CarswellAlta 1761, [2003] A.J. No. 1529, 2003 ABPC 210, 46 M.V.R. (4th) 282 (Alta. Prov. Ct.).

In *R. v. Appapillai* (1995) (Ont. Gen. Div.), Drinking & Driving Law, Vol. XI, no. 4, p. 29, an accused who started a vehicle so someone else could drive it was not in care and control. For similar cases see *R. v. Greenan* (1995), 18 M.V.R. (3d) 315 (P.E.I. T.D.); *R. v. Johnson* (1996), 182 A.R. 140 (Alta. Prov. Ct.).

An accused cannot be said to be in care or control of a motor vehicle on the basis that he or she had the power to designate the driver and turned the keys over to another to drive: *R. v. Moreau*, 162 Sask. R. 103, [1998] 6 W.W.R. 409 (Sask. Q.B.), Drinking & Driving Law, Vol. XIII, no. 7, p. 68. The accused was not found to be in care or control in these situations as well: where the vehicle was stuck in a ditch: *R. v. Dosa* (1999), 40 M.V.R. (3d) 253 (Ont. Gen. Div.); *R. v. Wheeler* (1989), 77 Sask. R. 13 (Sask. Prov. Ct.); where the accused was in his vehicle, which was lodged in a ditch and was attached to a tow truck by a chain: *R. v. Brala* (1989), 22 M.V.R. (2d) 324 (Ont. Dist. Ct.); or waiting for his wife to get him: *R. v. Sedore*, [2006] B.C.J. No. 1482, 2006 BCPC 307, 2006 CarswellBC 1609 (B.C. Prov. Ct.) (Baird Ellan P.C.J.) where he was sitting in the driver's seat of his car with his keys in his pocket waiting for a cab: *R. v. Burns* (1993), 117 Sask. R. 152 (Sask. Prov. Ct.); where he went into the vehicle to smoke marijuana and started the engine so he could use the heater; where the accused simply attempted to unlock his truck door: *R. v. Letestu* (1988), 8 M.V.R. (2d) 170, 69 Sask. R. 288 (Sask. Q.B.). In *R. v. Sharun* (2000), 2000 CarswellAlta 334, 81 Alta. L.R. (3d) 267, 262 A.R. 189, [2000] A.J. No. 400 (Alta. Q.B.), an appeal by the accused from a conviction for "over 80" care and control was allowed and an acquittal entered where the accused was sitting in his immobilized vehicle keeping warm while awaiting a tow truck. Care and control was held proved where the accused got behind the wheel with the engine running with the intention of putting it in park and shutting off the engine: *R. v. Lockerby* (1999), 175 N.S.R. (2d) 123, 534 A.P.R. 123 (N.S. S.C), affirmed 180 N.S.R. (2d) 115, 557 A.P.R. 115, 139 C.C.C. (3d) 314, 48 M.V.R. (3d) 54, 1999 NSCA 122, 1999 CarswellNS 316 (N.S. C.A.); the accused was behind the steering wheel of a vehicle with the engine running but the vehicle was inoperable and not capable of being put into motion: *R. v. Koziolek* (1999), 40 M.V.R. (3d) 304 (Ont. Gen. Div.); the accused was discovered standing seven or eight feet from his vehicle, which had gone into a ditch: *R. v. Rishy-Maharaj* (1995), 16 M.V.R. (3d) 147 (Ont. Gen. Div.); the accused was behind the steering wheel of a vehicle while it was being towed from a ditch: *R. v. Johal* (1998), 33 M.V.R. (3d) 87, 124 C.C.C. (3d) 249 (Ont. Gen. Div.); the accused was behind the steering wheel of a vehicle which was in a ditch and the keys were in his pocket: *R. v. McCue* (1997), 27 M.V.R. (3d) 85 (Ont. Gen. Div.); the accused was approached by a police officer just as he opened the driver door of the vehicle and responded to the question, "Where are you going?" with "Just out for a drive to cruise around": *R. v. Chartrand* (1998), 125 Man. R. (2d) 238 (Man. Q.B.).

In some cases, the accused has been found to be in care or control notwithstanding that he or she was found sleeping in the vehicle. In the following cases, however, the court held that a sleeping driver was not in care or control: *R. v. Hibbs* (2007), [2007] O.J. No. 1031, 47 M.V.R. (5th) 111, 2007 CarswellOnt 2620 (Ont. S.C.J.); *R. v. Snow*, [2008] M.J. No. 230, 2008 CarswellMan 229, 2008 MBQB 85 (Man. Q.B.); *R. v. Baumber*, [2007] A.J. No. 849, 2007 CarswellAlta 1004, 2007 ABPC 203 (Alta. Prov. Ct.); *R. v. Kawai*, [2007] B.C.J. No. 1754, 2007 CarswellBC 1821, 2007 BCPC 243 (B.C. Prov. Ct.); *R. v. Legrow*, [2007] N.S.J. No. 11, 2007 CarswellNS 13, 2007 NSSC 4, 41 M.V.R. (5th) 196, 251 N.S.R. (2d) 117, 802 A.P.R. 117 (N.S. S.C.), affirmed 255 N.S.R. (2d) 317, 814 A.P.R. 317, 49 M.V.R. (5th) 25, 2007 NSCA 74, 2007 CarswellNS 269 (N.S. C.A.), leave to appeal refused (2008), 2008 CarswellNS 33, 2008 CarswellNS 32 (S.C.C.) (D.L. MacLellan J.); *R. v. Christie*, [2006] B.C.J. No. 3397, 2006 CarswellBC 3314, 2006 BCPC 588

(B.C. Prov. Ct.) (Saunders Prov. Ct. J.); *R. v. Benoit* (2006), [2006] O.J. No. 3861, 2006 CarswellOnt 5851 (Ont. S.C.J.). *R. v. Cove*, [2006] A.J. No. 399, 2006 CarswellAlta 436, 2006 ABQB 264, 57 Alta. L.R. (4th) 117, 32 M.V.R. (5th) 63 (Alta. Q.B.); *R. v. Yakobchuk*, [2005] A.J. No. 1033, 2005 CarswellAlta 1148, 2005 ABPC 189, 22 M.V.R. (5th) 63, 383 A.R. 304 (Alta. Prov. Ct.); *R. v. Stephenson*, [2005] A.J. No. 1533, 2005 CarswellAlta 1663, 2005 ABPC 263, 389 A.R. 53 (Alta. Prov. Ct.); *R. v. Bird* (1999), 1999 CarswellSask 342 (Sask. Prov. Ct.); *R. v. Sherbrook*, 164 Sask. R. 183, [1998] 6 W.W.R. 602 (Sask. Q.B.); *R. v. Amendt* (1997), 1997 CarswellBC 2847, [1997] B.C.J. No. 2965, 1997 BCSC 3408 (B.C. S.C.), Drinking & Driving Law, Vol. XIII, no. 6, p. 41; *R. v. Martindale* (1995), 20 M.V.R. (3d) 263, 45 C.R. (4th) 111 (B.C. S.C.); *R. v. Barber* (1998), [1998] S.J. No. 708 (Sask. Prov. Ct.), Drinking & Driving Law, Vol. XIV, no. 2, p. 11; *R. v. Boyd* (1990), 95 N.S.R. (2d) 367, 251 A.P.R. 367 (N.S. Co. Ct.); *R. v. Bleau* (1991) [1991] O.J. No. 1524 (Ont. Gen. Div.), Drinking & Driving Law, Vol. VII, no. 3, pp. 23-24; *R. v. Boudreau* (1996), [1995] O.J. No 4990 (Ont. Gen. Div.), Drinking & Driving Law, Vol. XI, no. 4, p. 25; *R. v. Walton* (1996), 186 A.R. 180 (Alta. Prov. Ct.); *R. v. Nielsen* (1996), 186 A.R. 18 (Alta. Prov. Ct.); *R. v. Poulos* (1999), 1999 CarswellOnt 1448 (Ont. S.C.J.).

The Crown has successfully proved that the accused was in care or control of a motor vehicle where: the accused was asleep in the front seat with the engine running: *R. v. Murtaugh* (1998), 36 M.V.R. (3d) 284 (Ont. Prov. Div.); *R v. Morey* (1998), 1998 CarswellOnt 3145 (Ont. Gen. Div.); *R. c. Rousseau* (1997), 34 M.V.R. (3d) 41, (*sub nom. R. v. Rousseau*) 121 C.C.C. (3d) 571 (C.A. Qué.); *R. v. Clarke* (1997), 27 M.V.R. (3d) 91, 188 N.B.R. (2d) 123, 480 A.P.R. 123 (N.B. C.A.); the accused was asleep in the front seat with the keys in the ignition but the engine was not running: *R. v. Diotte* (1991), 28 M.V.R. (2d) 177, 64 C.C.C. (3d) 209 (N.B. C.A.); the accused was asleep in a disabled car which could not be moved because the parking brake was on and also the transmission linkage lever had been unhooked: *R. v. Moffat* (1988), 9 M.V.R. (2d) 237, 66 C.R. (3d) 155 (Ont. C.A.), leave to appeal refused (1989), 101 N.R. 157n (S.C.C.); the accused was asleep behind the steering wheel of a vehicle which was in a ditch and could not move under its own power: *Saunders v. R.*, 1 C.R.N.S. 249, [1967] 3 C.C.C. 278, [1967] S.C.R. 284, 61 D.L.R. (2d) 645 (S.C.C.); the accused was sitting in the driver's seat with his eyes closed and head tilted back, and the keys were on the floor: *R. v. Pilon* (1998), 39 M.V.R. (3d) 1, 131 C.C.C. (3d) 236, 115 O.A.C. 324, 1998 CarswellOnt 4425, [1998] O.J. No. 4755 (Ont. C.A.); *R. v. Ingram* (2007), [2007] A.J. No. 1160, 2007 CarswellAlta 1409, 84 Alta. L.R. (4th) 70, 2007 ABQB 631, 55 M.V.R. (5th) 148, [2008] 3 W.W.R. 647 (Alta. Q.B.); *R. v. Buckingham*, [2007] S.J. No. 138, 293 Sask. R. 42, 397 W.A.C. 42, 46 C.R. (6th) 284, 218 C.C.C. (3d) 203, 45 M.V.R. (5th) 165, [2007] 6 W.W.R. 73, 2007 CarswellSask 142, 2007 SKCA 32 (Sask. C.A.); *R. v. Snow*, [2008] M.J. No. 230, 2008 CarswellMan 229, 2008 MBQB 85 (Man. Q.B.) (sleeping driver convicted).

When a trial judge accepts that the accused went to sleep in his vehicle so he had no intention of driving at the time, the accused is not guilty of the care and control offence: *R. v. Grover* (2000), [2000] A.J. No. 1272, 2000 ABQB 779, 6 M.V.R. (4th) 237, [2001] 3 W.W.R. 182, 87 Alta. L.R. (3d) 276, 276 A.R. 77, 2000

CarswellAlta 1204 (Alta. Q.B.). A sleeping accused also found not guilty in *R. v. Gerrard*, [2000] A.J. No. 1354, 2000 ABPC 182, 8 M.V.R. (4th) 45, 275 A.R. 122, 2000 CarswellAlta 1282 (Alta. Prov. Ct.) and *R. v. Shuparski* (2001), [2001] S.J. No. 220, 2001 CarswellSask 197, 206 Sask. R. 299 (Sask. Prov. Ct.), affirmed (October 4, 2001), Doc. Regina Q.B.G. 1110/01 (Sask. Q.B.), affirmed 2003 CarswellSask 165, [2003] S.J. No. 147, 2003 SKCA 22, 9 C.R. (6th) 270, 173 C.C.C. (3d) 97 , 38 M.V.R. (4th) 17, 232 Sask. R. 1, 294 W.A.C. 1, [2003] 6 W.W.R. 428 (Sask. C.A.), leave to appeal refused (2003), [2003] S.C.C.A. No. 167, 2003 CarswellSask 614, 2003 CarswellSask 615, 176 C.C.C. (3d) vi, 254 Sask. R. 319 (note), 336 W.A.C. 319 (note), 321 N.R. 397 (note) (S.C.C.). All the precedents regarding sleeping accused were carefully analyzed in *R. v. Hannemann* (2001), [2001] O.J. No. 1686, 2001 CarswellOnt 1538, 43 C.R. (5th) 168, 17 M.V.R. (4th) 151 (Ont. S.C.J.) and *R. v. Miron* (2001), [2001] O.J. No. 1610, 2001 CarswellOnt 1506, 20 M.V.R. (4th) 145 (Ont. C.J.). In *R. v. Geoffroy*, [2003] A.J. No. 461, 2003 CarswellAlta 509, 2003 ABPC 50, 338 A.R. 182 (Alta. Prov. Ct.), the sleeping driver accused was found guilty of care and control offences.

In *R. v. Decker*, 2002 CarswellNfld 40, 2002 NFCA 9, 209 Nfld. & P.E.I.R. 44, 626 A.P.R. 44, 162 C.C.C. (3d) 503, 24 M.V.R. (4th) 26, [2002] N.J. No. 38, 2 C.R. (6th) 352 (Nfld. C.A.), leave to appeal refused (2002), 2002 CarswellNfld 316, 2002 CarswellNfld 317, [2002] S.C.C.A. No. 145 , 231 Nfld. & P.E.I.R. 355 (note), 686 A.P.R. 355 (note), 303 N.R. 397 (note) (S.C.C.) a divided appeal court considered in detail the elements of the offence of care or control in the case of a driver found sleeping in the vehicle, and in the result the Crown appeal from the accused's acquittal of care or control while impaired was dismissed by a 2:1 majority.

Similarly the sleeping accused was acquitted in *R. v. McNabb*, 2003 CarswellSask 547, [2003] S.J. No. 537, 2003 SKPC 118 (Sask. Prov. Ct.). See also *R. v. Kuokkanen*, 2005 CarswellOnt 1778, 2005 ONCJ 148 (Ont. C.J.).

Care and control while impaired not held made out where accused asleep lying on the front seat: *R. v. Bailey* (December 6, 2001), Doc. 535/01, [2001] O.J. No. 5697 (Ont. S.C.J.), or where accused found sleeping in vehicle driver's seat with motor running found not guilty of care and control while impaired: *R. v. Bishop*, 2002 CarswellBC 395, 2002 BCPC 6, [2002] B.C.J. No. 79 (B.C. Prov. Ct.). Similarly, driver planning to sleep, not drive, not guilty of care and control: *R. v. Redondo*, 2001 CarswellBC 2854, 2001 BCSC 1728, [2001] B.C.J. No. 2659 (B.C. S.C.).

See also *R. v. Merkley* (2003), 2003 CarswellOnt 1515, [2003] O.J. No. 1606 (Ont. S.C.J.) and *R. v. Geoffroy*, 2003 CarswellAlta 509, [2003] A.J. No. 461, 2003 ABPC 50, 338 A.R. 182 (Alta. Prov. Ct.) and *R. v. Peill* (2003), 2003 CarswellMan 90, [2003] M.J. No. 77, 171 Man. R. (2d) 270 (Man. Prov. Ct.).

10.2 ADMISSIONS

- Did your client admit to being the driver of the motor vehicle?

- If the admission was made to a person in authority, was the admission "voluntary"?
- Was the admission made after your client was arrested or "detained"?
- If so, did the admission comply with the section 10(*b*) requirements that provide for the accused's right to retain and instruct counsel without delay? *Without compliance with section 10(b) of the Charter, the statement may be excluded from evidence.*
- Did police questioning of your client cease until he or she had a reasonable opportunity to consult counsel?
- Did your client have the opportunity to consult counsel in private?

The client's admission of facts establishing that the client was in care or control of the motor vehicle at the material time is a common type of evidence establishing that fact.

Any such admission constitutes a statement by an accused and, if made to a person in authority such as a police officer, must be "voluntary" within the rules of evidence in that regard.

Any such admission made after an accused has been arrested or, as is more often the case, has been "detained" by a police officer must comply with the requirements of section 10(*b*) of the *Charter of Rights and Freedoms*. That is, it must be preceeded by the section 10(*b*) reminder given to the accused upon arrest or detention that he or she has the right to retain and instruct counsel without delay. Without compliance with section 10(*b*) the statement may be excluded from evidence under section 24(2) of the *Charter*.

See section 5.3 above for a detailed discussion of the right to counsel under section 10(*b*), issues around waiving the right and the exclusion of evidence under section 24(2) consequent upon a breach.

10.3 OTHER WITNESSES

- Is the matter of your client being in care or control in issue?
- Are there witnesses identifying your client as being in care or control? *Consult evidence texts on the eyewitness evidence caselaw in an appropriate case.*

The fact of the accused's identity as the person in care or control of the motor vehicle at the material time may also be established by witnesses who identify the client as such. In many cases this is not in dispute because one or more police officers may identify the accused as the person at the time they came into contact with the vehicle.

Where the identity of the person in care or control of the motor vehicle is in issue, evidence of witnesses identifying the accused constitutes a form of eyewitness identification and should be treated as such by counsel. The law of evidence views eyewitness identification with well-justified suspicion and there are numerous evidence cases outlining the proper approach to the reliability of eyewitness identification. Counsel should consult evidence texts for that body of caselaw in an appropriate case.

10.4 OWNERSHIP

- Ownership does not identify the driver and has no probative value.

The mere fact of vehicle ownership in and of itself has no probative value with regard to the identity of the person in care or control of a motor vehicle where such is disputed. There is no presumption that an owner is liable for the purposes of criminal guilt which must be proved beyond a reasonable doubt.

11

CAUSING BODILY HARM OR DEATH

11.1 CAUSATION

In order to convict the accused of the more serious offences of impaired driving causing bodily harm or impaired driving causing death, the Crown must establish a causal connection between the driver's condition and the ensuing bodily harm or death. One must bear in mind the distinction between a motorist driving in an impaired condition who is involved in an accident, and the motorist driving in an impaired condition whose impaired driving ability (as evidenced by driving conduct, failure to react, or failure to make a certain judgment) comprises a contributing cause of death or bodily harm outside the *de minimis* range: *R. v. Andrew* (1994), 6 M.V.R. (3d) 293, 91 C.C.C. (3d) 97 (B.C. C.A.).

It is not appropriate for the judge to consider whether a ''sober driver'' might have driven in a manner similar to that of the accused. The test is whether it is a reasonable inference that the accused's drinking was a cause, at least beyond the *de minimis* range, of the faulty driving and the injury to the victim: *R. v. Deprez* (1994), 9 M.V.R. (3d) 101, 95 C.C.C. (3d) 29, 97 Man. R. (2d) 272 (Man. C.A.); *R. v. Fisher* (1992), 36 M.V.R. (2d) 6, 13 C.R. (4th) 222 (B.C. C.A.); *R. v. Petersen* (1989), 16 M.V.R. (2d) 250 (Ont. Dist. Ct.). This principle, that the impaired condition of the accused must have been at least a contributing cause of the bodily harm or death outside the *de minimis* range, has also been approved in the following cases: *R. v. Pinske* (1988), 6 M.V.R. (2d) 19, 30 B.C.L.R. (2d) 114 (B.C. C.A.), affirmed 18 M.V.R. (2d) xxxiv, [1989] 2 S.C.R. 979, 40 B.C.L.R. (2d) 151, 100 N.R. 399 (S.C.C.); *R. v. F. (D.L.)* (1989), 18 M.V.R. (2d) 62, 73 C.R. (3d) 39, 52 C.C.C. (3d) 357, 100 A.R. 122 (Alta. C.A.); *R. v. Larocque* (1988), 5 M.V.R. (2d) 221 (Ont. C.A.); *R. v. Singhal* (1988), 5 M.V.R. (2d) 173 (B.C. C.A.); *R. v. Halkett* (1988), 11 M.V.R. (2d) 109, 73 Sask. R. 241 (Sask. C.A.).

The *de minimis* test was succinctly summarized in *R. v. Ewart* (1989), 18 M.V.R. (2d) 55, 53 C.C.C. (3d) 153, 100 A.R. 118 (Alta. C.A.), additional reasons at (1990), 53 C.C.C. (3d) 153 at 159, 105 A.R. 348 (Alta. C.A.), leave to appeal refused (1990), 109 A.R. 320 (note) (S.C.C.) as requiring that the underlying impaired driving must be shown to have been a ''real factor'' in bringing about any bodily harm or death which follows.

The fact that a collision may be combined with breathalyzer readings in excess of the legal limit, without evidence of anything unusual in the operation of the accused's vehicle prior to the collision, is not sufficient to establish that the accused's impairment was at least a contributing cause outside the *de minimis* range: *R. v. Fisher* (1992), 13 C.R. (4th) 222, 36 M.V.R. (2d) 6, [1992] B.C.J. No. 721, 1992 CarswellBC 462, 7 B.C.A.C. 264, 15 W.A.C. 264 (B.C. C.A.).

There is no requirement of a marked departure from the norm or other graduated standard in order to find a causal connection between the impairment and the collision: *R. v. White* (1994), 3 M.V.R. (3d) 283, 28 C.R. (4th) 160, 89 C.C.C. (3d) 336, 130 N.S.R. (2d) 143, 367 A.P.R. 143 (N.S. C.A.).

In the following situations, the court was not satisfied beyond a reasonable doubt that the impairment of the accused was a cause of the accident: the accused was distracted and did not see a pedestrian; the pedestrian did not see the vehicle before the impact; speed was not a material cause of the accident: *R. v. Angel* (1990), 27 M.V.R. (2d) 111, 100 N.S.R. (2d) 56, 272 A.P.R. 56 (N.S. Co. Ct.); the roads were very icy; the accused was driving carefully at or below the speed limit; the rear tires and brake drums were in poor condition: *R. v. Gairdner* (1999), 40 M.V.R. (3d) 133 (B.C. S.C.); the driving conditions were difficult; no excessive speed: *R. v. Halkett* (1988), 11 M.V.R. (2d) 109, 73 Sask. R. 241 (Sask. C.A.); two vehicles collided in an intersection controlled by traffic lights; neither vehicle attempted to brake; the deceased were also highly intoxicated: *R. v. Peck* (1989), 14 M.V.R. (2d) 136, 57 Man. R. (2d) 223 (Man. C.A.).

12

PROOF: MOTOR VEHICLE, ETC.

12.1 GENERAL

A motor vehicle is:

- driven by other than muscular power
- not railway equipment
- a motor vehicle even if incapable of being driven for some reason.

A motor vehicle is any vehicle driven by other than muscular power (excluding railway equipment): section 2. A motor vehicle incapable of being driven for some reason or other is still a motor vehicle: *Saunders v. R.*, 1 C.R.N.S. 249, [1967] 3 C.C.C. 278 (S.C.C.).

13

THE DEFENCE

13.1 GENERAL

In many cases the defence is based upon seeking to find a reasonable doubt concerning an essential element that the prosecution must establish to make out its case of guilt and secure a conviction. Such reasonable doubt may arise from the prosecution's own evidence or from defence evidence.

13.1.1 ESSENTIAL ELEMENTS OF THE OFFENCE TO BE ESTABLISHED BY THE PROSECUTION

A failure by the prosecution to establish the following matters beyond a reasonable doubt may, in an appropriate case, prevent conviction by negating an essential element required:

- whether the vehicle was a motor vehicle? See Chapter 12.

- whether the accused was the driver (operator)? See Chapter 9.

- whether the accused had care or control? See Chapter 10.

    - whether there was conduct or actions associated with the vehicle which involved a risk of putting the vehicle in motion so that it could become dangerous? See heading 10.1.
    - whether the accused was occupying the driver's seat? If so, has the accused established that he or she did not occupy that seat for the purpose of putting the vehicle in motion? See heading 10.1.

- whether the accused's blood alcohol level was over .08?

  - whether the factual matters required for the statutory presumption to apply have been proved? See headings 8.1.1 (breathalyzer tests) and 8.2.1 (blood tests).
  - whether the factual matters assumed in any expert opinion have been proved? See headings 8.1.1(a) (breathalyzer tests) and 8.2.1(a) (blood tests).
  - whether the source breathalyzer or blood test results have been proved?
  - whether the statutory prerequisites to any certificate evidence have been proved? See headings 8.1 (breathalyzer tests) and 8.2 (blood tests).
  - whether the statutory prerequisites to the taking of the blood or breath tests have been proved? See headings 8.1.1(a) (breathalyzer tests) and 8.2.1(a) (blood tests).

- whether the accused's ability to drive a motor vehicle was impaired by alcohol?

  - whether the factual matters required for the statutory presumption to apply have been proved? See headings 7.9.1(a)(i) (breathalyzer tests) and 7.9.2(a)(i) (blood tests).
  - whether the factual matters assumed in any expert opinion have been proved? See headings 7.9.1(a)(ii) (breathalyzer tests) and 7.9.2(a)(ii) (blood tests).
  - whether the source breathalyzer or blood test results have been proved?
  - whether the statutory prerequisites to any certificate evidence have been proved? See headings 7.9.1 (breathalyzer tests) and 7.9.2 (blood tests).
  - whether the statutory prerequisites to the taking of the blood or breath tests have been proved? See headings 7.9.1(a)(i) (breathalyzer tests) and 7.9.2(a)(i) (blood tests).
  - whether the relationship between a proved blood alcohol level and impairment has been proved? See headings 7.9.1(b) and 7.9.2(b).
  - whether other evidence bearing on impairment is credible and probative? See Chapter 7.

13.1.2 DEFENCE EVIDENCE DISPROVING AN ELEMENT OF THE OFFENCE

In other cases the defence may rely upon the adducing of defence evidence from the accused or from some other witness. Below are certain situations that commonly arise. Most of these negate the prosecution by adducing "evidence to the contrary" to rebut the presumption of blood alcohol level that would otherwise apply for the prosecution by virtue of the statutory provisions considered above.

It is always open to an accused to discharge this presumption by adducing evidence as to the amount and time of alcohol consumption. How much, when and under what circumstances he or she drank are facts peculiarly within his knowledge: *R. v. Ballem* (1990), 22 M.V.R. (2d) 14, 58 C.C.C. (3d) 46 (P.E.I. C.A.).

It should be noted that where the accused testifies to defend against the Crown's case and his evidence then discloses his guilt at an earlier point in time, the Crown cannot shift its case and claim a conviction based upon the admitted earlier transaction of drinking and driving: *R. v. Springer* (1980), 6 M.V.R. 146, 1980 CarswellSask 4 (Sask. Dist. Ct.); *R. v. MacDougall* (1998), [1998] O.J. No. 357, 1998 CarswellOnt 368 (Ont. Gen. Div.); *R. v. Wynnychuk* (1962), 132 C.C.C. 227, 37 W.W.R. 381, 1962 CarswellAlta 10, 37 C.R. 216 (Alta. C.A.); *R. v. Woodhouse* (1982), 38 O.R. (2d) 351, 15 M.V.R. 28, 1982 CarswellOnt 7 (Ont. Co. Ct.); *R. v. Pendleton* (1982), 1 C.C.C. (3d) 228, 1982 CarswellOnt 37, 18 M.V.R. 78, [1982] O.J. No. 132 (Ont. C.A.).

(a) "Last Drink" Defence

Where an accused is stopped shortly after the completion of consumption, and especially where the final consumption was the hasty consumption of a significant quantity, then because alcohol absorption takes time, it is possible that the accused's blood alcohol level was below the legal limit at the material time of driving but rose above the legal limit at the time of breathalyzer testing. This category of case obviously requires a breathalyzer reading not too much over the legal blood alcohol level of .08, in the order of .1 or .11. In such a case, the accused's evidence concerning his or her drinking, coupled with expert testimony calculating actual blood alcohol level at the time of driving, and confirming that these facts would have also given the breathalyzer readings actually obtained the hour or so later, will constitute "evidence to the contrary" negating the presumption and resulting in an acquittal (unless the accused's evidence concerning consumption is wholly rejected and disbelieved). In these cases the defence is not inconsistent with the actual breathalyzer readings obtained, but merely shows a pattern of consumption consistent with innocence and yet occasioning the actual readings obtained.

(b) "*Carter*" Defence

In other cases, the accused's evidence concerning his or her drinking, coupled with expert testimony calculating actual blood alcohol level at the time of driving, will constitute "evidence to the contrary" negating the presumption and resulting in an acquittal (unless the accused's evidence concerning consumption is wholly rejected and disbelieved). However, in these cases the defence is inconsistent with the actual breathalyzer readings obtained. The defence expert will be cross-examined to show that the accused's version of his or her actual drinking could not have led to the breathalyzer readings actually obtained. The prosecution will then argue that the trial judge should reject the accused's evidence concerning his or her consumption so that there is no "evidence to the contrary" to rebut the statutory presumption. Then, the prosecution will argue, relying upon the breathalyzer readings and applying the statutory presumption, a conviction should be entered. This defence, as considered in the leading case of *R. v. Carter* (1985), 31 M.V.R. 1, 19 C.C.C. (3d) 174 (Ont. C.A.), emphasized that in such cases for a conviction the trial judge must specifically reject the accused's evidence concerning consumption. If the trial judge is left with a reasonable doubt then the evidence remains as "evidence to the contrary" and the defence prevails. *Carter* also emphasized that it is not for the defence to show or speculate why the breathalyzer readings were allegedly erroneous. The subsequent case of *R. v. Gilbert* (1994), 7 M.V.R. (3d) 39, 92 C.C.C. (3d) 266, 19 O.R. (3d) 724 (Ont. C.A.) must not be misunderstood as casting doubt on *Carter*'s continued validity.

While Carter was confirmed to a large extent by the subsequent case of *R. v. Suttie*, [2004] O.J. No. 3345, 2004 CarswellOnt 3288, 24 C.R. (6th) 3, 72 O.R. (3d) 388, 10 M.V.R. (5th) 24, 188 C.C.C. (3d) 167, 189 O.A.C. 148 (Ont. C.A.), the matter has now been put beyond doubt by the majority decision of the Supreme Court of Canada in *R. c. Boucher*, [2005] S.C.J. No. 73, 2005 CarswellQue 10750, 2005 CarswellQue 10751, 2005 SCC 72, 33 C.R. (6th) 32, 259 D.L.R. (4th) 508, 202 C.C.C. (3d) 34, 25 M.V.R. (5th) 1, [2005] 3 S.C.R. 499, 342 N.R. 42 (S.C.C.):

> Breathalyzer results cannot be used to assess the credibility of a witness... [I]it would be circular to rely on the results to determine whether there is evidence that could raise a doubt regarding those very results...

Some courts subsequently have limited this holding to cases where certificate evidence of blood alcohol readings is involved, rather than *viva voce* evidence: *R. v. Snider*, [2006] O.J. No. 879, 2006 CarswellOnt 1321, 2006 ONCJ 65, 37 C.R. (6th) 61, 31 M.V.R. (5th) 296 (Ont. C.J.); *R. v. Lilek* (2006), [2006] O.J. No. 1158, 2006 CarswellOnt 1764 (Ont. S.C.J.). See also *R. v. Arrechea* (2006), [2006] O.J. No. 1562, 2006 CarswellOnt 2352, 31 M.V.R. (5th) 213 (Ont. C.J.). Since the difference is simply in how the machine results are being reported, rather than any additional evidence that might defeat the circular logic, it is submitted *Boucher* applies in both types of cases.

Nevertheless it is fair to say the debate still goes on as to the full meaning and application of the Boucher decision: *R. v. Sousa* (2007), 55 M.V.R. (5th) 104, [2007]

O.J. No. 3530, 2007 CarswellOnt 5880 (Ont. S.C.J.); *R. v. Doell*, [2007] S.J. No. 264, 221 C.C.C. (3d) 336, 293 Sask. R. 262, 397 W.A.C. 262, 50 M.V.R. (5th) 9, 158 C.R.R. (2d) 365, [2007] 9 W.W.R. 51, 2007 SKCA 61, 2007 CarswellSask 287 (Sask. C.A.) (Boucher stands for the proposition that breath test results cannot be used to assess the credibility of a witness in the context of the inquiry into whether the accused has presented evidence to the contrary. It does not address the question of whether those test results may be considered in determining if a .08 offence has been established.").

Mere uncertainty as to the size of the drinks the accused consumed is not enough to defeat the defence where it is a reasonable inference commercially-served drinks contained one ounce of alcohol: *R. v. Crayne* (1999), 40 M.V.R. (3d) 185, 175 Sask. R. 234, 1999 CarswellSask 107, [1999] S.J. No. 136 (Sask. Q.B.) at p. 191 [M.V.R.].

> Even though the size of the drinks were not specifically stated by the appellant, as all of the drinks that were consumed were purchased in a commercial establishment, it is logical to conclude that they were one ounce drinks.

Absent expert evidence the impact of drinking on the accused's memory and recollection cannot be considered by the court to reject the accused's evidence of consumption: *R. v. Hoffner* (2005), [2005] O.J. No. 3862, 2005 CarswellOnt 4347, 24 M.V.R. (5th) 280 (Ont. S.C.J.).

Independent evidence of the alcohol content of beer is not necessary and a defence toxicology expert's evidence is sufficient along with accused's evidence of consumption to rebut the breathalyser presumption: *R. v. Enright*, [2001] S.J. No. 170, 2001 SKQB 117, 2001 CarswellSask 199, 205 Sask. R. 100 (Sask. Q.B.).

To succeed with an "evidence to the contrary" defence the accused need not explain why the breath machine readings are inaccurate: *R. v. Durnie*, [2005] B.C.J. No. 2347, 2005 CarswellBC 2557, 2005 BCPC 484 (B.C. Prov. Ct.). The fact the machine passed its internal tests is also not determinative since again such amounts at best to an assertion that where the Court is left without explanation as to why the readings might be inaccurate, it must reject otherwise credible defence testimony.

13.2 "EVIDENCE TO THE CONTRARY"

Previously, evidence to the contrary was evidence which tends to establish that the proportion of alcohol in the accused's blood at the time the offence was alleged to have been committed was not the same as that indicated by the prosecution's analysis: *R. v. Moreau* (1979), 1 M.V.R. 1, 42 C.C.C. (2d) 525 (S.C.C.); *R. v. St. Pierre* (1995), 9 M.V.R. (3d) 1, 36 C.R. (4th) 273, 96 C.C.C. (3d) 385, 22 O.R. (3d) 127 (note) (S.C.C.). However, s. 258l(d.1) has now been amended to require "... evidence tending to show that the concentration of alcohol in the blood of the accused at the time when the offence was alleged to have been committed did not exceed 80 milligrams of alcohol in one hundred millilitres of blood...". Thus mere difference is not enough but the possibility of a level below the legal limit must also be disclosed by the evidence.

In *R. v. Heideman* (2002), [2002] O.J. No. 3461, 2002 CarswellOnt 2930, 162 O.A.C. 270, 168 C.C.C. (3d) 542, 34 M.V.R. (4th) 18 (Ont. C.A.), it was held that expert evidence that an ''average person of the height and weight of the [accused]'' would be under the legal limit of that ''if the [accused] was a slow or fast eliminator the range could be between 47 and 95 milligrams'' is not evidence to the contrary to rebut the breathalyzer test result presumption in the absence of evidence of the accused's elimination rate.

A cogent argument to the contrary is found in *R. v. Bray*, [2006] S.J. No. 631, 2006 SKPC 83, 2006 CarswellSask 618, 287 Sask. R. 244 (Sask. Prov. Ct.) (Koskie Prov. Ct. J.): "Clearly, if the evidence before me (which includes the expert opinion suggesting 90% of the population would be at less than 80 mg. % in this case) is not evidence to the contrary, it might be argued that the accused is required to prove his innocence beyond a reasonable doubt in order to obtain an acquittal." "Credibility combined with probability can and should constitute reasonable doubt."

R. v. Hughes, 420 A.R. 348, [2007] A.J. No. 740, 2007 CarswellAlta 916, 2007 ABPC 180 (Alta. Prov. Ct.); *R. v. Abercrombie*, 54 M.V.R. (5th) 69, [2007] A.J. No. 940, 2007 ABPC 226, 2007 CarswellAlta 1128 (Alta. Prov. Ct.).

The law in Saskatchewan is that evidence to the contrary to rebut the breathalyzer presumptions can be constituted by consumption and expert evidence resulting in "straddle readings" in which the evidence of the expert gives to the court a range of possible alcohol concentrations in the accused's blood that range both below and above 80 milligrams of alcohol in 100 millilitres of blood (.08): *R. v. Eddingfield*, 54 M.V.R. (5th) 160, 2007 CarswellSask 454, 2007 SKQB 248, 300 Sask. R. 63, [2007] S.J. No. 436 (Sask. Q.B.); *R. v. Gibson* (1992), 1992 CarswellSask 16, 13 C.R. (4th) 165, 72 C.C.C. (3d) 28, 18 W.A.C. 88, 100 Sask. R. 88, 36 M.V.R. (2d) 144 (Sask. C.A.); *R. v. Doell*, [2007] S.J. No. 264, 221 C.C.C. (3d) 336, 293 Sask. R. 262, 397 W.A.C. 262, 50 M.V.R. (5th) 9, 158 C.R.R. (2d) 365, [2007] 9 W.W.R. 51, 2007 SKCA 61, 2007 CarswellSask 287 (Sask. C.A.). Such "straddle readings" evidence is not as a matter of law incapable of constituting evidence to the contrary.

Of course if the accused is tested and can adduce expert evidence of an elimination rate leading to a exculpatory blood alcohol level the *Heideman* precedent does not apply: *R. v. Young*, [2005] A.J. No. 1091, 2005 CarswellAlta 1201, 2005 ABPC 230 (Alta. Prov. Ct.).

The Supreme Court of Canada considered the matter in *R. v. Gibson*, EYB 2008-820, [2008] S.C.J. No. 16, 2008 CarswellNS 201, 2008 CarswellNS 202, 59 M.V.R. (5th) 19, 2008 SCC 16 (S.C.C.) and the majority of the Court also rejected the stringent pro-Crown Ontario view. Only four of the nine justices held that straddle evidence was incapable of being evidence to the contrary. Two dissented and held it could be, using an average elimination rate of 15 mg per hour as a marker when evaluating the probative value of straddle evidence, unless there was expert evidence of the accused's specific elimination rate. The remaining three justices held that straddle evidence could be evidence to the contrary depending upon all the evidence in the case. A wide "straddle range", "such as those in the present appeals (40-105 mg for Mr. Gibson and 64-109 mg for Mr. MacDonald), cannot be considered evidence to the contrary of the breathalyzer result, since it does not tend to prove that the accused was at or under the legal limit" the Judges said. Similarly, a range that is overwhelmingly above the legal limit may be of limited probative value. A narrower range, or one whose values lie overwhelmingly below the legal limit, will generally have greater probative value. In the end, the more that is known about probabilities within the range, the more probative the evidence may be." Thus straddle evidence may depending on the scope of the straddle and the probabilities and possibilities proved by the evidence in fact be capable of being evidence to the contrary.

13.3 POST-DRIVING CONSUMPTION

Alcohol consumption after the alleged offence is "evidence to the contrary" to rebut the breathalyzer test presumption: *R. v. St. Pierre* (1995), 9 M.V.R. (3d) 1, 36 C.R. (4th) 273, 96 C.C.C. (3d) 385, 22 O.R. (3d) 127 (note) (S.C.C.):

> (per Iacobucci J.) Evidence to the contrary, as articulated in s. 258(1)(*c*) of the *Criminal Code*, means evidence sufficient to show that the temporal presumption, or as Arbour J.A. calls it the presumption of identity, should not operate to deem the blood alcohol level of the motorist at the time of breathalyzer testing to be the same as the blood alcohol level at the time of driving.
>
> . . .
>
> In the result, I would agree with Arbour J.A. in dissent in the Court of Appeal, and with the trial judge and summary conviction appeal judge, and hold that evidence that the accused drank two small bottles of vodka is "evidence to the contrary" with the meaning of s. 258(1)(*c*). Therefore, the Crown cannot rely on the presumption that her blood alcohol level at the time of the testing was the same as her blood alcohol level at the time of the offence. Since there was no other evidence establishing her blood alcohol level at the time of the offence, she must be acquitted. Accordingly, I would allow the appeal, set aside the judgment of the Ontario Court of Appeal, and restore the acquittal.

However, s. 258(d.1) has now been amended to require ". . . evidence tending to show that the concentration of alcohol in the blood of the accused at the time when the offence was alleged to have been committed did not exceed 80 milligrams of alcohol in one hundred millilitres of blood. . .". Thus mere difference is not enough but the possibility of a level below the legal limit must also be disclosed by the evidence.

13.4 INDEPENDENT BLOOD SAMPLE ANALYSIS

Section 258(4) provides for the application by the accused for release of the extra blood sample taken for independent analysis.

- The application must be made to the superior or district or county court by way of summary application.

- It must be made within six months from the day the blood samples were taken.

- The judge can order the release of one of the samples for analysis.

13.5 PRACTICE TIP: EXPERT EVIDENCE IN WRITING

Section 657.3 of the *Criminal Code* may be useful to defence counsel, for example, in drinking and driving cases to perhaps obviate the necessity for a toxicologist to do their blood alcohol calculation in person.

The section provides:

Expert testimony

657.3 (1) In any proceedings, the evidence of a person as an expert may be given by means of a report accompanied by the affidavit or solemn declaration of the person, setting out, in particular, the qualifications of the person as an expert if

(a) the court recognizes that person as an expert; and
(b) the party intending to produce the report in evidence has, before the proceeding, given to the other party a copy of the affidavit or solemn declaration and the report and reasonable notice of the intention to produce it in evidence.

Attendance for examination

(2) Notwithstanding subsection (1), the court may require the person who appears to have signed an affidavit or solemn declaration referred to in that subsection to appear before it for examination or cross-examination in respect of the issue of proof of any of the statements contained in the affidavit or solemn declaration or report.

Notice for expert testimony

(3) For the purpose of promoting the fair, orderly and efficient presentation of the testimony of witnesses,

(a) a party who intends to call a person as an expert witness shall, at least thirty days before the commencement of the trial or within any other period fixed by the justice or judge, give notice to the other party or parties of his or her intention to do so, accompanied by
  (i) the name of the proposed witness,
  (ii) a description of the area of expertise of the proposed witness that is sufficient to permit the other parties to inform themselves about the area of expertise, and
  (iii) a statement of the qualifications of the proposed witness as an expert;
(b) in addition to complying with paragraph (a), a prosecutor who intends to call a person as an expert witness shall, within a reasonable period before trial, provide to the other party or parties

(i) a copy of the report, if any, prepared by the proposed witness for the case, and

(ii) if no report is prepared, a summary of the opinion anticipated to be given by the proposed witness and the grounds on which it is based; and

(c) in addition to complying with paragraph (a), an accused, or his or her counsel, who intends to call a person as an expert witness shall, not later than the close of the case for the prosecution, provide to the other party or parties the material referred to in paragraph (b).

If notices not given

(4) If a party calls a person as an expert witness without complying with subsection (3), the court shall, at the request of any other party,

(a) grant an adjournment of the proceedings to the party who requests it to allow him or her to prepare for cross-examination of the expert witness;

(b) order the party who called the expert witness to provide that other party and any other party with the material referred to in paragraph (3)(b); and

(c) order the calling or recalling of any witness for the purpose of giving testimony on matters related to those raised in the expert witness's testimony, unless the court considers it inappropriate to do so.

Additional court orders

(5) If, in the opinion of the court, a party who has received the notice and material referred to in subsection (3) has not been able to prepare for the evidence of the proposed witness, the court may do one or more of the following:

(a) adjourn the proceedings;

(b) order that further particulars be given of the evidence of the proposed witness; and

(c) order the calling or recalling of any witness for the purpose of giving testimony on matters related to those raised in the expert witness's testimony.

Use of material by prosecution

(6) If the proposed witness does not testify, the prosecutor may not produce material provided to him or her under paragraph (3)(c) in evidence without the consent of the accused.

No further disclosure

(7) Unless otherwise ordered by a court, information disclosed under this section in relation to a proceeding may only be used for the purpose of that proceeding.

1997, c. 18, s. 80; 2002, c. 13, s. 62

Notice of expert evidence is now required. Subsections 657.3(3) – (7), which came into force September 23, 2002 provide for notice of expert testimony and sets out the consequences if notice is not given.

Notice of expert testimony has to be given by prosecutors and defence at least 30 days before the beginning of the trial or within such other period fixed by the court. The notice has to include the name of the proposed expert witness, a description of the witness' area of expertise, and a statement of the witness' qualifications. A copy of any report prepared by the expert or, if no report has been prepared, a summary of the opinion expected to be given by the witness, has to be provided to the other side, in the case of the prosecutor within a reasonable period before trial and in the case of the defence not later than the close of the case for the prosecution.

Where a party calls an expert without having complied with the notice requirements the court shall grant an adjournment of the proceedings to the party who requests it to allow him or her to prepare for cross-examination of the expert witness; order the part who called the expert witness to provide the other party and any other party with a copy of the report, or where it does not exist, a summary of the anticipated evidence, so as to allow for preparation for cross-examination, and order, where appropriate, the recalling or calling of any witnesses.

Even where a party has complied with the notice provisions, the court may where a party has not been able to prepare properly, to adjourn the proceedings, to order that further particulars be given of the evidence of the proposed witness; and order the calling or recalling of any witness for the purpose of giving testimony on matters related to those raised in the expert witness's testimony.

13.6 VARIOUS CHARTER ISSUES

There are various recurring *Charter* issues that may lead to success in defending drinking and driving cases.

13.6.1 DISCLOSURE

(a) Test Ampoule

In *R. v. Walker*, 2002 CarswellSask 437, 2002 SKQB 291, [2002] S.J. No. 413, [2002] 9 W.W.R. 168, 26 M.V.R. (4th) 59, 221 Sask. R. 249, 101 C.R.R. (2d) 167 (Sask. Q.B.), a drinking and driving charge was held properly stayed at the request of the defence because of the Crown's failure to make disclosure of the test ampoule and standard test solution.

(b) Video

The requirement for disclosure is undoubted: *R. v. Maxwell*, [2006] O.J. No. 4604, 148 C.R.R. (2d) 345, 2006 ONCJ 439, 2006 CarswellOnt 7233 (Ont. C.J.) (Lipson J.). *R. v. Zhu*, [2007] O.J. No. 4775, 2007 CarswellOnt 7905, 2007 ONCJ 580 (Ont. C.J.); *R. v. Phillips*, [2007] O.J. No. 4932, 2007 CarswellOnt 8146, 2007 ONCJ 591 (Ont. C.J.). In *R. v. Chechel* (1999), [1999] O.J. No. 5167 (Ont. C.J.) and *R. v. Terzo* (2004), [2004] O.J. No. 5529, 2004 CarswellOnt 6899 (Ont. C.J.), a stay of a drinking and driving charge was granted where the police booking video was not available. *R. v. Maghdoori*, 2008 CarswellOnt 1666, [2008] O.J. No. 1109, 2008 ONCJ 129 (Ont. C.J.) (police policy to only keep tape for 60 days); *R. v. Yu*, [2008] O.J. No. 1277, 2008 CarswellOnt 1889, 2008 ONCJ 153 (Ont. C.J.)

R. v. Leung, [2008] O.J. No. 1008, 2008 ONCJ 110, 2008 CarswellOnt 1411 (Ont. C.J.), Armstrong J. summarizes all the cases.

See also *R. v. Terzo* (2004), [2004] O.J. No. 5529, 2004 CarswellOnt 6899 (Ont. C.J.) (Shaw J.); *R. v. Li* (1999), [1999] O.J. No. 5163, 1999 CarswellOnt 5110 (Ont. C.J.); *R. v. Benincasa* (October 17, 2001), Doc. 00 06963, [2001] O.J. No. 6032 (Ont. C.J.); *R. v. Bormotko* (2002), [2002] O.J. No. 945, 2002 CarswellOnt 5552 (Ont. C.J.); *R. v. Hakkarainen* (2003), [2003] O.J. No. 3210, 2003 CarswellOnt 3097, 41 M.V.R. (4th) 62, 112 C.R.R. (2d) 24 (Ont. C.J.); *R. v. Biasiotto* (2004), [2004] O.J. No. 2640, 2004 CarswellOnt 8805 (Ont. C.J.); *R. v. Persichetti*, [2004] O.J. No. 3344, 2004 CarswellOnt 3306, 2004 ONCJ 139 (Ont. C.J.), *R. v. Singh* (December 7, 2005), Doc. 04-00696, [2005] O.J. No. 5754 (Ont. C.J.); *R. v. Iakouchev*, [2006] O.J. No. 642, 2006 CarswellOnt 895, 2006 ONCJ 44 (Ont. C.J.).

(c) Machine Manuals and Records

In *R. v. Shorter*, [2006] S.J. No. 772, 2006 CarswellSask 763, 42 M.V.R. (5th) 157, 2006 SKPC 38, 290 Sask. R. 166 (Sask. Prov. Ct.) (Bell Prov. Ct. J.), the defence application was granted for disclosure of operating manuals for the approved screening and the Intoxilyzer 5000C.

Maintenance records kept by the police with respect to the Intoxilyzer 5000C and its accessories represent materials properly related to the defendant's ability to prepare his defence: *R. v. Campbell* (2005), [2005] O.J. No. 3037, 26 M.V.R. (5th) 262, 2005 CarswellOnt 3130 (Ont. C.J.) (Pugsley J.).

Disclosure of calibration records was considered (and ordered) *R. v. Scurr*, [2008] A.J. No. 203, 2008 CarswellAlta 269, 2008 ABQB 127 (Alta. Q.B.).

13.6.2 UNLAWFUL ARRESTS AND SEARCHES

R. v. Petri (2001), 2001 CarswellMan 597, 22 M.V.R. (4th) 108, [2001] M.J. No. 540 (Man. Prov. Ct.), reversed 2003 CarswellMan 2, [2003] M.J. No. 1, 2003 MBCA 1, 32 M.V.R. (4th) 109, 170 Man. R. (2d) 238, 285 W.A.C. 238, 171 C.C.C. (3d) 553, 9 C.R. (6th) 170, 104 C.R.R. (2d) 95 (Man. C.A.), additional reasons at 2003 CarswellMan 43, 2003 MBCA 25, 171 C.C.C. (3d) 567, 173 Man. R. (2d) 96, 293 W.A.C. 96, [2003] 6 W.W.R. 599 (Man. C.A.) held that the arrest without warrant of the accused at his residence for a drinking and driving offence violated *Charter*.

In *R. v. Bissonnette* (2001), 2001 CarswellOnt 3294, 16 M.V.R. (4th) 146, 87 C.R.R. (2d) 363, [2001] O.J. No. 3737 (Ont. S.C.J.) it was held that the arresting officer's approach to the accused's car and his opening of the car door while it was parked in a hotel parking lot constituted an unreasonable search contrary to section 8 of the *Charter*.

In *R. v. Samuels*, [2008] O.J. No. 786, 2008 CarswellOnt 1111, 2008 ONCJ 85 (Ont. C.J.) an 'Over 80' charge was stayed because the accused driver unconstitutionally strip searched at police station.

13.6.3 ARBITRARY DETENTION

In *R. v. Simmons*, 2002 CarswellBC 970, 2002 BCPC 144, [2002] B.C.J. No. 936 (B.C. Prov. Ct.), drinking and driving charges were stayed because the accused was arbitrarily detained in custody after breathalyzer samples. Based upon the accused's readings a police supervisor decided he should be detained. The Court held that the accused's subsequent detention for 6 hours violated the *Charter* and a stay of proceedings was the appropriate remedy.

Similarly, in *R. v. Lewis*, 2001 CarswellBC 3077, 2001 BCPC 426, [2001] B.C.J. No. 2856 (B.C. Prov. Ct.) the overnight detention of the accused drinking driver was held to be in breach of the *Charter* and resulted in a stay of charges.

13.6.4 ABUSE OF PROCESS

In *R. v. Faulkner*, 2002 CarswellSask 187, 216 Sask. R. 212, 2002 SKQB 131, 24 M.V.R. (4th) 271, [2002] S.J. No. 174 (Sask. Q.B.), it was held to be an abuse of process to renew proceedings against the accused in the adjacent province after an original information was lost.

13.6.5 TRIAL PROCEDURES

A *Charter* voir dire is always separate proceeding within the trial and the accused has theright, even where the trial proceeded on consent as a blended proceeding, to testify on the s. 10(b) *Charter* voir dire and obtain a ruling on s. 10(b) issues before the accused has to make his election to call evidence and commence his defence case. Furthermore, he is entitled to testify on the *Charter* voir dire with his testimony and cross-examination restricted to the *Charter* issue and the Crown is not allowed to cross-examine him at large on the merits as if he was testifying in his own defence on the trial proper: *R. v. Phoenix* (2006), [2006] O.J. No. 2581, 2006 CarswellOnt 3874, 144 C.R.R. (2d) 284 (Ont. S.C.J.) (D.G. Stinson J.).

13.6.6 UNCONSTITUTIONAL SENTENCES

In *R. v. Middlebrook* (2002), 2002 CarswellOnt 5651, [2002] O.J. No. 666 (Ont. C.J.) the Court held that the mandatory minimum sentence of 90 days for impaired operation offence violates section 12 of the *Charter*.

In *R. v. Sanghera* (2002), 2002 CarswellOnt 203, 22 M.V.R. (4th) 155, [2002] O.J. No. 173 (Ont. C.J.), the *Charter* was held violated by the Crown seeking to rely in a drinking and driving case sentencing on a previous impaired conviction 12 years earlier where the Crown policy had been to only seek mandatory stepped-up penalty for previous offences within five years. The notice filed by the Crown was held to be nullified in the circumstances by a constitutional exemption in order to avoid an unconstitutional punishment.

In *R. v. Sever*, [2006] O.J. No. 1593, 2006 CarswellOnt 2407, 2006 ONCJ 138, 34 M.V.R. (5th) 87, 141 C.R.R. (2d) 44 (Ont. C.J.) it was held that s. 12 of the *Charter* requires that a driver guilty of impaired care or control who had prior convictions in 1987 and 2002 be sentenced as a second and not a third offender.

> In this case, it can be inferred that Mr. Sever's 1987 conviction was treated by the Crown in 2002 as "spent" for sentencing purposes. The extensive gap in sentencing since then has only increased. The accused has not had the benefit of progressively more severe mandatory minimum sentences. His high readings were not combined with actual driving. The Crown asks that he be re-incarcerated after serving the equivalent of 38 days.
>
> I am of the view that to treat this most recent conviction in these circumstances as a third offence under the mandatory minimum sentencing regime would be unfair, disproportionately harsh and a breach of s. 12. A constitutional exemption will issue. Mr. Sever will be sentenced as for a second offence.

14

SENTENCING

14.1 FINES AND IMPRISONMENT

- For the offences of failure or refusal to comply with a breath or blood demand, driving "over '80" and impaired driving, section 255(1) provides a uniform penalty as follows:

  - for a first offence: a fine of not less than $600 (increased from $300 - the lesser fine will apply in respect to an offence that was committed before July 1, 1999, as per the transitional provision of the amendment [S.C. 1999, c. 32, s. 7].
  - for a second offence: imprisonment for not less than 14 days
  - for a subsequent offence: imprisonment for not less than 90 days

- Where prosecution is by way of summary conviction, the maximum penalty is 6 months' imprisonment. Where prosecution is by way of indictment, the maximum penalty is 5 years' imprisonment.

- Section 727 requires the Crown to serve the accused with a notice that a greater punishment will be sought on the basis of previous convictions. An accused will not be subject to a minimum term of imprisonment if the prosecution fails to serve such notice.

- Where bodily harm is caused during the offence of impaired operation, the offence is prosecuted by way of indictment and section 255(2) provides for a maximum penalty of 10 years' imprisonment.

- Where death is caused during the offence of impaired operation, the offence is prosecuted by way of indictment and section 255(3) provides for a maximum penalty of life imprisonment.

It is important to remember that a "second" or "subsequent" offence is limited to an offence committed after one or more prior convictions. All offences committed without any intervening conviction are in law "first" offences: *R. v. Skolnick* (1982), 16 M.V.R. 35, 29 C.R. (3d) 143, 68 C.C.C. (2d) 385 (S.C.C.); *R. v. Negridge* (1980), 6 M.V.R. 255, 17 C.R. (3d) 14, 54 C.C.C. (2d) 304 (Ont. C.A.).

Because the number of convictions governs, and not the progression of penalties, it is not necessary for a penalty to have been imposed on another offence as a second offence in order to impose the penalty for a third offence: *R. v. Checkley* (1995), 14 M.V.R. (3d) 279, 132 Sask. R. 238 (Sask. Q.B.); *R. v. Nicholson* (1987), 5 M.V.R. (2d) 113, 86 N.B.R. (2d) 41, 219 A.P.R. 41 (N.B. Q.B.). But in *R. v. Chisholm* (1997), 34 M.V.R. (3d) 123 (Ont. Prov. Div.), Drinking & Driving Law, Vol. XIII, no. 8, p. 57, the accused was treated as a second offender, not a third, notwithstanding that it was his third offence, because he had not been previously treated as a second offender.

By applying for a pardon in connection with previous drinking and driving convictions, a person may be able to avoid mandatory imprisonment. It was held in *R. v. A. (D.)* (1998), 43 M.V.R. (3d) 149, 1998 CarswellOnt 3334 (Ont. Prov. Div.), Drinking & Driving Law Vol. XIII, no. 4, p. 32, that where an accused has been pardoned for a previous offence, the mandatory minimum sentences for second or subsequent offences do not apply and the court is not bound to imprison the accused. There is no discretion with respect to issuing a pardon for summary conviction offences, so that entitlement to a pardon is automatic three years after the offence. The process for obtaining a pardon in such circumstances takes approximately four months, and most importantly, is not affected or delayed if an outstanding charge exists.

Juvenile convictions are to be considered a prior record for purposes of sentencing an adult under the escalating scheme of drinking and driving penalties: *R. v. Morris* (1978), 6 C.R. (3d) 36, 43 C.C.C. (2d) 129, [1979] 1 S.C.R. 405, 91 D.L.R. (3d) 161 (S.C.C.), affirming (1975), 30 C.R.N.S. 85 (Que. C.A.).

14.1.1 SENTENCING FACTORS

- The following matters should be considered for submissions on sentence in these offences:
  - age

  - plea of guilty
  - driving record
  - prior licence suspensions
  - criminal record
  - offences since or while on bail
  - amount to drink
  - excessive speed
  - attempt to evade responsibility
  - death or injury
  - employment
  - education
  - family situation
  - health
  - injuries to accused
  - collateral consequences: effect on insurance; employment;
  - treatment, past or future, including therapy for alcoholism, educational programs or Alcoholics Anonymous (if appropriate)

- Character references should be obtained in appropriate cases to be used as witnesses or to provide letters of reference for sentencing purposes.

- While courts have routinely considered particularly high blood/alcohol readings to be an aggravating factor for purposes of determining an appropriate sentence, the *Criminal Code* now specifically provides in s. 255.1 [S.C. 1999, c. 32, s. 4] that for all driving offences, evidence of a blood/alcohol level exceeding twice the legal limit (.160) shall be deemed to be an aggravating circumstance that the court must take into consideration in imposing sentence.

- A fatality cannot be taken into account in a conviction for impaired driving simpliciter. The Crown cannot accept a plea of guilty to the lesser offence of impaired driving simpliciter and then ask the court to consider facts during sentencing which would justify conviction for the more serious charge of impaired driving causing death: *R. v. Doerksen* (1990), 19 M.V.R. (2d) 16, 53 C.C.C. (3d) 509 (Man. C.A.); *R. v. Roy* (1995), 18 M.V.R. (3d) 292, 170 N.B.R. (2d) 204,

435 A.P.R. 204 (N.B. Q.B.); *R. v. Tozer* (1994), 7 M.V.R. (3d) 83, 151 N.B.R. (2d) 173, 387 A.P.R. 162, (N.B. Q.B.). This proposition also finds support in the dangerous driving case of *R. v. Brown*, 6 C.R. (4th) 353, 66 C.C.C. (3d) 1, 30 M.V.R. (2d) 1, [1991] 2 S.C.R. 518, 93 Sask. R. 81, 4 W.A.C. 81 (S.C.C.).

14.1.2 WHERE BODILY HARM OR DEATH IS CAUSED

- Sentences for impaired driving causing bodily harm can vary widely. The range of sentences includes: 2-year suspended sentence on two counts: *R. v. Roasting* (1999), 40 M.V.R. (3d) 54, 232 A.R. 136, 195 W.A.C. 136, 1999 CarswellAlta 97 (Alta. C.A.); 3-year suspended sentence on two counts: *R. v. Martin* (1996), 22 M.V.R. (3d) 316, 154 N.S.R. (2d) 268, 452 A.P.R. 268 (N.S. C.A.); 45 days' imprisonment on two counts: *R. v. Stubel* (1990), 25 M.V.R. (2d) 118, 109 A.R. 1 (Alta. C.A.); 90 days intermittent: *R. v. Howard* (1991), 35 M.V.R. (2d) 41, 120 A.R. 29 (Alta. C.A.); *R. v. Froman* (1999), 39 M.V.R. (3d) 315 (Ont. Gen. Div.); 6 months' imprisonment: *R. v. Maynard* (1999), 131 Man. R. (2d) 308, 187 W.A.C. 308, 1999 CarswellMan 23, [1999] M.J. No. 8 (Man. C.A.); 9 months open custody for a young offender: *R. v. N. (B.A.)* (1998), 172 Sask. R. 156, 185 W.A.C. 156 (Sask. C.A.); 9 months' imprisonment plus 2 years' probation: *R. v. Somers* (1998), 207 N.B.R. (2d) 201, 529 A.P.R. 201 (N.B. Q.B.); 15 months' imprisonment plus 2 years' probation: *R. v. Pittman* (1998), 39 M.V.R. (3d) 237, 173 Nfld. & P.E.I.R. 107, 530 A.P.R. 107 (Nfld. T.D.); 2 years less a day *R. v. Gaboury* (1994), 3 M.V.R. (3d) 264, 149 A.P.R. 221 (Alta. C.A.); 2 1/2 years' imprisonment: *R. v. Storr* (1995), 14 M.V.R. (3d) 34, 174 A.R. 65 (Alta. C.A.). In *R. v. Gomes*, [2003] A.J. No. 567, 2003 CarswellAlta 650, 2003 ABCA 149, 39 M.V.R. (4th) 222, 327 A.R. 288, 296 W.A.C. 288, 14 Alta. L.R. (4th) 95, 175 C.C.C. (3d) 125 (Alta. C.A.), a conditional sentence of imprisonment was upheld for impaired driving causing bodily harm pursuant to s. 255(2) of the *Criminal Code*. The Court agreed that the mandatory sentences applicable to basic drinking and driving offences and not applicable to impaired driving causing bodily harm or death offences. See 14.3 Conditional Sentences, below.

- Recent sentences for impaired driving causing death have included: 18 months' imprisonment: *R. v. Cunningham* (1998), 33 M.V.R. (3d) 59 (Ont. Gen. Div.), varied (1999), 118 O.A.C. 396, 43 M.V.R. (3d) 39, 1999 CarswellOnt 980 (Ont. C.A.); 20 months' imprisonment: *R. v. McMahon* (1998), 1998 CarswellMan 135 (Man. C.A.), refusing leave to appeal from (1998), 1998 CarswellMan 66 (Man. Prov. Ct.); 2 1/2 years' imprisonment (also convicted of three counts of impaired driving causing bodily harm): *R. v. Sherlock* (1998), 39 M.V.R. (3d) 47, 131 Man. R. (2d) 143, 187 W.A.C. 143, 1998 CarswellMan 545 (Man. C.A.), leave to appeal refused (1999), 239 N.R. 398 (note), 145 Man. R. (2d) 159 (note), 218 W.A.C. 159 (note) (S.C.C.); 3 years' imprisonment: *R. v. Bath* (1998), 164 Nfld. & P.E.I.R. 358, 507 A.P.R. 358 (Nfld. T.D); 3 1/2 years' imprisonment (also convicted of two counts of impaired driving causing bodily harm): *R. v. Hayward* (1997), 1997 CarswellOnt 3520, 38 O.T.C. 235 (Ont. Gen. Div.); 6 years' imprisonment (also convicted of three counts of impaired driving causing bodily harm): *R. v. Wallace* (1997), 92 B.C.A.C. 68 (B.C. C.A.); 7 years' imprisonment (two counts of impaired driving causing death and two counts of impaired driving causing bodily harm: *R. v. Abraham* (1998), 39 M.V.R. (3d) 82, 231 A.R. 344, 1998 CarswellAlta 1125, [1998] A.J. No. 1380 (Alta. Prov. Ct.), varied 2000 ABCA 159, 4 M.V.R. (4th) 35, 261 A.R. 192, 225 W.A.C. 192, 2000 CarswellAlta 538 (Alta. C.A.).

14.2 CURATIVE DISCHARGES

By section 255(5), which is not in force in all provinces (not having been proclaimed for British Columbia, Ontario, Quebec or Newfoundland), a court may instead of convicting an accused of impaired driving or driving ''over '80'', order the accused be discharged for treatment. The accused is then discharged on the conditions in a probation order, including a condition respecting the accused's attendance for curative treatment in relation to his or her alcohol or drug problem.

Before a curative discharge can be granted, a court must:

- hear medical or other evidence

- be of the opinion that your client is in need of curative treatment in relation to alcohol or drug consumption

- be of the opinion that granting the curative discharge would not be contrary to the public interest.

The failure of a province to proclaim section 255(5), which empowers the court to grant a curative discharge, does not violate the equality rights under section 15 of the *Charter* of an accused in that province: *R. v. Alton* (1989), 18 M.V.R. (2d) 186, 74 C.R. (3d) 124, 53 C.C.C. (3d) 252 (Ont. C.A.); *R. v. Ellsworth* (1988), 11 M.V.R. (2d) 129, 46 C.C.C. (3d) 442 (Que. C.A.), leave to appeal refused (1990), 56 C.C.C. (3d) vi (note) (S.C.C.); *R. v. Jackson* (1993), 46 M.V.R. (2d) 247, 80 C.C.C. (3d) 22, 104 Nfld. & P.E.I.R. 349, 329 A.P.R. 349 (Nfld. C.A.); *R. v. Van Vliet* (1988), 10 M.V.R. (2d) 190, 45 C.C.C. (3d) 481 (B.C. C.A.), leave to appeal refused (1990), 115 N.R. 291n (S.C.C.).

Relevant factors in considering whether it would not be contrary to the public interest to grant a curative discharge include the circumstances of the offence, the *bona fides* of the offender, the criminal record of the accused as it relates to alcohol-related driving offences, whether the accused was subject to a driving prohibition at the time of the offence, and whether the accused had previously received a curative discharge and what the results of that had been: *R. v. Storr* (1995), 14 M.V.R. (3d) 34, 174 A.R. 65, 33 Alta. L.R. (3d) 163, 102 W.A.C. 65 (Alta. C.A.); *R. v. Kalyniak* (1996), 183 A.R. 321 (Alta. Prov. Ct.). "There should be evidence before the Court, preferably from a medical practitioner, indicating that a careful assessment of the accused has been made... the accused is well motivated and has a reasonable chance of overcoming his alcoholism and related problems.

"... [S]ome of the factors to be looked at in determining if a curative discharge is appropriate... included: the circumstances and gravity of the offence; the motivation of the offender to rehabilitate, the alcohol related criminal record of the accused, whether the accused was subject to a driving prohibition at the time of the offence, whether the accused has received a prior curative discharge": *R. v. Manyshots*, [2007] A.J. No. 965, 2007 CarswellAlta 1145, 2007 ABPC 238 (Alta. Prov. Ct.). For other cases in which the principles applicable to curative discharges were considered, see *R. v. Bogdala* (August 22, 1988), Doc. 1152/88 (Ont. Dist Ct.), Drinking & Driving Law, Vol. IV, no. 7, pp. 53-55; *R. v. McPhee* (2000), 2000 CarswellNB 186, 227 N.B.R. (2d) 30, 583 A.P.R. 30, [2000] N.B.J. No. 199 (N.B. Q.B.); *R. v. MacCormack* (2000), 2000 CarswellNB 24, 224 N.B.R. (2d) 29, 574 A.P.R. 29 (N.B. C.A.).

For the court to grant a discharge under section 255(5), there must be a good prospect that the program will succeed — that it will be genuinely ''curative''. Availability of appropriate treatment, motivation of the accused and a reasonable expectation that his alcoholism will be overcome, are all implied in that word. The likelihood of success is also a factor in assessing public interest. It need only be shown that the granting of a discharge would not be contrary to the public interest; it does not have to be shown that the granting of a discharge is in the affirmative sense in the public interest: *R. v. Earle* (1989), 15 M.V.R. (2d) 138, 90 N.S.R. (2d) 138, 230 A.P.R. 138 (N.S. Co. Ct.).

In *R. v. McPhee* (2000), [2000] N.B.J. No. 199, 227 N.B.R. (2d) 30, 583 A.P.R. 30, 2000 CarswellNB 186 (N.B. Q.B.) a curative conditional discharge under sections 255(5) and 730 was substituted for imprisonment.

In *R. v. Place*, 2008 CarswellMan 108, [2008] M.J. No. 82, 2008 MBPC 7 (Man. Prov. Ct.). *R. v. Ahenakew* (2005), 2005 CarswellSask 490, 2005 SKCA 93, 200 C.C.C. (3d) 527, 269 Sask. R. 166, 357 W.A.C. 166, 25 M.V.R. (5th) 49, [2006] 4 W.W.R. 27 (Sask. C.A.), *R. v. Jeerh*, 2005 CarswellAlta 505, 17 M.V.R. (5th) 322, 2005 ABPC 76 (Alta. Prov. Ct.), and *R. v. McLean* (2002), 2002 CarswellMan 361, [2002] M.J. No. 331, 30 M.V.R. (4th) 124, 185 Man. R. (2d) 63 (Man. Prov. Ct.), the principles governing the granting of a conditional discharge pursuant to the curative provisions contained in s. 255(5) of the *Criminal Code* were considered in detail.

A prior drinking and driving record alone should not preclude granting a discharge, particularly where the evidence otherwise establishes genuine motivation and the likelihood of rehabilitation: *R. v. Ashberry* (1989), 11 M.V.R. (2d) 1, 68 C.R. (3d) 341, 47 C.C.C. (3d) 138, 30 O.A.C. 376 (Ont. C.A.), leave to appeal refused (1990), 116 N.R. 157n (S.C.C.); *R. v. Beaulieu* (1980), 7 M.V.R. 9, 53 C.C.C. (2d) 342, 21 A.R. 120 (N.W.T. S.C.).

14.3 CONDITIONAL SENTENCES

- Section 742.1 provides that a person may be ordered to serve his or her sentence in the community where the sentence imposed is less than two years and the court is satisfied that it would not endanger the safety of the community and would be consistent with the fundamental principles of sentencing set out in sections 718 to 718.2. However, a conditional sentence is unavailable where there is a mandatory minimum sentence of imprisonment. Accordingly, a sentence can only be ordered to be served in the community where the offence is a first offence under section 253 or 254 — in which case a term of incarceration is unlikely — or where the offence is impaired driving causing bodily harm or impaired driving causing death. *R. v. Cromwell*, [2005] N.S.J. No. 428, 2005 CarswellNS 460, 2005 NSCA 137, 23 M.V.R. (5th) 39, 202 C.C.C. (3d) 310,

238 N.S.R. (2d) 17, 757 A.P.R. 17 (N.S. C.A.) contains a detailed consideration of precedents governing conditional sentences for impaired driving offences occasioning bodily harm or death.

- The accused received a 6-month conditional sentence for two counts of impaired driving causing bodily harm: *R. v. Smith* (1998), 37 M.V.R. (3d) 311 (Ont. Gen. Div.). Other cases in which a conditional sentence was imposed for impaired driving causing bodily harm are: *R. v. Davison*, [2006] N.S.J. No. 569, 2006 CarswellNS 637, 824 A.P.R. 289, 2006 NSPC 73, 258 N.S.R. (2d) 289 (N.S. Prov. Ct.) (18 months); *R. v. Campbell* (1997), 157 Nfld. & P.E.I.R. 62, 486 A.P.R. 62 (Nfld. T.D.): 4-month conditional sentence; *R. v. Buffi* (1998), 1998 CarswellOnt 1236 (Ont. Gen. Div.): 1-year conditional sentence; *R. v. Goulais* (1999), 1999 CarswellOnt 206, [1999] O.J. No. 199 (Ont. Gen. Div.): 1-year conditional sentence; *R. v. Callan*, [2002] A.J. No. 1342, 2002 CarswellAlta 1315, 2002 ABPC 159 (Alta. Prov. Ct.): 1-year conditional sentence. Conditional sentences for impaired driving causing bodily harm and dangerous driving causing bodily harm were also imposed in *R. v. Chapman*, 2000 CarswellBC 437, 2000 BCCA 152, 3 M.V.R. (4th) 57, 135 B.C.A.C. 147, 221 W.A.C. 147, [2000] B.C.J. No. 435 (B.C. C.A.): conditional sentence of imprisonment of 2 years less 1 day upheld against Crown appeal; *R. v. MacDonald* (1999), [1999] M.J. No. 415, 138 Man. R. (2d) 194, 202 W.A.C. 194, 139 C.C.C. (3d) 524, 2 M.V.R. (4th) 116, 1999 CarswellMan 418 (Man. C.A.): 15 months conditional sentence; *R. v. Mischaud*, [2000] N.J. No. 205, 2000 NFCA 40, 190 Nfld. & P.E.I.R. 206, 576 A.P.R. 206, 2000 CarswellNfld 202 (Nfld. C.A.) (16 months); *R. v. Best*, [2001] P.E.I.J. No. 24, 2001 PESCTD 24, 198 Nfld. & P.E.I.R. 352, 595 A.P.R. 352, 2001 CarswellPEI 26, 17 M.V.R. (4th) 114 (P.E.I. T.D.) (15 months); *R. v. Mercer*, [2000] N.J. No. 183, 2000 NFCA 34, 189 Nfld. & P.E.I.R. 174, 571 A.P.R. 174, 2000 CarswellNfld 177, 15 M.V.R. (4th) 52 (Nfld. C.A.) (4 months); *R. v. Valladares* (2000), [2000] O.J. No. 2980, 5 M.V.R. (4th) 288, 2000 CarswellOnt 2762 (Ont. C.J.) (18 months); *R. v. Fisher* (2003), [2003] O.J. No. 3886, 2003 CarswellOnt 6686 (Ont. S.C.J.) (2 years less 1 day); *R. v. Merrill*, [2004] A.J. No. 924, 2004 CarswellAlta 1072, 13 M.V.R. (5th) 292, 2004 ABPC 135 (Alta. Prov. Ct.); *R. v. Baker*, [2005] A.J. No. 1405, 2005 CarswellAlta 1496, 2005 ABPC 269 (Alta. Prov. Ct.) (18 months conditional sentence); *R. v. Wood*, [2005] A.J. No. 1230, 2005 CarswellAlta 1354, 2005 ABPC 200, 26 M.V.R. (5th) 126, 388 A.R. 137 (Alta. Prov. Ct.) (15 month conditional sentence).

- Conditional sentences of 2 years less a day have been imposed for impaired driving causing death in *R. v. Colin*, 32 M.V.R. (3d) 298, [1998] N.W.T.R. 9 (N.W.T. S.C.); and *R. v. Boyd* (1998), 33 M.V.R. (3d) 37 (Ont. Gen. Div.) where there was also a conviction for criminal negligence causing death; *R. v. Shore*, [2002] S.J. No. 262, 2002 CarswellSask 288, 2002 SKPC 42, 225 Sask. R. 5 (Sask. Prov. Ct.); *R. c. Laford* (2002), [2002] A.N.-B. No. 143, 2002 CarswellNB 133, 249 N.B.R. (2^{e}) 337, 648 A.P.R. 337 (B.R. N.-B.). Conditional sentences were also imposed in *R. v. Jackson*, [2007] A.J. No. 807, 2007 CarswellAlta 982, 2007 ABPC 198 (Alta. Prov. Ct.); *R. v. Gallant*, [2008] P.E.I.J. No. 1, 228 C.C.C. (3d) 61, 830 A.P.R. 338, 272 Nfld. & P.E.I.R. 338, 55 M.V.R. (5th) 15, 2008 PESCAD 1, 2008 CarswellPEI 1 (P.E.I. C.A.) (18 months); *R. v. Carrier*, [2008] A.J. No. 398, 2008 CarswellAlta 445, 2008 ABCA 134 (Alta. C.A. [In Chambers]). *R. v. Kutsukake* (2006), [2006] O.J. No. 3771, 2006 CarswellOnt 5699, 213 C.C.C. (3d) 80, 216 O.A.C. 317, 36 M.V.R. (5th) 174 (Ont. C.A.); *R. c. Fortin* (2002), [2002] J.Q. n°. 444, 2002 CarswellQue 1000 (C.Q.): 22 month conditional sentence; *R. v. Meathrell* (2000), [2000] O.J. No. 2249 (Ont. S.C.J.): 18-month conditional sentence for impaired driving causing death; *R. v. Forward*, 2000 BCCA 153, 50 M.V.R. (3d) 300, 136 B.C.A.C. 274, 222 W.A.C. 274, 2000 CarswellBC 439, [2000] B.C.J. No. 436 (B.C. C.A.): Crown appeal dismissed from conditional sentence of two years less a day imposed on accused upon his plea of guilty to impaired driving causing death. His three-year-old daughter died when the vehicle he was driving left the road and struck a culvert: *R. v. Bettridge* (2000), 50 M.V.R. (3d) 231, 2000 CarswellOnt 300, [2000] O.J. No. 363 (Ont. S.C.J.): conditional sentence of imprisonment of 2 years less 1 day imposed on accused's pleas of guilty to two counts of impaired driving causing death and six counts of impaired driving causing bodily harm, all arising from a motor vehicle collision; *R. v. Mould* (1999), 1999 CarswellOnt 4548, 3 M.V.R. (4th) 111 (Ont. S.C.J.), affirmed (2000), 2000 CarswellOnt 2890, 6 M.V.R. (4th) 150, 135 O.A.C. 294, [2000] O.J. No. 3040 (Ont. C.A.): 15-month conditional sentence of imprisonment imposed upon accused convicted of impaired driving causing death and impaired driving causing bodily harm; *R. v. Logan* (1999), 45 M.V.R. (3d) 224, 139 C.C.C. (3d) 57, 125 O.A.C. 152 (Ont. C.A.): 20 months' conditional sentence of imprisonment for impaired driving causing death and causing bodily harm; *R. v. Godfree* (2000), [2000] O.J. No. 3409, 136 O.A.C. 49, 7 M.V.R. (4th) 60, 2000 CarswellOnt 3316 (Ont. C.A.) (20 months); *R. v. McKenzie*, [2000] M.J. No. 370, 2000 MBCA 57, 148 Man. R. (2d) 63, 224 W.A.C. 63, 2000 CarswellMan 379 (Man. C.A.) (20 months); *R. v. Travers* (2001), [2001] M.J. No. 250, 2001 CarswellMan 227, 16 M.V.R. (4th) 113 (Man. Prov. Ct.) (2 years less 1 day); *R. v. Meathrell* (2000), [2000] O.J. No. 2249 (Ont. S.C.J.) (18 months); *R. v. Doust* (2001), [2001] O.J. No. 4389, 2001 CarswellOnt 4291, 20 M.V.R. (4th) 123 (Ont. S.C.J.) (18 months); *R. v. Shave* (2005), [2005] M.J. No. 16, 2005 CarswellMan 348, 25 M.V.R. (5th) 285 (Man. Prov. Ct.) (2 years less 1 day); *R. v. Singh*, 2004 CarswellBC 1755, [2004] B.C.J. No. 1621, 2004 BCPC 262, 6 M.V.R. (5th) 239 (B.C. Prov. Ct.) (2 years less 1 day).

- Section 742.1 of the *Criminal Code* dealing with conditional sentences of imprisonment does not allow blended sentences that are partly actual imprisonment and partly conditional: *R. v. Maynard* (1999), 131 Man. R. (2d) 308, 187 W.A.C. 308 (Man. C.A.); *R. v. Sanderson*, 189 Sask. R. 171, 216 W.A.C. 171, 2000 SKCA 26, 2000 CarswellSask 131 (Sask. C.A.); *R. v. Fisher* (2000), 143 C.C.C. (3d) 413,

47 O.R. (3d) 397, 129 O.A.C. 92, 2000 CarswellOnt 329 (Ont. C.A.).

- Conditional sentence of imprisonment of 2 years less 1 day were imposed on pleas of guilty to impaired operation causing death and bodily harm in *R. v. Kyle*, 2001 CarswellAlta 1004, 2001 ABPC 136, 16 M.V.R. (4th) 294, 291 A.R. 201, [2001] A.J. No. 1009 (Alta. Prov. Ct.). The case provides detailed consideration of principles and precedents dealing with sentencing in drinking and driving cases as well as conditional sentences.

14.4 LICENSE PROHIBITION ORDERS

A person convicted of any of the drinking and driving offences will be subject to a mandatory driving prohibition order under the *Criminal Code* and a driver's license suspension under provincial legislation.

14.4.1 CRIMINAL CODE DRIVING PROHIBITION ORDERS

- Section 259(1) provides that upon conviction of a person under section 253 or 254 the court must impose a driving prohibition order. The length of the mandatory prohibition is as follows:

  - for a first offence, the driving prohibition is between 1 year and 3 years in addition to any period of imprisonment

  - for a second offence, the driving prohibition is between 2 years and 5 years in addition to any period of imprisonment

  - for a third offence, the driving prohibition is not less than 3 years in addition to any period of imprisonment. Note that the previous maximum term, which was 3 years, is now the minimum term of prohibition. There is no longer a maximum period of prohibition.

- Where a person is convicted of a driving offence committed before July 1, 1999, that person will still be subject to the previous minimum mandatory driving prohibitions [S.C. 1999, c. 32, s. 7]:
  - for a first offence, the driving prohibition is between 3 months and 3 years in addition to any period of imprisonment
  - for a second offence, the driving prohibition is between 6 months and 3 years in addition to any period of imprisonment
  - for a third offence, the driving prohibition is between 1 year and 3 years in addition to any period of imprisonment
- It should be noted that in provinces in which a program governing the use of an alcohol ignition interlock device has been established, the minimum driving prohibition of not less than one year for a first offender is reduced to not less than 3 months if the offender participates in the program during the remainder of the one year period: s. 259(1.1) [S.C. 1999, c. 32, s. 5(1)].
- Where an accused is convicted of impaired driving causing bodily harm, the court has discretion to make an order prohibiting the accused from driving for up to 10 years in addition to any period of imprisonment: Section 259(2)(b).
- Where an accused is convicted of impaired driving causing death, the court has the discretion to make an order prohibiting the accused from driving for any period that the court considers proper: Section 259(2)(a).
- The procedure to be followed upon the making of an order of prohibition under section 259(1) or 259(2) is set out in section 260.
- A lifetime prohibition on operating a motor vehicle pursuant to s. 259(1)(c) of the *Criminal Code* is an increased penalty

by virtue of prior convictions and requires notice in compliance with section 727 of the *Criminal Code*: *R. v. Sheppard*, 2004 CarswellOnt 4577, 11 M.V.R. (5th) 318, 2004 ONCJ 247 (Ont. C.J.).

- A driving prohibition begins the day the order is made. A judge has no jurisdiction to order it to commence on some date in the future: *R. v. Laycock* (1989), 17 M.V.R. (2d) 1, 51 C.C.C. (3d) 65 (Ont. C.A.).

- It is an offence to operate a motor vehicle during a period of prohibition: section 259(4) — operation while disqualified.

14.4.2 PROVINCIAL LICENSE SUSPENSIONS

- There are various ways in which a drinking driver can lose the right to drive under provincial legislation:

- A number of provinces have enacted 90-day administrative license suspensions: Ontario — *Highway Traffic Act* R.S.O. 1990, c. H-8, s. 48.3, British Columbia — *Motor Vehicle Act*, R.S.B.C. 1996, c. 318, ss. 94.1-94.6, Manitoba — *Highway Traffic Act*, S.M. 1985-86, c. 3, C.C.S.M., c. H60, ss. 263.1 and 263.2, and Nova Scotia — *Motor Vehicle Act*, R.S.N.S. 1989, c. 293, ss. 279A and 279B. Prince Edward Island - *Highway Traffic Act*, R.S.P.E.I. 1988, c. H-5 (as amended by S.P.E.I. 1996, c. 19), ss. 277.2-277.7. This legislation requires a police officer to serve notice of a 90-day driving prohibition on a driver who refuses to comply with a breath or blood sample demand, or who has a blood/alcohol reading over 80. These administrative license suspension provisions have withstood constitutional challenges based on their being beyond provincial powers and their being in violation of rights guaranteed by the *Canadian Charter of Rights and Freedoms*: *Horsefield v. Ontario (Registrar of Motor Vehicles)* (1999), 42 M.V.R. (3d) 1, 134 C.C.C. (3d) 161, 172 D.L.R. (4th) 43, 118 O.A.C. 291, 62 C.R.R. (2d) 161, 44 O.R. (3d) 73, 1999 CarswellOnt 919, [1999] O.J. No. 967 (Ont. C.A.), varied

(1999), 44 M.V.R. (3d) 204, 144 C.C.C. (3d) 190, 185 D.L.R. (4th) 711, 1999 CarswellOnt 1382 (Ont. C.A.); *R. v. MacCormack* (1998), (*sub nom. R. v. MacCormick*) 34 M.V.R. (3d) 266, (*sub nom. R. v. MacCormick*) 163 Nfld. & P.E.I.R. 1, (*sub nom. R. v. MacCormick*) 503 A.P.R. 1 (P.E.I. T.D. [In Chambers]), affirmed (1999), 134 C.C.C. (3d) 351, 180 Nfld. & P.E.I.R. 314, 548 A.P.R. 314, 1999 CarswellPEI 28 (P.E.I. C.A.).

- The police have the authority in several provinces to suspend a driver's license temporarily at roadside (e.g. Ontario — s. 48 of the *Highway Traffic Act* empowers a police officer to suspend a person's driver's license for 12 hours where that person registers a "Warn" or "Alert" on an approved screening device, blows "over 50" on a breathalyzer test, or is charged with refusing to provide a breath or blood sample; Alberta — s. 110 of the *Motor Vehicle Administration Act* authorizes a police officer to suspend a driver's license for 24 hours where the officer "reasonably suspects" that the driver has consumed alcohol, drugs or other substances "in such quantity as to affect the driver's physical or mental ability"; British Columbia — s. 215 of the *Motor Vehicle Act* entitles a peace officer to suspend a driver's license for 24 hours where the officer has "reasonable and probable grounds to believe" that the driver's ability to drive a motor vehicle is affected by alcohol or a drug).

- There is an automatic minimum license suspension in most provinces where a person is convicted of a *Criminal Code* drinking and driving offence. The duration of these automatic suspensions varies from jurisdiction to jurisdiction, typically becoming longer for successive offences (e.g. Ontario — s. 41 of the *Highway Traffic Act*: one year for first conviction, three years for second conviction, and then indefinitely; Alberta — s. 83 of the *Traffic Safety Act*: license suspensions range from six months to five years; British Columbia — s. 99 of the *Motor Vehicle Act*: automatic minimum suspension for one year, but s. 98 gives the convicting court the discretion to impose a prohibition for any definite period of time).

- In most provinces, the Registrar (or Superintendent) of Motor Vehicles or the appropriate provincial Minister has broad discretionary authority to suspend or revoke a driver's license for any "sufficient" reason: Ontario — s. 47(1) of the *Highway Traffic Act*; Alberta — s. 57(1) of the *Motor Vehicle Administration Act*; British Columbia — s. 93(1) of the *Motor Vehicle Act*.

14.4.3 IGNITION INTERLOCK DEVICE PROGRAM

Section 259 of the *Criminal Code* relating to Mandatory orders of licence prohibition has now had new subsections (1.1) and (1.2) added (in force December 18, 2001) allowing a court when a mandatory licence prohibition is imposed to "authorize the offender to operate a motor vehicle equipped with an alcohol ignition interlock device during the prohibition period if the offender registers in an alcohol ignition interlock device program established under the law of the province in which the offender resides."

However, this authorization can only be effective after a certain minimum period of the prohibition has been served:

- at least 3 months, for a first offence;
- at least 6 months, for a second offence; and
- at least 12 months, for each subsequent offence.

The authorization requires registration in the provincial interlock program to be effective (subsection (1.4)) and can be switched to another province if the accused changes his province of residence (subsection (1.3)).

The interlock exemption cannot be applied for or granted before the province has in fact established the program, notwithstanding provincial legislation authorizing the relevant regulations has been passed: *R. v. Kaczala* (2008), 2008 CarswellOnt 1405, [2008] O.J. No. 994 (Ont. S.C.J.). The required regulations must be enacted first.

14.5 PROBATION

- Where an offender is fined or sentenced to imprisonment for a term not exceeding two years, the court may also make an order for probation for a period not exceeding three years. In addition to the compulsory conditions of the probation order, which are set out in s. 732.1(2), the court may also prescribe other optional conditions: s. 732.1(3). For example, the terms of probation may require the offender to perform up to 240 hours of community service, or to abstain from drinking or using non-prescription drugs. The court has wide discretion as to the conditions it may include in the order for probation. Any reasonable condition "for protecting society and for faciliating the offender's successful reintegration into the community" may be made: s. 732.1(3)(h).

- Section 732.1(3) was amended by S.C. 1999, c. 32, s. 6 (in force July 1, 1999). Two more options in prescribing conditions of probation have been made available to the courts:
  - In provinces in which a program for curative treatment has been established the court may order that the offender attend a designated treatment facility for assessment and curative treatment.
  - In provinces in which a program governing the use of an alcohol ignition interlock device has been established, the court may order that the offender comply with the program, but only if the offender consents to participate in the program.

14.6 FORFEITURE OF AUTOMOBILE

- Section 490.1(1) of the *Criminal Code* allows the forfeiture of "offence-related" property. In *R. v. Waite*, [2004] N.B.J. No. 455, 2004 CarswellNB 595, 2004 NBPC 29 (N.B. Prov. Ct.) the accused's motor vehicle was forfeited pursuant to section 490.1(1) of the *Criminal Code* upon his conviction for "over 80". This was the accused's ninth similar conviction and the accused had lifetime driving prohibition. The Court made it clear such forfeiture very much depended upon the extreme circumstances of the case: "I hasten to add that in my opinion the principle of proportionality might dictate against the granting of a forfeiture order in different circumstances. For example, where there are fewer drinking and driving offences, or again where it is a much more expensive vehicle, or where there is a diverse usage for family means of transportation or work; otherwise such an order might be pushing towards cruel and unusual punishment. . ."

See also *R. v. Adamson*, 48 M.V.R. (5th) 130, 2007 BCSC 745, 2007 CarswellBC 1189, [2007] B.C.J. No. 1143 (B.C. S.C.): forfeiture upon conviction for dangerous driving causing bodily harm contrary to s. 249(3) and failing to provide a breathe sample on demand, contrary to s. 254(5).

14.7 STAY PENDING APPEAL

- By section 261, where an appeal is taken a judge of the court appealed to may direct that any driving prohibition order be stayed pending the appeal. This requires a specific application to the court appealed to and the mere filing of a notice of appeal does not automatically stay any licence prohibition order.

- Where an appellant seeks an order staying a driving prohibition pending appeal to the *Supreme Court of Canada*, section 261 applies in preference to the more general provision of section 65.1 of the *Supreme Court Act*. As a result, jurisdiction to hear the application lies with the "a judge of the court being appealed to" and not with "the court appealed from" i.e. the Supreme Court of Canada, not the Court of Appeal: *R. v. Reed* (1997), 120 C.C.C. (3d) 556, 31 M.V.R. (3d) 320, 100 B.C.A.C. 161, 163 W.A.C. 161 (B.C. S.C. [In Chambers]).

- The court's power under section 261 is a discretionary one. To satisfy the requirements for the exercise of judicial discretion, the applicant must show that the appeal is not frivolous, that there is some arguable point to be presented to the appeal court, and that the prohibition is not necessary in the public interest. The court concluded that a stay of enforcement of penalty would be not be adverse to public interest in circumstances where the accused was a first offender and the period of prohibition would expire before the hearing of the appeal: *Carpenter v. R.* (1991), 28 M.V.R. (2d) 69, (*sub nom. R. v. Carpenter*) 89 Nfld. & P.E.I.R. 19, (*sub nom. R. v. Carpenter*) 278 A.P.R. 19 (Nfld. T.D.).

- An additional requirement to show that granting the stay would not detrimentally affect the confidence of the public in the effective enforcement and administration of criminal law was placed upon the appellant in *R. v. Jay* (1987), 50 M.V.R. 137, 66 Nfld. & P.E.I.R. 84, 204 A.P.R. 84 (P.E.I. S.C.).

- There should be in depth information before the court as to the circumstances giving rise to the grounds of appeal. Factors to be taken into account by the court in considering whether a stay will be contrary to the public interest are: the accused's driving record; hardship to the accused; the seriousness of the charge; the circumstances of the offence; indicia of intoxication; the background of the accused; facts relating to the risk of recurrence; and other factors such as driving ability, addiction to drugs or alcohol and psychological makeup that impinge on the conduct of the accused and the potential risk to the public in staying a driving prohibition: *Holloway v. R.* (1987), 48 M.V.R. 270 (Ont. Dist. Ct.).

- For cases in which the appellant was granted a stay of a driving prohibition order pending appeal, see *R. v. Berkach* (1992), 102 Sask. R. 223 (Sask. Q.B.); *R. v. O'Brien* (1989), 19 M.V.R. (2d) 214, 79 Nfld. & P.E.I.R. 45, 246 A.P.R. 45 (Nfld. T.D.); *R. v. McPherson*, [1999] B.C.J. No. 2489, 47 M.V.R. (3d) 55, 140 C.C.C. (3d) 316, 130 B.C.A.C. 254, 211 W.A.C. 254, 1999 BCCA 638, 1999 CarswellBC 2388 (B.C. C.A. [In Chambers]).

- The stay can be partial to allow the accused to drive only for employment: *R. v. Smith* (1993), 50 M.V.R. (2d) 307 (B.C. C.A.). In the following cases, the appellant was permitted to drive only as required by his employment: *R. v. Cunningham*, [2006] A.J. No. 53, 2006 CarswellAlta 74, 2006 ABCA 24 (Alta. C.A.); *R. v. Claus*, 19 M.V.R. (2d) 73, [1989] N.W.T.R. 369 (N.W.T. S.C.); *R. v. Murphy* (1994), 14 M.V.R. (3d) 103, 134 N.S.R. (2d) 393, 383 A.P.R. 393 (N.S. C.A.); *R. v. Cole* (1994), 7 M.V.R. (3d) 293, 49 B.C.A.C. 318, 80 W.A.C. 318 (B.C. C.A.); *R. v. Lockerby* (1999), 175 N.S.R. (2d) 329, 534 A.P.R. 329 (N.S. C.A. [In Chambers]).

- In *R. v. Petruk* (1997), 1997 CarswellBC 1854 (B.C. S.C.), the grounds of appeal were all directed toward a *Charter* breach in connection with the detention of the accused overnight in police cells. The court concluded that where the substantive offence was not under appeal, as here, it was not appropriate that the prohibition be stayed.

- The mandatory licence suspension under provincial highway traffic legislation is generally automatically stayed pending an appeal upon the relevant provincial ministry being informed of the appeal. This is usually accomplished by the delivery to the ministry of a certified copy of the notice of appeal with proof of filing.

Appendix A

Record of Information from Initial Interview

1. Name:

2. Address:

3. Age:
   Date of Birth:

4. Occupation:

5. Telephone: Home:
   Work:

6. Height:
   Weight:

7. Family Background (briefly):

8. Prior Record:

9. Language Fluency:

10. Medical and Physical Condition (such as weariness, a limp, etc., which may be responsible for symptoms taken by the officer as indicative of intoxication):

11. If Accident, any Injuries:

12. Consumption of Alcohol:
    Amount:
    Kind and Brand:
    Time Started:
    Time Finished:

13. Consumption of Food:
    Amount:
    When Consumed:

14. Documentation Showing Amount of Consumption (such as restaurant bills, credit card slips):

15. Outline of events from initial consumption of alcohol to and including arrest (including any videotapes) and release:

16. Name and Addresses of All Witnesses (to any or all events, especially witnesses who saw accused immediately before, during or immediately after police contact):

17. Name of any Lawyer Spoken to (in exercise of right to counsel):

Appendix B

Disclosure Request

<u>SENT BY FACSIMILE: [Fax #1]</u>

[Date]

Disclosure Clerk

Crown Attorney's Office

[Address]

[City], Ontario [Postal Code]

Dear Madam or Sir:

Re: [Client Name] (dob. [DOB])

Charges: [List Charges]

Next Court Date: [Next Court Date]

I am counsel for the above mentioned individual and I am requesting full disclosure in his matter. Without limiting the generality of the foregoing, I am requesting the following items:

[Choose as appropriate for each case]

1. The notes of all officers that had dealings with my client, including booking officers **OR** Notes of the following officers who had relevant dealings in this matter: **[list names]**
2. Complete copies of any demands made to **[Client]**.
3. Any videotape or images of **[Client]** police custody, including booking, cell, in-car and any other videos.
4. Notes of any ambulance and fire crews who attended the scene of the incident **[**, including but not limited to: **list names]**.
5. All relevant police **[and ambulance, etc.]** communications with corresponding communication logs, and mobile data transmissions or searches, including complete copies of all recordings, computer screens and printouts, and 911 communications.
6. All information pertaining to the RIDE program for which my client was stopped.
7. All information from any computer inquiries and data searches of any police databases in relation to my **[client, client's vehicle, etc.]**
8. Complete copies of any and all photographs or other images taken at the scene of the incident.
9. All records regarding the Standard alcohol solution and test solution.
10. All calibration, maintenance records, and usage logs of **[Intoxilyzer machine including serial number & Screening device]**.

11. All reports created at the booking of **[Client]**, including any reports listing the property taken from **[Client]**.
12. Certificate of Analysis for **[Name Item]**.
13. Certificate of Analyst for the Standard Alcohol Solution.
14. All information, including any reports filled out, with respects to searches done on **[Client]** while in police custody, including strip searches.
15. All Use of Force Reports completed as a result of the incident.
16. All reports, bulletins or other material relating to police procedure with respect to **[list subjects; ex. Crows Control, Dealing with Parking Violations, Use of Force, Use of pepper spray, Taking witness statements]**
17. All disciplinary proceedings, either complete or still pending, for **[name of or list of officer(s)]**.
18. Complete copies of the criminal record of the complainant and all other witnesses including disclosure of outstanding charges, previous police reports, and other material affecting credibility. In the case of police officers, disclosure of all discipline records.
19. Complete copies of all audio/video statements made by **[my client, witnesses, complainant(s), and/or co-accused]** with corresponding transcript.
20. The Record of Arrest and complete copies of all documents used to create the record of arrest in this case.
21. An inventory, with justifications, of all other material in the possession of the Crown or other authorities relating to this matter and the persons involved in this case that is not being disclosed for any reason, including lack of relevance.

If the Crown refuses to disclose any of the above information, please provide written reasons for such refusal.

Please contact our office at the number listed above when disclosure is ready to be picked up. Thank you for your attention to this matter.

Appendix C

Regulations

ORDER APPROVING BLOOD SAMPLE CONTAINERS

SOR/2005-37

Approved Containers

1. The following containers, being containers of a kind that is designed to receive a sample of blood of a person for analysis, are hereby approved as suitable, in respect of blood samples, for the purposes of section 258 of the *Criminal Code*:

(*a*) Vacutainer® XF947;
(*b*) BD Vacutainer™ 367001;
(*c*) Vacutainer® 367001; and
(*d*) Tri-Tech Inc. TUG10.

APPROVED BREATH ANALYSIS INSTRUMENTS ORDER

SI/85-201, as amended

Approved Instruments

2. The following instruments, each being an instrument of a kind that is designed to receive and make an analysis of a sample of the breath of a person in order to measure the concentration of alcohol in the blood of that person, are hereby approved as suitable for the purposes of section 258 of the *Criminal Code*:

(*a*) Breathalyzer®, Model 800;
(*b*) Breathalyzer®, Model 900;
(*c*) Breathalyzer®, Model 900A;
(*d*) Intoximeter Mark IV;
(*e*) Alcolmeter AE-D1;
(*f*) Intoxilyzer 4011AS;
(*g*) Alcotest® 7110;
(*h*) Intoxilyzer® 5000 C;
(*i*) Breathalyzer®, Model 900B;
(*j*) Intoxilyzer 1400;
(*k*) BAC Datamaster C;
(*l*) Alco-Sensor IV-RBT IV;
(*m*) Breathalyzer® 7410-CDN with Printer;
(*n*) Alco-Sensor IV/RBT IV-K; and
(*o*) Alcotest 7110 MKIII Dual C.
(*p*) Intoxilyzer® 8000 C; and
(*q*) DataMaster DMT-C.

SI/92-105; SI/92-167; SI/93-61; SI/93-175; SOR/94-422; SOR/94-572; SOR/95-312; SOR/2000-200; SOR/2002–99, s. 1; SOR/2007-197, s. 1; SOR/ 2008-106, s. 1

APPROVED SCREENING DEVICES ORDER

SI/85-200, as amended

Approved Screening Devices

2. The following devices, each being a device of a kind that is designed to ascertain the presence of alcohol in the blood of a person, are hereby approved for the purposes of section 254 of the *Criminal Code*:

(*a*) Alcolmeter S-L2;
(*b*) Alco-sûr;
(*c*) Alcotest® 7410 PA3;
(*d*) Alcotest® 7410 GLC;
(*e*) Alco-Sensor IV DWF;
(*f*) Alco-Sensor IV PWF; and
(*g*) Intoxilyzer 400D.

Am. SI/88-136; SOR/93-263; SOR/94-193; SOR/94-423; SOR/96-81; SOR/97-116.

EVALUATION OF IMPAIRED OPERATION (DRUGS AND ALCOHOL) REGULATIONS

SOR/2008-196

Qualification Required of Evaluating Officer

1. An evaluating officer must be a certified drug recognition expert accredited by the International Association of Chiefs of Police.

Physical Coordination Tests

2. The physical coordination tests to be conducted under paragraph 254(2)(*a*) of the *Criminal Code* are the following standard field sobriety tests:

(a) the horizontal gaze nystagmus test;

(b) the walk-and-turn test; and

(c) the one-leg stand test.

Evaluation Tests and Procedures

3. The tests to be conducted and the procedures to be followed during an evaluation under subsection 254(3.1) of the *Criminal Code* are

(a) a preliminary examination, which consists of measuring the pulse and determining that the pupils are the same size and that the eyes track an object equally;

(b) eye examinations, which consist of

(i) the horizontal gaze nystagmus test,

(ii) the vertical gaze nystagmus test, and

(iii) the lack-of-convergence test;

(c) divided-attention tests, which consist of

(i) the Romberg balance test,

(ii) the walk-and-turn test referred to in paragraph 2(*b*),

(iii) the one-leg stand test referred to in paragraph 2(*c*), and

(iv) the finger-to-nose test, which includes the test subject tilting the head back and touching the tip of their index finger to the tip of their nose in a specified manner while keeping their eyes closed;

(d) an examination, which consists of measuring the blood pressure, temperature and pulse;

(e) an examination of pupil sizes under light levels of ambient light, near total darkness and direct light and an examination of the nasal and oral cavities;

(f) an examination, which consists of checking the muscle tone and pulse; and

(g) a visual examination of the arms, neck and, if exposed, the legs for evidence of injection sites.

Coming into Force

4. These Regulations come into force on July 2, 2008.

Appendix D

PROVINCIAL LICENCE SUSPENSIONS

Editor's Note: Throughout this Appendix, legislation which has not come into force as at date of publication appears in shaded text.

Alberta

***Traffic Safety Act*, R.S.A. 2000, c. T-6, sections 31, 64(r), 82-85, 87-90, 92-94, 96-100, 172-175, 179-181, 189, 190 and the Schedule.**

Action taken re reviews

31. On conducting a review or considering an application under section 30 the board may,

(a) where a person's ability or attitude regarding the operation of a motor vehicle has been considered by the Board,

(i) disqualify the person from driving a motor vehicle in Alberta for a definite or indefinite period of time;

(ii) with respect to that person, prescribe any measure or course of remedial education or treatment as a condition of acquiring or holding an operator's licence;

(iii) prescribe terms and conditions governing that person's operator's licence;

(b) where the suspension of a person's operator's licence or the disqualification of a person to hold an operator's licence arises out of that person being found guilty under section 253 or 254 of the *Criminal Code* (Canada),

(i) on the expiration of a suspension or disqualification imposed by a court, set aside the operation of the suspension or disqualification imposed under this Act on the condition that the person who is subject to the suspension or disqualification

(A) does not operate a motor vehicle unless the vehicle is equipped with an alcohol-sensing device that meets the approval of the Board, and

(B) complies with any terms or conditions imposed by the Board;

(ii) on the expiration of the suspension or disqualification imposed under this Act, direct that the reinstatement or issuance of an operator's licence to the person who was subject to the suspension or disqualification be on the condition that the person, in addition to complying with the requirements imposed under this Act,

(A) does not operate a motor vehicle unless the vehicle is equipped with an alcohol-sensing device that meets the approval of the Board, and

(B) complies with any terms or conditions imposed by the Board.

. . .

Regulations

64. The Minister may make regulations

(r) governing alcohol-sensing devices and their installation, use and removal;

. . .

PART 4

DISQUALIFICATION FROM DRIVING

Division 1
Disqualifications Arising from Offences

Operator's licence suspended

82. When a person is disqualified from driving a motor vehicle in Alberta;

(a) that person's operator's licence, if that person holds a subsisting operator's licence, is suspended, and

(b) that person is disqualified from holding an operator's licence,

during the time that the person is disqualified from driving.

Disqualification for impaired driving

83.(1) When a person is found guilty under section 253 or 254 of the *Criminal Code* (Canada) anywhere in Canada, that person on being found guilty becomes disqualified from driving a motor vehicle for a period of one year from the day of the finding of guilt.

(2) Notwithstanding subsection (1), if a person

(a) is found guilty under section 253 or 254 of the *Criminal Code* (Canada) anywhere in Canada, and

(b) has, in the preceding 10 years, been found guilty of an offence under section 253 or 254 of the *Criminal Code* (Canada) anywhere in Canada,

that person on being found guilty of the offence referred to in clause (a) becomes disqualified from driving a motor vehicle in Alberta for a period of 3 years from the day of the finding of guilt.

(3) Notwithstanding anything in this section, when a person

(a) is found guilty under section 253 or 254 of the *Criminal Code* (Canada) anywhere in Canada, and

(b) has, in the preceding 10 years, been found guilty of

(i) 2 offences under section 253 or 254 of the *Criminal Code* (Canada), or

(ii) one offence under section 253 of the *Criminal Code* (Canada) and one offence under section 254 of the *Criminal Code* (Canada)

anywhere in Canada, unless those 2 offences arose out of the same incident,

that person on being found guilty of the offence referred to in clause (a) becomes disqualified from driving a motor vehicle in Alberta for a period of 5 years from the day of the finding of guilt.

(4) When a person who holds an operator's licence is found guilty under section 253 or 254 of the *Criminal Code* (Canada), the court hearing the case shall forward the operator's licence of that person to the Registrar.

(5) If a person is found guilty of 2 or more offences under section 253 or 254 of the *Criminal Code* (Canada) anywhere in Canada and the offences arose out of the same incident,

(a) the findings of guilty for those offences shall, for the purposes of subsections 2(b) and (3)(b), be considered to constitute only one finding of guilt, which shall be considered to have occurred on the day of the earliest finding of guilt respecting those offences, and

(b) for the purposes of subsection (1), the period of disqualification shall be one year and shall run from the day of the earliest finding of guilt respecting those offences.

(6) For the purposes of subsections (2) and (3), a finding of guilt for an offence

(a) under section 234 or 236 of the *Criminal Code* (Canada) as it read immediately prior to December 4, 1985 is deemed to be a finding of guilt for an offence under section 237 of the *Criminal Code* (Canada) as it read immediately after December 3, 1985, and

(b) under section 234.1 or 235 of the *Criminal Code* (Canada) as it read immediately prior to December 4, 1985 is deemed to be a finding of guilt for an offence under section 238 of the *Criminal Code* (Canada) as it read immediately after December 3, 1985.

(7) For the purposes of subsections (2) and (3), a finding of guilt for an offence

(a) under section 237 of the *Criminal Code* (Canada) as it read immediately prior to December 12, 1988 is deemed to be a finding of guilt for an offence under section 253 of the *Criminal Code* (Canada) as it read immediately after December 11, 1988, and

(b) under section 238 of the *Criminal Code* (Canada) as it read immediately prior to December 12, 1988 is deemed to be a finding of guilt for an offence under section 254 of the *Criminal Code* (Canada) as it read immediately after December 11, 1988.

(8) For the purposes of subsections (2) and (3), a finding of guilt for an offence under section 253 of the *Criminal Code* (Canada) as it read immediately prior to November 1, 1989 is deemed to be a finding of guilt for an offence under section 253 of the *Criminal Code* (Canada) as it read immediately after October 31, 1989.

Driving while prohibited under Criminal Code

84. If a person is found guilty anywhere in Canada of an offence under section 259(4) of the *Criminal Code* (Canada), that person on being found guilty becomes disqualified from driving a motor vehicle in Alberta for a period of 6 months from the day of the finding of guilt.

Disqualification arising under National Defence Act (Canada)

85. (1) When a person is found guilty under section 130 of the *National Defence Act* (Canada) by reason that the person contravened section 253 or 254 of the *Criminal Code* (Canada) anywhere in or out of Canada that person on being found guilty becomes disqualified from driving a motor vehicle in Alberta for a period of one year from the day of the finding of guilt.

(2) Notwithstanding subsection (1), if a person

(a) is found guilty under section 130 of the *National Defence Act* (Canada) by reason that the person contravened section 253 or 254 of the *Criminal Code* (Canada) anywhere in or out of Canada, and

(b) has, in the preceding 10 years, been found guilty of an offence under section 130 of the *National Defence Act* (Canada) by reason that the person contravened section 253 or 254 of the *Criminal Code* (Canada) anywhere in or out of Canada.

that person on being found guilty of the offence referred to in clause (a) becomes disqualified from driving a motor vehicle in Alberta for a period of 3 years from the day of the finding of guilt.

(3) Notwithstanding anything in subsection (1) or (2), when a person

(a) is found guilty under section 130 of the *National Defence Act* (Canada) by reason that the person contravened section 253 or 254 of the *Criminal Code* (Canada) anywhere in or out of Canada, and

(b) has, in the preceding 10 years, been found guilty of 2 offences under the *National Defence Act* (Canada) by reason that the person, in the preceding 10 years.

(i) twice contravened section 253 or 254 of the *Criminal Code* (Canada), or

(ii) once contravened section 253 of the *Criminal Code* (Canada) and once contravened section 254 of the *Criminal Code* (Canada),

anywhere in or out of Canada, unless those 2 offences arose out of the same incident,

that person on being found guilty of the offence referred to in clause (a) becomes disqualified from driving a motor vehicle in Alberta for a period of 5 years from the day of the finding of guilt.

(4) If a person is found guilty of 2 or more offences under section 130 of the *National Defence Act* (Canada) by reason that the person contravened section 253 or 254 of the *Criminal Code* (Canada) anywhere in or out of Canada and the offences arose out of the same incident.

(a) the findings of guilt for those offences shall, for the purposes of subsection, (2)(b) and (3)(b), be considered to constitute only one finding of guilt, which shall be considered to have occurred on the day of the earliest finding of guilt respecting those offences, and

(b) for the purposes of subsection (1), the period of disqualification shall be one year and shall run from the day of the earliest finding of guilt respecting those offences.

(5) For the purposes of subsections (2) and (3), a finding of guilt for an offence under section 120 of the *National Defence Act* (Canada) as the *National Defence Act* (Canada) read immediately prior to December 12, 1988, by reason that a person contravened

(a) section 234 or 236 of the *Criminal Code* (Canada) as the *Criminal Code* (Canada) read immediately prior to December 4, 1985 is deemed to be a finding of guilt under section 120 of the *National Defence Act* (Canada) as the *National Defence Act* (Canada) read immediately prior to December 12, 1988 by reason that the person contravened section 237 of the *Criminal Code* (Canada) as the *Criminal Code* (Canada) read immediately after December 3, 1985, and

(b) section 234.1 or 235 of the *Criminal Code* (Canada) as the *Criminal Code* (Canada) read immediately prior to December 4, 1985 is deemed to be a finding of guilt under section 120 of the *National Defence Act* (Canada) as the *National Defence Act* (Canada) read immediately prior to December 12, 1988 by reason that the person contravened section 238 of the *Criminal Code* (Canada) as the *Criminal Code* (Canada) read immediately after December 3, 1985.

(6) For the purposes of subsections (2) and (3), a finding of guilt for an offence under section 120 of the *National Defence Act* (Canada) as the *National Defence Act* (Canada) read immediately prior to December 12, 1988 by reason that a person contravened

(a) section 237 of the *Criminal Code* (Canada) as the *Criminal Code* (Canada) read immediately prior to December 12, 1988 is deemed to be a finding of guilt under section 130 of the *National Defence Act* (Canada) by reason that the person contravened section 253 of the *Criminal Code* (Canada) as the *Criminal Code* (Canada) and the *National Defence Act* (Canada) read immediately after December 11, 1988, and

(b) section 238 of the *Criminal Code* (Canada) as the *Criminal Code* (Canada) read immediately prior to December 12, 1988 is deemed to be a finding of guilt under section 130 of the *National Defence Act* (Canada) by reason that the person contravened section 254 of the *Criminal Code* (Canada) as the *Criminal Code* (Canada) and the *National Defence Act* (Canada) read immediately after December 11, 1988.

(7) For the purposes of subsections (2) and (3), a finding of guilt for an offence under section 130 of the *National Defence Act* (Canada) by reason that a person contravened section 253 of the *Criminal Code* (Canada) as the *Criminal Code* (Canada) read immediately prior to November 1, 1989 is deemed to be a finding of guilt under section 130 of the *National Defence Act* (Canada), by reason that the person contravened section 253 of the *Criminal Code* (Canada) as the *Criminal Code* (Canada) read immediately after October 31, 1989.

(8) When a person is found guilty anywhere in or out of Canada of an offence under section 130 of the *National Defence Act* (Canada) by reason that the person contravened subsection 249(1), 249.1(1) or 252(1) of the *Criminal Code* (Canada), that person on being found guilty becomes disqualified from driving a motor vehicle in Alberta for a period of one year from the day of the finding of guilt.

(9) When a person is found guilty anywhere in or out of Canada of an offence under section 130 of the *National Defence Act* (Canada) by reason that the person contravened subsection 249(3) or (4), 249.1(3), 252(1.2) or (1.3) or 255(2) or (3) of the *Criminal Code* (Canada), that person on being found guilty becomes disqualified from driving a motor vehicle in Alberta for a period of 5 years from the day of the finding of guilt.

(10) When a person is found guilty anywhere in or out of Canada of an offence under section 130 of the *National Defence Act* (Canada) committed by means of a motor vehicle by reason that the person contravened section 220, 221 or 236 of the *Criminal Code* (Canada), that person on being found guilty becomes disqualified from driving a motor vehicle in Alberta for a period of 5 years from the day of the finding of guilt.

(11) If a person is found guilty under section 130 of the *National Defence Act* (Canada) by reason that the person contravened subsection 259(4) of the *Criminal Code* (Canada),

(a) that person on being found guilty becomes disqualified from driving a motor vehicle in Alberta for a period of 6 months, and

(b) if that person is under suspension or under a prohibition at the time of the finding of guilt, the period of disqualification shall run consecutively with that suspension or prohibition.

2001, c. 14, s. 10

. . .

Licence disqualification

87. (1) When a person is found guilty under subsection 249(1), 249.1(1) or 252(1) of the *Criminal Code* (Canada) anywhere in Canada, that person on being found guilty becomes disqualified from driving a motor vehicle in Alberta for a period of one year from the day of the finding of guilt.

(2) When a person is found guilty under subsection 249(3) or (4), 249.1(3), 252(1.2) or (1.3) of the *Criminal Code* (Canada) anywhere in Canada, that person on being found guilty becomes disqualified from driving a motor vehicle in Alberta for a period of 5 years from the day of the finding of guilt.

(3) When a person is found guilty under section 220, 221 or 236 of the *Criminal Code* (Canada) of an offence anywhere in Canada committed by means of a motor vehicle, that person on being found guilty becomes disqualified from driving a motor vehicle in Alberta for a period of 5 years from the day of the finding of guilt.

2001, c. 14, s. 12

3- and 6- month suspensions, etc.

88. (1) In this section,

(a) **"alcohol-related driving of a motor vehicle"** means those circumstances referred to in subsection (2)(a) and (b);

(b) **"bodily harm"** means any hurt or injury to a person that interferes with the health or comfort of the person and that is more than merely transient or trifling in nature;

(c) **"notice of disqualification"** means a notice of disqualification referred to in subsection (2);

(d) **"notice of suspension"** means a notice of suspension referred to in subsection (2);

(e) **"peace officer"** means a police officer as defined in section 1 of the *Police Act*;

(f) **"temporary operator's permit"** means a temporary operator's permit issued under subsection (2).

(2) Where

(a) a peace officer has reasonable and probable grounds to believe that a person drove a motor vehicle, and

(b) in relation to that person driving that motor vehicle, the peace officer

(i) by reason of an analysis of the breath or blood of the person, has reasonable and probable grounds to believe that the person has consumed alcohol in such a quantity that the concentration of alcohol in that person's blood exceeds 80 milligrams of alcohol in 100 millilitres of blood, or

(ii) has reasonable and probable grounds to believe that the person while having alcohol in that person's body failed or refused, without a reasonable excuse, to comply with a demand made on that person to supply a sample of that person's breath or blood under section 254 of the *Criminal Code* (Canada),.

the peace officer shall, on behalf of the Registrar,

(c) in the case of a person who holds an operator's licence,

(i) require that person to surrender to the peace officer that operator's licence and issue to that person a temporary operator's permit, and

(ii) serve on that person a notice of suspension of that person's operator's licence;

(d) in the case of a person who holds a temporary operator's permit,

(i) require that person to surrender to the peace officer that temporary operator's permit, and

(ii) serve on that person a notice of suspension of that temporary operator's permit;

(e) in the case of a person who holds a licence or permit issued in another jurisdiction that permits the person to operate a motor vehicle, serve on that person a notice of disqualification

(i) disqualifying that person from operating a motor vehicle, and

(ii) disqualifying that person from applying for or holding an operator's licence;

(f) in the case of a person who does not hold an operator's licence, serve on that person a notice of disqualification disqualifying that person from applying for or holding an operator's licence.

(3) Where

(a) a person's operator's licence is surrendered and a temporary operator's permit is issued under subsection (2)(c),

(i) that person is immediately disqualified from driving a motor vehicle in Alberta and remains so disqualified until the temporary operator's permit comes into effect,

(ii) the temporary operator's permit comes into effect at the expiration of 24 hours from the time that the disqualification referred to in subclause (i) came into effect, and

(iii) the temporary operator's permit expires at the end of the 21st day following the day on which the temporary operator's permit came into effect;

(b) a notice of suspension is served on a person under subsection (2)(c), the suspension, with respect to the surrendered operator's licence, takes effect immediately on the expiration of the temporary operator's permit issued in respect of the surrendered operator's licence;

(c) a notice of suspension is served on a person under subsection (2)(d), the suspension, with respect to the surrendered temporary operator's permit, takes effect immediately on the service of the notice;

(d) a notice of disqualification is served on a person under subsection (2)(e),

(i) that person is immediately disqualified from driving a motor vehicle in Alberta, but that disqualification temporarily ceases to have effect at the end of 24 hours from the time that the notice of disqualification was served on that person, and

(ii) that person is, at the end of the 21st day following the day on which the disqualification temporarily ceased to have effect under subclause (i), once again disqualified from driving a motor vehicle in Alberta;

(e) a notice of disqualification is served on a person under subsection (2)(f), the disqualification takes effect immediately on the service of the notice.

(4) A temporary operator's permit, during the period of time that it is in effect, stands in the place of the surrendered operator's licence and is subject to the same terms and conditions as those to which the surrendered operator's licence was subject.

(5) A suspension or disqualification that comes into effect under subsection (3)(b), (d) or (e) is in effect, unless otherwise directed by the Board pursuant to an appeal under section 39, until the end of the 3-month period that commences on the day that the suspension or disqualification takes effect.

(6) Notwithstanding subsection (5), where a peace officer on reasonable and probable grounds believes that the alcohol-related driving of a motor vehicle by a person has caused bodily harm to or the death of another person, a suspension or disqualification that comes into effect under subsection (3)(b), (d) or (e) is in effect

unless otherwise directed by the Board pursuant to an appeal under section 39, until the end of the 6-month period that commences on the day that the suspension or disqualification takes effect.

(6.1) For the purposes of subsections (5) and (6), a disqualification referred to in subsection (3)(d) is deemed to come into effect when the disqualification once again comes into effect, under subsection (3)(d)(ii).

(7) Notwithstanding that a person refuses or fails

(a) to accept from a peace officer service of a notice of suspension or a notice of disqualification, that notice is deemed to have been served at the time that the peace officer attempted to serve that notice on that person;

(b) to surrender an operator's licence or a temporary operator's permit, that refusal or failure does not prevent the suspension or disqualification from taking effect;

(c) to accept service of a notice of suspension or a notice of disqualification, that refusal or failure does not prevent the suspension or disqualification from taking effect.

2001, c. 14, s. 13

24-hour disqualification re alcohol or drug

89. (1) If a peace officer reasonably suspects that the driver of a motor vehicle has consumed alcohol or otherwise introduced into the driver's body any alcohol, drug or other substance in such a quantity so as to affect the driver's physical or mental ability, the peace officer may require the driver to surrender the driver's operator's licence to the peace officer.

(2) On being required by a peace officer to surrender the driver's operator's licence under subsection (1), the driver

(a) is disqualified from driving a motor vehicle in Alberta, and

(b) shall forthwith surrender the driver's operator's licence, if the driver is the holder of an operator's licence, to the peace officer.

(3) The refusal or other failure of a driver to surrender an operator's licence under subsection (2) does not prevent the disqualification from driving from taking effect.

(4) A disqualification from driving arising pursuant to this section terminates at the end of 24 hours from the time that the disqualification came into effect.

(5) Notwithstanding subsection (4), if the disqualification from driving arises in respect of the use of alcohol and the driver voluntarily,

(a) at a place designated by the peace officer, undergoes a test the purpose of which is to show the proportion of alcohol in the driver's blood, and the result of that test indicates that the proportion of alcohol in the driver's blood does not exceed 80 milligrams of alcohol in 100 millilitres of blood, or

(b) produces to the peace officer a certificate signed by a physician stating that the driver's blood, as tested by the physician after the commencement of the disqualification from driving, did not contain more than 80 milligrams of alcohol in 100 millilitres of blood, the peace officer shall forthwith return the operator's licence, if any, to the driver and the disqualification from driving is terminated.

(6) With respect to a driver of a vehicle, this section does not apply to a case arising out of the circumstances described in subsection (1)

(a) when a peace officer decides to lay an information against the driver alleging that the driver has, in contravention of the *Criminal Code* (Canada), committed any offence

(i) involving the actual driving of a motor vehicle by the driver, and

(ii) involving

(A) the condition of the driver or the amount of alcohol in the driver's blood, as the case may be, resulting from the consumption by the driver of alcohol, or

(B) the condition of the driver resulting from the introduction by the driver into the driver's body of any drug or other substance,

or

(b) where the driver's operator's licence is suspended or the driver is disqualified from driving a motor vehicle under section 88.

2001, c. 14, s. 14

One-month suspension re novice driver

90. (1) In this section,

(a) **"approved screening device"** means a device that is designed to ascertain the presence of alcohol in a person's blood and that is

(i) an approved screening device within the meaning of section 254 of the *Criminal Code* (Canada), or

(ii) approved under this Act by the Lieutenant Governor in Council to be used for the purposes of this section;

(b) **"notice of suspension"** means a notice of suspension referred to in subsection (4);

(c) **"novice driver"** means a person who holds a novice operator's licence;

(d) **"novice operator's licence"** means an operator's licence classified as a learner's operator's licence or a probationary operator's licence;

(e) **"peace officer"** means a police officer as defined in section 1 of the *Police Act*;

Proposed Amendment—90(1)(e)

(e) "peace officer" means a police officer as defined in section 1 of the *Police Act* and for the purposes of subsections (2) to (8) includes a peace officer appointed under the *Peace Officer Act* for the purposes of this section;

2005, c. 34, s. 20 [Not in force at date of publication. Amended 2006, c. P-3.5, s. 45.]

(f) **"temporary novice operator's permit"** means a temporary novice operator's permit issued under subsection (4).

(2) If a peace officer reasonably suspects that the driver of a motor vehicle who is a novice driver, having consumed alcohol, drove the motor vehicle, the peace officer may require that the novice driver forthwith provide a breath sample into an approved screening device.

(3) On being required to provide a breath sample under subsection (2), the novice driver must provide a breath sample forthwith.

(4) Where a novice driver

(a) provides a breath sample under subsection (3) and the breath sample registers a result on the approved screening device that indicates the presence of alcohol in that driver's blood, or

(b) without a reasonable excuse fails or refuses to provide a breath sample when required to do so by a peace officer under subsection (2),

the peace officer shall, on behalf of the Registrar

(c) in the case of a person who holds a novice operator's licence,

(i) require that person to surrender to the peace officer that novice operator's licence and issue to that person a temporary novice operator's permit, and

(ii) serve on that person a notice of suspension of that person's novice operator's licence;

(d) in the case of a person who holds a temporary novice operator's permit,

(i) require that person to surrender to the peace officer that temporary novice operator's permit, and

(ii) serve on that person a notice of suspension of that temporary novice operator's permit.

(5) Where

(a) a person's novice operator's licence is surrendered and a temporary novice operator's permit is issued under subsection (4)(c),

(i) that person is immediately disqualified from driving a motor vehicle in Alberta and remains so disqualified until the temporary novice operator's permit comes into effect,

(ii) the temporary novice operator's permit comes into effect at the expiration of 24 hours from the time that the disqualification referred to in subclause (i) came into effect, and

(iii) the temporary novice operator's permit expires at the end of the 7th day following the day on which the temporary novice operator's permit came into effect,

(b) a notice of suspension is served on a person under subsection (4)(c), the suspension, with respect to the surrendered novice operator's licence, takes effect immediately on the expiration of the temporary novice operator's permit issued in respect of the surrendered novice operator's licence;

(c) a notice of suspension is served on a person under subsection (4)(d), the suspension, with respect to the surrendered temporary novice operator's permit, takes effect immediately on the service of the notice.

(6) A temporary novice operator's permit, during the period of time that it is in effect, stands in the place of the surrendered novice operator's licence and is subject to the terms and conditions as those to which the surrendered novice operator's licence was subject.

(7) A suspension that comes into effect under subsection (5)(b) is in effect, unless otherwise directed by the Board pursuant to an appeal under section 39.1, until the end of the one-month period that commences on the day that the suspension takes effect.

(8) Notwithstanding that a person refuses or fails

(a) to accept from a peace officer service of a notice of suspension, that notice is deemed to have been served at the time that the peace officer attempted to serve that notice on that person;

(b) to surrender a novice operator's licence or a temporary novice operator's permit, that refusal or failure does not prevent the suspension from taking effect;

(c) to accept service of a notice of suspension, that refusal or failure does not prevent the suspension or disqualification from taking effect.

(9) With respect to a driver of a vehicle, this section does not apply to a case arising out of the circumstances described in subsection (2)

(a) when a peace officer decides to lay an information against the driver alleging that the driver has, in contravention of the *Criminal Code* (Canada), committed any offence

(i) involving the actual driving of a motor vehicle by the driver, and

(ii) involving

(A) the condition of the driver or the amount of alcohol in the driver's blood, as the case may be, resulting from the consumption by the driver of alcohol, or

(B) the condition of the driver resulting from the introduction by the driver into the driver's body of any drug or other substance,

or

(b) where the driver's operator's licence is suspended or the driver is disqualified from driving a motor vehicle under section 88.

(10) [Repealed 2001, c. 14, s. 15.]

(11) [Repealed 2001, c. 14, s. 15.]

2001, c. 14, s. 15

. . .

Removal of requirements disqualification

92. (1) If under this Act or by an order or judgment made under this or anyother Act a person is disqualified from driving a motor vehicle in Alberta, orthe person's licence was suspended or cancelled, the disqualification,suspension or cancellation remains in effect notwithstanding that the period ofdisqualification, suspension or cancellation has expired until the Registrarremoves the disqualification, suspension or cancellation.

(2) For the purpose of satisfying the Registrar as to a person's competencyto drive a motor vehicle without endangering the safety of the general public,the Registrar may as a condition of removing the disqualification, suspension orcancellation referred to in subsection (1) require that person to do one or moreof the following at any time before or after the removal of thedisqualification, suspension or cancellation:

(a) attend interviews conducted by or on behalf of the Registrar;

(b) take and successfully complete training, educational or rehabilitationprograms or courses as required by the Registrar;

(c) provide to the Registrar medical and other reports prepared byphysicians and other health care providers;

(d) take and successfully complete any examinations or other tests as may be required by the Registrar.

2003, c. 42, s. 15(3)

Exceptions, etc.

93. (1) Notwithstanding that a person is disqualified from driving a motor vehicle in Alberta, that person may, subject to subsection (2), operate implements of husbandry or industrial equipment that is

(a) designed primarily for agricultural use, construction, maintenance, land clearing, ditching or other related tasks, and

(b) not required to be licensed under this Act,

unless that person is disqualified under the *Criminal Code* (Canada) from operating a motor vehicle.

(2) If, for medical reasons, a person is disqualified from driving a motor vehicle under this Act, the Registrar may also disqualify that person from driving implements of husbandry or industrial equipment of the kind referred to in subsection (1).

(3) Notwithstanding that a person is disqualified from driving a motor vehicle in Alberta, a person may operate a vehicle, on any terms or conditions the Registrar may prescribe, while engaged in any course of remedial education or treatment under section 31.

Prohibition re driving while unauthorized

94. For the purposes of this section, a person is an unauthorized driver if

(a) that person's operator's licence is suspended or cancelled under this Act,

(b) that person is disqualified from driving a motor vehicle in Alberta,

(c) that person's licence or permit to operate a motor vehicle in a jurisdiction outside Alberta is suspended or cancelled, or

(d) that person's privilege to secure a licence or permit to operate a motor vehicle in a jurisdiction outside Alberta is suspended or cancelled.

(2) A person shall not drive a motor vehicle on a highway at any time during which that person is an unauthorized driver.

2003, c. 42, s. 15(4)

. . .

Suspension continues after licence expires

96. (1) If a person's operator's licence is suspended or cancelled under this Act, the suspension or cancellation continues in effect notwithstanding the expiration of the licence during the period of the suspension or cancellation.

(2) If a person's operator's licence is suspended or cancelled under this Act, the suspension or cancellation operates to suspend or cancel any operator's licence held by that person during the period of suspension or cancellation, whether or not so stated in the suspension or cancellation.

Extended period of disqualification

97. Notwithstanding anything in this Act, where

(a) a person is found guilty of an offence under

(i) the *Criminal Code* (Canada) anywhere in Canada, or

(ii) the *National Defence Act* (Canada) anywhere in or out of Canada,

(b) in respect of the conviction referred to in clause (a), that person is prohibited from operating a motor vehicle, and

(c) the period of prohibition is for a period of time that is greater than the period of disqualification from driving provided for under this Act,

that person is, on the coming into effect of the prohibition, disqualified from driving a motor vehicle in Alberta during the period that the prohibition is in effect.

Disqualifications to run consecutively

98. Where

(a) a person is disqualified from driving a motor vehicle in Alberta, and

(b) during the period of disqualification referred to in clause (a), that person is disqualified from driving a motor vehicle in Alberta under section 94 or anywhere in Canada under section 259 of the *Criminal Code* (Canada).

that 2nd mentioned disqualification referred to in clause (b) shall run consecutively to any previous disqualification that is still in effect or waiting to go into effect, as the case may be.

Setting aside suspension, etc. re demerit points

99. Where a person's operator's licence is, by reason of the accumulation of demerit points, suspended or cancelled, the Registrar may, on the application by that person, review the matter and if the Registrar considers it appropriate set aside the operation of the suspension or cancellation and reinstate that person's operator's licence subject to any terms or conditions imposed by the Registrar.

Regulations

100. The Minister may make regulations

(a) governing the information and the form of information to be provided to the Registrar by peace officers with respect to the suspensions or the disqualifications referred to in sections 88, 89 and 90;

(b) governing the handling of operator's licences and other documents surrendered under sections 88, 89 and 90;

(c) prescribing and governing the use of forms to be used for the purposes of sections 88, 89 and 90;

(d) designating

(i) any of the Rules of the Road and any other regulations under this Act, and

(ii) the regulations under the *National Parks Act* (Canada)

to which section 86 applies.

. . .

24-hour seizure or immobilization of vehicle

172. Where a person has been charged with an offence under

(a) section 253 or 254 of the *Criminal Code* (Canada),

(b) section 130 of the *National Defence Act* (Canada) by reason of that person contravening section 253 or 254 of the *Criminal Code* (Canada), or

(c) section 115(2)(c) or (d), where a peace officer believes that the safety of the public may be at risk, then, notwithstanding sections 169 and 170,

a peace officer or another person authorized by a peace officer may, for a period of time not exceeding 24 hours from the time that the person was charged, seize or immobilize the motor vehicle that was being operated by that person at the time that the person was charged.

2005, c. 34, s. 32

Seizure or immobilization of motor vehicle

173. (1) Where a person has been charged with an offence under

(a) section 94,

(b) subsection 259(4) of the *Criminal Code* (Canada), or

(c) section 130 of the *National Defence Act* (Canada) by reason of that person's contravening subsection 259(4) of the *Criminal Code* (Canada), a peace officer, the Registrar or a person authorized by a peace officer or the Registrar shall seize or immobilize the motor vehicle that was being operated by that person at the time that the person was charged.

(2) Where a motor vehicle is seized or immobilized under subsection (1), the seizure or immobilization is in effect for

(a) 30 days from the day that the motor vehicle is seized or immobilized, or

(b) if a shorter period of time is provided for by regulation, that shorter period of time.

(3) Notwithstanding subsection (2), where

(a) a person has previously been charged with an offence referred to in subsection (1),

(b) as a result of that charge, the motor vehicle that was being operated by that person was seized or immobilized under subsection (1),

(c) that seizure or immobilization has not been revoked or rescinded,

(d) within 3 years from the day that the motor vehicle referred to in clause (b) was seized or immobilized, the person referred to in clause (a) is once again charged with an offence referred to in subsection (1), and

(e) as a result of the charge referred to in clause (d), the motor vehicle that was being operated by that person has been seized or immobilized under subsection (1),

the seizure or immobilization of the motor vehicle referred to in clause (e) is in effect for

(f) 60 days from the day that the motor vehicle is seized or immobilized, or

(g) if a shorter period of time is provided for by regulation, that shorter period of time.

(4) Subsection (3) applies only where the person who is the registered owner of the motor vehicle referred to in subsection (3)(e) at the time that that vehicle is seized or immobilized was the registered owner of the motor vehicle referred to in subsection (3)(b) at the time that the vehicle referred to in subsection (3)(b) was seized or immobilized.

(5) Subject to the regulations, no person shall release a motor vehicle from seizure or immobilization while the seizure or immobilization of the motor vehicle is in effect.

2001, c. 14, s. 19; 2005, c. 34, s. 33

Seizure of vehicle in prostitution related offences

173.1 (1) Where a person has been charged with an offence under section 211, 212 or 213 of the *Criminal Code* (Canada), a peace officer or a person authorized by a peace officer may seize or immobilize the motor vehicle that was being operated by that person at the time that the person was charged.

(2) Where a motor vehicle is seized or immobilized under subsection (1), a peace officer may release the vehicle to the registered owner, or a person authorized by the registered owner, if the officer is satisfied that

(a) the vehicle was stolen,

(b) every person

(i) who was in the vehicle at the time it was seized, and

(ii) who the peace officer had reasonable grounds to believe had committed an offence referred to in subsection (1),

is eligible for, and consents to be dealt with by way of, a program of alternative measures authorized under section 717((1)(a) of the *Criminal Code* (Canada), or

(c) seizure of the vehicle is causing or will cause undue financial hardship.

(3) Subject to subsection (2) and any decision of the Board in an appeal commenced pursuant to section 40, when a person who is in a motor vehicle at the time it is seized or immobilized under subsection (1) is convicted of an offence referred to in that subsection, the vehicle is forfeited to the Government subject to any security interest registered under the Personal Property Security Act before the seizure or immobilization.

(4) If no person is convicted of an offence in respect of which a motor vehicle is seized under this section, a peace officer shall release the vehicle.

2003, c. 48, s. 6 [Amended 2005, c. 34, s. 34(3).]

Claim by owner for expenses

174. Where

(a) a motor vehicle has been seized or immobilized under section 172, 173 or 173.1.

(b) the person driving the vehicle at the time of the seizure or immobilization was not the owner of the vehicle, and

(c) the owner of the vehicle incurs expenses in respect of the release of the vehicle,

the owner of the motor vehicle may claim against the person who was driving the vehicle at the time of the seizure or immobilization any expenses incurred by the owner with respect to the release of the vehicle from the seizure or immobilization.

2003, c. 48, s. 7

Personal property

175. (1) In this section, **"personal property"** means personal property other than personal property that is a part of a motor vehicle.

(2) Where personal property is in or on a motor vehicle that is seized or immobilized under section 172, 173 or 173.1, that personal property is not subject to the seizure or immobilization and, subject to the regulations, shall, on request, be returned to the person having claim to that personal property.

2003, c. 48, s. 7

. . .

Guilty pleas

179. For the purposes of this Act, a person who pleads guilty to an offence referred to in this Act is deemed to have been found guilty of that offence

Surrender of operator's licence

180. When, after a finding of guilt,

(a) the operator's licence of a person is suspended, or

(b) a person is disqualified from holding an operator's licence,

the court shall by order require that person to surrender that person's operator's licence to the court and on the surrender of the licence the court shall cause the operator's licence to be forwarded to the Registrar.

Appeal

181. (1) If a person who has been disqualified from driving a motor vehicle in Alberta appeals against that person's conviction, applies for leave to appeal against that person's conviction, the disqualification remains in effect unless

(a) the court being appealed to or to which the application is made orders that the disqualification be stayed pending the disposition of the appeal or application, and

(b) the appellant or applicant serves on the Registrar by personal service or by registered mail

(i) a copy of the notice of appeal, stated case, notice of motion or other document by which the appeal or application is commenced,

(ii) a copy of the document by which the application to stay the disqualification from driving a motor vehicle is commenced,

(iii) a copy of the order staying the disqualification, and

(iv) a notice setting out the person's full name, address, date of birth and operator's licence number.

(2) An application for a stay of the disqualification under subsection (1) must be brought by

(a) a notice of motion, if the application is to be made in the same court as the appeal, application for leave to appeal or application to quash the conviction, or

(b) an originatin notice, if the application is not to be made in the same court as the appeal, application for leave to appeal or application to quash the conviction.

(3) The applicant must serve a copy of the application referred to in subsection (2) and the supporting documents on the Minister of Justice and Attorney General or that Minister's agent on not less than 2 days' notice of the application.

(4) If the court on an appeal or application under subsection (1) confirms the finding of guilt,

(a) a disqualification from driving a motor vehicle in Alberta that has been stayed under subsection (1) is revived on the day that the finding of guilt is confirmed, and

(b) the period of time during which the qualification was stayed shall not be included in calculating the termination day of the disqualification.

(5) If an appeal, or an application described in subsection (1), of a person whose disqualification is stayed under subsection (1) is abandoned, withdrawn, discontinued or dismissed, the disqualification that has been stayed under subsection (1)

(a) is automatically revived on the day the appeal or application is abandoned, withdrawn, discontinued or dismissed, and

(b) the period of time during which the disqualification was stayed shall not be included in calculating the termination day of the disqualification.

(6) If a disqualification from driving a motor vehicle in Alberta is revived under subsection (4) or (5), the person disqualified from driving is deemed to have knowledge of that revival and notice under this Act is not required to be served on that person.

. . .

Transitional provisions

189. (1) In this section, **"previous legislation"** means

(a) the *Highway Traffic Act*;

(b) the *Motor Transport Act* (R.S.A. 1980, c. M-20);

(c) the *Motor Transport Act* (S.A. 1992, c. M-20.1);

(d) the *Motor Vehicle Administration Act*;

(e) the *Off-highway Vehicle Act*.

(2) Where on the coming into force of this Act

(a) a proceeding is in progress or pending

(i) before the Alberta Motor Transport Board, that proceeding shall be continued under this Act before the Alberta Transportation Safety Board, or

(ii) before the Driver Control Board, that proceeding shall be continued under this Act before the Alberta Transportation Safety Board;

(b) a reference is made in any enactment, order in council, agreement or document to the Alberta Motor Transport Board or the Driver Control Board, that reference is deemed to be a reference to the Alberta Transportation Safety Board;

(c) a reference is made to a provision of any Act repealed pursuant to this Act, that reference is deemed to be a reference to the appropriate corresponding provision of this Act;

(d) a person is subject to a prosecution for a failure to comply with an Act repealed pursuant to this Act, that prosecution shall be carried on as if that repealed Act had not been repealed;

(e) a person is disqualified from driving in Alberta, that person is disqualified under this Act from driving in Alberta;

(f) the registration of a vehicle has been suspended or cancelled, that registration is suspended or cancelled, as the case may be, under this Act;

(g) any licence plates issued in respect of a vehicle have been suspended or cancelled, those licence plates are suspended or cancelled, as the case may be, under this Act;

(h) a person's operator's licence is suspended, that operator's licence is suspended under this Act;

(i) any reference in any provision of an enactment, other than a provision that is amended by sections 192 to 214, to a vehicle that is a public vehicle as defined in the *Motor Transport Act*, R.S.A. 1980, c. M-20, is deemed to be a reference to a commercial vehicle;

(j) subject to clauses (a) to (i), any order, rule, regulation, direction, permit, instrument or document that was made, issued, created, registered or otherwise dealt with and every action taken, decision made or thing done under an Act repealed pursuant to this Act that could have been made, issued, created, registered, dealt with, taken or done under this Act if this Act had been then in force and that is still valid at the commencement of this section is deemed to have been made, issued, created, registered, dealt with, taken or done under this Act.

(3) The Minister may make regulations

(a) respecting the transition of any matter from the previous legislation;

(b) to deal with any difficulty or impossibility resulting from the transition from the previous legislation.

Transitional

190. (1) In this section,

(a) **"Schedule"** means the Schedule to this Act;

(b) a reference to a suspension or disqualification is a reference to a suspension or disqualification under the Schedule and that is still in effect on the coming into force of sections 39 and 88 of this Act;

(c) a reference to an ongoing appeal is a reference to an appeal commenced under section 3 of the Schedule and that is still continuing on the coming into force of sections 39 and 88 of this Act;

(d) a reference to a right of appeal is a reference to a right of appeal provided for under section 3 of the Schedule and that has not expired before the coming into force of sections 39 and 88 of this Act.

(2) On the coming into force of sections 39 and 88 of this Act,

(a) all suspensions and disqualifications continue under those provisions;

(b) all ongoing appeals continue and shall be determined under those provisions;

(c) all rights of appeal continue under and are subject to those provisions;

(d) notwithstanding clause (c), a right of appeal expires on the day provided for in the Schedule as if the Schedule had not been repealed.

. . .

SCHEDULE [Repealed R.S.A. 2000, c. T-6, s. 214(g).]

British Columbia

***Motor Vehicle Act*, R.S.B.C. 1996, c. 318, sections 1 (in part), 25.1, 89, 90.1–90.4, 93, 94.1–94.6, 95–104, 105.1–105.3, 105.5, 105.9, 215–215.4, 224–229, 232, 233, and 241–248.**

Definitions

1. In this Act:

. . .

"motor vehicle related Criminal Code offence" means

(a) an offence committed before December 4, 1985 under section 203, 204, 219, 233, 234, 235 or 236 of the *Criminal Code* as it then was,

(b) an offence committed on or after December 4, 1985 and before December 12, 1988 under section 203, 204, 219, 233, 236, 237, 238, 239 or 242 of the *Criminal Code* as it then was,

(c) an offence committed on or after December 12, 1988 under section 220, 221, 236, 249(1)(a), (3) or (4), 252(1), 253(a) or (b), 254(5), 255(2) or (3) or 259(4) of the *Criminal Code*, or

(d) an offence committed under section 249.1 of the *Criminal Code* on or after a date prescribed by the Lieutenant Governor in Council

if the offence arose out of or was related to the operation, care or control of a motor vehicle or that was committed by means of a motor vehicle;

. . .

Remedial courses and programs for drivers

25.1 (1) This section applies if a person has a driving record that in the opinion of the superintendent is unsatisfactory or the superintendent considers that, with respect to the person's driving skills, fitness or ability to drive and operate a motor vehicle, it is in the public interest for the person to attend or participate in one or more of the following:

(a) a driver training course specified by the superintendent;

(b) a remedial program or a component of it specified by the superintendent;

(c) an ignition interlock program specified by the superintendent.

(2) The superintendent may require a statement in, endorsement on or attachment to the person's driver's licence, adding as a condition of the driver's licence that the person must, in order to continue to hold the licence, attend or participate in and complete, to the satisfaction of the superintendent, a course or program referred to in subsection (1) if it is not, in the superintendent's opinion, contrary to the public interest to allow the person to hold a driver's licence while attending or participating in the course or program.

(3) The superintendent may

(a) as part of a condition of a driver's licence under subsection (2), specify a date by which or a period of time during which the person must complete the program, and

(b) at any time extend, change or cancel a date or period of time specified under paragraph (a).

(4) Section 25(13) applies to a condition imposed in respect of a person's driver's licence under this section.

(5) If it is, in the superintendent's opinion, contrary to the public interest to allow the person to hold a driver's licence while attending or participating in a course or program referred to in subsection (1), the superintendent may require that the person attend and complete, to the satisfaction of the superintendent, a course or program referred to in subsection (1)(a) or (b) before being eligible to apply for a driver's licence under section 25.

(6) A person who is required to attend or participate in and complete a program referred to in subsection (1) must pay the prescribed fees.

(7) Nothing in this section limits the application of sections 25(12), 29, 92 and 93.

2004, c. 68, s. 2

Deemed suspension

89. (1) A person's driver's licence and his or her right to apply for or obtain a driver's licence are deemed to be suspended if the person

(a) is prohibited from driving a motor vehicle

(i) under this Act, the *Youth Justice Act*, the *Youth Criminal Justice Act* (Canada) or the *Criminal Code*,

(ii) before April 1, 2003, under the *Young Offenders Act* (Canada), as it then was, or

(iii) before April 1, 2004, under the *Young Offenders (British Columbia) Act,* as it then was,

(b) pleads guilty to or is found guilty of an offence under an Act referred to in paragraph (a) of this subsection, the *Commercial Transport Act* or the *Insurance (Vehicle) Act* and is prohibited from driving a motor vehicle while waiting to be sentenced for that offence, or

(c) as a condition of an order of judicial interim release under the *Criminal Code*, may not drive a motor vehicle.

(2) A judge, registrar, deputy registrar or court clerk may notify the Insurance Corporation of British Columbia if a person

(a) is prohibited from driving a motor vehicle under the *Youth Justice Act*, the *Youth Criminal Justice Act* (Canada) or the *Criminal Code*,

(b) pleads guilty to an offence under an Act referred to in subsection (1)(a), the *Commercial Transport Act* or the *Insurance (Vehicle) Act* and is prohibited from driving a motor vehicle while waiting to be sentenced for that offence, or

(c) as a condition of an order of judicial interim release under the *Criminal Code*, may not drive a motor vehicle.

2003, c. 85, s. 68; 2004, c. 68, ss. 7, 22

. . .

90.1 [Repealed 2006, c. 33, s. 1 (2)(j).]

90.2 [Repealed 2006, c. 33, s. 1 (2)(j).]

12 hour suspension

90.3 (1) In this section:

"approved screening device" means a device prescribed for the purposes of this section;

"driver" means a driver who holds a driver's licence on which a condition is imposed under section 25(10.1) and includes any such person having the care or control of a motor vehicle on a highway or industrial road whether or not the motor vehicle is in motion.

(2) A peace officer may, at any time or place on a highway or industrial road if the peace officer has reasonable and probable grounds to believe that a driver has alcohol in his or her body,

(a) request the driver to drive the motor vehicle, under the direction of the peace officer, to the nearest place off the travelled portion of the highway or industrial road, and

(b) by demand made to that driver, require the driver to promptly provide a sample of breath that, in the opinion of the peace officer, is necessary to enable a proper analysis of the breath to be made by means of an approved screening device and, if necessary, to accompany the peace officer for the purpose of enabling that sample of breath to be taken.

(3) If

(a) a driver, without a reasonable excuse, fails or refuses to comply with a demand made under subsection (2)(b), or

(b) the peace officer, pursuant to an analysis of the breath of the driver under subsection (2)(b), has reasonable and probable grounds to believe that the driver has alcohol in his or her body,

the peace officer may

(c) serve the driver with a notice of licence suspension, and

(d) if the driver is in possession of a driver's licence, request the driver to surrender that licence.

(4) If a peace officer requests a driver to surrender the driver's licence under subsection (3)(d), the driver must promptly surrender the driver's licence to the peace officer.

(5) A person's driver's licence is automatically suspended for a period of 12 hours from the time the peace officer served the driver with a notice of licence suspension under subsection (3)(c).

(6) [Repealed 2004, c. 68, s. 8(b).]

(a) states that the blood alcohol level of the driver did not exceed 3 mg of alcohol in 100 ml of blood at the time the certificate was signed, and

(b) was signed after the person's driver's licence was suspended,

the suspension of the driver's licence is terminated.

(7) A peace officer acting under subsection (3) need not hold the opinion that the blood alcohol level of the driver exceeds 3 mg of alcohol in 100 ml of blood.

(8) If a peace officer serves a notice of licence suspension under subsection (3)(c), the peace officer must cause a report of the suspension to be delivered to the Insurance Corporation of British Columbia.

(9) The report referred to in subsection (8) must be in a form established by the Insurance Corporation of British Columbia.

(10) The Lieutenant Governor in Council may prescribe an approved screening device for the purposes of this section.

R.S.B.C. 1996 (Supp.), c. 318, s. 21; 1997, c. 31, s. 14; 2004, c. 68, s. 8

Driving while suspended

90.4 (1) A person who holds a driver's licence on which a condition has been imposed under section 25(10.1) commits an offence if the person drives a motor vehicle on a highway or industrial road knowing that the person's driver's licence has been suspended under section 90.1 or 90.3.

(2) If a person is charged with an offence under subsection (1), the court hearing the charge may admit into evidence a certificate of the Insurance Corporation of British Columbia if the offence pertains to a suspension under section 90.3, or a certificate of the superintendent if the offence pertains to a suspension under section 90.1, stating the information required by subsection (3).

(3) If a person is charged with an offence under subsection (1), the certificate referred to in subsection (2) must state that the suspension was in effect on the date of the alleged offence and that the records of the Insurance Corporation of British Columbia or superintendent, as the case may be,

(a) show that a notice of suspension was mailed by registered mail or certified mail to the person at the person's most recent address recorded in the records of the corporation and that the corporation or superintendent subsequently received a copy of a confirmation of delivery provided by Canada Post showing a recipient's signature that, from a comparison with the signature on the records of the corporation, appears to be that of the person to whom the notice of suspension was sent,

(b) contain a document that

(i) indicates that the person charged

(A) has acknowledged that the person's driver's licence is suspended, or

(B) has acknowledged that the person has received from the corporation or the superintendent a notice of suspension, and

(ii) is signed by a signature that, from a comparison with the signature on the records of the corporation, appears to be that of the person whose driver's licence was suspended or to whom the corporation or the superintendent mailed a notice of suspension, or

(c) contain a document that indicates that the person charged has surrendered the person's driver's licence to the corporation or the superintendent subsequent to receiving from the corporation a notice of suspension.

(4) If the certificate of the Insurance Corporation of British Columbia or the superintendent, as the case may be, is admitted into evidence, it is proof that the defendant had knowledge of the suspension in effect at the time of the alleged offence.

(5) This section applies to any document contained in the records of the Insurance Corporation of British Columbia or of the superintendent, whether that document was signed before, on or after the date this subsection comes into force.
R.S.B.C. 1996 (Supp.), c. 318, s. 21; 1997, c. 31, s 14; 1999, c. 39, s. 46

. . .

Prohibition against driving by superintendent

93. (1) Even though a person is or may be subject to another prohibition from driving, if the superintendent considers it to be in the public interest, the superintendent may, with or without a hearing, prohibit the person from driving a motor vehicle

(a) if the person

(i) has failed to comply with this Act or the regulations, or

(ii) has a driving record that in the opinion of the superintendent is unsatisfactory,

(b) if the person's privilege of driving a motor vehicle has been suspended or cancelled in any jurisdiction in Canada or in the United States of America, or

(c) for any cause not referred to in paragraph (a) or (b) that relates to the use or operation of motor vehicles.

(2) In forming an opinion as to whether a person's driving record is unsatisfactory the superintendent may consider all or any part of the person's driving record, including but not limited to any part of the driving record previously taken into account by a court or by the superintendent in making any order prohibiting the person from driving a motor vehicle.

(3) If under this section the superintendent prohibits a person from driving a motor vehicle on the grounds of an unsatisfactory driving record, a prohibition so made must not be held invalid on the grounds that the superintendent did not examine or consider other information or evidence.

. . .

Notice of driving prohibition

94.1 (1) If a peace officer has reasonable and probable grounds to believe

(a) by reason of an analysis of the breath or blood of a person, that a person operated a motor vehicle or had care or control of a motor vehicle having consumed alcohol in such a quantity that the concentration of alcohol in the person's blood exceeded 80 milligrams of alcohol in 100 millilitres of blood at any time within 3 hours after operating or having care or control of the motor vehicle, or

(b) that a person failed or refused, without a reasonable excuse, to comply with a demand made on the person to supply a sample of his or her breath or blood under section 254 of the *Criminal Code* in respect of the operation or care or control of a motor vehicle,

the peace officer must,

(c) if the person holds a valid licence or permit issued under this Act to operate a motor vehicle,

(i) take possession of the person's licence or permit if the person has it in his or her possession, and

(ii) serve on the person a notice of driving prohibition, or

(d) if the person

(i) holds a valid document issued in another jurisdiction that allows the person to operate a motor vehicle, or

(ii) does not hold a valid licence or permit to operate a motor vehicle,

serve on the person a notice of driving prohibition.

(2) If a person referred to in subsection (1)(c) is not in possession of his or her licence or permit issued under this Act to operate a motor vehicle at the time the person is served with the notice of driving prohibition, the person must promptly send the licence or permit to the Insurance Corporation of British Columbia.

(3) The notice of driving prohibition must be in the prescribed form and must contain

(a) a statement of the right to have the driving prohibition reviewed by the superintendent under section 94.4,

(b) prescribed instructions describing how to apply for that review, and

(c) a statement that if the person on whom the notice of driving prohibition is served does not apply for a review under section 94.4, the person will be prohibited from operating a motor vehicle for a period of 90 days.

R.S.B.C. 1996 (Supp.), c. 318, ss. 23, 42; 2000, c. 9, s. 32

Effect of notice of driving prohibition

94.2 (1) If a person is served with a notice of driving prohibition under

(a) section 94.1(1)(c),

(i) subject to subsection (2), the notice acts as a temporary driver's licence that expires 21 days from the date it is served, and

(ii) despite the fact the person is or may be subject to another prohibition from driving, the person is prohibited from operating a motor vehicle for 90 days effective on the expiration of the temporary driver's licence referred to in subparagraph (i), or

(b) section 94.1(1)(d), despite the fact the person is or may be subject to another prohibition from driving, the person is prohibited from operating a motor vehicle for 90 days effective 21 days from the date the notice is served.

(2) If a person is subject to a driving prohibition under section 215 at the time the person is served with a notice of driving prohibition under section 94.1, the temporary driver's licence referred to in subsection (1)(a)(i) is valid only on expiry of the driving prohibition under section 215.

(3) The temporary driver's licence referred to in subsection (1)(a)(i)

(a) is of the same class, and

(b) is subject to all of the same restrictions and conditions

as the licence or permit taken by the peace officer or sent to the Insurance Corporation of British Columbia under section 94.1.

R.S.B.C. 1996 (Supp.), c. 318, ss. 23, 42

Duties of peace officer

94.3 A peace officer who serves a notice of driving prohibition on a person under section 94.1 must promptly forward to the superintendent

(a) the person's licence or permit to operate a motor vehicle, if the peace officer took the licence or permit into possession,

(b) a copy of the notice of driving prohibition,

(c) a certificate of service, in the form established by the superintendent, showing that the notice of driving prohibition was personally served on the person subject to the driving prohibition,

(d) a report, in the form established by the superintendent, sworn or solemnly affirmed by the peace officer, and

(e) a copy of any certificate of analysis under section 258 of the *Criminal Code* with respect to the person.

R.S.B.C. 1996 (Supp.), c. 318, s. 23; 2002, c. 25, s. 47

Review of driving prohibition

94.4 (1) A person may, within 7 days of being served with a notice of driving prohibition under section 94.1, apply to the superintendent for a review of the driving prohibition by

(a) filing an application for review with the superintendent,

(b) paying to the superintendent

(i) the prescribed application fee, and

(ii) the prescribed hearing fee, and

(c) if it has not been taken by the peace officer or sent to the superintendent under section 94.1, surrendering to the Insurance Corporation of British Columbia his or her licence or permit to operate a motor vehicle unless the person completes and files with the superintendent a statutory declaration stating that the licence or permit has been lost, stolen or destroyed.

(2) An application for review must be in the form, contain the information and be completed in the manner required by the superintendent.

(3) An applicant may attach to the application for review any sworn statements or other evidence that the applicant wishes the superintendent to consider.

(4) The filing of an application for review does not stay the driving prohibition.

(5) The superintendent is not required to hold an oral hearing unless the applicant

(a) requests an oral hearing at the time of filing the application for review, and

(b) pays the prescribed oral hearing fees.

(6) If a person requests an oral hearing and fails to appear on the date and at the time and place arranged for the hearing, without prior notice to the superintendent, the right to an oral hearing is deemed to have been waived by the person.

R.S.B.C. 1996 (Supp.), c. 318, ss. 23, 24; 2002, c. 25, s. 48

Considerations

94.5 (1) In a review of a driving prohibition under section 94.4, the superintendent must consider

(a) any relevant sworn or solemnly affirmed statements and any other relevant information,

(b) the report of the peace officer forwarded under section 94.3(d),

(c) a copy of any certificate of analysis under section 258 of the *Criminal Code* with respect to the person served with the notice of driving prohibition, and

(d) if an oral hearing is held, in addition to the matters referred to in paragraphs (a) to (c), any relevant evidence given or representations made at the hearing.

(2) The superintendent may consider a copy of the certificate referred to in subsection (1)(c) without proof

(a) of the identity and official character of the person appearing to have signed the certificate, or

(b) that the copy is a true copy.

(3) In a review of a driving prohibition under section 94.4, no person may be cross examined.

R.S.B.C. 1996 (Supp.), c. 318, s. 23; 2002, c. 63, s. 16

Decision of the superintendent

94.6 (1) If after considering an application for review under section 94.4, the superintendent is satisfied that

(a) the person operated or had care or control of a motor vehicle having consumed alcohol in such a quantity that the concentration of alcohol in the person's blood exceeded 80 milligrams of alcohol in 100 millilitres of blood at any time within 3 hours after operating or having care or control of the motor vehicle, or

(b) the person failed or refused, without a reasonable excuse, to comply with a demand made on the person to supply a sample of his or her breath or blood under section 254 of the *Criminal Code* in respect of the operation or care or control of a motor vehicle

the superintendent must confirm the driving prohibition.

(2) If after considering an application for review under section 94.4, the superintendent is satisfied that

(a) the person did not, because of alcohol consumption prior to or while operating or having care or control of a motor vehicle, have concentration of alcohol in his or her blood that exceeded 80 milligrams of alcohol in 100 millilitres of blood at any time within 3 hours after operating or having care or control of the motor vehicle,

(b) the person

(i) did not fail or refuse to comply with a demand made on the person to supply a sample of his or her breath or blood under section 254 of the *Criminal Code* in respect of the operation or care or control of a motor vehicle, or

(ii) had a reasonable excuse for failing or refusing to comply with the demand referred to in subparagraph (i),

the superintendent must

(c) revoke the driving prohibition,

(d) direct the Insurance Corporation or British Columbia to return any licence or permit to operate a motor vehicle taken into possession by the peace officer or sent to the Corporation, and

(e) direct that the application and hearing fees paid be refunded to the applicant.

(3) Subject to subsection (4), the decision of the superintendent, and the reasons for the decision, must be in writing and a copy must be sent to the applicant within 21 days of the date the notice of driving prohibition was served on the applicant under section 94.1

(4) If the superintendent is unable to send the decision to the applicant within the 21 day period set out in subsection (3), the superintendent may extend that period for a period determined by the superintendent.

(5) If the superintendent extends the period for sending a decision to the applicant under subsection (4), the superintendent must

(a) stay the driving prohibition imposed on the applicant under section 94.2 for the period of the extension determined under subsection (4), and

(b) if the applicant held a valid licence or permit issued under this Act to operate a motor vehicle at the time the applicant was served with the notice of driving prohibition under section 94.1, direct the Insurance Corporation of British Columbia to issue to the applicant a temporary driver's licence that

(i) is valid on the expiration of the temporary driver's licence referred to in section 94.2(1)(a)(i), and

(ii) expires with the period of extension determined under subsection (4).

(6) The temporary driver's licence issued under subsection (5)(b)

(a) is of the same class, and

(b) is subject to all of the same restrictions and conditions

as the licence or permit taken by the peace officer or sent to the Insurance Corporation of British Columbia under section 94.1.

(7) The superintendent must promptly give the applicant notice of an extension made under subsection (4).

(8) The copy referred to in subsection (3) and the notice referred to in subsection (7) must be sent to the applicant

(a) at the last known address of the applicant as shown in the records maintained by the Insurance Corporation of British Columbia, or

(b) at the address shown in the application for review, if that address is different from the address in the Insurance Corporation of British Columbia's records.

(9) A notice of extension given under subsection (7) is deemed to be a notice of prohibition for the purposes of section 95(4)(a) or (b).

R.S.B.C. 1996 (Supp.), c. 318, ss. 23, 25, 42; 1997, c. 31, s. 16; 1997, c. 43, s. 15; 2000, c. 9, s. 33

Driving while prohibited

95. (1) A person who drives a motor vehicle on a highway or industrial road knowing that

(a) he or she is prohibited from driving a motor vehicle under section 91, 92, 93, 94.2 or 215, or

(b) the person's licence or the person's right to apply for or obtain a driver's licence is suspended under section 25, 83, 87, 88, 94 or 214X of the *Motor Vehicle Act*, R.S.B.C. 1979, c. 288, as the section was before its repeal and replacement or its amendment came into force under the *Motor Vehicle Amendment Act, 1982*,

commits an offence and is liable,

(c) on a first conviction, to a fine of not less than $500 and not more than $2 000 or to imprisonment for not more than 6 months, or to both and

(d) on a subsequent conviction, regardless of when the contravention occurred, to a fine of not less than $500 and not more than $2 000 or to imprisonment for not less than 14 days and not more than one year.

(2) If a person is charged with an offence under subsection (1) that pertains to a prohibition under section 91 or 215, the court hearing the charge may admit into evidence

(a) a certificate of the Insurance Corporation of British Columbia, or

(b) a certificate of the superintendent dated before the date this paragraph comes into force

stating the information required by subsection (4) and if the certificate is admitted into evidence it is proof that the defendant had knowledge of the prohibition in effect at the time of the alleged offence.

(3) If a person is charged with an offence under subsection (1) that pertains to a prohibition under section 92, 93 or 94.2, or to a suspension under section 25, 83, 87, 88, 94 or 214X of the *Motor Vehicle Act*, R.S.B.C. 1979, c. 288, as the section was before its repeal and replacement or its amendment came into force under the *Motor Vehicle Amendment Act, 1982*, the court hearing the charge may admit into evidence a certificate of the superintendent stating the information required by subsection (4) and if the certificate of the superintendent is admitted into evidence it is proof that the defendant had knowledge of the prohibition or suspension in effect at the time of the alleged offence.

(4) If a person is charged with an offence under subsection (1), the certificate referred to in subsection (2) or (3), as the case may be, must state that the prohibition or suspension was in effect on the date of the alleged offence and that the records of the Insurance Corporation of British Columbia or the superintendent, as the case may be,

(a) show that a notice of the prohibition or suspension was mailed by registered or certified mail to the person at the person's most recent address recorded in the records of the corporation and that the corporation or superintendent subsequently received a copy of the confirmation of delivery provided by Canada Post showing a recipient's signature that, from a comparison with the signature on the records of the corporation, appears to be that of the person to whom the notice of prohibition or suspension was sent,

(b) contain a document that

(i) indicates that the person so charged

(A) has acknowledged that he or she is prohibited from driving a motor vehicle, or that his or her driver's licence or his or her right to apply for or to obtain a driver's licence is suspended,

(B) has acknowledged that he or she has received from the corporation or the superintendent a notice of prohibition against driving a motor vehicle or a notice of suspension of his or her driver's licence or of his or her right to apply for or to obtain a driver's licence, or

(C) has surrendered his or her driver's licence to the corporation or the superintendent subsequent to receiving from the corporation or the superintendent a notice of prohibition, relating to a prohibition under section 91, 92 or 93, or a notice of suspension, and

(ii) is signed with a signature that, from a comparison with the signature on the records of the corporation, appears to be that of the person whom the corporation or superintendent intended to prohibit from driving a motor vehicle, or whose driver's licence or right to apply for or to obtain a driver's licence the corporation or superintendent intended to suspend, or to whom the corporation or superintendent mailed a notice of prohibition or suspension, or

(c) contain a certificate of service prescribed under section 94.3(c) showing that a notice of driving prohibition under section 94.1 was personally served on the person.

(5) This section applies to any document contained in the records of the Insurance Corporation of British Columbia or the superintendent, whether that document was signed before, on or after the date this subsection comes into force.
R.S.B.C. 1996 (Supp.), c. 318, s. 26; 1997, c. 31, s. 17; 1999, c. 39, s. 47; 2002, c. 25, s. 49; 2004, c. 68, s. 10 [Amended 2005, c. 2, s. 12.]

Driver to surrender licence

96. (1) If a person is prohibited from driving a motor vehicle under section 91, 92 or 93, he or she must,

(a) if notified of the prohibition by mail, immediately send his or her driver's licence, or any document issued in another jurisdiction that allows him or her to drive a motor vehicle, to the Insurance Corporation of British Columbia, and

Proposed Amendment—96(1)

(1) If a person is prohibited from driving a motor vehicle under section 91, 92 or 93, or if the person's driver's licence is suspended under section 90.1, he or she must,

(a) if notified of the prohibition or suspension by mail, immediately send his or her driver's licence, or any document issued in another jurisdiction that allows him or her to drive a motor vehicle, to the Insurance Corporation of British Columbia, and
1997, c. 43, s. 16(a), (b) [Not in force at date of publication.]

(b) if notified by personal service by a peace officer, sheriff or person authorized by the Insurance Corporation of British Columbia or the superintendent, surrender the person's driver's licence, or any document issued in another jurisdiction that allows the person to drive a motor vehicle, to the service peace officer, sheriff or person for forwarding to the corporation.

(2) A person must immediately surrender his or her driver's licence, or any document issued in another jurisdiction that allows him or her to drive a motor vehicle, to the justice, court clerk or sheriff for forwarding to the Insurance Corporation of British Columbia if the person is prohibited from driving a motor vehicle

(a) under section 98, 99 or 100 of this Act, the *Youth Justice Act*, the *Youth Criminal Justice Act* (Canada) or the *Criminal Code*,

(b) before April 1, 2003, under the *Young Offenders Act* (Canada), as it then was, or

(c) before April 1, 2004, under the *Young Offenders (British Columbia) Act*, as it then was.

(3) If a person fails to comply with subsection (2), a peace officer or sheriff, at the request of the Insurance Corporation of British Columbia, may recover the driver's licence issued to that person under this Act or any document issued in another jurisdiction that allows him or her to drive a motor vehicle.

(4) If a peace officer serves on a person, who is in control of a motor vehicle on a highway or industrial road, a document containing notice that the person is prohibited from driving a motor vehicle, the notice acts as a temporary driver's licence to expire at the time noted on its face, and the prohibition from driving starts immediately on the expiration of the temporary driver's licence.

Proposed Amendment—96(4)

(4) If a peace officer serves on a person, who is in control of a motor vehicle on a highway or industrial road, a document containing notice that the person is prohibited from driving a motor vehicle or that his or her driver's licence is suspended, the notice acts as a temporary driver's licence to expire at the time noted on its face, and the prohibition from driving or the licence suspension, as the case may be, starts immediately on the expiration of the temporary driver's licence. 1997, c. 43, s. 16(c) [Not in force at date of publication.]

(5) A temporary driver's licence issued under subsection (4) is subject to all restrictions and conditions of the driver's licence of the person who is prohibited from driving a motor vehicle.

Proposed Amendment—96(5)

(5) A temporary driver's licence issued under subsection (4) is subject to all restrictions and conditions of the driver's licence of the person who is prohibited from driving a motor vehicle or whose driver's licence is suspended, as the case may be.

1997, c. 43, s. 16(c) [Not in force at date of publication.]

(6) Subsection (4) does not apply if the peace officer serves a person who is already prohibited from driving a motor vehicle or if the person's driver's licence or right to apply for or obtain a driver's licence is already under suspension.

1997, c. 31, s. 18; 2003, c. 85, s. 69; 2004, c. 68, s. 4

Notice of prohibition

97. (1) A prohibition under section 91 is not invalid and must not be held to be invalid on the grounds that the notice of prohibition sent to the person being prohibited from driving under that section is not signed by an officer of the Insurance Corporation of British Columbia.

(2) A prohibition under section 92 or 93 is not invalid and must not be held to be invalid on the grounds that the notice of prohibition sent to the person being prohibited from driving under either of those sections is not signed by the superintendent or deputy superintendent.

1997, c. 31, s. 19

Proposed Amendment—97

Notice of prohibition or licence suspension

97. (1) A prohibition under section 91 is not invalid and must not be held to be invalid on the grounds that the notice of prohibition sent to the person being prohibited from driving under that section is not signed by an officer of the Insurance Corporation of British Columbia.

(2) A prohibition under section 92 or 93, or a licence suspension under section 90.1, is not invalid and must not be held to be invalid on the grounds that the notice of prohibition or of licence suspension, as the case may be, sent to the person being prohibited from driving under section 92 or 93, or sent to the person whose licence is being suspended under section 90.1, is not signed by the superintendent or deputy superintendent.

1997, c. 43, s. 17 [Not in force at time of publication.]

. . .

Prohibition against driving by court

98. (1) For the purpose of this section, **"convicts"** includes the granting of an absolute or conditional discharge and the determination under section 123(2) of the *Motor Vehicle Act*, R.S.B.C. 1979, c. 288, that a contravention took place.

(2) If a court convicts a person of

(a) an offence under this Act, or

(b) [Repealed 2007, c. 14, s. 156]

(c) a motor vehicle related *Criminal Code* offence,

the court may

(d) consider the person's driving record, and

(e) even though the person is or may be subject to another prohibition from driving, prohibit the person from driving a motor vehicle for a definite period of time if the court considers that the facts of the case or the person's driving record or both the facts of the case and his or her driving record when taken together justify the prohibition.

(3) Subsection (2) does not apply if the defendant is convicted of an offence under section 83 or 83.1.

(4) If a court prohibits a person from driving a motor vehicle under this section, the court must order that the prohibition

(a) take effect immediately,

(b) continue for the full day of each day of the prohibition, and

(c) continue for consecutive days.

(5) A person, who is prohibited from driving a motor vehicle under this section for a period of more than 3 years, may make an application to the court that prohibited him or her from driving for a review of the length of the prohibition, after 3 years of the prohibition have elapsed and after notifying the Insurance Corporation of British Columbia.

(6) On an application under subsection (5), the court may, if it considers that it is not contrary to public interest, reduce the length of the prohibition or cancel the prohibition.

(7) If the court reduces the length of a prohibition or cancels a prohibition under subsection (6), it must forthwith notify the Insurance Corporation of British Columbia of its decision.

1997, c. 31, s. 20; 1997, c. 43, s. 18; 2007, c. 14, s. 156

Automatic prohibition against driving on conviction

99. (1) For the purpose of this section, "**convicted**" includes the granting of an absolute or conditional discharge.

(2) A person who is convicted of

(a) an offence under section 95, 102, 224 or 226(1), or

(b) a motor vehicle related *Criminal Code* offence

is automatically and without notice prohibited from driving a motor vehicle for 12 months from the date of sentencing, the date that the passing of sentence is suspended, the date of being granted an absolute or conditional discharge or the date a court imposes a sentence under the *Youth Criminal Justice Act* (Canada) or the *Youth Justice Act*.

2003, c. 85, s. 70

Prohibition against driving for failing to stop

100. (1) A driver of a motor vehicle commits an offence if

(a) he or she

(i) is signalled or requested to stop by a peace officer who is readily identifiable as a peace officer, and

(ii) fails to come to a safe stop, and

(b) a peace officer pursues the driver in order to require him or her to stop.

(2) If a person commits an offence under subsection (1), he or she is liable to a fine of not less than $300 and not more than $2 000 or to imprisonment for not less than 7 days and not more than 6 months, or to both.

Proposed Amendment—100(2)

(2) If a person commits an offence under subsection (1), he or she is liable to a fine of not less than $500 and not more than $2 000 or to imprisonment for not less than 7 days and not more than 6 months, or to both.

1997, c. 30, s. 1 [Not in force at date of publication.]

(3) If a person is convicted of an offence under subsection (1), the court must, even though the person is or may be subject to another prohibition from driving under this Act, prohibit the person from driving a motor vehicle for a period of 2 years from the date of sentencing if the person is also convicted of contravening any of the following provisions of the *Criminal Code* with respect to the same incident:

(a) section 220;

(b) section 221;

(c) section 236;

(d) section 249(1)(a), (3) or (4).

(4) Section 98(4) applies to a prohibition ordered under this section.

(5) If a person is charged with an offence under subsection (1) and the evidence does not prove the offence but does prove a contravention of section 73(1), the person may be convicted of contravening section 73(1).

Stay of prohibition against driving

101. (1) In this section:

"appellate court" means a court to which a person who is prohibited from driving appeals a conviction;

"conviction" means a conviction under which a prohibition has been imposed, and includes the granting of an absolute or conditional discharge and the determination under section 123(2) of the *Motor Vehicle Act*, R.S.B.C. 1979, c. 288, that a contravention took place;

"licence" means a licence authorizing a person to drive, and includes a document issued in another jurisdiction authorizing a person to drive;

"prohibition" means a prohibition on a person from driving a motor vehicle, imposed

(a) under section 98, 99 or 100 of this Act,

(b) under the *Youth Justice Act*, or

(c) before April 1, 2004, by or under the *Young Offenders (British Columbia) Act*, as it then was, and **"prohibited from driving"** has a corresponding meaning;

"stay" means a stay of a prohibition, granted under subsection (2).

(2) A judge of the appellate court may stay a prohibition for a period the judge considers appropriate if a person,

(a) appeals a conviction, and

(b) applies to a judge of the appellate court for an order to stay the prohibition imposed pursuant to the conviction.

(3) An application for a stay shall not be heard unless written notice has been served on the Attorney General not less than 2 days before the day the application is heard.

(4) The Attorney General may appear as respondent on an application for a stay.

(5) On application of

(a) the person who applied for a stay, or

(b) a respondent to vary a stay,

a judge of the appellate court may, in the judge's discretion, vary the period of the stay, extend the stay or, where a stay has expired, grant a new stay.

(6) If a judge of the appellate court orders a stay in respect of a person, the clerk of that court must

(a) return that person's licence, and

(b) send a copy of the order to the Insurance Corporation of British Columbia.

(7) On receiving a copy of an order referred to in subsection (6), the Insurance Corporation of British Columbia must return the licence to the person to whom it was issued.

(8) A prohibition is automatically and without notice reimposed on the day

(a) a stay expires, or

(b) an appeal from the conviction in respect of which a person is prohibited from driving is dismissed.

(9) If a prohibition is reimposed by subsection (8), the number of days during which the prohibition was stayed must be added to the original period of the prohibition, and the prohibition continues for that additional number of days, but

(a) a further stay may be ordered under subsection (2), and

(b) if an appeal from the conviction in respect of which the prohibition from driving was imposed is allowed, the prohibition ends.

(10) If a prohibition is reimposed by subsection (8)(a), the person must forthwith cause his or her licence to be sent to the Insurance Corporation of British Columbia.

(11) If a prohibition is reimposed by subsection (8)(b),

(a) the person must cause his or her licence to be surrendered to the court as soon as practicable after the dismissal, and the prohibition has effect from the date of reimposition whether or not the licence has been surrendered, and

(b) the court must forthwith cause

(i) the surrendered licence to be sent to the Insurance Corporation of British Columbia, and

(ii) the Insurance Corporation of British Columbia to be notified of the dismissal.

(12) If an appeal from a conviction is allowed, the court must forthwith cause the Insurance Corporation of British Columbia to be notified.
1997, c. 31, s. 20; 2003, c. 85, s. 71; 2004, c. 68, s. 4; 2007, c. 14, s. 201 (Sched. 1, item 43)

Driving while prohibited by court order or operation of law

102. A person who drives a motor vehicle on a highway or industrial road while

(a) he or she is prohibited from driving a motor vehicle

(i) under section 98, 99 or 100 of this Act,

(ii) under the *Youth Justice Act*, or

(iii) before April 1, 2004, under the *Young Offenders (British Columbia) Act*, as it then was, or

(b) his or her driver's licence or his or her right to apply for or obtain a driver's licence is suspended under section 82 or 92 of the *Motor Vehicle Act*, R.S.B.C. 1979, c. 288, as the section was before its repeal and replacement came into force under the *Motor Vehicle Amendment Act, 1982*,

commits an offence and is liable,

(c) on a first conviction, to a fine of not less than $500 and not more than $2 000 and to imprisonment for not more than 6 months, or to both, and

(d) on a subsequent conviction, regardless of when the contravention occurred, to a fine of not less than $300 and not more than $2 000 and to imprisonment for not less than 14 days and not more than one year.

Proposed Amendment—102(d)

(d) on a subsequent conviction, regardless of when the contravention occurred, to a fine of not less than $500 and not more than $2 000 and to imprisonment for not less than 14 days and not more than one year.

2004, c. 68, s. 11(b) [Not in force at date of publication.]

2003, c. 85, s. 72; 2004, c. 68, ss. 4, 11(a)

Deemed prior convictions

103. If a person who is convicted of an offence under section 95 or 102 has previously been convicted of an offence under

(a) section 95 or 102, or

(b) section 88.1 or 94.1 of the *Motor Vehicle Act*, R.S.B.C. 1979, c. 288, as the section was before its repeal and replacement came into force under the *Motor Vehicle Amendment Act, 1982*,

that prior conviction is conclusively deemed to be a first conviction for the purpose of determining the punishment to which the person is subject under section 95 or 102.

Reporting conviction or judgment

104. (1) A judge of any court, with respect to each conviction made by the judge for, or each conditional or absolute discharge given by the judge in respect of,

(a) an offence under this Act,

(b) an offence under the *Commercial Transport Act*,

(c) an offence under the *Insurance (Vehicle) Act*, or

(d) a motor vehicle related *Criminal Code* offence,

and every registrar, deputy registrar or court clerk must immediately send the Insurance Corporation of British Columbia a certificate, transcript, copy or record of the conviction.

(2) Every registrar, deputy registrar or court clerk, with respect to each order or judgment of the court in an action for damages resulting from bodily injury to or

the death of a person or from damage to property occasioned by or arising out of the ownership, maintenance, operation or use of a motor vehicle, must immediately send the Insurance Corporation of British Columbia a certificate, transcript or certified copy of the order or judgment.

(3) A certificate, transcript, copy or record sent to the Insurance Corporation of British Columbia under subsection (1) is evidence of the conviction, appeal or proceedings to which it refers.

(4) If a person

(a) is convicted of an offence or given an absolute or conditional discharge, and

(b) is a resident of or has a document from another jurisdiction that allows him or her to drive a motor vehicle,

the Insurance Corporation of British Columbia must send a certificate, transcript of or certified copy of the person's conviction to the person in charge of the registration of motor vehicles or licensing of drivers in the jurisdiction in which the person resides or from which the person has a document that allows him or her to drive a motor vehicle, as the case may be.

(5) If the Insurance Corporation of British Columbia has received notice that a person

(a) is or was prohibited from driving a motor vehicle, or his or her right to apply for or obtain a driver's licence is or was suspended,

(i) under this Act, the *Youth Justice Act*, the *Youth Criminal Justice Act* (Canada) or the *Criminal Code*,

(ii) before April 1, 2003, under the *Young Offenders Act* (Canada), as it then was, or

(iii) before April 1, 2004, under the *Young Offenders (British Columbia) Act*, as it then was, and

(b) is a resident of or has a document from another jurisdiction that allows him or her to drive a motor vehicle,

the corporation must send

(c) a notice of the prohibition or suspension containing a brief statement of the reasons for it, and

(d) the document that allows the person to drive a motor vehicle, if it is in the corporation's possession,

to the person in charge of the registration of motor vehicles or licensing of drivers in the jurisdiction in which the person resides or from which he or she has a document that allows him or here to drive a motor vehicle, as the case may be.
2003, c. 85, s. 73; 2004, c. 68, s. 4; 2003, c. 94, s. 43 (Sched.); 2007, c. 14, ss. 157, 215 (Sched. 15, item 58)

. . .

Impoundment of a motor vehicle: prohibited drivers

105.1 (1) If a peace officer has reasonable and probable grounds to believe that a person has operated a motor vehicle while

(a) the person is prohibited from driving a motor vehicle under

(i) section 92, 93, 94.2, 98, 99 or 215 of this Act,

(ii) the *Youth Justice Act*, the *Youth Criminal Justice Act* (Canada) or the *Criminal Code*,

(iii) the *Young Offenders Act* (Canada), as it read before its repeal by the *Youth Criminal Justice Act* (Canada), or

(iv) the *Young Offenders (British Columbia) Act*, as it read before its repeal by the *Youth Justice Act*, or

(b) the person's driver's licence and his or her right to apply for or obtain a driver's licence are suspended under section 89(1)(b) or (c), 232 or 233,

(c) [Repealed 2004, c. 68, s. 13.]

(d) [Repealed 2004, c. 68, s. 13.]

the peace officer must cause the motor vehicle to be taken to and impounded at a place directed by the peace officer.

(2) If a peace officer is satisfied that the impoundment of a motor vehicle under subsection (1) would

(a) jeopardize the safety of the occupants of the motor vehicle, or

(b) leave the occupants stranded,

the peace officer must arrange for transportation of the occupants of the motor vehicle to the nearest safe area where they can summon an alternative form of transportation.

(3) Personal property present in a motor vehicle that has been impounded under subsection (1), other than personal property attached to or used in connection with the operation of the motor vehicle, must be returned to the owner on request.

(4) Despite subsection (1), if, at any time before a review is conducted under section 105.5, the superintendent is satisfied that a motor vehicle impounded under subsection (1) is stolen property, the superintendent must

(a) order the person who has custody of the motor vehicle under the impoundment to release the motor vehicle to the owner or a person authorized by the owner, if the owner completes a statutory declaration, and

(b) pay to the person having custody of the motor vehicle under the impoundment the costs and charges referred to in section 105.4(2).

(5) Despite subsection (1), if, at any time before a review is conducted under section 105.5, a peace officer is satisfied that a motor vehicle impounded under subsection (1) of this section is stolen property, the peace officer must

(a) order the person who has custody of the motor vehicle under the impoundment to release the motor vehicle to the owner or a person authorized by the owner, and

(b) promptly give notice to the superintendent of the release of the impounded motor vehicle.

(6) After receiving the notice referred to in subsection (5)(b), the superintendent must pay to the person who had custody of the motor vehicle the impoundment costs and charges referred to in section 105.4(2)

R.S.B.C. 1996 (Supp.), c. 318, s. 37; 1997, c. 43, s. 22; 2002, c. 25, s. 54; 2003, c. 85, s. 75; 2004, c. 68, s. 13

Period of impoundment

105.2 (1) A motor vehicle impounded under section 105.1 is to remain impounded for a period of 60 days from the day it is impounded.

(2) Despite subsection (1), if a motor vehicle impounded under section 105.1 is owned by a person who, within 2 years before the day of the impoundment, was the owner of a motor vehicle that was impounded under section 105.1 and that impoundment was not revoked under section 105.7, the motor vehicle is to remain impounded for a period of 90 days from the date it is impounded.

(3) If a motor vehicle is subject to the period of impoundment authorized under subsection (2), the superintendent must give notice to

(a) the registered owner of the motor vehicle, and

(b) the person who has custody of the motor vehicle under the impoundment

that, subject to the superintendent revoking the impoundment under section 105.7 or reducing the period of impoundment under section 105.8, the motor vehicle will not be released until the expiry of the period of impoundment authorized under subsection (2).

(4) The notice required by subsection (3)(a) must be sent by mail to the last known address of the registered owner as shown in the records maintained by the Insurance Corporation of British Columbia.

R.S.B.C. 1996 (Supp.), c. 318, ss. 37, 42; 2002, c. 25, s. 51; 2004, c. 68, s. 14

Duties of peace officer

105.3 (1) A peace officer who impounds a motor vehicle under section 105.1 must

(a) complete a notice of impoundment,

(b) give a copy of the notice of impoundment to the driver and the person who has custody of the motor vehicle under the impoundment,

(c) forward to the superintendent

(i) a report, in the form established by the superintendent, sworn or solemnly affirmed by the peace officer, and

(ii) a copy of the notice of impoundment, and

(d) retain a copy of the notice of impoundment.

(2) When the superintendent receives a copy of the notice of impoundment under subsection (1)(c)(ii), the superintendent must promptly send a copy of that

notice by mail to the last known address of the registered owner of the motor vehicle as shown in the records maintained by the Insurance Corporation of British Columbia.

(3) The notice of impoundment must contain

(a) a statement of the right to have the impoundment reviewed by the superintendent under section 105.5,

(b) instructions describing how to apply for that review,

(c) a statement that if the owner of the motor vehicle does not apply for a review under section 105.5, the vehicle will be impounded for the period authorized under section 105.2, and

(d) a statement that if the owner of the motor vehicle does not pay the costs and charges referred to in section105.4(2), the motor vehicle may be disposed of under the *Warehouse Lien Act* or under section 105.4(6) of this Act.

R.S.B.C. 1996 (Supp.), c. 318, ss. 37, 38; 2002, c. 25, ss. 51, 55

. . .

Review of impoundment

105.5 (1) The owner of a motor vehicle impounded under section 105.1 may, within 30 days of becoming aware of the impoundment, apply to the superintendent for a review of the impoundment by

(a) filing an application for review with the superintendent, and

(b) paying to the superintendent

(i) the prescribed application fee, and

(ii) the prescribed hearing fee.

(2) The application for review must be in the form, contain the information and be completed in the manner required by the superintendent.

(3) The applicant may attach to the application for review any sworn statements or other evidence that the applicant wishes the superintendent to consider.

(4) The filing of an application for review does not stay the impoundment of the motor vehicle.

(5) The superintendent is not required to hold an oral hearing unless the applicant

(a) requests an oral hearing at the time of filing the application for review, and

(b) pays the prescribed oral hearing fees.

(6) If a person requests an oral hearing and fails to appear on the date and at the time and place arranged for the hearing, without prior notice to the superintendent, the right to an oral hearing is deemed to have been waived by the person.

R.S.B.C. 1996 (Supp.), c. 318, s. 41

. . .

Compassionate release of motor vehicle

105.9 (1) Any person who

(a) holds a valid licence or permit, issued under this Act or in another jurisdiction, to operate a motor vehicle,

(b) is not prohibited from driving a motor vehicle

(i) under this Act, the *Youth Justice Act*, the *Youth Criminal Justice Act* (Canada) or the *Criminal Code*,

(ii) before April 1, 2003, under the *Young Offenders Act* (Canada), as it then was, or

(iii) before April 1, 2004, under the *Young Offenders (British Columbia) Act*, as it then was, and

(c) is cohabiting with the owner of a motor vehicle at the time the vehicle is impounded under section 105.1,

is eligible to apply for the release of the motor vehicle under subsection (2).

(2) An eligible person, within 30 days of the impoundment of the motor vehicle under section 105.1, may apply to the superintendent for the release of the vehicle on the grounds that

(a) the impoundment of the motor vehicle

(i) will cause the eligible person to suffer a loss or curtailment of employment or educational opportunities, or

(ii) will prevent the eligible person, or someone under the care of the eligible person, from obtaining medical treatment, and

(b) the eligible person has no reasonable alternative form of transportation, including public transportation, that would

(i) prevent the loss or curtailment referred to in paragraph (a)(i), or

(ii) allow the medical treatment referred to in paragraph (a)(ii) to be obtained.

(3) The applicant must

(a) apply in a form acceptable to the superintendent,

(b) provide the superintendent with any information the superintendent may reasonably require, and

(c) pay to the superintendent the prescribed application fee.

(4) If the superintendent is satisfied, with respect to an application, that the grounds set out in subsection (2) have been established, the superintendent may,

(a) with the consent of the owner of the motor vehicle, and

(b) on receiving payment of the prescribed vehicle release fee,

subject to the lien described in section 105.4(2), order the person who has custody of the motor vehicle under the impoundment to release the motor vehicle to the applicant.

(5) If a motor vehicle has been released under this section during the course of an impoundment that occurred in respect of a particular period of prohibition under a provision referred to in section 105.1(1), no further application for the release of a motor vehicle may be made under this section with respect to an impoundment that occurred in respect of that same period of prohibition.

R.S.B.C. 1996 (Supp.), c. 318, s. 41; 2003, c. 85, s. 76; 2004, c. 68, s. 4

. . .

24 hour prohibition

215. (1) In this section,

"approved screening device" means a device prescribed by the Lieutenant Governor in Council for the purposes of this section;

"driver" includes a person having the care or control of a motor vehicle on a highway or industrial road whether or not the motor vehicle is in motion.

(2) A peace officer may, at any time or place on a highway or industrial road if the peace officer has reasonable and probable grounds to believe that a driver's ability to drive a motor vehicle is affected by alcohol,

(a) request the driver to drive the motor vehicle, under the direction of the peace officer, to the nearest place off the travelled portion of the highway or industrial road,

(b) serve the driver with a notice of driving prohibition, and

(c) if the driver is in possession of a driver's licence, request the driver to surrender that licence.

(3) A peace officer may, at any time or place on a highway or industrial road if the peace officer has reasonable and probable grounds to believe that a driver's ability to drive a motor vehicle is affected by a drug, other than alcohol,

(a) request the driver to drive the motor vehicle, under the direction of the peace officer, to the nearest place off the travelled portion of the highway or industrial road,

(b) serve the driver with a notice of driving prohibition, and

(c) if the driver is in possession of a driver's licence, request the driver to surrender that licence.

(4) If a peace officer requests a driver to surrender his or her driver's licence under this section, the driver must forthwith surrender to the peace officer his or her driver's licence issued under this Act or any document issued in another jurisdiction that allows him to drive or operate a motor vehicle.

(5) Unless the prohibition from driving a motor vehicle is terminated under subsection (6) or (8), the driver is automatically prohibited from driving a motor vehicle for a period of 24 hours from the time the peace officer served the driver with a notice of driving prohibition under subsection (2) or (3).

(6) If a driver, who is served with a notice of driving prohibition under subsection (2), forthwith requests a peace officer to administer and does undergo as soon as practicable a test that indicates that his or her blood alcohol level does not

exceed 50 mg of alcohol in 100 mL of blood, the prohibition from driving is terminated.

(6.1) A test referred to in subsection (6) may be performed with an approved screening device.

(6.2) Despite subsection (6), a driver who is served with a notice of driving prohibition does not have a right to request or undergo a test under subsection (6) if

(a) the peace officer who served the notice first performed a test of the driver's blood alcohol level with an approved screening device,

(b) the test indicated that the driver's blood alcohol level exceeded 50 mg of alcohol in 100mL of blood, and

(c) the peace officer used the results of the test as part of the basis on which the peace officer formed reasonable and probable grounds to believe that the driver's ability to drive a motor vehicle was affected by alcohol.

(7) [Repealed 2004, c. 68, s. 18(d).]

(8) If a driver, who is served with a notice of driving prohibition under subsection (3), satisfies a peace officer having charge of the matter that his or her ability to drive a motor vehicle is not affected by a drug, other than alcohol, the prohibition from driving is terminated.

(9) A peace officer acting under subsection (2) need not hold the opinion that the blood alcohol level of the driver exceeds 50 mg of alcohol in 100 mL of blood.

(10) If a peace officer prohibits a person from driving a motor vehicle under this section, the peace officer shall cause a report of the prohibition to be delivered to the Insurance Corporation of British Columbia unless the prohibition from driving a motor vehicle is terminated under subsection (6).

(11) The report referred to in subsection (10) shall be in a form established by the Insurance Corporation of British Columbia.

(12) The Lieutenant Governor in Council may prescribe an approved screening device for the purposes of this section.

1997, c. 31, s. 8; 2004, c. 68, s. 18

Review of driving prohibition

215.1 (1) A person may, within the prescribed number of days after being served with a notice of driving prohibition under section 215(2), apply to the superintendent for a review of the driving prohibition by

(a) filing an application for review with the superintendent, and

(b) paying to the superintendent the application fee prescribed by the Lieutenant Governor in Council.

(2) For the purposes of subsection (1), the Lieutenant Governor in Council may prescribe the number of days, which number must not be less than 7, within which a person may apply for a review of a driving prohibition.

(3) An application for review must be in the form, contain the information and be completed in the manner required by the superintendent.

(4) An applicant may attach to the application for review any written statements or other evidence that the applicant wishes the superintendent to consider.

(5) The superintendent must conduct a review under this section on the basis of written submissions and must not hold an oral hearing.

2004, c. 68, s. 19

Considerations

215.2 In a review of a driving prohibition under section 215.1, the superintendent may only consider

(a) the report of the prohibition delivered under section 215(10) and other relevant information provided by the peace officer with the report, and

(b) relevant information provided by the person on whom the notice of driving prohibition was served.

2004, c. 68, s. 19

Decision of the superintendent

215.3 If, after considering an application for review under section 215.1, the superintendent is satisfied that

(a) the person on whom the notice of driving prohibition was served had the right to request and requested that the peace officer administer a test to indicate his or her blood alcohol level but the peace officer failed to provide the person with the opportunity to undergo the test, or

(b) the person on whom the notice of driving prohibition was served was not a driver within the meaning of section 215(1), the superintendent must revoke the driving prohibition.

2004, c. 68, s. 19

24 hour impoundment of motor vehicle

215.4 (1) If a peace officer serves a driver with a notice of driving prohibition under section 215(2) or (3), the peace officer may, if the peace officer believes that impoundment is necessary to prevent the driver from driving or operating the motor vehicle before the prohibition expires, immediately cause the motor vehicle that the driver was operating or of which the driver had care or control to be taken to a place directed by the peace officer and impounded there for a period of 24 hours.

(2) If a peace officer is satisfied that the impoundment of a motor vehicle under subsection (1) would

(a) jeopardize the safety of the occupants of the motor vehicle, or

(b) leave the occupants stranded, the peace officer must arrange for transportation of the occupants of the motor vehicle to the nearest safe area where they can summon an alternative form of transportation.

(3) The owner or driver of a motor vehicle that is impounded under subsection (1) may remove any cargo or other personal property that is in or on the motor vehicle.

(4) If a motor vehicle is impounded under subsection (1), the peace officer must take all reasonable steps to notify the owner of the motor vehicle.

(5) A person must not remove or permit the removal of a motor vehicle from the place where it is impounded under subsection (1) before the end of the 24 hour period unless the person is authorized to do so by a peace officer or a court.

(6) All the costs and charges for towing, care and storage of a motor vehicle impounded under subsection (1) are a lien on the motor vehicle, and the lien may be enforced in the manner provided under the *Warehouse Lien Act.*

2004, c. 68, s. 19

Driving with more than 80 milligrams of alcohol in blood

224. Everyone who, on a highway or industrial road, drives a motor vehicle or has the care or control of a motor vehicle, whether it is in motion or not, having consumed alcohol in such a quantity that the proportion of alcohol in his or her blood exceeds 80 milligrams of alcohol in 100 millilitres of blood, commits an offence and is liable on conviction to a fine of not less than $100 and not more than $2 000 or to imprisonment for not less than 7 days and not more than 6 months, or to both.

Demand for blood sample

225. (1) If a peace officer on reasonable and probable grounds believes that a person has, within the preceding 2 hours, committed an offence under section 224, the peace officer may, by demand made to that person forthwith or as soon as practicable, require him or her to provide then or as soon after that as is practicable a sufficient sample of his or her blood, as in the opinion of the person taking the sample is necessary, to enable a proper analysis to be made in order to determine the proportion, if any, of alcohol in his or her blood, and to accompany the peace officer for the purpose of enabling that sample to be taken.

(2) If the person referred to in subsection (1) is incapable, due to physical or mental trauma, of comprehending the nature of a demand under subsection (1), a sufficient sample of his or her blood, as in the opinion of the person taking the sample is necessary, to enable a proper analysis to be made in order to determine the proportion, if any, of alcohol in his or her blood, may be taken from that person without a demand being made under subsection (1).

(3) A blood sample may be taken under this section only by a person or class of persons approved by order of the Attorney General or a medical practitioner or registered nurse authorized under an enactment to practice as a medical practitioner or registered nurse in British Columbia.

(4) A blood sample taken under this section may only be analyzed by a person or class of persons approved by order of the Attorney General using a method approved as suitable for the purposes of this section by order of the Attorney General.

2003, c. 57, s. 54 [Amended 2004, c. 23, s. 13]

Refusal to give blood sample

226. (1) A person who without reasonable excuse fails or refuses to comply with a demand made under section 225(1) commits an offence and is liable on conviction to a fine of not less than $100 and not more than $2 000 or to imprisonment for not less than 7 days and not more than 6 months, or to both.

(2) [Repealed 1997, c. 43, s. 31.]

1997, c. 43, s. 31

Proof of blood sample

227. (1) In a proceeding under section 224, if a blood sample of the defendant was taken

(a) under a demand made under section 225(1) or pursuant to section 225(2), and

(b) as soon as practicable after the time when the offence was alleged to have been committed and in any event no later than 2 hours after that time,

evidence of the result of an analysis of the blood sample is, in the absence of any evidence to the contrary, proof of the proportion of alcohol in the blood of the defendant at the time when the offence was alleged to have been committed.

(2) In a proceeding under section 224, if a blood sample of the defendant was taken under a demand made under section 225(1) or under section 225(2), a certificate of a person referred to in section 225(3) or (4) stating that he or she has

(a) taken the blood sample of the defendant, or

(b) made an analysis of the blood sample of the defendant and stating the result of his or her analysis

is evidence of the statements contained in the certificate without proof of the signature of the person appearing to have signed the certificate.

(3) In a proceeding under section 224, if a blood sample of the defendant was taken under section 225(2), a certificate of a medical practitioner stating that, in his or her opinion, at the time the blood sample was taken the defendant was incapable, due to physical or mental trauma, of comprehending the nature of a demand under section 225(1) is evidence of the statements contained in the certificate without proof of the signature of the person appearing to have signed the certificate.

(4) In a proceeding under section 224, if a blood sample of the defendant was taken under a demand made under section 225(1) or under section 225(2), the proportion of alcohol in the blood sample of the defendant at the time of the analysis is deemed to be the same as the proportion of alcohol in the blood of the defendant when the sample was taken, unless the defendant proves otherwise.

(5) A defendant against whom a certificate described in subsection (2) or (3) is produced may, with leave of the court, require the attendance of the person who made the certificate for the purposes of cross examination.

(6) A certificate must not be received in evidence under subsection (2) or (3) unless, before the trial, the defendant has received reasonable notice that the certificate will be introduced and has received a copy of the certificate.

(7) The Lieutenant Governor in Council may prescribe the form and content of certificates to be used in this section.

Civil liability

228. No action lies, for damages or otherwise, against any person as a result of the taking or analyzing of a blood sample under section 225 except an action for damages arising out of negligence in technical procedures used in taking the blood.

No legal obligation

229. Notwithstanding anything in sections 224 to 228, a person authorized to take a blood sample under section 225(3) may decline to take a blood sample from a person if to do so would, in the opinion of a medical practitioner, endanger that person's health or life.

. . .

Suspension on conviction for certain offences

232. (1) In this section:

"convicted" includes the granting of an absolute or conditional discharge;

"date of sentencing" includes

(a) the date that the passing of sentence is suspended,

(b) the date that an absolute or a conditional discharge is granted, or

(c) the date that a court

(i) imposes a sentence under the *Youth Justice Act* or the *YouthCriminal Justice Act* (Canada), or

(ii) makes a disposition under the *Young Offenders (British Columbia)Act*, as it read before its repeal by the *Youth Justice Act*, or a disposition under the *Young Offenders Act* (Canada), as it read before its repeal by the *Youth Criminal Justice Act* (Canada);

"motor vehicle related Criminal Code offence" does not include an offence under section 259(4) of the *Criminal Code*.

(2) If a person is convicted of a motor vehicle related *Criminal Code* offence or under a provision that is enacted by a state of the United States of America and that is designated by regulation, his or her driver's licence and his or her right to apply for or obtain a driver's licence are deemed to be suspended for the period referred to in subsection (3).

(3) A suspension under subsection (2) is effective from the date of sentencing, and is, subject to section 233, effective for the following period:

(a) on the first conviction, for one year;

(b) on the first subsequent conviction, whether or not that conviction is under the same provision as the conviction referred to in paragraph (a), for 3 years;

(c) on the second subsequent conviction or an additional subsequent conviction, whether or not that conviction is under the same provision as the convictions referred to in paragraph (a) or (b), indefinitely.

(4) Subsection (3) applies only if,

(a) for subsection (3)(a), the conviction is in respect of an offence committed after the coming into force of this section,

(b) for subsection (3)(b), the first subsequent conviction is in respect of an offence committed after the coming into force of this section and the previous conviction was not more than 5 years before the date on which this section comes into force, and

(c) for subsection (3)(c), the second subsequent conviction or the additional subsequent conviction is in respect of an offence committed after the coming into force of this section and the previous convictions were not more than 5 years before the date on which this section comes into force.

(5) Subsection (3)(b) and (c) does not apply if the subsequent conviction is more than 10 years after the previous conviction.

(6) Despite subsection (3), if the subsequent conviction is within 10 years after the previous conviction, a conviction that preceded the previous conviction by less than 10 years must be taken into account for the purpose of subsection (3)(b) and (c).

1997, c. 43, s. 33; 2003, c. 85, s. 77; B.C. Reg. 346/2006, s. 1(i) (Sched., item 13)

Reinstatement of suspended licence

233. (1) In this section, **"program"** means a remedial program or component of it or an ignition interlock program specified by the superintendent.

(2) The superintendent must notify the Insurance Corporation of British Columbia of a person's right

(a) to have his or her suspended driver's licence reinstated or to apply for a new driver's licence, as the case may be, in the following circumstances:

(i) the person's driver's licence is suspended and the person's right to apply for or obtain a driver's licence is suspended under section 232(2) and (3)(a) or (b);

(ii) the person has,

(A) to the satisfaction of the superintendent, attended or participated in and completed a program as required by the superintendent, and

(B) paid the prescribed fees, or

(b) to apply for a driver's licence at the end of a suspension period of 5 years in the following circumstances:

(i) the person's driver's licence is suspended and the person's right to apply for or obtain a driver's licence is suspended under section 232(2) and (3)(c);

(ii) the person has,

(A) to the satisfaction of the superintendent, attended or participated in and completed a program as required by the superintendent, and

(B) paid the prescribed fees.

(3) If it is, in the superintendent's opinion, in the public interest for a person in the circumstances referred to in subsection (2)(a) or (b) to participate in an ignition interlock program specified by the superintendent and the person pays the prescribed fees for the ignition interlock program, the superintendent may require a statement in, endorsement on or attachment to the person's driver's licence adding a condition of the driver's licence that the person participate in and complete the ignition interlock program, to the satisfaction of the superintendent.

(4) The superintendent may

(a) as part of a condition of a driver's licence under subsection (3), specify a date by which or a period of time during which the person must complete the program, and

(b) at any time extend, change or cancel a date or period of time specified under paragraph (a).

(5) Section 25(13) applies to a condition imposed in respect of a person's driver's licence under this section.

(6) If the superintendent notifies the Insurance Corporation of British Columbia

(a) under subsection (2)(a), the corporation must,

(i) on the expiry of the suspension, reinstate the driver's licence if

(A) the driver's licence has not expired or been cancelled,

(B) the person is otherwise qualified to hold the licence, and

(C) there is no other suspension, cancellation or prohibition under this Act in respect of the driver's licence or the person, or

(ii) on receipt of the notification, allow the person to apply for a new driver's licence, subject to any other suspension, cancellation or prohibition under this Act, or

(b) under subsection (2)(b), the corporation must, at the expiry of the suspension period, allow the person to apply for a new driver's licence, subject to any other suspension, cancellation or prohibition under this Act.

(7) The suspension of a person's driver's licence and of the person's right to apply for or obtain a driver's licence is extended

(a) if, on the expiry of a suspension under section 232(2) and (3)(a) or (b), the person has not

(A) attended or participated in and completed a program to the satisfaction of the superintendent, and

(B) paid the prescribed fees, and

(b) until the person has done the things referred to in paragraph (a).

1997, c. 43, s. 33; 2004, c. 68, s. 20

. . .

Definitions

241. In this Part:

"race" means circumstances in which, taking into account the condition of the road, traffic, visibility and weather, the operator of a motor vehicle is operating the motor vehicle without reasonable consideration for other persons using the highway or in a manner that may cause harm to an individual, by doing any of the following:

(a) outdistancing or attempting to outdistance one or more other motor vehicles;

(b) preventing or attempting to prevent one or more other motor vehicles from passing;

(c) driving at excessive speed in order to arrive at or attempt to arrive at a given destination ahead of one or more other motor vehicles;

"serious offence" means any of the following:

(a) a motor vehicle related *Criminal Code* offence;

(b) an offence under section 90.4, 95, 100, 102, 224, 226 or 234(1) of this Act;

(c) an offence under section 144(1) or 148 of this Act, if the charge is to be commenced by the laying of an information in Form 2 of the *Offence Act*.

2002, c. 49, s. 2

Impoundment of a motor vehicle for racing

242. (1) If a peace officer has reasonable and probable grounds to believe that a person has operated a motor vehicle on a highway in a race and the peace officer intends to charge the person who operated the motor vehicle with a serious offence, the peace officer may cause the motor vehicle to be taken to, and impounded for 48 hours at, a place directed by the peace officer.

(2) If a peace officer is satisfied that the impoundment of a motor vehicle under subsection (1) would

(a) jeopardize the safety of the occupants of the motor vehicle, or

(b) leave the occupants stranded,

the peace officer must arrange for transportation of the occupants of the motor vehicle to the nearest safe area where they can summon an alternative form of transportation.

(3) The owner or operator of a motor vehicle impounded under subsection (1) may remove any cargo or other personal property that is in or on the motor vehicle.

(4) Despite subsection (1), if a peace officer is satisfied that a motor vehicle impounded under that subsection is stolen property, the peace officer must

(a) order the person who has custody of the impounded motor vehicle to release the motor vehicle to the owner or a person authorized by the owner, and

(b) promptly give notice to the superintendent of the release of the impounded motor vehicle.

(5) After receiving the notice referred to in subsection (4)(b), the superintendent must pay to the person who had custody of the motor vehicle the impoundment costs and charges referred to in section 105.4(2).

(6) If a motor vehicle is impounded under subsection (1), the peace officer must take all reasonable steps to notify the owner of the motor vehicle.

(7) A person must not remove or permit the removal of a motor vehicle from the place where it is impounded under subsection (1) before the end of the 48 hour period unless the person is authorized to do so

(a) by an order of a peace officer under subsection (4), (8) or (11), or

(b) by an order of a court.

(8) A peace officer must order the release of a motor vehicle on request by an owner, if

(a) the owner is not the person whose operation of the motor vehicle is the reason for the impoundment, and

(b) the motor vehicle is to be released, after payment of the costs and charges referred to in section 105.4(2), to the owner or a person other than the person whose operation of the motor vehicle is the reason for the impoundment.

(9) When the impoundment period referred to in subsection (1) has elapsed, the owner or a person authorized by the owner may obtain the release of the motor vehicle after paying the costs and charges referred to in section 105.4(2).

(10) An impoundment under this section must be considered to be an impoundment for the purposes of section 243(1)(b) unless the impoundment is withdrawn by the peace officer under subsection (11) of this section.

(11) A peace officer may withdraw an impoundment before the 48 hour period has elapsed and may order the release of the motor vehicle, subject to payment of the costs and charges referred to in section 105.4(2).

(12) Sections 105.4 and 105.92 apply to an impoundment under sections 242 and 243.

(13) Sections 105.9(1) to (4), 105.91, 105.93, 105.94 and 105.95(1) to (3) apply to an impoundment under section 243.

2002, c. 49, s. 2

30 day impoundment

243. (1) A peace officer may cause a motor vehicle to be taken to, and impounded for 30 days at, a place directed by the peace officer if the peace officer has reasonable and probable grounds to believe that

(a) a person has operated the motor vehicle on a highway in a race and the peace officer intends to charge the person who operated the motor vehicle with a serious offence, and

(b) the person who operated the motor vehicle had, within 2 years before the day of the impoundment, operated a motor vehicle that was impounded under section 242, and that impoundment was not withdrawn under section 242(11).

(2) If a peace officer is satisfied that the impoundment of a motor vehicle under subsection (1) would

(a) jeopardize the safety of the occupants of the motor vehicle, or

(b) leave the occupants stranded,

the peace officer must arrange for transportation of the occupants of the motor vehicle to the nearest safe area where they can summon an alternative form of transportation.

(3) The owner or operator of a motor vehicle impounded under subsection (1) may remove any cargo or other personal property that is in or on the motor vehicle.

(4) Despite subsection (1), if, at any time before a review is conducted under section 246, the superintendent is satisfied that a motor vehicle impounded under subsection (1) of this section is stolen property, the superintendent must

(a) order the person who has custody of the impounded motor vehicle to release the motor vehicle to the owner or a person authorized by the owner, if the owner completes a statutory declaration, and

(b) pay to the person who has custody of the impounded motor vehicle the costs and charges referred to in section 105.4(2).

(5) Despite subsection (1), if, at any time before a review is conducted under section 246, a peace officer is satisfied that a motor vehicle impounded under subsection (1) of this section is stolen property, the peace officer must

(a) order the person who has custody of the impounded motor vehicle to release the motor vehicle to the owner or a person authorized by the owner, and

(b) promptly give notice to the superintendent of the release of the impounded motor vehicle.

(6) After receiving the notice referred to in subsection (5)(b), the superintendent must pay to the person who had custody of the motor vehicle the impoundment costs and charges referred to in section 105.4(2).

2002, c. 49, s. 2

Duties of peace officer

244. (1) A peace officer who impounds a motor vehicle under section 242 or 243 must complete, retain a copy of, and forward to the superintendent an incident report, in the form established by the superintendent, detailing the circumstances that resulted in the impoundment, the serious offence with which the operator is being charged and any other relevant information.

(2) The incident report forms part of the driving record of the operator of the impounded motor vehicle and may be used, in conjunction with any other relevant information, for the purposes of imposing a prohibition under section 93.

(3) A peace officer who impounds a motor vehicle under section 242 or 243 must do all of the following:

(a) complete a notice of impoundment;

(b) give a copy of the incident report to the operator of the motor vehicle;

(c) give a copy of the notice of impoundment to the operator of the motor vehicle and to the person who has custody of the impounded motor vehicle;

(d) unless an impoundment is withdrawn under section 242(11), forward to the superintendent

(i) the motor vehicle impoundment report, in the form established by the superintendent, sworn or solemnly affirmed by the peace officer, and

(ii) a copy of the notice of impoundment,

(e) retain a copy of the notice of impoundment.

(4) When the superintendent receives a copy of the notice of impoundment under subsection (3)(d)(ii), the superintendent must promptly send a copy of that notice by mail to the last known address of the registered owner of the motor vehicle as shown in the records maintained by the Insurance Corporation of British Columbia.

(5) The notice of impoundment for an impoundment for 48 hours must contain all of the following:

(a) a statement of the right of the owner to have the motor vehicle released under section 242(8);

(b) a statement that the motor vehicle will be impounded for 48 hours;

(c) a statement that if the owner of the motor vehicle does not pay the costs and charges referred to in section 105.4(2), the motor vehicle may be disposed of under the *Warehouse Lien Act* or under section 105.4(6) of this Act.

(6) The notice of impoundment for an impoundment for 30 days must contain all of the following:

(a) a statement of the right to have the impoundment reviewed by the superintendent under section 246;

(b) instructions describing how to apply for that review;

(c) a statement that if the owner of the motor vehicle does not apply for a review under section 246, the motor vehicle will be impounded for 30 days.

(d) a statement that if the owner of the motor vehicle does not pay the costs and charges referred to in section 105.4(2), the motor vehicle may be disposed of under the *Warehouse Lien Act* or under section 105.4(6) of this Act.

2002, c. 49, s. 2

Release to owner who was not the operator

245. (1) The superintendent must authorize the release of a motor vehicle impounded under section 243 on request by an owner in accordance with subsection (2) of this section, if

(a) the owner is not the person whose operation of the motor vehicle is the reason for the impoundment, and

(b) the motor vehicle is to be released to the owner or a person other than the person whose operation of the motor vehicle is the reason for the impoundment.

(2) A request by an owner under subsection (1) must be in the form, contain the information and be completed in the manner required by the superintendent.

2002, c. 49, s. 2

Review of impoundment

246. The owner of a motor vehicle who operated the motor vehicle in a manner that resulted in the motor vehicle being impounded under section 243 may, within 30 days of the impoundment, apply to the superintendent for a review of the impoundment and section 105.5 applies.

2002, c. 49, s. 2

Considerations for review under section 246

247. In a review under section 246, the superintendent must consider all of the following:

(a) the driving record of the applicant;

(b) an incident report forwarded under section 244(1);

(c) a motor vehicle impoundment report forwarded under section 244(3)(d)(i);

(d) if an oral hearing is held, in addition to the reports referred to in paragraphs (b) and (c), any relevant evidence given or representations made at the hearing;

(e) any relevant sworn or solemnly affirmed statements and any other relevant information, including any report to Crown counsel or other information forwarded by the peace officer.

2002, c. 49, s. 2

Decision of the superintendent

248. (1) If, after considering an application for review under section 246 in respect of a motor vehicle impounded under section 243(1), the superintendent is satisfied that at the time of the impoundment the motor vehicle was not operated as described in section 243(1)(a) or that the applicant was not subject to a 30 day impoundment under section 243, the superintendent must do all of the following:

(a) revoke the impoundment;

(b) order the person who has custody of the impounded motor vehicle to release the motor vehicle to the owner or a person authorized by the owner;

(c) pay to the person who has custody of the impounded motor vehicle the costs and charges referred to in section 105.4(2);

(d) direct that the application and hearing fees paid be refunded to the applicant.

(2) The decision of the superintendent under subsection (1), and the reasons for the decision, must be in writing and a copy must be sent to the applicant within 7 days of the date the application was considered or the oral hearing was held.

(3) The copy referred to in subsection (2) must be sent to the applicant

(a) at the last known address of the applicant as shown in the records of the Insurance Corporation of British Columbia, or

(b) at the address shown in the application for review, if that address is different from the last known address in the records of the Insurance Corporation of British Columbia.

2002, c. 49, s. 2

Ontario

Highway Traffic Act, R.S.O. 1990, c. H.8, sections 41, 41.1–41.3, 42–44, 46, 47(1), 47.1, 48, 48.1–48.3, 50.1–50.3, 55.1 and 198.5

Suspension on conviction for certain offences

41. (1) Subject to subsections 41.1(1), (2) and (3), the driver's licence of a person who is convicted of an offence,

(a) under section 220, 221 or 236 of the *Criminal Code* (Canada) committed by means of a motor vehicle or a street car within the meaning of this Act or a motorized snow vehicle within the meaning of the *Motorized Snow Vehicles Act*;

(b) under section 249, 249.1, 249.2, 249.3, 249.4 or 252 of the *Criminal Code* (Canada) committed while driving or having the care, charge or control of a motor vehicle or street car within the meaning of this Act or a motorized snow vehicle within the meaning of the *Motorized Snow Vehicles Act*;

(b.1) under section 253 or 255 of the *Criminal Code* (Canada) committed while,

(i) driving or having the care, charge or control of a motor vehicle or street car within the meaning of this Act or a motorized snow vehicle within the meaning of the *Motorized Snow Vehicles Act*, or

(ii) operating or having the care or control of a vessel within the meaning of section 48;

(c) under section 254 of the *Criminal Code* (Canada) committed in relation to,

(i) driving or having the care, charge or control of a motor vehicle or street car within the meaning of this Act or a motorized snow vehicle within the meaning of the *Motorized Snow Vehicles Act*, or

(ii) operating or having the care or control of a vessel within the meaning of section 48;

(d) under a provision that is enacted by a state of the United States of America and that is designated by the regulations; or

(e) referred to in a predecessor to this subsection,

is thereupon suspended,

(f) upon the first conviction, for one year;

(g) upon the first subsequent conviction, for three years; and

(h) upon the second subsequent conviction or an additional subsequent conviction, indefinitely.

Determining subsequent conviction

(2) In determining whether a conviction is a subsequent conviction or an additional subsequent conviction, as the case may be, for the purpose of clauses

(1)(g) and (h), the only question to be considered is the sequence of convictions and no consideration shall be given to the sequence of commission of offences or whether any offence occurred before or after any conviction.

Ten-year limitation

(3) Clauses (1)(g) and (h) do not apply when the subsequent conviction is more than 10 years after the previous conviction.

Exception

(3.01) Despite subsection (3), when the subsequent conviction is within 10 years after the previous conviction, all previous convictions that were not followed by a 10-year period without a conviction shall be taken into account for the purpose of clauses (1)(g) and (h).

Transition

(3.02) Despite subsections (3) and (3.01), a conviction that was more than five years before the date on which this subsection comes into force shall not be taken into account for the purpose of clauses (1)(g) and (h).

Suspension concurrent with s. 48.3 suspension

(3.1) The licence suspension under this section runs concurrently with the remaining portion, if any, of a suspension under section 48.3.

Order extending suspension

(4) Where the court or judge, as the case may be, making the conviction referred to in subsection (1) considers it to be desirable for the protection of the public using the highways, the court or judge may make an order extending the suspension of the licence,

(a) for any period in addition to the period specified in subsection (1) that the court or judge considers proper, if the person is liable to imprisonment for life in respect of the offence; or

(b) for any period in addition to the period specified in subsection (1) that the court or judge considers proper but not exceeding three years, if the person is not liable to imprisonment for life in respect of the offence.

Reduced suspension with ignition interlock condition

(4.1) A person whose driver's licence is suspended under subsection (1) for an offence listed in clause (1)(b.1) or (c) may apply to the Registrar for the reinstatement of his or her licence before the end of the licence suspension period, and the Registrar may reinstate the person's licence before the end of the licence suspension period, if the person has been notified under section 57 that he or she is required to participate in a conduct review program under that section that consists of or includes an ignition interlock program.

Order for discharge

(5) This section applies in the same manner as if a person were convicted of an offence if the person pleads guilty to or is found guilty of an offence referred to in subsection (1) and,

(a) an order directing that the accused be discharged is made under section 730 of the *Criminal Code* (Canada) or under a provision that is enacted by a state of the United States of America and that is designated by the regulations; or

(b) a disposition is made under section 20 or sections 28 to 32 of the *Young Offenders Act* (Canada) or a youth sentence is imposed under section 42, 59, 94, 95 or 96 of the *Youth Criminal Justice Act* (Canada) or an adult sentence is imposed under the *Youth Criminal Justice Act* (Canada), including a confirmation or variation of the disposition or sentence.

Appeal

(6) An appeal may be taken from an order for additional suspension made under subsection (4) and the provisions of the *Criminal Code* (Canada) applying to an appeal from the conviction referred to in subsection (1) apply in respect of an appeal from an order made under subsection (4).

Stay of order on appeal

(7) Where an appeal is taken under subsection (6), the court being appealed to may direct that the order being appealed from shall be stayed pending the final disposition of the appeal or until otherwise ordered by that court.

No cause of action

(8) No person whose licence is or was suspended under subsection (1) or a predecessor thereof has a cause of action against the Registrar of Motor Vehicles or Her Majesty the Queen in right of Ontario for any misapplication of, or misadvice about, the suspension period under subsection (1) or predecessor thereof.
1996, c. 20, s. 5; 1997, c. 12, s. 1; 2000, c. 26, Sched. O, s. 1; 2001, c. 9, Sched. O, s. 2; 2006, c. 19, Sched. D, s. 9(2); 2006, c. 20, s. 1; 2007, c. 13, s. 6

Reinstatement of suspended licence

41.1 (1) Where the Registrar is satisfied that a person whose driver's licence is suspended under clause 41(1)(f) or (g) has completed the prescribed assessments and remedial programs that are applicable to the person, if any, and meets the prescribed requirements that are applicable to the person, if any, the Registrar shall reinstate the driver's licence upon the expiry of the suspension, subject to any other suspension under this Act.

Reduction of indefinite suspension and reinstatement of licence

(2) Where the Registrar is satisfied that a person whose driver's licence is suspended under clause 41(1)(h) for a second subsequent conviction has completed the prescribed assessments and remedial programs that are applicable to the person, if any, and meets the prescribed requirements that are applicable to the person, if any, the Registrar shall reduce the period of the suspension to 10 years and shall reinstate the driver's licence upon the expiry of the reduced suspension, subject to any other suspension under this Act.

Further suspension

(3) If, upon the expiry of a suspension under subsection 41(1), the person whose driver's licence is suspended has not satisfied the Registrar that he or she

has completed the prescribed assessments and remedial programs that are applicable to the person, if any, and meets the prescribed requirements that are applicable to the person, if any, the Registrar shall suspend the person's driver's licence until such time as the Registrar is so satisfied.

Effective date of further suspension

(4) A suspension under subsection (3) takes effect from the time notice of the suspension is given, in accordance with section 52, to the person whose driver's licence is suspended.

Parties to judicial review

(5) The parties to any judicial review brought in respect of this section are the Registrar and the person whose driver's licence is suspended.

Documents privileged

(6) Documents filed with the Ministry for the purposes of this section are privileged for the information of the Ministry only and shall not be open for public inspection.

Persons authorized to provide programs

(6.1) The Minister may authorize or require any person or class of persons to provide or conduct assessments and programs for the purposes of this section and may require them to prepare, keep and submit reports to the Ministry as specified by the Ministry.

Protection from personal liability

(7) No action or other proceeding for damages shall be instituted against a person authorized or required to conduct an assessment or program or submit a report for the purposes of this section, unless the person was negligent in the conduct of the assessment or program or in the preparation or submission of the report.

Same

(8) No action or other proceeding for damages shall be instituted against the Registrar or any employee of the Ministry for the suspension or reinstatement of a driver's licence in good faith in the execution or intended execution of a duty under this section.

Crown not relieved of liability

(9) Despite subsections 5(2) and (4) of the *Proceedings Against the Crown Act*, subsections (7) and (8) do not relieve the Crown of liability in respect of a tort committed by a person mentioned in subsection (7) or (8) to which it would otherwise be subject.

Regulations

(10) The Lieutenant Governor in Council may make regulations,

(a) governing the assessments and remedial programs required under this section and prescribing what constitutes their completion;

(b) prescribing fees for assessments and remedial programs;

(c) [Repealed 2007, c. 13, s. 7(3).]

(d) respecting documents required to be filed with the Registrar to satisfy him or her with respect to the completion of assessments and remedial programs;

(e) prescribing the requirements to be met by a person in order to have his or her suspension reduced or his or her driver's licence reinstated under this section;

(f) prescribing conditions that the Minister may impose on a driver's licence reinstated under this section;

(g) prescribing the length of time that conditions imposed on a driver's licence reinstated under this section will apply, or a method for determining it;

(h) requiring a person whose licence is suspended under subsection 41(1) or whose licence is reinstated under this section to attend an interview with an official of the Ministry and prescribing the circumstances where the interview will be required and the purposes of the interview;

(i) defining classes of persons, based on the nature of the offence or offences for which a driver's licence may be suspended under section 41 and on the number of convictions a person has for offences described in subsection 41(1);

(j) providing that this section, or any part of it, applies to a class or classes of persons or exempting any class or classes of persons from this section or any part of it, prescribing conditions for any such applications or exemptions and prescribing circumstances in which any such applications or exemptions apply.

Same

(11) A regulation made under subsection (10) may provide differently for different classes of persons and in different parts of Ontario.

1997, c. 12, s. 2; 2007, c, 13, s. 7

Reinstated licence subject to condition: first conviction

41.2 (1) If a person's driver's licence is suspended under section 41 as a result of a first conviction for an offence under section 253, 254 or 255 of the *Criminal Code* (Canada) and his or her driver's licence is reinstated under section 41.1, and not under subsection 41(4.1) it is a condition of the person's driver's licence that he or she is prohibited from driving any motor vehicle that is not equipped with an approved ignition interlock device.

Application to remove condition

(2) A person mentioned in subsection (1) may apply to the Registrar to remove the condition prohibiting him or her from driving any motor vehicle that is not equipped with an approved ignition interlock device.

Time Limit

(3) An application under subsection (2) may not be made earlier than one year from the day the person's driver's licence was reinstated under section 41.1

Prescribed criteria must be met

(4) On receiving an application made in accordance with subsections (2) and (3), the Registrar shall remove the condition, if the person meets the criteria prescribed for the purpose of this subsection.

Reinstated licence subject to condition: second conviction

(5) If a person's driver's licence is suspended under section 41 as a result of a second conviction for an offence under section 253, 254 or 255 of the *Criminal Code* (Canada) and his or her driver's licence is reinstated under section 41.1, it is a condition of the person's driver's licence that he or she is prohibited from driving any motor vehicle that is not equipped with an approved ignition interlock device.

Application to remove condition

(6) A person mentioned in subsection (5) may apply to the Registar to remove the condition prohibiting him or her from driving any motor vehicle that is not equipped with an approved ignition interlock device.

Time limit

(7) An application under subsection (6) may not be made earlier than three years from the day the person's driver's licence was reinstated under section 41.1

Prescribed criteria must be met

(8) On receiving an application made in accordance with subsections (6) and (7), the Registrar shall remove the condition, if the person meets the criteria prescribed for the purpose of this subsection.

Reinstated licence subject to permanent condition

(9) If, in accordance with subsection 41.1(2), the Registrar reduces an indefinite licence suspension that was imposed for a second subsequent conviction or an additional subsequent conviction of an offence under section 253, 254 or 255 of the *Criminal Code* (Canada), and reinstates a person's driver's licence, it is a permanent condition of the person's driver's licence that he or she is prohibited from driving any motor vehicle that is not equipped with an approved ignition interlock device.

Responsibility of owner of motor vehicle

(10) No person who is the owner or is in possession or control of a motor vehicle that is not equipped with an approved ignition interlock device shall knowingly permit a person to drive the vehicle, if that person is prohibited from driving any motor vehicle that is not equipped with such a device.

No tampering with devices

(11) Except in accordance with an authorization under subsection (14), no person shall tamper with an approved ignition interlock device.

Inspections

(12) If, under the authority of this Act, a police officer stops a motor vehicle, inspects a person's driver's licence and determines that the person is prohibited

from driving any motor vehicle that is not equipped with an approved ignition interlock device, the police officer may, without warrant or court order, inspect the vehicle to the extent that is reasonably necessary to determine,

(a) whether the vehicle is equipped with such a device; and

(b) if the vehicle has the device, whether the device has been tampered with in any manner.

Penalty

(13) Every person who drives a motor vehicle that is not equipped with an approved ignition interlock device while prohibited from doing so or who contravenes subsection (10) or (11) is guilty of an offence and on conviction is liable,

(a) in the case involving a commercial motor vehicle within the meaning of subsection 16(1), to a fine of not less than $200 and not more than $20,000;

(b) in every other case, to a fine of not less than $200 and not more than $1,000.

Authorization to install devices

(14) The Minister may in writing authorize any person to install, maintain and remove approved ignition interlock devices.

Authorization to charge fees

(15) Where, under subsection (14), the Minister has authorized a person to install, maintain and remove approved ignition interlock devices, the Minister may in writing authorize that person to charge a fee for the installation, maintenance and removal of such devices.

Regulations

(16) The Lieutenant Governor in Council may make regulations,

(a) approving ignition interlock devices for the purpose of this section;

(b) respecting the standards governing the installation, operation and maintenance of approved ignition interlock devices for the purposes of this section and Part III.1 of the *Civil Remedies Act, 2001* and requiring persons authorized under subsection (14) to comply with those standards;

(c) providing for the purposes of this section that "motor vehicle" includes a streetcar or a motorized snow vehicle;

(d) prescribing exemptions from subsection (1), (5) or (9) and providing that an exemption is subject to restrictions or conditions specified in the regulations and providing that any such restriction or condition shall be deemed to be a condition contained on a person's driver's licence;

(e) prescribing criteria for the purpose of subsections (4) and (8);

(f) requiring a driver who is prohibited from driving any motor vehicle that is not equipped with an approved ignition interlock device to attend upon a person authorized under subsection (14) for the purpose of enabling that person to gather information from the device;

(g) governing reports that shall be made to the Ministry by persons authorized under subsection (14) in respect of information gathered under clause (f);

(h) respecting programs of supervision for persons prohibited from driving a motor vehicle that is not equipped with an approved ignition interlock device;

(i) respecting any other matter necessary for the administration of this section.

Same

(17) A regulation made under subsection (16) may be general or particular in its application.

Adoption of codes in regulations

(18) A regulation under clause (16)(b) may adopt by reference, in whole or in part, with such changes as the Lieutenant Governor in Council considers necessary, any code, standard, protocol, procedure or policy, and may require compliance with any code, standard, protocol, procedure or policy.

Amendments to codes

(19) The power to adopt by reference and require compliance with a code, standard, protocol, procedure or policy in subsection (18) includes the power to adopt a code, standard, protocol, procedure or policy as it may be amended from time to time.

Definitions

(20) In this section and in section 41.3,

"approved" means approved under clause (16)(a); ("approuvé")

"driver's licence" includes a driver's licence issued by any other jurisdiction; ("permis de conduire")

"ignition interlock device" means a device designed to ascertain the presence of alcohol in the driver's body and to prevent a motor vehicle from being started if the concentration of alcohol in the driver's body exceeds the prescribed limit. ("dispositif de verrouillage du système de démarrage")

2000, c. 35, s. 1; 2002, c. 18, Sched. P, s. 13; 2007, c. 13, s. 8

Parties to judicial review

41.3 (1) The parties to any judicial review brought in respect of section 41.2 are the Registrar and the person whose driver's licence is subject to the condition prohibiting him or her from driving any motor vehicle that is not equipped with an approved ignition interlock device.

Documents privileged

(2) Documents filed with the Ministry for the purposes of section 41.2 are privileged for the information of the Ministry only and shall not be open for public inspection.

Protection from personal liability

(3) No action or other proceeding for damages shall be instituted against a person authorized under subsection 41.2(14) to install or maintain an approved

ignition interlock device, unless the person was negligent in the performance of his or her duties and responsibilities under section 41.2

Same

(4) No action or other proceeding for damages shall be instituted against the Registrar or any employee of the Ministry for the removal of a condition prohibiting a person from driving a motor vehicle that is not equipped with an approved ignition interlock device or for the failure to remove the condition, if the Registrar or employee acted in good faith in the execution or intended execution of his or her duties under section 41.2

Crown not relieved of liability

(5) Despite subsections 5(2) and (4) of the *Proceedings Against the Crown Act*, subsections (3) and (4) do not relieve the Crown of liability in respect of a tort committed by a person mentioned in subsection (3) and (4) to which it would otherwise be subject.

2000, c. 35, s. 1

Suspension for driving while disqualified

42. (1) The driver's licence of a person who is convicted of an offence under subsection 259(4) of the *Criminal Code* (Canada) or under a provision that is enacted by a state of the United States of America and that is designated by the regulations is thereupon suspended for a period of,

(a) upon the first conviction, one year; and

(b) upon a subsequent conviction, two years,

in addition to any other period for which the licence is suspended and consecutively thereto.

Determining subsequent conviction

(2) In determining whether a conviction is a subsequent conviction for the purposes of subsection (1), the only question to be considered is the sequence of convictions and no consideration shall be given to the sequence of commission of offences or whether any offence occurred before or after any conviction.

Five-year limitation

(3) Clause (1)(b) does not apply when the subsequent conviction is more than five years after the previous conviction.

Order for discharge

(4) This section applies in the same manner as if a person were convicted of an offence if the person pleads guilty to or is found guilty of an offence referred to in subsection (1) and,

(a) an order directing that the accused be discharged is made under section 730 of the *Criminal Code* (Canada) or under a provision that is enacted by a state of the United States of America and that is designated by the regulations; or

(b) a disposition is made under section 20 or sections 28 to 32 of the *Young Offenders Act* (Canada) or a youth sentence is imposed under section 42, 59, 94, 95 or 96 of the *Youth Criminal Justice Act* (Canada) or an adult sentence is imposed under the *Youth Criminal Justice Act* (Canada), including a confirmation or variation of the disposition or sentence.

Regulations

(5) The Lieutenant Governor in Council may make regulations designating provisions enacted by a state of the United States of America for purposes of this section and section 41.

1993, c. 27, Sched.; 2000, c. 26, Sched. O, s. 2; 2006, c. 19, Sched. D, s. 9(3)

Suspension while prohibited from driving

43. (1) Where the licence of a person who is subject to an order made under section 259 of the *Criminal Code* (Canada), if the order is the result of an offence committed while operating a motor vehicle or street car within the meaning of this Act, a vessel within the meaning of section 48 or a motorized snow vehicle within the meaning of the *Motorized Snow Vehicles Act*, is suspended under subsection 41(1) or under subsection 42(1), the licence shall remain suspended during the period of prohibition set out in the order despite the expiration of any other period of suspension.

Expanded meaning of order

(2) For the purposes of subsection (1), "**an order made under section 259 of the *Criminal Code* (Canada)**" includes an order made under subsection 238(1) of the *Criminal Code* (Canada) before the 26th day of April, 1976.

2006, c. 20, s. 2

Increased suspension time

44. (1) Where an order is made under section 259 of the *Criminal Code* (Canada) or under subsection 41(4) of this Act and the court or judge, when sentencing the offender or making the conviction, orders the imprisonment of the offender and that the period of prohibition or suspension, as the case may be, shall start to run on the termination of the imprisonment, the suspension imposed by subsection 41(1) of this Act is thereupon increased by the period of imprisonment.

Modification to increased suspension

(2) Where the period of imprisonment referred to in subsection (1) is less than that ordered by the court or judge, the length of the increased suspension imposed by subsection (1) shall, upon the application of the offender, be reduced by a period equal to that by which the period of imprisonment was reduced.

. . .

Defaulted fine

46. (1) This section applies if a fine is imposed on conviction for an offence and the offence is an offence,

(a) under this Act or the regulations;

(b) under any other Act listed in the Schedule to this section or under the regulations made under such an Act;

(c) under clause 17(1)(a) or subsection 24(1) of the *Fish and Wildlife Conservation Act, 1997*,

(d) under subsection 32(1) of the *Liquor Licence Act*; or

(e) that was committed with a motor vehicle under section 249, 249.1, 249.2, 249.3, 249.4, 252, 253, 254, 255 or 259 of the *Criminal Code* (Canada).

Order or direction

(2) If the payment of a fine imposed on conviction for an offence is in default, an order or direction may be made under section 69 of the *Provincial Offences Act* directing that the convicted person's driver's licence be suspended and that no driver's licence be issued to him or her until the fine is paid.

Suspension by Registrar

(3) On being informed of an outstanding order or direction referred to in subsection (2), the Registrar shall suspend the person's driver's licence if it has not already been suspended under another order or direction referred to in subsection (2).

Proposed Amendment—46(3)

(3) On being informed of an outstanding order or direction referred to in subsection (2), the Registrar shall suspend the person's driver's licence.

1996, c. 20, s. 6(1) [Not in force at date of publication.]

Reinstatement

(4) On being informed that the fine and any applicable administrative fee for reinstatement of the person's driver's licence have been paid, the Registrar shall reinstate the licence, unless he or she has also been informed that;

(a) another order or direction referred to in subsection (2) is outstanding;

(b) the licence is suspended under any other order or direction or under another statute;

(c) interest charged or a penalty imposed under subsection 5(2) has not been paid; or

(d) an applicable prescribed administrative fee for handling a dishonoured cheque has not been paid.

Proposed Amendment—46(4)(d)

(d) an applicable prescribed administrative fee for handling a dishonoured payment has not been paid.

1996, c. 20, s. 6(2) [Not in force at date of publication.]

Regulations

(5) The Lieutenant Governor in Council may make regulations prescribing forms and procedures and respecting any matter considered necessary or advisable to carry out effectively the intent and purpose of this section.

SCHEDULE

(Section 46)

Compulsory Automobile Insurance Act
Dangerous Goods Transportation Act
Motorized Snow Vehicles Act
Off-Road Vehicles Act
Public Vehicles Act

1993, c. 27, Sched.; 1993, c. 31, s. 2(6); 1997, c. 41, s. 120; 2001, c. 9, Sched. O, s. 3; 2002, c. 18, Sched. P, s. 14; 2007, c. 13, s. 9

Suspension and cancellation of licence, etc., general

47. (1) Subject to section 47.1, the Registrar may suspend or cancel,

(a) the plate portion of a permit as defined in Part II;

(b) a driver's licence; or

(c) a CVOR certificate,

on the grounds of,

(d) misconduct for which the holder is responsible, directly or indirectly, related to the operation or driving of a motor vehicle;

(e) conviction of the holder for an offence referred to in subsection 210(1) or (2);

(f) the Registrar having reason to believe, having regard to the safety record of the holder or of a person related to the holder, and any other information that the Registrar considers relevant, that the holder will not operate a commercial motor vehicle safely or in accordance with this Act, the regulations and other laws relating to highway safety; or

(g) any other sufficient reasons not referred to in clause (d), (e) or (f).

. . .

1996, c. 33, s. 7

Notice of proposed action

47.1 (1) Before taking any action under clause 47(1)(a) or (c) or subsection 47(2), the Registrar shall notify the person whose plate portion of a permit or CVOR certificate is to be affected of his or her proposed action.

Notice of safety record concerns

(1.1) The Registrar may also notify an operator at any time if the Registrar has reason to believe that the operator may not operate a commercial motor vehicle safely or in accordance with this Act, the regulations or other laws relating to highway safety.

Method of giving notice

(2) Notice under subsection (1) or (1.1), or withdrawal of such a notice, is sufficiently given,

(a) if it is delivered personally;

(b) if it is delivered by registered mail addressed to the person at the latest address for the person appearing on the Ministry records; or

(c) if it is sent by telephone transmission of a facsimile or by some other electronic or other transmission medium permitted by the regulations to the person at the latest facsimile number or other medium address for the person provided by the person to the Ministry.

Same

(3) Unless the person establishes that the person did not, acting in good faith, through absence, accident, illness or other cause beyond the person's control, receive the notice,

(a) notice given by registered mail shall be deemed to have been received on the fifth day after it was mailed;

(b) notice given by telephone transmission of a facsimile or by some other electronic or other transmission medium shall be deemed to have been received on the first business day after it was sent.

Restrictions on vehicle transfers

(4) If a notice under subsection (1) or (1.1) is issued to an operator, no person shall, without the consent of the Registrar, transfer or lease any commercial motor vehicle or trailer for which the operator's name is on the vehicle or plate portion of the permit or do anything that will result in a change of name on the vehicle or plate portion of the permit for any such vehicle or trailer.

Duration of restrictions

(4.1) Subsection (4) is effective in respect of notice under subsection (1) from the earlier of the date the notice is actually received by the operator and the date the notice is deemed by subsection (3) to have been received by the operator,

(a) in the case of proposed suspension or fleet limitation, until the end of the suspension or fleet limitation;

(b) in the case of proposed cancellation, forever.

Same

(4.2) Despite subsection (4.1), subsection (4) ceases to apply in respect of notice under subsection (1),

(a) if the Registrar withdraws the proposal to suspend or cancel the plate portion of the permit or the CVOR certificate or to impose a fleet limitation; or

(b) if the suspension, cancelation or limitation is set aside on appeal.

Same

(5) Subsection (4) is effective in respect of a notice under subsection (1.1) from the earlier of the date notice is actually received by the operator and the date the notice is deemed by subsection (3) to have been received by the operator,

(a) if a notice under subsection (1) is issued to the operator on or before the first anniversary of the date the notice under subsection (1.1) was issued, until earlier of the date the notice under subsection (1) is actually received by the operator and the date the notice under subsection (1) is deemed by subsection (3) to have been received by the operator;

(b) if a notice under subsection (1) is not issued to the operator on or before the first anniversary of the date the notice under subsection (1.1) was issued, until the earlier of the date the Registrar withdraws the notice under subsection (1.1) or the first anniversary of the date the notice under subsection (1.1) was issued.

Registrar not to withhold consent without reason

(6) The Registrar shall not withhold consent under subsection (4) if the operator satisfies him or her that the transfer, lease or other action is not being made for the purpose of avoiding an action under clause 47(1) (a) or (c) or subsection 47(2).

Regulations

(7) The Lieutenant Governor in Council may, for the purpose of subsection (3), make regulations,

(a) prescribing other methods of transmission;

(b) governing the giving of notice by telephone transmission of a facsimile or by a method prescribed by clause (a).

1996, c. 33, s. 8; 2001, c. 9, Sched. O, s. 5

Spot checks

48. (1) A police officer, readily identified as such, may require the driver of a motor vehicle or operator of a vessel to stop for the purpose of determining whether or not there is evidence to justify making a demand under section 254 of the *Criminal Code* (Canada).

Licence suspensions: screening device test

(2) Where, upon demand of a police officer made under section 254 of the *Criminal Code* (Canada), a person provides a sample of breath which, on analysis by an approved screening device as defined in that section, registers "Warn" or "Alert", the police officer may request the person to surrender his or her driver's licence.

Idem: breathalyzer test

(3) Where, upon demand of a police officer made under section 254 of the *Criminal Code* (Canada), a person provides a sample of breath which, on analysis by an instrument approved as suitable for the purpose of section 254 of the *Criminal Code* (Canada), indicates that the concentration of alcohol in his or her blood is 50 milligrams or more of alcohol in 100 millilitres of blood, a police officer may request the person to surrender his or her driver's licence.

Refusal to supply a breath sample

(4) Where a person is charged with an offence under section 254 of the *Criminal Code* (Canada) or any procedure is taken pending the laying of such a charge to assure the person's attendance in court on the charge, a police officer may request the person to surrender his or her driver's licence.

Surrender of licence and suspension for twelve hours

(5) Upon a request being made under subsection (2), (3) or (4), the person to whom the request is made shall forthwith surrender his or her driver's licence to the police officer and, whether or not the person is unable or fails to surrender the licence to the police officer, his or her licence is suspended and invalid for any purpose for a period of twelve hours from the time the request is made.

Suspension concurrent with s. 48.3 suspension

(5.1) The licence suspension under this section runs concurrently with a suspension, if any, under section 48.3.

Second analysis

(6) Where an analysis of the breath of a person is made under subsection (2) and registers "Warn" or "Alert", the person may require a further analysis to be performed in the manner provided in subsection (3), in which case the result obtained on the second analysis governs and any suspension resulting from an analysis under subsection (2) continues or terminates accordingly.

Calibration of screening device

(7) For the purposes of subsection (2), the approved screening device shall not be calibrated to register "Warn" or "Alert" if the concentration of alcohol in the blood of the person whose breath is being analyzed is less than 50 milligrams of alcohol in 100 millilitres of blood.

Idem

(8) It shall be presumed, in the absence of proof to the contrary, that any approved screening device used for the purposes of subsection (2) has been calibrated as required under subsection (7).

Intent of suspension

(9) The suspension of a licence under this section is intended to safeguard the licensee and the public and does not constitute an alternative to any proceeding or penalty arising from the same circumstances or around the same time.

Duty of officer

(10) Every officer who asks for the surrender of a licence under this section shall keep a written record of the licence received with the name and address of the person and the date and time of the suspension and, at the time of receiving the licence, shall return the Photo Card portion of the licence, if the licence consists of a Photo Card and Licence Card, and provide the licensee with a written statement of the time from which the suspension takes effect, the length of the period during

which the licence is suspended, and the place where the licence or Licence Card portion thereof may be recovered.

Removal of vehicle

(11) If the motor vehicle of a person whose licence is suspended under this section is at a location from which, in the opinion of a police officer, it should be removed and there is no person available who may lawfully remove the vehicle, the officer may remove and store the vehicle or cause it to be removed and stored, in which case, the officer shall notify the person of the location of the storage.

Cost of removal

(12) Where a police officer obtains assistance for the removal and storage of a motor vehicle under this section, the costs incurred in moving and storing the vehicle are a lien on the vehicle that may be enforced under the *Repair and Storage Liens Act* by the person who moved or stored the vehicle at the request of the officer.

Definitions

(13) In this section,

"driver's licence" includes a motorized snow vehicle operator's licence and a driver's licence issued by any other jurisdiction; ("permis de conduire")

"motor vehicle" includes a motorized snow vehicle. ("véhicule automobile")

"vessel" means a vessel within the meaning of section 214 of the *Criminal Code* (Canada). ("bateau")

1993, c. 40, s. 4; 1996, c. 20, s. 7; 2006, c. 20, s. 3

Proposed Amendment — 48

Administrative licence suspension for blood alcohol concentration above .05

Determining whether to make a demand

48. (1) A police officer, readily identifiable as such, may require the driver of a motor vehicle to stop for the purpose of determining whether or not there is evidence to justify making a demand under section 254 of the Criminal Code (Canada).

Screening device breath test

(2) Where, upon demand of a police officer made under section 254 of the Criminal Code (Canada), the driver of a motor vehicle or the operator of a vessel provides a sample of breath which, on analysis by an approved screening device as defined in that section, registers "Warn" or "Alert" or otherwise indicates that the concentration of alcohol in the person's blood is 50 milligrams or more of alcohol in 100 millilitres of blood, the police officer may request that the person surrender his or her driver's licence.

Approved instrument test

(3) Where, upon demand of a police officer made under section 254 of the Criminal Code (Canada), the driver of a motor vehicle or the operator of a vessel

provides a sample of breath which, on analysis by an instrument approved as suitable for the purpose of section 254 of the Criminal Code (Canada), indicates that the concentration of alcohol in his or her blood is 50 milligrams or more of alcohol in 100 millilitres of blood, a police officer may request that the person surrender his or her driver's licence.

Licence suspension

(4) Upon a request being made under subsection (2) or (3), the person to whom the request is made shall forthwith surrender his or her driver's licence to the police officer and, whether or not the person is unable or fails to surrender the licence to the police officer, his or her driver's licence is suspended from the time the request is made for the period of time determined under subsection (14).

Suspension concurrent with s. 48.3 suspension

(5) The licence suspension under this section runs concurrently with a suspension, if any, under section 48.3.(5.1) [Repealed 2007, c. 13, s. 10. Not in force at date of publication.]

Opportunity for a second analysis

(6) Where an analysis of the breath of a person is made under subsection (2) and registers "Warn" or "Alert" or otherwise indicates that the concentration of alcohol in the person's blood is 50 milligrams or more of alcohol in 100 millilitres of blood, the person may require a further analysis to be performed in the manner provided in subsection (3), in which case the result obtained on the second analysis governs and any suspension resulting from an analysis under subsection (2) continues or terminates accordingly.

Calibration of screening device

(7) For the purposes of subsection (2), the approved screening device shall not be calibrated to register "Warn" or "Alert" or to otherwise indicate that the concentration of alcohol in the person's blood is 50 milligrams or more of alcohol in 100 millilitres of blood if the concentration of alcohol in the blood of the person whose breath is being analyzed is less than 50 milligrams of alcohol in 100 millilitres of blood.

Same

(8) It shall be presumed, in the absence of proof to the contrary, that any approved screening device used for the purposes of subsection (2) has been calibrated as required under subsection (7).

No appeal or hearing

(9) There is no appeal from, or right to be heard before, the suspension of a driver's licence under this section, but this subsection does not affect the taking of any proceeding in court.

Intent of suspension

(10) The suspension of a licence under this section is intended to safeguard the licensee and the public and does not constitute an alternative to any proceeding or penalty arising from the same circumstances or around the same time.

Duties of officer

(11) Every officer who asks for the surrender of a licence under this section shall,

(a) notify the Registrar of that fact, or cause the Registrar to be so notified, in the form and manner and within the time prescribed by the regulations;

(b) keep a record of the licence received with the name and address of the person and the date and time of the suspension; and

(c) as soon as practicable after receiving the licence, provide the licensee with a notice of suspension showing the time from which the suspension takes effect and the period of time for which the licence is suspended.

Removal of vehicle

(12) If the motor vehicle of a person whose licence is suspended under this section is at a location from which, in the opinion of a police officer, it should be removed and there is no person available who may lawfully remove the vehicle, the officer may remove and store the vehicle or cause it to be removed and stored, in which case the officer shall notify the person of the location of the storage.

Cost of removal

(13) Where a police officer obtains assistance for the removal and storage of a motor vehicle under this section, the costs incurred in moving and storing the vehicle are a lien on the vehicle that may be enforced under the Repair and Storage Liens Act by the person who moved or stored the vehicle at the request of the officer.

Period of suspension

(14) A driver's licence suspended under subsection (4) shall be suspended for,(a) three days, in the case of a first suspension under this section;(b) seven days, in the case of a second suspension under this section;(c) 30 days, in the case of a third or subsequent suspension under this section.

Same

(15) The following previous suspensions shall not be taken into account in determining whether the current suspension is a first, second or subsequent suspension for the purpose of subsection (14):1. A previous suspension that took effect more than five years before the current suspension takes effect.2. A previous suspension that took effect before section 10 of the Safer Roads for a Safer Ontario Act, 2007 comes into force.

Police officer's other powers unchanged

(16) Subsection (1) shall not be construed so as to prevent a police officer from requiring a driver stopped under that subsection to surrender any licence, permit, card or other document that the officer is otherwise authorized to demand under this Act or the Compulsory Automobile Insurance Act or from requiring a driver to submit a vehicle to examinations and tests under subsection 82(2) of this Act.

Regulations

(17) The Lieutenant Governor in Council may make regulations,(a) respecting the form, manner and time within which the Registrar must be notified under subsection (11);(b) prescribing other material or information to be forwarded to the Registrar under subsection (11).

Definitions

(18) In this section,**"driver's licence"** includes a motorized snow vehicle operator's licence and a driver's licence issued by any other jurisdiction;

"motor vehicle" includes a motorized snow vehicle;

"vessel" means a vessel within the meaning of section 214 of the Criminal Code (Canada).

2007, c. 13, s. 10 [Not in force at date of publication.]

Application of subss. (2), (3) and (4)

48.1 (1) Subsections (2) and (3) apply and subsection (4) does not apply if the police officer who stops a novice driver uses one screening device for the purposes of section 48 and another screening device for the purposes of this section, and subsection (4) applies and subsections (2) and (3) do not apply if the police officer uses one screening device for the purposes of both section 48 and this section.

Screening device test, novice drivers

(2) Where a novice driver has been brought to a stop by a police officer under the authority of this Act and has provided a sample of breath under section 48 which, on analysis registers ''Pass'', but the police officer reasonably suspects that the novice driver has alcohol in his or her body, the police officer may, for the purposes of determining compliance with the regulations respecting novice drivers, demand that the novice driver provide within a reasonable time such a sample of breath as, in the opinion of the police officer, is necessary to enable a proper analysis of breath to be made by means of a provincially approved screening device and, where necessary, to accompany the police officer for the purpose of enabling such a sample of breath to be taken.

Proposed Amendment — 48.1(2)

Screening device test, novice drivers

(2) Where a novice driver has been brought to a stop by a police officer under the authority of this Act and has provided a sample of breath under section 48 which, on analysis registers "Pass" or otherwise indicates that the novice driver has no alcohol in his or her body, but the police officer reasonably suspects that the novice driver has alcohol in his or her body, the police officer may, for the purposes of determining compliance with the regulations respecting novice drivers, demand that the novice driver provide within a reasonable time such a sample of breath as, in the opinion of the police officer, is necessary to enable a proper analysis of the breath to be made by means of a provincially approved screening device and, where necessary, to accompany the police officer for the purpose of enabling such a sample of breath to be taken.

2007, c. 13, s. 11(1) [Not in force at date of publication.]

Surrender of licence

(3) Where, upon demand of a police officer made under subsection (2), a novice driver fails or refuses to provide a sample of breath or provides a sample of breath which, on analysis by a provincially approved screening device, registers ''Presence of Alcohol'', the police officer may request the novice driver to surrender his or her driver's licence.

Proposed Amendment — 48.1(3)

Surrender of licence

(3) Where, upon demand of a police officer made under subsection (2), a novice driver fails or refuses to provide a sample of breath or provides a sample of breath which, on analysis by a provincially approved screening device, registers "Presence of Alcohol" or otherwise indicates that the novice driver has alcohol in his or her body, the police officer may request the novice driver to surrender his or her driver's licence.

2007, c. 13, s. 11(2) [Not in force at date of publication.]

Same

(4) Where a novice driver has been brought to a stop by a police officer under the authority of this Act and has provided a sample of breath under section 48 which, on analysis registers ''Warn'', ''Alert'' or ''Presence of Alcohol'', or, upon demand of a police officer made under section 254 of the *Criminal Code* (Canada), fails or refuses to provide a sample of breath, the police officer may request the novice driver to surrender his or her licence.

Proposed Amendment — 48.1(4)

Same

(4) Where a novice driver has been brought to a stop by a police officer under the authority of this Act and has provided a sample of breath under section 48 which, on analysis registers "Warn", "Alert" or "Presence of Alcohol" or otherwise indicates that the novice driver has alcohol in his or her body, or, upon demand of a police officer made under section 254 of the Criminal Code (Canada), fails or refuses to provide a sample of breath, the police officer may request the novice driver to surrender his or her licence.

2007, c. 13, s. 11(3) [Not in force at date of publication.]

Suspension of licence for twelve hours

(5) Upon a request being made under subsection (3) or (4), the novice driver to whom the request is made shall forthwith surrender his or her driver's licence to the police officer and, whether or not the novice driver is unable or fails to surrender the licence to the police officer, his or her licence is suspended and invalid for any purpose for a period of twelve hours from the time the request is made.

Proposed Amendment — 48.1(5)

Suspension of licence for twelve hours

(5) Upon a request being made under subsection (3) or (4), the novice driver to whom the request is made shall forthwith surrender his or her driver's licence to the police officer and, whether or not the novice driver is unable or fails to surrender the licence to the police officer, his or her licence is suspended for a period of twelve hours from the time the request is made.

2007, c. 13, s. 11(4) [Not in force at date of publication.]

Further analysis

(6) Where an analysis of the breath of the novice driver under subsection (3) or (4) registers ''Warn'', ''Alert'' or ''Presence of Alcohol'', the novice driver may require a further analysis to be performed in the manner provided in subsection 48(3), in which case the result obtained on the further analysis governs and any suspension resulting from an analysis under subsection (3) or (4) continues or terminates accordingly.

Proposed Amendment — 48.1(6)

Further analysis

(6) Where an analysis of the breath of the novice driver under subsection (3) or (4) registers "Warn", "Alert" or "Presence of Alcohol" or otherwise indicates that the novice driver has alcohol in his or her body, the novice driver may require a further analysis to be performed in the manner provided in subsection 48(3), in which case the result obtained on the further analysis governs and any suspension resulting from an analysis under subsection (3) or (4) continues or terminates accordingly.

2007, c. 13, s. 11(5) [Not in force at date of publication.]

Calibration of screening device

(7) For the purposes of this section, the provincially approved screening device shall be calibrated to register ''Presence of Alcohol'' if the concentration of alcohol in the blood of the person whose breath is being analyzed is as prescribed by the regulations, and despite anything in this section, the reading on a provincially approved screening device for ''Presence of Alcohol'' may be another term or symbol that conveys the same meaning.

Same

(8) It shall be presumed, in the absence of proof to the contrary, that any provincially approved screening device used for the purposes of this section has been calibrated as required by the regulations.

Intent of suspension

(9) The suspension of a licence under this section is intended to ensure that novice drivers acquire experience and develop or improve safe driving skills in controlled conditions and to safeguard the licensee and the public and does not

constitute an alternative to any proceeding or penalty arising from the same circumstances or around the same time.

Duty of officer

(10) Every officer who asks for the surrender of a licence under this section shall keep a written record of the licence received with the name and address of the person and the date and time of the suspension and, at the time of receiving the licence, shall return the Photo Card portion of the licence, if the licence consists of a Photo Card and Licence Card, and provide the licensee with a written statement of the time from which the suspension takes effect, the length of the period during which the licence is suspended and the place where the licence or Licence Card portion of it may be recovered.

Removal of vehicle

(11) If the motor vehicle of a person whose licence is suspended under this section is at a location from which, in the opinion of a police officer, it should be removed and there is no person available who may lawfully remove the vehicle, the officer may remove and store the vehicle or cause it to be removed and stored, in which case, the officer shall notify the person of the location of the storage.

Cost of removal

(12) Where a police officer obtains assistance for the removal and storage of a motor vehicle under this section, the costs incurred in moving and storing the vehicle are a lien on the vehicle that may be enforced under the *Repair and Storage Liens Act* by the person who moved or stored the vehicle at the request of theofficer.

Offence

(13) Every person commits an offence who, without reasonable excuse, fails or refuses to comply with a demand made to him or her by a police officer under this section.

Definitions

(14) In this section,

"novice driver" has the meaning prescribed by the regulations made under section 57.1; ("conducteur débutant")

"provincially approved screening device" means a device of a kind that is designed to ascertain the presence of alcohol in the blood of a person and that is prescribed for the purposes of this section by the regulations made under section 57.1. ("appareil de détention approuvé par la province").

1993, c. 40, s. 5

Screening device test, accompanying driver

48.2 (1) Where a police officer has brought a novice driver to a stop under the authority of this Act, and the police officer reasonably suspects that the accompanying driver has alcohol in his or her body, the police officer may, for the purposes of determining whether the novice driver is in compliance with the regulations respecting novice drivers, demand that the accompanying driver provide forthwith a sample of breath into an approved screening device as defined in section 254 of the *Criminal Code* (Canada) as if he or she was the person operating the motor vehicle.

Direction to novice driver

(2) Where, upon demand of a police officer made under subsection (1), an accompanying driver fails or refuses to provide a sample of breath or provides a sample of breath which, on analysis by an approved screening device, as defined in section 254 of the *Criminal Code* (Canada), registers ''Warn'', ''Alert'' or ''Fail'', the police officer may direct the novice driver not to drive a motor vehicle on a highway except in compliance with the regulations respecting novice drivers.

Proposed Amendment — 48.2(2)

Direction to novice driver

(2) Where, upon demand of a police officer made under subsection (1), an accompanying driver fails or refuses to provide a sample of breath or provides a sample of breath which, on analysis by an approved screening device, as defined in section 254 of the Criminal Code (Canada), registers "Warn", "Alert" or "Fail" or otherwise indicates that the concentration of alcohol in the accompanying driver's blood is 50 milligrams or more of alcohol in 100 millilitres of blood, the police officer may direct the novice driver not to drive a motor vehicle on a highway except in compliance with the regulations respecting novice drivers.

2007, c. 13, s. 12(1) [Not in force at date of publication.]

Second analysis

(3) Where an analysis of the breath of an accompanying driver is made under subsection (2) and registers ''Warn'', ''Alert'' or ''Fail'', the accompanying driver may require an analysis to be performed in the manner provided by subsection 48(3), in which case the result obtained on the second analysis governs and any direction given by the police officer under subsection (2) continues or terminates accordingly.

Proposed Amendment — 48.2(3)

Second analysis

(3) Where an analysis of the breath of an accompanying driver is made under subsection (2) and registers "Warn", "Alert" or "Fail" or otherwise indicates that the concentration of alcohol in the accompanying driver's blood is 50 milligrams or more of alcohol in 100 millilitres of blood, the accompanying driver may require an analysis to be performed in the manner provided by subsection 48(3), in which case the result obtained on the second analysis governs and any direction given by the police officer under subsection (2) continues or terminates accordingly.

2007, c. 13, s. 12(2) [Not in force at date of publication.]

Calibration of screening device

(4) For the purposes of subsection (2), the approved screening device referred to in that subsection shall not be calibrated to register ''Warn'' or ''Alert'' if the

concentration of alcohol in the blood of the person whose breath is being analyzed is less than 50 milligrams of alcohol in 100 millilitres of blood.

Same

(5) It shall be presumed, in the absence of proof to the contrary, that any approved screening device used for the purposes of subsection (2) has been calibrated as required under subsection (4).

Intent of direction

(6) The direction under this section to a novice driver not to drive a motor vehicle on a highway is intended to ensure that novice drivers acquire experience and develop or improve safe driving skills in controlled conditions and to safeguard the licensee and the public and does not constitute an alternative to any proceeding or penalty arising from the same circumstances or around the same time.

Removal of vehicle

(7) If the motor vehicle of a person who is directed not to drive under this section is at a location from which, in the opinion of a police officer, it should be removed and there is no person available who may lawfully remove the vehicle, officer may remove and store the vehicle or cause it to be removed and stored, in which case, the officer shall notify the person of the location of the storage.

Cost of removal

(8) Where a police officer obtains assistance for the removal and storage of a motor vehicle under this section, the costs incurred in moving and storing the vehicle are a lien on the vehicle that may be enforced under the *Repair and Storage Liens Act* by the person who moved or stored the vehicle at the request of the officer.

Offence

(9) Every person commits an offence who, without reasonable excuse, fails or refuses to comply with a demand made to him or her by a police officer under this section.

Definitions

(10) In this section, **"accompanying driver"** and **"novice driver"** have the meanings prescribed by the regulations made under section 57.1.

1993, c. 40, s. 5

Registrar notified by police

48.3 (1) Where a police officer is satisfied that a person driving or having the care, charge or control of a motor vehicle or operating or having the care or control of a vessel meets one of the criteria set out in subsection (3), the officer shall notify the Registrar of that fact, or cause the Registrar to be so notified, in the form and manner and within the time prescribed by the regulations.

Suspension of driver's licence for ninety days

(2) Upon being notified under subsection (1), the Registrar shall suspend a person's driver's licence for a period of ninety days.

No right to be heard

(2.1) A person has no right to be heard before or after the notification by the officer, or before or after the Registrar suspends the licence, but this subsection does not affect the taking of any proceeding in Court.

Criteria

(3) The criteria for the purpose of subsection (1) are:

1. The person is shown, by an analysis of breath or blood taken pursuant to a demand made under section 254(3) of the *Criminal Code* (Canada) or pursuant to section 256 of the *Criminal Code* (Canada), to have a concentration of alcohol in his or her blood in excess of 80 milligrams in 100 millilitres of blood.

2. The person failed or refused to provide a breath or blood sample in response to a demand made under section 254 of the *Criminal Code* (Canada).

Effective date

(4) The suspension takes effect from the time notice of the suspension is given, in accordance with section 52, to the person whose licence is suspended.

Surrender of licence

(5) If notice of the suspension is delivered personally to the person by a police officer, the officer may request the person to surrender his or her driver's licence and, upon the request, the person shall forthwith surrender his or her driver's licence to the police officer.

Same

(6) If notice of the suspension is given to the person by mail, the person shall forthwith surrender to the Registrar his or her driver's licence, except the Photo Card portion of the licence, if the licence consists of a Photo Card and Licence Card.

Licence invalid

(7) Whether or not the person is unable or fails to surrender his or her driver's licence under subsection (5) or (6), the licence is suspended and invalid for any purpose for a period of ninety days from the time notice is given to the person.

Proposed Amendment — 48.3(7)

Licence invalid

(7) Whether or not the person is unable or fails to surrender his or her driver's licence under subsection (5) or (6), the licence is suspended for a period of ninety days from the time notice is given to the person.

2007, c. 13, s. 13 [Not in force at date of publication.]

Photo card portion returned

(8) Every police officer to whom a driver's licence is surrendered under this section shall return the Photo Card portion of the licence to the person, if the licence consists of a Photo Card and Licence Card.

Licence delivered to Registrar

(9) A police officer who has notified the Registrar under subsection (1) or a police officer who personally delivered notice of the suspension to the person shall, as soon as practicable, forward to the Registrar,

(a) the person's driver's licence, except the Photo Card portion, if the licence was surrendered to the police officer; and

(b) such other material or information as may be prescribed by the regulations.

Intent of suspension

(10) The suspension of a driver's licence under this section is intended to safeguard the public and does not constitute an alternative to any proceeding or penalty arising from the same circumstances or around the same time.

Removal of vehicle

(11) If the motor vehicle of a person whose licence is suspended under this section is at a location from which, in the opinion of a police officer, it should be removed and there is no person available who may lawfully remove the vehicle, the officer may remove and store the vehicle or cause it to be removed and stored, in which case the officer shall notify the person of the location of the storage.

Cost of removal

(12) Where a police officer obtains assistance for the removal and storage of a motor vehicle under this section, the costs incurred in moving and storing the vehicle are a lien on the vehicle that may be enforced under the *Repair and Storage Liens Act* by the person who moved or stored the vehicle at the request of the officer.

Protection from personal liability

(13) No action or other proceeding for damages shall be instituted against the Registrar or any employee of the Ministry for the suspension of a licence in good faith in the execution or intended execution of a duty under this section.

Crown not relieved of liability

(14) Despite subsections 5(2) and (4) of the *Proceedings Against the Crown Act*, subsection (13) does not relieve the Crown of liability in respect of a tort committed by a person mentioned in subsection (13) to which it would otherwise be subject.

Regulations

(15) The Lieutenant Governor in Council may make regulations,

(a) respecting the form, manner and time within which the Registrar must be notified under subsection (1);

(b) respecting the information to be provided to persons whose licences are suspended under this section;

(c) prescribing other material or information to be forwarded to the Registrar under subsection (9).

Definitions

(16) In this section and in section 50.1,

"driver's licence" includes a motorized snow vehicle operator's licence and a driver's licence issued by any other jurisdiction;

"motor vehicle" includes a street car and a motorized snow vehicle.

"vessel" means a vessel within the meaning of section 214 of the *Criminal Code* (Canada). ("bateau")

Meaning of suspension for out-of-province licences

(17) With respect to a driver's licence issued by another jurisdiction, instead of suspending the person's driver's licence, the Registrar shall suspend the person's privilege to drive a motor vehicle in Ontario for a period of ninety days, and this section and section 50.1 apply to the suspension of that privilege with necessary modifications.

1996, c. 20, s. 8; 1997, c. 12, s. 3; 2006, c. 20, s. 4

. . .

Appeal of ninety day suspension

50.1 (1) A person whose driver's licence is suspended under section 48.3 may appeal the suspension of the Tribunal.

Grounds for appeal

(2) The only grounds on which a person may appeal under subsection (1) and the only grounds on which the Tribunal may order that the suspension be set aside are,

(a) that the person whose licence was suspended is not the same individual to whom a demand for a sample of breath or blood was made, or from whom a sample of breath or blood was taken, as the case may be, under or pursuant to the provisions of the *Criminal Code* (Canada) referred to in subsection 48.3(3); or

(b) that the person failed or refused to comply with a demand made under section 254 of the *Criminal Code* (Canada) to provide a sample of breath or blood because he or she was unable to do so for a medical reason.

Supporting material

(3) A person who appeals to the Tribunal under subsection (1) shall file such written material in support of the appeal as may be required by the regulations made under clause 49(4)(c), together with such other material as the person may wish to submit, and the Tribunal shall not hold a hearing until all the supporting material is filed.

Powers of Tribunal

(4) The Tribunal may confirm the suspension or may order that the suspension be set aside.

Licence reinstated

(5) If the Tribunal orders that the suspension be set aside, it shall give written notice of the order to the appellant and the registrar and, upon receipt of such notice, the Registrar shall reinstate the appellant's driver's licence, subject to any other suspension under this Act.

Decision final

(6) The decision of the Tribunal under this section is final and binding.

Suspension not stayed

(7) The suspension under section 48.3 continues to apply despite the filing of an appeal under this section unless the Registrar reinstates the licence pursuant to the Tribunal's order that the suspension be set aside, and this subsection prevails over the *Statutory Powers Procedure Act*.

When oral hearing required

(8) The Tribunal is not required to hold an oral hearing under this section unless the appellant requests an oral hearing at the time of filing the appeal and bases the appeal on one of the grounds set out in subsection (2).

Exception

(9) Despite a request by the appellant for an oral hearing, the Tribunal may order that the suspension be set aside on the basis of the material filed with the Tribunal without holding an oral hearing.

(10) [Repealed 1999, c. 12, Sched. G, s. 24(11).]
1996, c. 20, s. 10; 1997, c. 12, s. 4; 1999, c. 12, Sched. G, s. 24(8), paras. 2-4(11)]

Appeal of order to impound

50.2 (1) The owner of a motor vehicle that is subject to an order to impound under section 55.1 may, upon paying the prescribed fee, appeal the order to the Tribunal.

Parties

(2) The owner and the Registrar are the parties to an appeal under this section.

Grounds for appeal

(3) The only grounds on which an owner may appeal under subsection (1) and the only grounds on which the Tribunal may set aside the order to impound are,

(a) that the motor vehicle that is subject to the order was stolen at the time in respect of which the order was made;

(b) that the driver's licence of the driver of the motor vehicle at the time in respect of which the order was made was not then under suspension;

(c) that the owner of the motor vehicle exercised due diligence in attempting to determine that the driver's licence of the driver of the motor vehicle at the time in respect of which the order was made was not then under suspension; or

(d) that the order will result in exceptional hardship.

Exception

(4) Clause (3)(d) does not apply if an order to impound under section 55.1 was previously made with respect to any motor vehicle then owned by the same owner.

Powers of Tribunal

(5) The Tribunal may confirm or set aside the order to impound.

Notice of decisions

(6) The Tribunal shall give written notice of its decision to the owner and the Registrar.

Registrar's actions if order set aside

(7) If the Tribunal sets aside the order, the Registrar, upon receipt of the notice,

(a) shall issue an order to release the vehicle;

(b) shall pay on behalf of the owner the amount incurred by the owner, as a result of the order to impound, for removing and impounding the vehicle, not including any amount for economic losses; and

(c) shall pay the operator or the owner the amount incurred by the operator or owner, as a result of the order to impound, for removing the load or drawn vehicle from the motor vehicle, not including any amount for economic losses.

Decision final

(8) The decision of the Tribunal under this section is final and binding.

Impoundment not stayed

(9) Despite the *Statutory Powers Procedure Act*, the filing of an appeal under this section does not suspend or terminate the order to impound under section 55.1.

Civil Remedies Act, 2001 prevails

(10) Subsection (7) does not apply if the vehicle is subject to an order under Part III.1 of the Civil Remedies Act, 2001.

Definitions

(11) In this section,

"operator" has the same meaning as in section 55.1; ('utilisateur")

"owner" means each person whose name appears on the certificate of registration for the vehicle but in subsection (4) "owner" means the person whose name appears on the plate portion of a permit in cases where the certificate of registration consists of a vehicle portion and a plate portion and different persons are named on each portion. ("propriétaire")

1997, c. 12, s. 5; 1999, c.12, Sched. G, s. 24(12), (13); 2000, c. 26, Sched. O, s. 3; 2007, c. 13, s. 14

Appeal of order to impound and suspend

50.3 (1) The owner of a commercial motor vehicle or trailer that is subject to an order to impound and suspend under section 82.1 may, upon paying the prescribed fee, appeal the order to the Tribunal.

Parties

(2) The owner and the Registrar are the parties to an appeal under this section.

Grounds for appeal

(3) The only grounds on which an owner may appeal under subsection (1) and the only grounds on which the Tribunal may set aside the order to impound and suspend are,

(a) that the commercial motor vehicle or trailer that is subject to the order was stolen at the time the order was made; or

(b) that the commercial motor vehicle or trailer had no critical defects at the time of the inspection under section 82.1

Effect of withdrawal of appeal

(4) If the owner withdraws the appeal after the Registrar has ordered the release of the vehicle pursuant to an order by the Court (General Division) under section 82.1, the Registrar shall order the owner of the commercial motor vehicle or trailer to return it, without any load, to an impound facility at a location and within the time specified in the Registrar's order, failing which the security deposited in the Court (General Division) under section 82.1 shall be forfeited to the Crown.

Proposed Amendment—50.3(4)

Effect of withdrawal of appeal

(4) If the owner withdraws the appeal after the Registrar has ordered the release of the vehicle pursuant to an order by the Superior Court of Justice under section

82.1, the Registrar shall order the owner of the commercial motor vehicle or trailer to return it, without any load, to an impound facility at a location and within the time specified in the Registrar's order, failing which the security deposited in the Court of Justice under section 82.1 shall be forfeited to the Crown.

1999, c. 12, Sched. R, s. 10(1) [Not in force at date of publication.]

Powers of Tribunal

(5) The Tribunal may confirm or set aside the order to impound and suspend.

Notice of decision

(6) The Tribunal shall give written notice of its decision to the owner and the Registrar.

Owner must return vehicle to impound facility if order confirmed

(7) If the Tribunal confirms the order, the Registrar shall order the owner of the commercial motor vehicle or trailer, if the vehicle had been previously released from the impound facility, to return it, without any load, to an impound facility at a location and within the time specified in the Registrar's order and for the period set out in the original order to impound and suspend less the number of days the vehicle was impounded prior to its release under subsection 82.1(24), failing which the security deposited in the Court (General Division) under section 82.1 shall be forfeited to the Crown.

Proposed Amendment—50.3(7)

Owner must return vehicle to impound facility if order confirmed

(7) If the Tribunal confirms the order, the Registrar shall order the owner of the commercial motor vehicle or trailer, if the vehicle had been previously released from the impound facility, to return it, without any load, to an impound facility at a location and within the time specified in the Registrar's order and for the period set out in the original order to impound and suspend less the number of days the vehicle was impounded prior to its release under subsection 82.1(24), failing which the security deposited in the Superior Court of Justice under section 82.1 shall be forfeited to the Crown.

1999, c. 12, Sched. R. s. 10(2) [Not in force at date of publication.]

Registrar's actions if order set aside

(8) If the Tribunal sets aside the order, the Registrar, upon receipt of the notice,

(a) shall issue an order to release the vehicle;

(b) shall reinstate the vehicle portion of the permit that was suspended;

(c) shall pay the owner the amount incurred by the owner, as a result of the order to impound and suspend, for removing and impounding the vehicle, not including any amount for economic losses;

(d) shall pay the operator of the vehicle the amount incurred by the operator, as a result of the order to impound and suspend, for removing the load from the vehicle, not including any amount for economic loss.

Vehicle cannot be operated until made safe

(9) Despite the fact that an order to impound and suspend is set aside and the vehicle portion of the permit is reinstated, no person shall drive or operate on a highway the vehicle that was the subject of the order until it has been placed in a safe condition.

Proposed Amendment—50.3(9)

(9) Despite the fact that an order to impound and suspend is set aside and the vehicle portion of the permit is reinstated, no person shall drive or operate on a highway the vehicle that was the subject of the order until all defects prescribed under section 82 has been repaired and the vehicle is in a safe condition.

1999, c. 12, Sched. R, s. 10(3) [Not in force at date of publication.]

Decision final

(10) The decision of the Tribunal section is final and binding.

Impoundment not stayed

(11) Despite the *Statutory Powers Procedure Act*, the filing of an appeal under this section does not suspend or terminate the order to impound and suspend under section 82.1.

Quorum

(12) [Repealed 1999, c. 12, Sched. G, s. 24 (15).]

Definitions

(13) In this section,

"commercial motor vehicle", **"operator"**, **"owner"** and **"permit"** have the same meanings as in section 82.1.

1997, c. 12, s. 6; 1999, c. 12, Sched. G, s. 24(14), (15)

. . .

Definitions

55.1(1) In this section,

"operator" means

(a) the person directly or indirectly responsible for the operation of a commercial vehicle, including the conduct of the driver of, and the carriage of goods or passengers, if any, in the commercial motor vehicle or combination of vehicles, and

(b) in the absence of evidence to the contrary, where no CVOR certificate, as defined in subsection 16(1), or lease applicable to a commercial motor vehicle, is produced, the holder of the plate portion of the permit for the commercial motor vehicle;

"owner" means the person whose name appears on the certificate of registration for the vehicle, and, where the certificate of registration for the vehicle consits of a vehicle portion and plate portion and different persons are named on each portion, means,

(a) in subsections (5), (8) and (14), the person whose name appears on the vehicle portion, and

(b) in subsections (3), (5), (6), (8), (10), (11), (12), (13), (14), (16), (18.1) and (21), the person whose name appears on the plate portion. ("propriétaire")

Driving while under suspension, registrar notified

(2) Where a police officer or officer appointed for carrying out the provisions of this Act is satisfied that a person was driving a motor vehicle on a highway while his or her driver's licence is under suspension under section 41, 42 or 43, even if it is under suspension at the same time for any other reason, the officer shall,

(a) notify the Registrar of the fact or cause the Registrar to be notified; and

(b) detain the motor vehicle that was being driven by the person whose driver's licence is under suspension under the Registrar issues an order under subsection (3).

Order to impound or release

(3) Upon notification under subsection (2), the Registrar may, without a hearing, issue an order to release the motor vehicle or issue an order to impound the motor vehicle that was being driven by the driver whose driver's licence is under suspension, as follows:

1. For 45 days, if an order to impound under this section has not previously been made, within a prescribed period, with respect to any motor vehicle then owned by the owner of the vehicle currently being impounded.

2. For 90 days, if one order to impound under this section has previously been made, within a prescribed period, with respect to any motor vehicle then owned by the owner of the vehicle currently being impounded.

3. For 180 days, if more than one order to impound under this section has previously been made, within a prescribed period, with respect to any motor vehicle then owned by the owner of the vehicle currently being impounded.

Intent of order to impound

(4) The order to impound issued under this section is intended to promote compliance with this Act and to thereby safeguard the public and does not constitute an alternative to any proceeding or penalty arising from the same circumstances or around the same time.

Notification to police

(5) The Registrar shall notify a police officer or officer appointed for carrying out the provisions of this Act of an order made under subsection (3) and shall send notice of the order to the owner of the motor vehicle at the most recent address for the owner appearing in the records of the Ministry.

Release of vehicle

(6) Upon notification of the Registrar's order to release the motor vehicle, a police officer or officer appointed for carrying out the provisions of this Act shall forthwith release the motor vehicle to its owner.

Service of order to impound

(7) Upon notification of the Registrar's order to impound the motor vehicle, a police officer or officer appointed for carrying out the provisions of this Act shall serve the order or notice of it on the driver.

Service on driver is deemed service on owner and operator

(8) Service of the order, or notice of it, on the driver of the motor vehicle shall be deemed to be service on and sufficient notice to the owner of the vehicle and the operator of the vehicle, if there is an operator.

Surrender of documents, information re trip and goods carried

(9) If the motor vehicle that is the subject of the order to impound contains goods, the police officer or officer appointed for carrying out the provisions of this Act may require the driver and any other person present who is in charge of the motor vehicle to surrender all documents in his or her possession or in the vehicle that relate to the operation of the vehicle or to the carriage of the goods and to furnish all information within the person's knowledge relating to the details of the current trip and the ownership of the goods.

Operator, owner to remove load

(10) Upon being served, or being deemed to have been served, with the order to impound or notice of it, the operator of the motor vehicle, or if there is no operator, the owner, shall forthwith remove any vehicle drawn by the motor vehicle and any load from the motor vehicle.

Application of Dangerous Goods Transportation Act

(11) If the goods are dangerous goods, within the meaning of *Dangerous Goods Transportation Act*, the operator, or if there is no operator, the owner, shall remove them in accordance with that Act.

Officer may remove load, trailer at operator's cost, risk

(12) If, in the opinion of a police officer or officer appointed for carrying out the provisions of this Act, the operator or owner fails to remove a drawn vehicle or load as required by subsection (10) within a reasonable time after being served or being deemed to have been served with the order to impound, the officer may cause the drawn vehicle or load to be removed and stored or disposed of at the cost and risk of the operator, or if there is no operator, the owner.

Same

(13) If a police officer or officer appointed for carrying out the provisions of this Act is of the opinion that the operator or owner has not made appropriate arrangements for the removal of a drawn vehicle or load, having regard to the nature of the goods, including the fact that they are or appear to be dangerous goods, within

the meaning of the *Dangerous Goods Transportation Act*, or are perishable, the officer may cause the drawn vehicle or load to be removed, stored or otherwise disposed of at the cost and risk of the operator, or if there is no operator, the owner.

Vehicle impounded

(14) Upon service or deemed service of the order to impound or notice of it being effected, or, if the motor vehicle that is subject to the order was drawing a vehicle or had a load, once the drawn vehicle and load have been removed, the motor vehicle shall, at the cost of and risk to the owner,

(a) be removed to an impound facility as directed by a police officer or officer appointed for carrying out the provisions of this Act; and

(b) be impounded for the period set out in the order to impound or until ordered to be released by the Registrar under section 50.2

Release of vehicle before end of impound period

(14.1) Despite any order to impound issued under this section, the Registrar may, on application by a person belonging to a class of persons prescribed by regulation, release an impounded motor vehicle of a prescribed class prior to the end of the impound period specified in the order on such conditions as he or she considers just.

Consequences of order to release

(14.2) Where an order to release is made under subsection (14.1), the order to impound shall not be considered a previously made order to impound for the purposes of subsection (3) or subsection 50.2(4).

Personal property in vehicle available to owner

(15) Any personal property that is left in the impounded motor vehicle and that is not attached to or used in connection with its operation shall, upon request and proof of ownership, be made available, at reasonable times, to the owner of the property.

Vehicle released from impound facility

(16) Upon the expiry of the period of impoundment, the Registrar shall order that the motor vehicle be released to its owner from the impound facility.

Release to holder of vehicle portion

(16.1) Despite subsection (16), the holder of the vehicle portion of a certificate of registration may apply to the Registrar for the motor vehicle to be released to that holder upon the expiry of the period of impoundment, rather than to the holder of the plate portion, and the Registrar may order the motor vehicle released to the applicant on such conditions as he or she considers appropriate.

Rescission of previously made order

(16.2) Where the Registrar decides to make an order under subsection (16.1), he or she may rescind any order previously made with respect to the motor vehicle under subsection (16).

Obligations of holder of vehicle portion

(16.3) An order under subsection (16.1) has the effect of making the applicant liable for meeting the owner's obligations under subsection (18.1).

Costs to be paid before release

(17) Despite being served with an order under subsection (14.1), (16) or (16.1), the person who operates the impound facility is not required to release the motor vehicle to the person named in the order until the removal and impound costs related to the order to impound have been paid.

Lien on vehicle for removal, impound costs

(18) The costs incurred by the person who operates the impound facility in respect of an order to impound under this section are a lien on the motor vehicle, which may be enforced in the manner provided under Part III of the *Repair and Storage Liens Act*.

Impound costs

(18.1) The costs incurred by the person who operates the impound facility in respect of an order to impound under this section are a debt due by the owner and the driver of the motor vehicle at the time the order was made to the person, for which the owner and the driver are jointly and severally liable, and the debt may be recovered in any court of competent jurisdiction.

Defence

(18.2) It is a defence to an action referred to in subsection (18.1) that the owner sold or transferred the motor vehicle to another person prior to the date of the order to impound.

Debt due to Crown

(19) The costs incurred by the Crown in removing, storing or disposing of a drawn vehicle or load from a motor vehicle under subsection (12) or (13) are a debt due to the Crown and may be recovered by the Crown in any court of competent jurisdiction.

Civil Remedies Act, 2001 prevails

(19.1) Despite subsections (6), (14.1), (16) and (16.1), a vehicle that is subject to an order under Part III.1 of the *Civil Remedies Act, 2001* shall not be released from detention or the impound facility except in accordance with the terms of that order, or another order, made under that Act.

Impound, removal service providers are independent contractors

(20) Persons who provide removal services or load removal services or who operate impound facilities, and their subcontractors, are independent contractors and not agents of the Ministry for the purposes of this section; such persons shall not charge more for their services in connection with this section than is permitted by regulation.

Owner may recover losses from driver

(21) The owner of a motor vehicle that is subject to an order to impound under this section may bring an action against the driver of the motor vehicle at the time the order was made to recover any costs or other losses incurred by the owner in connection with the order.

Holder of vehicle portion may recover costs

(21.1) The holder of the plate portion of the permit and the driver of the motor vehicle at the time the order to impound was made are jointly and serverally liable to the holder of the vehicle portion of the permit who obtains an order under subsection (16.1) for any costs or losses incurred in connection with the order, and the costs and losses may be recovered in any court of competent jurisdiction.

Protection from personal liability

(22) No action or other proceeding for damages shall be instituted against the Registrar or any employee of the Ministry for any act done in good faith in the execution or intended execution of his or her duty under this section or for any alleged neglect or default in the execution in good faith of that duty.

Crown not relieved of liability

(23) Despite subsections 5(2) and (4) of the *Proceedings Against the Crown Act*, subsection (22) does not relieve the Crown of liability in respect of a tort committed by a person mentioned in that subsection to which it would otherwise be subject.

Offence

(24) Every person who fails to comply with subsection (10) or with a requirement of a police officer or officer appointed for carrying out the provisions of this Act under subsection (9) is guilty of an offence and on conviction is liable to a fine of not less than $200 and not more than $20,000.

Same

(25) Every person who drives or operates or removes a motor vehicle that is subject to an order to impound under this section and every person who causes or permits such a motor vehicle to be driven, operated or removed is guilty of an offence and on conviction is liable to a fine of not less than $200 and not more than $20,000.

Same

(26) Every person who provides removal services or who operates an impound facility and who charges fees for services provided in connection with this section in excess of those permitted by regulation is guilty of an offence and on conviction is liable to a fine of not less than $100 and not more than $1,000.

Same

(27) Every person who obstructs or interferes with a police officer or officer appointed for carrying out the provisions of this Act in the performance of his or her duties under this section is guilty of an offence and on conviction is liable to a

fine of not less than $200 and not more than $20,000 or to imprisonment for a term of not more than six months, or to both.

Decision without hearing is final

(27.1) The Registrar shall assess applications made under subsections (14.1) and (16.1) without a hearing and the Registrar's decision is final.

Regulations

(28) The Lieutenant Governor in Council may make regulations,

(a) prescribing the period for the purpose of subsection (3);

(b) prescribing a schedule of fees that may be charged by independent contractors for services in connection with this section;

(c) prescribing the manner in which orders may be issued and notification of them given under this section;

(d) prescribing methods for and rules of service for any notices or orders required to be served under this section;

(e) classifying persons and motor vehicles and exempting any class of person or any class of motor vehicle from any provision of this section or any regulation made under this section and prescribing conditions for any such exemptions:

Proposed Addition — 55.1 (28) (e.1), (e.2)

(e.1) prescribing a period of time during which all persons and motor vehicles are exempt from paragraphs 2 and 3 of subsection (3) and providing that an order to impound for 45 days under paragraph 1 of subsection (3) shall be made during that period where paragraph 2 or 3 of subsection (3) would otherwise apply;

(e.2) classifying persons and motor vehicles and exempting any class of person or motor vehicle from paragraphs 2 and 3 of subsection (3) and providing that an order to impound for 45 days under paragraph 1 of subsection (3) shall be made with respect to that class of person or motor vehicle where paragraph 2 or 3 of subsection (3) would otherwise apply, and prescribing conditions for any such exemption.

1999, c. 12, Sched. R, s. 11 [Not in force at date of publication.]

(f) prescribing fees for the administration of this section;

(g) prescribing the time within which an appeal may be brought under section 50.2 with respect to an order under this section, and governing any other time requirements in the appeal process;

(h) prescribing criteria to be considered, and criteria not to be considered, by the Tribunal in determining in an appeal under section 50.2 whether exceptional hardship will result from an order to impound that is made under this section;

(i) prescribing classes of persons and motor vehicles for the purposes of subsection (14.1) and specifying eligibility criteria;

(j) prescribing rules, time periods and procedures with respect to applications under subsection (14.1).

Forms

(29) The Minister may require that forms approved by the Minister be used for any purpose of this section.

1997, c. 12, s. 8; 1999, c. 12, Sched. G, s. 24(16); 2000, c. 26, Sched. O, s. 5; 2002, c. 18, Sched. P, s. 18; 2007, c. 13, s. 15

. . .

Proposed Addition—198.5

Suspension on conviction, procuring, etc.

198.5 (1) The driver's licence of a person is suspended on his or her conviction of an offence under section 211, 212 or 213 of the *Criminal Code* (Canada) that was committed while the person was driving or had care, charge or control of a motor vehicle.

Period of suspension

(2) The period of the suspension is,

(a) one year if in the five years before the date of the conviction the person has not been convicted of an offence under section 211, 212 or 213 of the *Criminal Code* (Canada) that would have resulted in a suspension of his or her driver's licence under this section; or

(b) two years if in the five years before the date of the conviction the person has been convicted of an offence under section 211, 212 or 213 of the *Criminal Code* (Canada) that would have resulted in a suspension of his or her driver's licence under this section.

Order for discharge

(3) This section applies in the same manner as if the person were convicted if,

(a) the person pleads guilty or is found guilty of the offence; and

(b) an order under the *Criminal Code* (Canada), a disposition under the *Young Offenders Act* (Canada) or a sentence imposed under the *Youth Criminal Justice Act* (Canada) directs that the person be discharged.

Proposed Amendment—Conditional Amendment—198.5(3)(b)

On the later of the coming into force of 2002, c. 5, s. 32 [Not i force at date of publication.] and the day the *Good Government Act, 2006* receives Royal Assent [S.O. 2006, c. 19 received Royal Assent June 22, 2006.], clause 198.5(3)(b) is replaced by the following:

(b) an order under the *Criminal Code* (Canada), a disposition under the *Young Offenders Act* (Canada) or a sentence imposed under the *Youth Criminal Justice Act* (Canada) directs that person be discharged.

2006, c. 19, s 9(4) [Conditions not yet satisfied.]

Increased suspension

(4) The period of suspension under this section is increased by the period equal to any sentence of imprisonment that is imposed on the person on the conviction.

Protection from personal liability

(5) No action or other proceeding for damages shall be instituted against any person for the suspension or reinstatement of a driver's licence in good faith in the execution or intended execution of a duty under this section or for any incorrect information about or misapplication of the suspension period under subsection (2).

Crown not relieved of liability

(6) Despite subsections 5(2) and (4) of the *Proceedings Against the Crown Act*, subsection (5) does not relieve the Crown from liability for a tort committed by a person for which the Crown would otherwise be liable.

Transitional

(7) This section applies only on convictions of offences committed on or after the day this section comes into force.

2002, c. 5, s. 32 [Not in force at date of publication.]

Appendix E

Notice and Certificates

NOTICE OF INTENTION TO PRODUCE
CERTIFICATE(S) S.258 (7)

IN THE ______________ COURT OF JUSTICE

HER MAJESTY THE QUEEN
vs

____

TAKE NOTICE that the Crown intends to tender into evidence at your trial on a charge under subsection(s)

253(a) ("impaired") ☐
253(b) ("over 80") ☐
255(2) ("impaired causing bodily harm") ☐
253(3) ("impaired causing death") ☐

of the Criminal Code of Canada alleged to have been committed by means of a

motor vehicle ☐
vessel ☐
aircraft ☐

at ______________________ on the ________ day of ______________________

20 ______ , a certificate/certificates pursuant to paragraph(s)

258(1)(e) ☐	258(1)(h)(i) ☐
258(1)(f) ☐	258(1)(h)(ii) ☐
258(1)(g) ☐	258(1)(h)(iii) ☐
258(1)(i) ☐	

of the Criminal Code a copy/copies of which is/are given to you.

Dated at ____

this ______________ day of ______________________________, 20 ____

Time Served ______________ hrs

Served by ______________ ______________ ______________ ______________
Signature of Officer Badge No. Rank Division

I acknowledge receipt of a copy of this Notice and a copy/copies of the certificate(s) attached hereto

____
Signature and name of accused

NOTE: FOR COURT PURPOSES THE SERVING OFFICER MUST COMPARE THE ORIGINAL AND COPIES TO ENSURE THEY ARE IDENTICAL

PRP 50

Distribution
Copy - Insert in Crown Envelope
Copy - To Person Tested (Accused)
Copy - For Person Serving Notice

CERTIFICATE OF QUALIFIED TECHNICIAN (BREATH SAMPLES)
(Sec. 258(1)(g))

TOP 18, 1994/02

I, ..., a person designated by the Solicitor General of the Province of Ontario pursuant to subsection 254(1) of the Criminal Code of Canada as a qualified technician, qualified to operate the approved instrument Intoxilyzer ® 5000C,

DO HEREBY CERTIFY:

That at ....
Address where samples taken

in the Municipality of Metropolitan Toronto, in the Province of Ontario, pursuant to a demand made under subsection 254(3) of the Criminal Code of Canada, I took samples of the breath of a person identified to me as:

....

of ....
Home Address

THAT at .... a.m./p.m. on the .... day of .... 20.........., I completed taking the first of the said samples and at .... a.m./p.m. on the .... day of .... 20.........., I commenced taking the second of the said samples;

THAT the time required to take each of the said samples was less than one minute;

THAT each of the said samples was received directly into an Intoxilyzer ® 5000C, an approved instrument as defined in subsection 254(1) of the Criminal Code and operated by me;

THAT an analysis was made of each of the said samples by means of the said instrument which was operated by me and which I ascertained to be in proper working order by means of an alcohol standard suitable for use with said instrument and identified as

....;

THAT I found the result of the analysis of the first of the said breath samples to be .... milligrams of alcohol in 100 millilitres of blood; and

THAT I found the result of the analysis of the second of the said breath samples to be .... milligrams of alcohol in 100 millilitres of blood.

Dated this .... day of ...., 20......., at .... in the Municipality of Metropolitan Toronto, in the Province of Ontario.

Alcohol Influence Report Serial Number: ....

....
Signature of Qualified Technician *Name, Rank, Number, Unit*

Served .... a.m./p.m; ...., 20.................

By: ....
Signature *Name, Rank, Number, Unit*

Distribution: *White* - *Insert in Confidential Crown Envelope*
Pink - *To Person Tested*
Yellow - *Technicians' Copy*

APPENDIX E

Ontario
Provincial
Police

CERTIFICATE OF QUALIFIED TECHNICIAN (BREATH SAMPLES)

(Sec. 258(1)(g))

I, ______________________________, a person designated by the Solicitor General of the Province of Ontario pursuant to subsection 254(1) of the Criminal Code of Canada as a qualified technician, qualified to operate the approved instrument Intoxilyzer ® 5000C,

DO HEREBY CERTIFY:

That at ____ in the Municipality of Metropolitan Toronto, in the Province of Ontario, pursuant to a demand made under section 254(3) of the Criminal Code of Canada, I took samples of the breath of a person identified to me as:

____

of (Home Address) ____

THAT at ___________ a.m./p.m. on the _________ day of __________________ 20_____, I completed taking the first of the said samples and at ___________ a.m./p.m. on the _________ day of __________________ 20_____ commenced taking the second of the said samples;

THAT the time required to take each of the said samples was less than one minute;

THAT each of the said samples was received directly into an Intoxilyzer ® 5000C, an approved instrument as defined in subsection 254(1) of the Criminal Code and operated by me;

THAT an analysis was made of each of the said samples by means of the said instrument which was operated by me and which I ascertained to be in proper working order by means of an alcohol standard suitable for use with said instrument and identified as

____.

THAT I found the result of the analysis of the first of the said breath samples to be _________ milligrams of alcohol in 100 milliliters of blood.

THAT I found the result of the analysis of the second of the said breath samples to be _________ milligrams of alcohol in 100 milliliters of blood.

Dated this _________ day of __________________, 20_____, at ____________________________ in the Municipality of Metropolitan Toronto, in the Province of Ontario.

Alcohol Influence Report Serial Number ____________________________

____

Signature of Qualified Technician - Name, Rank, Number

Served_____________ a.m./p.m; ____________________________, 20_____

By: ____

Signature - Name, Rank, Number

NOTICE IN ACCORDANCE WITH SECTION 258(7) OF THE CRIMINAL CODE

YOU are hereby notified that is intended to produce this certificate at your trial ____________________________

I acknowledge receipt of a true copy of this certificate ____________________ served by ____________________

Dated this _____ day of __________________ 20_____ at ______________________ in the Province of Ontario.

Appendix F

Charges

CANADA
PROVINCE OF ONTARIO
PROVINCE DE L'ONTARIO
TORONTO REGION
RÉGION DE TORONTO

Information of
Dénonciation de

of/*de*

(occupation/*profession*)

The informant says
Le dénonciateur

that he/she believes on reasonable grounds that
déclare qu'il a des motifs raisonnables de croire que

of
de

(1) on or about the .... day of .... 20 ....., at the Municipality of Metropolitan Toronto, in the Toronto Region
le ou vers le .... jour de .... dans la municipalité de la communauté urbaine de Toronto, dans la région de Toronto,

without reasonable excuse, failed or refused to comply with a demand made to him/her by a peace officer under section 254(2) of the Criminal Code in the circumstances therein mentioned, to provide forthwith, such sample of his/her breath, as in the opinion of the police officer, is necessary to enable a proper analysis of his/her breath to be made by means of an approved screening device and to accompany the peace officer for the purpose of enabling such a sample of his/her breath to be taken, contrary to section 254(5) of the Criminal Code.

a fait défaut ou a refusé d'obtempérer, sans excuse raisonnable, à l'ordre que lui a donné un agent de la paix en vertu du paragraphe 254(2) du Code criminel, dans les circonstances y mentionnées, de lui fournir l'échantillon d'haleine que l'agent de la paix estimait nécessaire pour l'analyser à l'aide d'un appareil de détection approuvé et de suivre l'agent de la paix pour que cet échantillon d'haleine puisse être prélevé, en violation du paragraphe 254(5) du Code criminel.

Sworn before me at the Municipality of Metropolitan Toronto, in the Toronto Region
Assermenté devant moi dans la municipalité de la communauté urbaine de Toronto, dans la région de Toronto,

this ....
le

day of .... 20 ......
jour de

.... A Justice of the Peace in and for the Province of Ontario/*Juge de paix dans et pour la province de l'Ontario*

.... Informant/*Dénonciateur*

☐ Appearance Notice / *Citation à comparaître* ☐ Promise to Appear / *Promesse de comparaître* ☐ Recognizance for / *Engagement pour le* ...... 20 ...... ☐ Confirmed on / *Confirmé(e) le* ...... 20 ...... J P

Date

Crown Elects to Proceed / *Choix du poursuivant*: ☐ Summarily / *Procédure sommaire* ☐ By Indictment / *Acte d'accusation* ☐ Summary Conviction (Offence(s) / *Infraction(s) punissable(s) sur déclaration de culpabilité par procédure sommaire*

Accused Elects Trial by / *Choix de l'accusé(e)*: ☐ Judge (General Division) / *Juge seul (Division générale)* ☐ Judge and Jury / *Juge et jury*

☐ Discharged / *Libéré(e)* ☐ Committed / *Renvoyé(e) à procès* ☐ Ordered to Stand Trial / *Astreint(e) en jugement* ☐ With Consent of Accused and Prosecutor, / *Avec le consentement de l'accusé(e) et du poursuivant*

Without Taking or Recording / *Sans recueillir ou consigner*: ☐ Any Evidence (or) / *de preuve (ou)* ☐ Further Evidence / *de preuve supplémentaire* Bail $ / *Cautionnement* $

☐ Accused Elects Trial by a Judge (Provincial Division) / *L'accusé(e) choisit d'être jugé(e) (Division provinciale)* ☐ Absolute Jurisdiction / *Juridiction absolue*

Pleads / *Plaide*: ☐ Guilty / *Coupable* ☐ Not Guilty / *Non coupable* ☐ Withdrawn / *Accusation(s) retirée(s)*

Found / *Reconnu(e)*: ☐ Guilty / *Coupable* ☐ Not Guilty / *Non coupable* ☐ In Absentia / *Ex parte*

☐ Absolute Discharge / *Absolution inconditionnelle* ☐ Conditional Discharge / *Absolution sous condition*

Fined $ / *Amende de* ...... & $ / *$ et de* ...... costs / *$ pour les dépens* Time to Pay / *Délai de paiement*

or / *ou*

Date of Birth / *Date de naissance*: Day *Jour* | Mo. *Mois* | Yr. *Année*

Probation for / *Période de probation de*

Sentenced to Imprisonment for / *Peine d'emprisonnement*

FAIL TO PROVIDE SAMPLE OF BREATH, Code, Sec. 254(5) (screening device)
DÉFAUT DE FOURNIR UN ÉCHANTILLON D'HALEINE, Art. 254(5) du Code (appareils de detection)

Judge *Juge*

YC 0877 (rev. 05/90)

CANADA
PROVINCE OF ONTARIO
PROVINCE DE L'ONTARIO
TORONTO REGION
RÉGION DE TORONTO

Information of
Dénonciation de
of/*de*

(occupation/*profession*)

The informant says
Le dénonciateur

that he/she believes on reasonable grounds that
déclare qu'il a des motifs raisonnables de croire que

of
de

(1) on or about the day of 20 , at the Municipality of Metropolitan Toronto, in the Toronto Region
le ou vers le jour de dans la municipalité de la communauté urbaine de Toronto, dans la région de Toronto,
ability to operate a motor vehicle was impaired by alcohol or a drug, operated a motor vehicle, contrary to section 253(a) of the Criminal Code
a conduit un véhicule à moteur alors que sa capacité de conduire un véhicule à moteur était affaiblie par l'effet de l'alcool ou d'une drogue, en violation de l'alinéa 253(a) du Code criminel

(2) and further that
et en outre que

on or about the day of 20 , at the Municipality
le ou vers le jour de dans la municipalité
of Metropolitan Toronto, without reasonable excuse, failed or refused to comply with a demand made to him/her by a peace officer under section 254(3) of
de la communauté urbaine de Toronto, a fait défaut ou a refusé d'obtempérer, sans excuse raisonnable, à l'ordre que lui a donné un agent de la paix
the Criminal Code in the circumstances therein mentioned to provide then, or as soon thereafter as is practicable, such samples of his/her breath as
en vertu du paragraphe 254(3) du Code criminel, dans les circonstances y mentionnées, de lui fournir immédiatement ou dès que possible, les
in the opinion of a qualified technician referred to in section 254 of the Criminal Code are necessary to enable a proper analysis to be made in order
échantillons d'haleine qui, de l'avis d'un technicien qualifié défini à l'article 254 du Code criminel, étaient nécessaires à une analyse convenable pour
to determine the concentration, if any, of alcohol in his/her blood, and to accompany the peace officer for the purpose of enabling such samples to be
permettre de déterminer son alcoolémie et de suivre l'agent de la paix pour le prélèvement des échantillons, en violation du paragraphe 254(5) du
taken, contrary to section 254(5) of the Criminal Code
Code criminel.

Sworn before me at the Municipality of Metropolitan Toronto, in the Toronto Region
Assermenté devant moi dans la municipalité de la communauté urbaine de Toronto, dans la région de Toronto,

this
le

day of 20
jour de

A Justice of the Peace in and for the Province of Ontario/*Juge de paix dans et pour la province de l'Ontario*

Informant/*Dénonciateur*

☐ Appearance Notice / *Citation à comparaître* ☐ Promise to Appear / *Promesse de comparaître* ☐ Recognizance for / *Engagement pour le* 20 ☐ Confirmed on / *Confirmé(e) le* 20 J.P.

Date

Crown Elects to Proceed / *Choix du poursuivant* ☐ Summarily / *Procédure sommaire* ☐ By Indictment / *Acte d'accusation* ☐ Summary Conviction (Offence(s) / *Infraction(s) punissable(s) sur déclaration de culpabilité par procédure sommaire*

Accused Elects Trial by / *Choix de l'accusé(e)* ☐ Judge (General Division) / *Juge seul (Division générale)* ☐ Judge and Jury / *Juge et jury*

☐ Discharged / *Libéré(e)* ☐ Committed / *Renvoyé(e) à procès* ☐ Ordered to Stand Trial / *Astreint(e) en jugement* ☐ With Consent of Accused and Prosecutor / *Avec le consentement de l'accusé(e) et du poursuivant*

Without Taking or Recording / *Sans recueillir ou consigner* ☐ Any Evidence (or) / *de preuve (ou)* ☐ Further Evidence / *de preuve supplémentaire* Bail $ / *Cautionnement* $

☐ Accused Elects Trial by a Judge (Provincial Division) / *L'accusé(e) choisit d'être jugé(e) (Division provinciale)* ☐ Absolute Jurisdiction / *Juridiction absolue*

Pleads / *Plaide* ☐ Guilty / *Coupable* ☐ Not Guilty / *Non coupable* ☐ Withdrawn / *Accusation(s) retirée(s)*

Found / *Reconnu(e)* ☐ Guilty / *Coupable* ☐ Not Guilty / *Non coupable* ☐ In Absentia / *Ex parte*

☐ Absolute Discharge / *Absolution inconditionnelle* ☐ Conditional Discharge / *Absolution sous condition*

Fined $ & $ costs Time to Pay
Amende de $ et de $ pour les dépens Délai de paiement

or
ou

Date of Birth / *Date de naissance*

Day *Jour*	Mo. *Mois*	Yr. *Année*

Probation for
Période de probation de

Sentenced to Imprisonment for
Peine d'emprisonnement

IMPAIRED DRIVING, Sec. 253(a)
FAIL TO PROVIDE SAMPLE OF BREATH, Code, Sec. 254(5)
CAPACITÉ DE CONDUITE AFFAIBLIE Art. 253(a)
DÉFAUT DE FOURNIR UN ÉCHANTILLON D'HALEINE, Art. 254(5) du Code

YC 0882 (rev. 05/90)

Judge *Juge*

CANADA
PROVINCE OF ONTARIO
PROVINCE DE L'ONTARIO
TORONTO REGION
RÉGION DE TORONTO

Information of
Dénonciation de
of/*de*

(occupation/*profession*)

The informant says
Le dénonciateur

that he/she believes on reasonable grounds that
déclare qu'il a des motifs raisonnables de croire que

of
de

(1) on or about the .... day of .... 20 ......, at the Municipality of Metropolitan Toronto, in the Toronto Region
le ou vers le *jour de* *dans la municipalité de la communauté urbaine de Toronto, dans la région de Toronto,*
without reasonable excuse, failed or refused to comply with a demand made to him/her by a peace officer under section 254(3) of the Criminal Code in the
a fait défaut ou a refusé d'obtempérer, sans excuse raisonnable, à un ordre que lui a donné un agent de la paix en vertu du paragraphe
circumstances therein mentioned to provide then, or as soon thereafter as is practicable, such samples of his/her breath as in the opinion of a qualified
254(3) du Code criminel, dans les circonstances y mentionnées, de lui fournir immédiatement ou dès que possible les échantillons d'haleine
technician referred to in section 254 of the Criminal Code are necessary to enable a proper analysis to be made in order to determine the concen-
qui, de l'avis d'un technicien qualifié défini à l'article 254 du Code criminel, étaient nécessaires à une analyse convenable pour permettre de déter-
tration, if any, of alcohol in his/her blood, and to accompany the peace officer for the purpose of enabling such samples to be taken, contrary to section
miner son alcoolémie et de suivre l'agent de la paix afin que soient prélevés les échantillons, en violation du paragraphe 254(5) du Code criminel.
254(5) of the Criminal Code.

Sworn before me at the Municipality of Metropolitan Toronto, in the Toronto Region
Assermenté devant moi dans la municipalité de la communauté urbaine de Toronto, dans la région de Toronto,

this
le

day of .... 20 ....
jour de

A Justice of the Peace in and for the Province of Ontario/*Juge de paix dans et pour la province de l'Ontario*

Informant/*Dénonciateur*

☐ Appearance Notice / *Citation à comparaître*
☐ Promise to Appear / *Promesse de comparaître*
☐ Recognizance for / *Engagement pour le* 20
☐ Confirmed on / *Confirmé(e) le* 20 J.P.

Date

Crown Elects to Proceed / *Choix du poursuivant*: ☐ Summarily / *Procédure sommaire* ☐ By Indictment / *Acte d'accusation* ☐ Summary Conviction (Offence(s) / *Infraction(s) punissable(s) sur déclaration de culpabilité par procédure sommaire*

Accused Elects Trial by / *Choix de l'accusé(e)*: ☐ Judge (General Division) / *Juge seul (Division générale)* ☐ Judge and Jury / *Juge et jury*

☐ Discharged / *Libéré(e)* ☐ Committed / *Renvoyé(e) à procès* ☐ Ordered to Stand Trial / *Astreint(e) en jugement* ☐ With Consent of Accused and Prosecutor, / *Avec le consentement de l'accusé(e) et du poursuivant*

Without Taking or Recording / *Sans recueillir ou consigner* ☐ Any Evidence (or) / *de preuve (ou)* ☐ Further Evidence / *de preuve supplémentaire* Bail $ / *Cautionnement* $

☐ Accused Elects Trial by a Judge (Provincial Division) / *L'accusé(e) choisit d'être jugé(e) (Division provinciale)* ☐ Absolute Jurisdiction / *Juridiction absolue*

Pleads / *Plaide*: ☐ Guilty / *Coupable* ☐ Not Guilty / *Non coupable* ☐ Withdrawn / *Accusation(s) retirée(s)*

Found / *Reconnu(e)*: ☐ Guilty / *Coupable* ☐ Not Guilty / *Non coupable* ☐ In Absentia / *Ex parte*

☐ Absolute Discharge / *Absolution inconditionnelle* ☐ Conditional Discharge / *Absolution sous condition*

Fined $ / *Amende de* & $ / $ *et de* costs. Time to Pay / $ *pour les dépens. Délai de paiement*

or / *ou*

Date of Birth / *Date de naissance*

Day/Jour	Mo/Mois	Yr/Année

Probation for / *Période de probation de*

Sentenced to Imprisonment for / *Peine d'emprisonnement*

FAIL TO PROVIDE SAMPLE OF BREATH, Code, Sec. 254(5) (approved instruments)
DÉFAUT DE FOURNIR UN ÉCHANTILLON D'HALEINE, Art. 254(5) du Code (alcootest approuvé)

Judge/*Juge*

YC 0889 (rev. 05/90)

CANADA
PROVINCE OF ONTARIO
PROVINCE DE L'ONTARIO
TORONTO REGION
RÉGION DE TORONTO

Information of
Dénonciation de
of/*de*

(occupation/*profession*)

The informant says
Le dénonciateur

that he/she believes on reasonable grounds that
déclare qu'il a des motifs raisonnables de croire que

of
de

(1) on or about the .... day of .... 20 .... , at the Municipality of Metropolitan Toronto, in the Toronto Region
le ou vers le *jour de* *dans la municipalité de la communauté urbaine de Toronto, dans la région de Toronto,*
while his ability to operate a motor vehicle was impaired by alcohol or a drug, had the care or control of a motor vehicle, contrary to the Criminal Code, section 253(a).
a eu la garde ou le contrôle d'un véhicule à moteur alors que sa capacité de conduire ce véhicule était affaiblie par l'effet de l'alcool ou d'une drogue, en violation de l'alinéa 253(a) du Code criminel.

Sworn before me at the Municipality of Metropolitan Toronto, in the Toronto Region
Assermenté devant moi dans la municipalité de la communauté urbaine de Toronto, dans la région de Toronto,

this ....
le

day of .... 20 ....
jour de

A Justice of the Peace in and for the Province of Ontario/*Juge de paix dans et pour la province de l'Ontario*

Informant/*Dénonciateur*

☐ Appearance Notice / *Citation à comparaître* ☐ Promise to Appear / *Promesse de comparaître* ☐ Recognizance for / *Engagement pour le* 20 ☐ Confirme and / *Confirmé(e) le* 20 J P

Date

Crown Elects to Proceed / *Choix du poursuivant* ☐ Summarily / *Procédure sommaire* ☐ By Indictment / *Acte d'accusation* ☐ Summary Conviction (Offence(s) / *Infraction(s) punissable(s) sur déclaration de culpabilité par procédure sommaire*

Accused Elects Trial by / *Choix de l'accusé(e)* ☐ Judge (General Division) / *Juge seul (Division générale)* ☐ Judge and Jury / *Juge et jury*

☐ Discharged / *Libéré(e)* ☐ Committed - / *Renvoyé(e) à procès* - ☐ Ordered to Stand Trial - / *Astreint(e) en jugement* - ☐ With Consent of Accused and Prosecutor, / *Avec le consentement de l'accusé(e) et du poursuivant*

Without Taking or Recording - / *Sans recueillir ou consigner* - ☐ Any Evidence (or) / *de preuve (ou)* - ☐ Further Evidence / *de preuve supplémentaire* Bail $ / *Cautionnement* $

☐ Accused Elects Trial by a Judge (Provincial Division) / *L'accusé(e) choisit d'être jugé(e) (Division provinciale)* ☐ Absolute Jurisdiction / *Juridiction absolue*

Pleads / *Plaide* ☐ Guilty / *Coupable* ☐ Not Guilty / *Non coupable* ☐ Withdrawn / *Accusation(s) retirée(s)*

Found / *Reconnu(e)* ☐ Guilty / *Coupable* ☐ Not Guilty / *Non coupable* ☐ In Absentia / *Ex parte*

☐ Absolute Discharge / *Absolution inconditionnelle* ☐ Conditional Discharge / *Absolution sous condition*

Fined $ / *Amende de* & $ / $ *et de* costs. Time to Pay / $ *pour les dépens. Délai de paiement*

or / *ou*

Date of Birth / *Date de naissance*

Day/Jour	Mo/Mois	Yr/Année

Probation for / *Période de probation de*

Exhibits Filed / *Pièces déposées* ☐ Yes / *Oui* ☐ No / *Non*

Sentenced to Imprisonment for / *Peine d'emprisonnement*

CARE OR CONTROL, WHILE IMPAIRED, Code, Sec. 253(a)
GARDE OU CONTRÔLE AVEC CAPACITÉ AFFAIBLIE, Art. 253(a) du Code

Judge/*Juge*

YC 0909 (rev. 05/90)

CANADA
PROVINCE OF ONTARIO
PROVINCE DE L'ONTARIO
TORONTO REGION
RÉGION DE TORONTO

Information of / *Dénonciation de* ....
of/*de* ....

.... (occupation/*profession*) .... The informant says / *Le dénonciateur*

that he/she believes on reasonable grounds that
déclare qu'il a des motifs raisonnables de croire que

.... of / *de* ....

(1) on or about the .... day of .... 20...... , at the Municipality of Metropolitan Toronto, in the Toronto Region
le ou vers le .... *jour de* .... *dans la municipalité de la communauté urbaine de Toronto, dans la région de Toronto,*

while his/her ability to operate a motor vehicle was impaired by alcohol or a drug, had the care or control of a motor vehicle, contrary to section 253(a)
avait la garde ou le contrôle d'un véhicule à moteur alors que sa capacité de conduire un véhicule était affaiblie par l'effet de l'alcool ou d'une drogue,

of the Criminal Code.
en violation de l'alinéa 253(a) du Code criminel.

(2) and further that
et en outre que

on or about the .... day of .... 20..... , at the Municipality
le ou vers le .... *jour de* .... *dans la municipalité*

of Metropolitan Toronto, in the Toronto Region, had the care or control of a motor vehicle, having consumed alcohol in such quantity that the concentration
de la communauté urbaine de Toronto, dans la région de Toronto, avait la garde ou le contrôle d'un véhicule à moteur alors qu'il avait consommé une quantité

thereof in his blood exceeded 80 milligrams of alcohol in 100 millilitres of blood, contrary to section 253(b) of the Criminal Code.
d'alcool telle que son alcoolémie dépassait quatre-vingts milligrammes d'alcool par cent millilitres de sang, en violation de l'alinéa 253(b) du Code criminel.

Sworn before me at the Municipality of Metropolitan Toronto, in the Toronto Region
Assermenté devant moi dans la municipalité de la communauté urbaine de Toronto,
dans la région de Toronto,

this / *le* ....

day of / *jour de* .... 20.......... ,

.... A Justice of the Peace in and for the Province of Ontario/*Juge de paix dans et pour la province de l'Ontario*

.... Informant/*Dénonciateur*

☐ Appearance Notice / *Citation à comparaître* ☐ Promise to Appear / *Promesse de comparaître* ☐ Recognizance for / *Engagement pour le* .... 20 .... ☐ Confirmed on / *Confirmé(e) le* .... 20 .... J P

Date

Crown Elects to Proceed / *Choix du poursuivant* ☐ Summarily / *Procédure sommaire* ☐ By Indictment / *Acte d'accusation* ☐ Summary Conviction (Offence(s) / *Infraction(s) punissable(s) sur déclaration de culpabilité par procédure sommaire*

Accused Elects Trial by / *Choix de l'accusé(e)* ☐ Judge (General Division) / *Juge seul (Division générale)* ☐ Judge and Jury / *Juge et jury*

☐ Discharged / *Libéré(e)* ☐ Committed - / *Renvoyé(e) à procès* - ☐ Ordered to Stand Trial - / *Astreint(e) en jugement* - ☐ With Consent of Accused and Prosecutor, / *Avec le consentement de l'accusé(e) et du poursuivant*

Without Taking or Recording - / *Sans recueillir ou consigner* - ☐ Any Evidence (or) / *de preuve (ou)* - ☐ Further Evidence / *de preuve supplémentaire* Bail $ / *Cautionnement* .... $

☐ Accused Elects Trial by a Judge (Provincial Division) / *L'accusé(e) choisit d'être jugé(e) (Division provinciale)* ☐ Absolute Jurisdiction / *Juridiction absolue*

Pleads / *Plaide* ☐ Guilty / *Coupable* ☐ Not Guilty / *Non coupable* ☐ Withdrawn / *Accusation(s) retirée(s)*

Found / *Reconnu(e)* ☐ Guilty / *Coupable* ☐ Not Guilty / *Non coupable* ☐ In Absentia / *Ex parte*

☐ Absolute Discharge / *Absolution inconditionnelle* ☐ Conditional Discharge / *Absolution sous condition*

Fined $ / *Amende de* .... & $ / *$ et de* .... costs. Time to Pay / *$ pour les dépens. Délai de paiement*

or / *ou*

Date of Birth / *Date de naissance*

Day/*Jour*	Mo/*Mois*	Yr/*Année*

Probation for / *Période de probation de*

Exhibits Filed / *Pièces déposées* ☐ Yes / *Oui* ☐ No / *Non*

Sentenced to Imprisonment for / *Peine d'emprisonnement*

CARE OR CONTROL WHILE IMPAIRED, Code, Sec. 253(a)
CARE OR CONTROL WHILE OVER 80 mgs, Code, Sec. 253(b)
CAPACITÉ DE CONDUIRE AFFAIBLIE, Art. 253(a) du Code
CONDUIRE LORSQUE L'ALCOOLÉMIE DÉPASSE 80 mg., Art. 253(b) du Code

YC 0910 (rev 05/90)

Judge/*Juge*

CANADA
PROVINCE OF ONTARIO
PROVINCE DE L'ONTARIO
TORONTO REGION
RÉGION DE TORONTO

Information of
Dénonciation de
of/*de*

(occupation/*profession*)

The informant says
Le dénonciateur

that he/she believes on reasonable grounds that
déclare qu'il a des motifs raisonnables de croire que

(1) on or about the ______ day of ______ 20 ___, at the Municipality of Metropolitan Toronto, in the Toronto Region
le ou vers le ______ jour de ______ dans la municipalité de la communauté urbaine de Toronto, dans la région de Toronto,
while his ability to operate a motor vehicle was impaired by alcohol or a drug, had the care or control of a motor vehicle, contrary to section 253(a) of the Criminal Code.
avait la garde ou le contrôle d'un véhicule à moteur alors que sa capacité de conduire un véhicule était affaiblie par l'effet de l'alcool ou d'une drogue, en violation de l'alinéa 253(a) du Code criminel.

(2) and further that
et en outre que

on or about the ______ day of ______ 20 ___, at the Municipality of Metropolitan Toronto, in the Toronto Region, without reasonable excuse, failed or refused to comply with a demand made to him/her by a peace officer under section 254(3) of the Criminal Code in the circumstances therein mentioned to provide then, or as soon thereafter as is practicable, such samples of his/her breath as in the opinion of a qualified technician referred to in section 254 of the Criminal Code are necessary to enable a proper analysis to be made in order to determine the concentration, if any, of alcohol in his/her blood, and to accompany the peace officer for the purpose of enabling such samples to be taken, contrary to section 254(5) of the Criminal Code.

le ou vers le ______ jour de ______ dans la municipalité de la communauté urbaine de Toronto, dans la région de Toronto, a fait défaut ou a refusé d'obtempérer, sans excuse raisonnable, à l'ordre que lui a donné un agent de la paix en vertu du paragraphe 254(3) du Code criminel, dans les circonstances y mentionnées, de lui fournir immédiatement ou dès que possible, les échantillons d'haleine qui, de l'avis d'un technicien qualifié défini à l'article 254 du Code criminel, étaient nécessaires à une analyse convenable pour permettre de déterminer son alcoolémie et de suivre l'agent de la paix afin que soient prélevés les échantillons, en violation du paragraphe 254(5) du Code criminel.

Sworn before me at the Municipality of Metropolitan Toronto, in the Toronto Region
Assermenté devant moi dans la municipalité de la communauté urbaine de Toronto, dans la région de Toronto,
this / *le* ______
day of / *jour de* ______ 20 ___.

A Justice of the Peace in and for the Province of Ontario/*Juge de paix dans et pour la province de l'Ontario*

Informant/*Dénonciateur*

☐ Appearance Notice / *Citation à comparaître* ☐ Promise to Appear / *Promesse de comparaître* ☐ Recognizance for / *Engagement pour le* ___ 20 ___ ☐ Confirmed on / *Confirmé(e) le* ___ 20 ___ J.P.

Date

Crown Elects to Proceed / *Choix du poursuivant*: ☐ Summarily / *Procédure sommaire* ☐ By Indictment / *Acte d'accusation* ☐ Summary Conviction (Offence(s)) / *Infraction(s) punissable(s) sur déclaration de culpabilité par procédure sommaire*

Accused Elects Trial by / *Choix de l'accusé(e)*: ☐ Judge (General Division) / *Juge seul (Division générale)* ☐ Judge and Jury / *Juge et jury*

☐ Discharged / *Libéré(e)* ☐ Committed - / *Renvoyé(e) à procès -* ☐ Ordered to Stand Trial - / *Astreint(e) en jugement -* ☐ With Consent of Accused and Prosecutor. / *Avec le consentement de l'accusé(e) et du poursuivant*

Without Taking or Recording - / *Sans recueillir ou consigner -* ☐ Any Evidence (or) / *de preuve (ou) -* ☐ Further Evidence / *de preuve supplémentaire* Bail $ / *Cautionnement* $

☐ Accused Elects Trial by a Judge (Provincial Division) / *L'accusé(e) choisit d'être jugé(e) (Division provinciale)* ☐ Absolute Jurisdiction / *Juridiction absolue*

Pleads / *Plaide*: ☐ Guilty / *Coupable* ☐ Not Guilty / *Non coupable* ☐ Withdrawn / *Accusation(s) retirée(s)*

Found / *Reconnu(e)*: ☐ Guilty / *Coupable* ☐ Not Guilty / *Non coupable* ☐ In Absentia / *Ex parte*

☐ Absolute Discharge / *Absolution inconditionnelle* ☐ Conditional Discharge / *Absolution sous condition*

Fined $ / *Amende de* ___ & $ / $ *et de* ___ costs. Time to Pay / $ *pour les dépens. Délai de paiement*

or / *ou*

Date of Birth / *Date de naissance*

Day/*Jour*	Mo/*Mois*	Yr/*Année*

Probation for / *Période de probation de*

Exhibits Filed / *Pièces déposées* ☐ Yes / *Oui* ☐ No / *Non*

Sentenced to Imprisonment for / *Peine d'emprisonnement*

CARE OR CONTROL WHILE IMPAIRED, Code, Sec. 253(a)
FAIL TO PROVIDE SAMPLE OF BREATH, Code, Sec. 254(5) (Breathalyzer)
GARDE OU CONTRÔLE AVEC CAPACITÉ AFFAIBLIE Art. 253(a)
DÉFAUT DE FOURNIR UN ÉCHANTILLON D'HALEINE, Art. 254(5) du Code (Alcootest)

Judge/*Juge*

YC 0911 (rev. 05/90)

APPENDIX F

CANADA
PROVINCE OF ONTARIO
PROVINCE DE L'ONTARIO
TORONTO REGION
RÉGION DE TORONTO

Information of ....
Dénonciation de:
of/*de* ....

.... The informant says
(*occupation/profession*) *Le dénonciateur*

that he/she believes on reasonable grounds that
déclare qu'il a des motifs raisonnables de croire que

.... of ....
de

(1) on or about the .... day of .... 20.........., at the Municipality of Metropolitan Toronto, while his/her
le ou vers le *jour de* *à la municipalité de la communauté urbaine de Toronto*
ability to operate a motor vehicle was impaired by alcohol or a drug, operated a motor vehicle, contrary to section 253(a) of the Criminal Code.
a conduit un véhicule à moteur lorsque sa capacité de conduire ce véhicule était affaiblie par l'effet de l'alcool ou d'une drogue, en violation de l'alinéa 253(a) du Code criminel.

(2) and further that
et en outre que

on or about the .... day of .... 20.........., at the Municipality of Metropolitan Toronto
le ou vers le *jour de* *à la municipalité de la communauté urbaine de Toronto*
operated a motor vehicle, having consumed alcohol in such a quantity that the concentration thereof in his/her blood exceeded 80 milligrams of alcohol in 100 millilitres of blood, contrary to section 253(b) of the Criminal Code.
a conduit un véhicule à moteur lorsqu'il avait consommé une quantité d'alcool telle que son alcoolémie dépassait quatre-vingts milligrammes d'alcool par cent millilitres de sang, en violation de l'alinéa 253 (b) du Code Criminel.

Sworn before me at the Municipality of Metropolitan Toronto
Assermenté devant moi à la municipalité de la communauté urbaine de Toronto

in the Toronto Region this ....
dans la région de Toronto le

day of .... 20 ....,
jour de

....
A Justice of the Peace in and for the Province of Ontario/*Juge de paix dans et pour la province de l'Ontario*

....
Informant/*Dénonciateur*

☐ Appearance Notice / *Citation à comparaître*
☐ Promise to Appear / *Promesse de comparaître*
☐ Recognizance for / *Engagement pour le* .... 20 ....
☐ Confirmed on / *Confirmé(e) le* .... 20 .... J.P.

Date

Crown Elects to Proceed / *Choix du poursuivant*: ☐ Summarily / *Procédure sommaire* ☐ By Indictment / *Acte d'accusation* ☐ Summary Conviction (Offence(s) / *Infraction(s) punissable(s) sur déclaration de culpabilité par procédure sommaire*

Accused Elects Trial by / *Choix de l'accusé(e)*: ☐ Judge (General Division) / *Juge seul (Division générale)* ☐ Judge and Jury / *Juge et jury*

☐ Discharged - / *Libéré(e)* ☐ Committed - / *Renvoyé(e) à procès* - ☐ Ordered to Stand Trial - / *Astreint(e) en jugement* - ☐ With Consent of Accused and Prosecutor, / *Avec le consentement de l'accusé(e) et du poursuivant*

Without Taking or Recording - / *Sans recueillir ou consigner* - ☐ Any Evidence (or) / *de preuve (ou)* - ☐ Further Evidence / *de preuve supplémentaire*

Bail $ / *Cautionnement* .... $

☐ Accused Elects Trial by a Judge (Provincial Division) / *L'accusé(e) choisit d'être jugé (Division provinciale)*
☐ Absolute Jurisdiction / *Juridiction absolue* ....

Pleads / *Plaide*: ☐ Guilty / *Coupable* ☐ Not Guilty / *Non coupable* ☐ Withdrawn / *Accusation(s) retirée(s)*

Found / *Reconnu(e)*: ☐ Guilty / *Coupable* ☐ Not Guilty / *Non coupable* ☐ In Absentia / *Ex parte*

☐ Absolute Discharge / *Absolution inconditionnelle* ☐ Conditional Discharge / *Absolution sous condition*

Fined $ .... & $ .... costs. Time to Pay
Amende de *$ et de* *$ pour les dépens. Délai de paiement*

or ....
ou

Date of Birth / *Date de naissance*

Day/Jour	Mo./Mois	Yr./Année

Probation for ....
Période de probation de

Exhibits Filed / *Pièces déposées* ☐ Yes / *Oui* ☐ No / *Non*

Sentenced to Imprisonment for ....
Peine d'emprisonnement

IMPAIRED DRIVING, Code, Sec. 253(a)
DRIVE WHILE OVER 80 mgs, Code, Sec. 253(b)
CAPACITÉ DE CONDUIRE AFFAIBLIE Art. 253(a)
CONDUIRE LORSQUE L'ALCOOLÉMIE DÉPASSE 80 mgs Art. 253(b) du Code

....
Judge/*Juge*

YC 0883 (rev. 10/90)

CANADA
PROVINCE OF ONTARIO
PROVINCE DE L'ONTARIO
TORONTO REGION
RÉGION DE TORONTO

Information of
Dénonciation de

of/*de*

(occupation/*profession*)

The informant says
Le dénonciateur

that he/she believes on reasonable grounds that
déclare qu'il a des motifs raisonnables de croire que

of
de

(1) on or about the .... day of .... 20...... at the Municipality of Metropolitan Toronto, in the Toronto Region
le ou vers le .... *jour de* .... *dans la municipalité de la communauté urbaine de Toronto, dans la région de Toronto,*

while his/her ability to operate a motor vehicle was impaired by alcohol or a drug, operated a motor vehicle, and did thereby cause bodily harm to ....
a conduit un véhicule à moteur alors que sa capacité de conduire ce véhicule était affaiblie par l'effet de l'alcool ou d'une drogue, et a causé

.... contrary to the Criminal Code, section 255(2)
ainsi des lésions corporelles à .... *en violation du paragraphe 255(2) du Code criminel*

Sworn before me at the Municipality of Metropolitan Toronto, in the Toronto Region
Assermenté devant moi dans la municipalité de la communauté urbaine de Toronto, dans la région de Toronto,

this ....
le

day of .... 20 ....
jour de

A Justice of the Peace in and for the Province of Ontario/*Juge de paix dans et pour la province de l'Ontario*

Informant/*Dénonciateur*

☐ Appearance Notice / *Citation à comparaître*
☐ Promise to Appear / *Promesse de comparaître*
☐ Recognizance for / *Engagement pour le* 20
☐ Confirmed on / *Confirmé(e) le* .... 20 .... J P

Date

Crown Elects to Proceed / *Choix du poursuivant*: ☐ Summarily / *Procédure sommaire* ☐ By Indictment / *Acte d'accusation* ☐ Summary Conviction (Offence(s) / *Infraction(s) punissable(s) sur déclaration de culpabilité par procédure sommaire*

Accused Elects Trial by / *Choix de l'accusé(e)*: ☐ Judge (General Division) / *Juge seul (Division générale)* ☐ Judge and Jury / *Juge et jury*

☐ Discharged / *Libéré(e)* ☐ Committed / *Renvoyé(e) à procès* ☐ Ordered to Stand Trial / *Astreint(e) en jugement* ☐ With Consent of Accused and Prosecutor / *Avec le consentement de l'accusé(e) et du poursuivant*

Without Taking or Recording / *Sans recueillir ou consigner* ☐ Any Evidence (or) / *de preuve (ou)* ☐ Further Evidence / *de preuve supplémentaire* Bail $ / *Cautionnement* $

☐ Accused Elects Trial by a Judge (Provincial Division) / *L'accusé(e) choisit d'être jugé(e) (Division provinciale)* ☐ Absolute Jurisdiction / *Juridiction absolue*

Pleads / *Plaide*: ☐ Guilty / *Coupable* ☐ Not Guilty / *Non coupable* ☐ Withdrawn / *Accusation(s) retirée(s)*

Found / *Reconnu(e)*: ☐ Guilty / *Coupable* ☐ Not Guilty / *Non coupable* ☐ In Absentia / *Ex parte*

☐ Absolute Discharge / *Absolution inconditionnelle* ☐ Conditional Discharge / *Absolution sous condition*

Fined $ / *Amende de* .... & $ / $ *et de* .... costs Time to Pay / $ *pour les dépens Délai de paiement*

or / *ou*

Date of Birth / *Date de naissance*

Day *Jour*	Mo *Mois*	Yr *Année*

Probation for / *Période de probation de*

Exhibits Filed / *Pièces déposées* ☐ Yes / *Oui* ☐ No / *Non*

Sentenced to Imprisonment for / *Peine d'emprisonnement*

IMPAIRED DRIVING: BODILY HARM, Code, Sec. 255(2)
CAPACITÉ DE CONDUIRE AFFAIBLIE CAUSANT DES LÉSIONS, Art. 255(2) du Code

YC 0914 (rev 05/90)

Judge/*Juge*

APPENDIX F

CANADA
PROVINCE OF ONTARIO
PROVINCE DE L'ONTARIO
TORONTO REGION
RÉGION DE TORONTO

Information of
Dénonciation de

of/*de*

(occupation/*profession*)

The informant says
Le dénonciateur

that he/she believes on reasonable grounds that
déclare qu'il a des motifs raisonnables de croire que

.... of
de

(1) on or about the .... day of .... 20 ....., at the Municipality of Metropolitan Toronto, in the Toronto Region
le ou vers le .... *jour de* .... *dans la municipalité de la communauté urbaine de Toronto, dans la région de Toronto,*
while his/her ability to operate a motor vehicle was impaired by alcohol or a drug, operated a motor vehicle, and did thereby cause the death of ....
a conduit un véhicule à moteur alors que sa capacité de conduire ce véhicule était affaiblie par l'effet de l'alcool ou d'une drogue, causant ainsi la mort de
.... contrary to the Criminal Code, section 255(3)
en violation de l'article 255(3) du Code criminel

Sworn before me at the Municipality of Metropolitan Toronto, in the Toronto Region
Assermenté devant moi dans la municipalité de la communauté urbaine de Toronto, dans la région de Toronto,

this ....
le

day of .... 20 ....
jour de

....
A Justice of the Peace in and for the Province of Ontario/*Juge de paix dans et pour la province de l'Ontario*

....
Informant/*Dénonciateur*

☐ Appearance Notice / *Citation à comparaître* ☐ Promise to Appear / *Promesse de comparaître* ☐ Recognizance for / *Engagement pour le* 20 ☐ Confirmed on / *Confirmé(e) le* 20 J P

Date

Crown Elects to Proceed / *Choix du poursuivant* ☐ Summarily / *Procédure sommaire* ☐ By Indictment / *Acte d'accusation* ☐ Summary Conviction (Offence(s) / *Infraction(s) punissable(s) sur déclaration de culpabilité par procédure sommaire*

Accused Elects Trial by / *Choix de l'accusé(e)* ☐ Judge (General Division) / *Juge seul (Division générale)* ☐ Judge and Jury / *Juge et jury*

☐ Discharged / *Libéré(e)* ☐ Committed - / *Renvoyé(e) à procès* - ☐ Ordered to Stand Trial - / *Astreint(e) en jugement* - ☐ With Consent of Accused and Prosecutor, / *Avec le consentement de l'accusé(e) et du poursuivant*

Without Taking or Recording - / *Sans recueillir ou consigner* - ☐ Any Evidence (or) / *de preuve (ou)* - ☐ Further Evidence / *de preuve supplémentaire* Bail $ / *Cautionnement* $

☐ Accused Elects Trial by a Judge (Provincial Division) / *L'accusé(e) choisit d'être jugé(e) (Division provinciale)* ☐ Absolute Jurisdiction / *Juridiction absolue*

Pleads / *Plaide* ☐ Guilty / *Coupable* ☐ Not Guilty / *Non coupable* ☐ Withdrawn / *Accusation(s) retirée(s)*

Found / *Reconnu(e)* ☐ Guilty / *Coupable* ☐ Not Guilty / *Non coupable* ☐ In Absentia / *Ex parte*

☐ Absolute Discharge / *Absolution inconditionnelle* ☐ Conditional Discharge / *Absolution sous condition*

Fined $ / *Amende de* & $ / $ *et de* costs Time to Pay / $ *pour les dépens* *Délai de paiement*

or / *ou*

Date of Birth / *Date de naissance*

Day/*Jour*	Mo/*Mois*	Yr/*Année*

Probation for / *Période de probation de*

Exhibits Filed / *Pièces déposées* ☐ Yes / *Oui* ☐ No / *Non*

Sentenced to Imprisonment for / *Peine d'emprisonnement*

IMPAIRED DRIVING: DEATH, Code, Sec. 255(3)
CAPACITÉ DE CONDUIRE AFFAIBLIE CAUSANT LA MORT, Art. 255(3) du Code

YC 0915 (rev 05/90)

....
Judge/*Juge*

CANADA
PROVINCE OF ONTARIO
PROVINCE DE L'ONTARIO
TORONTO REGION
RÉGION DE TORONTO

Information of
Dénonciation de
of/*de*

(occupation/*profession*)

The informant says
Le dénonciateur

that he/she believes on reasonable grounds that
déclare qu'il a des motifs raisonnables de croire que

of
de

(1) on or about the .... day of .... 20...., at the Municipality of Metropolitan Toronto, in the Toronto Region
le ou vers le .... *jour de* .... *dans la municipalité de la communauté urbaine de Toronto, dans la région de Toronto,*

without reasonable excuse, failed or refused to comply with a demand made to him/her by a peace officer under section 254(3) of the Criminal Code
a fait défaut ou a refusé, sans excuse raisonnable, d'obtempérer à un ordre que lui avait donné un agent de la paix en vertu de l'article 254(3)

in the circumstances therein mentioned to provide then, or as soon thereafter as is practicable, such samples of his/her blood, under the conditions
du Code criminel, dans les circonstances y mentionnées, de lui fournir immédiatement, ou dès que possible, l'échantillon de sang prévu au paragraphe

referred to in section 254(4) as in the opinion of a qualified medical practitioner/technician referred to in section 254(1) of the Criminal Code are necessary
Cross out inapplicable
254(4) du Code criminel et qui de l'avis d'un médecin ou d'un technicien qualifiés définis à l'article 254(1) du Code criminel était nécessaire pour permettre
biffer les mentions inutiles

to enable a proper analysis to be made in order to determine the concentration, if any, of alcohol in his/her blood, and to accompany the peace officer
de déterminer son alcoolémie et de suivre l'agent de la paix pour que cet échantillon puisse être prélevé, en violation de l'article 254(5) du

for the purpose of enabling such samples to be taken, contrary to section 254(5) of the Criminal Code.
Code criminel.

Sworn before me at the Municipality of Metropolitan Toronto, in the Toronto Region
Assermenté devant moi dans la municipalité de la communauté urbaine de Toronto, dans la région de Toronto,

this ....
le

day of .... 20.......
jour de

....
A Justice of the Peace in and for the Province of Ontario/*Juge de paix dans et pour la province de l'Ontario*

....
Informant/*Dénonciateur*

☐ Appearance Notice / *Citation à comparaître* ☐ Promise to Appear / *Promesse de comparaître* ☐ Recognizance for / *Engagement pour le* 20 ☐ Confirmed on / *Confirmé(e) le* 20 J.P.

Date

Crown Elects to Proceed / *Choix du poursuivant* ☐ Summarily / *Procédure sommaire* ☐ By Indictment / *Acte d'accusation* ☐ Summary Conviction (Offence(s) / *Infraction(s) punissable(s) sur déclaration de culpabilité par procédure sommaire*

Accused Elects Trial by / *Choix de l'accusé(e)* ☐ Judge (General Division) / *Juge seul (Division générale)* ☐ Judge and Jury / *Juge et jury*

☐ Discharged / *Libéré(e)* ☐ Committed / *Renvoyé(e) à procès* ☐ Ordered to Stand Trial / *Astreint(e) en jugement* ☐ With Consent of Accused and Prosecutor / *Avec le consentement de l'accusé(e) et du poursuivant*

Without Taking or Recording / *Sans recueillir ou consigner* ☐ Any Evidence (or) / *de preuve (ou)* ☐ Further Evidence / *de preuve supplémentaire* Bail $ / *Cautionnement* $

☐ Accused Elects Trial by a Judge (Provincial Division) / *L'accusé(e) choisit d'être jugé(e) (Division provinciale)* ☐ Absolute Jurisdiction / *Juridiction absolue*

Pleads / *Plaide* ☐ Guilty / *Coupable* ☐ Not Guilty / *Non coupable* ☐ Withdrawn / *Accusation(s) retirée(s)*

Found / *Reconnu(e)* ☐ Guilty / *Coupable* ☐ Not Guilty / *Non coupable* ☐ In Absentia / *Ex parte*

☐ Absolute Discharge / *Absolution inconditionnelle* ☐ Conditional Discharge / *Absolution sous condition*

Fined $ / *Amende de* & $ / *$ et de* costs Time to Pay / *$ pour les dépens. Délai de paiement*

or / *ou*

Date of Birth / *Date de naissance*

Day/*Jour*	Mo/*Mois*	Yr/*Année*

Probation for / *Période de probation de*

Exhibits Filed / *Pièces déposées* ☐ Yes / *Oui* ☐ No / *Non*

Sentenced to Imprisonment for / *Peine d'emprisonnement*

FAIL TO PROVIDE BLOOD SAMPLE, Code, Sec. 254(5)
DÉFAUT DE FOURNIR UN ÉCHANTILLON DE SANG, Art. 254(5) du Code

....
Judge/*Juge*

YC 0916 (rev 05/90)

Appendix G

Alcohol Influence Report

Ontario Provincial Police

Alcohol Influence Report

Occurrence / Case File Number

General

Location of interview			Time / date of interview Hrs. D M Y	Qualified technician	Badge no.	Det.
Arresting officer	Badge no.	Det.	Time / date delivered Hrs. D M Y	Presented by	Badge no.	Det.
Name of accused (Surname)	(G1)		(G2)	Driver's licence no.		
Address - Street / P.O. Box no.				Date of Birth (D, M, Y)		Age
City /Town	Province		Postal code	Sex	Height	Weight

Details of Arrest

Time of Offence / Accident Hrs.	Location of offence	Was caution given? ☐ Yes ☐ No	Was caution understood? ☐ Yes ☐ No
Time of Arrest Hrs.	Location of arrest ☐ Same as offence, or:		

Reason for arrest
☐ Impaired operation ☐ Fail A.L.E.R.T.
☐ Care or control ☐ Other, *(Specify)*:

Constitutional rights given by - Name | Rank

Was demand given? ☐ Yes ☐ No	Time of demand	Demand given by - Name	Rank

Interview *(Local practice may require caution [illegible])*

A. 1. Were you operating a vehicle / vessel? ☐ Yes ☐ No
2. At the time of the accident? ☐ Yes ☐ No
3. What time did the accident happen?
4. How long after the accident occurred did the first officer arrive?
5. When were you last operating your vehicle / vessel?

B. 1. Where were you going?
2. Where did you start from?
3. When did you start?
4. What time is it now? | Actual time

C. 1. Have you been drinking? ☐ Yes ☐ No
2. What have you been drinking?
3. What quantities?
4. Where were you drinking?
5. What time did you start?
6. What time did you have your last drink?
7. What was your last drink?
8. How long to consume the last drink?

D. 1. Have you been drinking since the accident? ☐ Yes ☐ No
2. What have you been drinking since the accident?
3. What quantities since the accident?
4. Where were you drinking since the accident?

Personal Health

Are you ill? ☐ Yes ☐ No
Are you taking medicine / pill? ☐ Yes ☐ No
If yes, specify medication
When was last dosage (time)? Hrs.

Did your doctor give any warning of effects of driving after taking this medication? ☐ Yes ☐ No
Did your doctor give you any warning about consuming alcohol while taking this medication? ☐ Yes ☐ No

Do you have any physical handicap(s)? ☐ No ☐ Yes, *(Describe)*:
How much sleep have you had in the previous 24 hours?
Are you injured? ☐ No ☐ Yes, *(Describe)*:

Is there any reason you are not able to provide a breath sample?

Remarks, additional observations

LE 061 (Rev. 05/90)

Observations *Check (✓) words describing condition of accused. Add words where necessary.*

Breath (Odour of an alcoholic beverage) ☐ Absent ☐ Present | Hair colour, style | ☐ Beard ☐ Moustache | Face colour ☐ Appears normal | ☐ Tanned ☐ Pale | ☐ Flushed ☐ Red

Eyes - Colour | Condition ☐ Appear normal ☐ Watery ☐ Glassy ☐ Bloodshot | Wearing glasses / contacts ☐ Yes ☐ No

Any visible scar(s) / mark(s) / injury ☐ Yes ☐ No | Speech ☐ Good ☐ Fair ☐ Slurred ☐ Stuttering ☐ Incoherent ☐ Accent

Clothes - Type | Condition ☐ Orderly ☐ Disarranged ☐ Soiled | Footwear - Type | Condition

Attitude ☐ Polite ☐ Cooperative ☐ Talkative ☐ Carefree ☐ Abusive ☐ Other | Unusual actions ☐ Hiccuping ☐ Belching ☐ Vomiting ☐ Fighting ☐ Crying ☐ Other

Coordination Tests: ☐ **Demonstrated**

A. Balance ☐ Sure ☐ Fair ☐ Swaying ☐ Unsure ☐ Unsteady ☐ Falling ☐ In a circle ☐ Side to side ☐ Back and forth

B. Finger to nose - Right ☐ Sure ☐ Hesitant ☐ Missed | Left ☐ Sure ☐ Hesitant ☐ Missed | Balance during test ☐ Sure ☐ Swaying ☐ Falling ☐ Unsteady

C. Walking (Heel to toe) ☐ Sure ☐ Swaying ☐ Unsteady ☐ Stumbling ☐ Lost balance | Turning ☐ Sure ☐ Swaying ☐ Unsteady ☐ Staggering ☐ Stumbling ☐ Falling

D. Others

Appeared to understand tests required? ☐ Yes ☐ No | Effects of alcohol ☐ Apparently none ☐ Slight ☐ Obvious ☐ Extreme | Conclusion - Ability to operate vehicle / vessel ☐ Apparently fit ☐ Impaired by the consumption of alcohol

☐ Accused refused | ☐ Demand explained and accused aware of consequences of refusal | Time of refusal Hrs. | Reason for refusal

Charge(s) laid

Subject knew of charge(s) ☐ Yes ☐ No | Comments

Accused returned to | Officer's name | Time Hrs.

Remarks, additional observations

Appendix H

Blood Alcohol Content Report

Alan D. Gold
Professional Corporation
Barristers

Alan D. Gold, B.Sc., LL.B.*
Vanessa G. Arsenault, B.A., M.Sc., LL.B.
R. Matthew Barteaux, B.Sc., LLB., LL.M.

Telephone: (416) 368-1726
Facsimile: (416) 368-6811
E-mail: adgold@on.aibn.com

*Certified by the Law Society as a Specialist in Criminal Litigation

SENT BY FACSIMILE

May 16, 2007

G.J. Kupferschmidt
Forcon Forensic Consulting Services
2046 Oxford Avenue
Oakville, Ontario
L6H 4K7

Dear Mr. Kupferschmidt,

Re:	**Toxicology Report**
Our File #:	**5627**
Charges:	**"Over 80/Impaired"**

I would like to retain you to prepare a Blood Alcohol Content Report based on the following information:

Personal Information:

Sex:	Male
Height:	5'9"
Weight:	180 lbs.
DOB:	April 4, 1951
Date of Incident:	January 16-17, 2007

Drinking Pattern on Day of Incident:

Assume this person woke up at approximately 8:00 a.m. after about 5 hours of sleep. This person had cereal for breakfast and had bacon and eggs for lunch around noon. Assume this person did not have anything else to eat that day. This person worked from 9:00 a.m. to 3:00 p.m. that day.

Assume that this person arrived at a bar that night at approximately 10:00 p.m. and ordered his first alcoholic drink of the day. From approximately 10:00 p.m. to 1:00 a.m. assume this individual consumed a total of: one beer, one (possibly two) rye & gingers and one shooter. This person first consumed the bottled Labatts Blue beer. Assume about an hour later he consumed a (single shot) rye and ginger-ale. This person may have consumed another (single shot) rye and ginger-ale, however, he cannot be certain. Before this individual left the bar he had a single-shot shooter. He cannot recall the type of shooter, however, he recalls that he consumed the shooter as a toast with three other people approximately 50 minutes after his last rye and ginger.

Assume this person left the bar at approximately 1:00 a.m., approximately 15 minutes after he finished the shooter. This person turned right out of the club parking lot, turned right on Melanie Drive and drove down Melanie Drive for about 1000 ft. He then turned left onto Steeles Avenue. He then drove from Bramalea Road, past Dixie and was just about to turn on to highway 410 south when he was stopped by the police at approximately 2:05 a.m. At 3:46 a.m. this person was given his first Intoxilyzer test and registered a BAL of .118 mgs/100mL. Assume that at 4:05 a.m. this person was given his second test and registered a BAL of .116 mgs/mL.

Summary of Police Evidence:

I have attached a copy of the police synopsis as well as the Intoxilyzer readings. Please note that these items have been edited to conceal the client's identity.

Should you require any additional information please contact my office.

Yours truly,

Alan D. Gold

APPENDIX H

FORCON
Forensic Consulting Services
a division of G. Kupferschmidt Consulting Services Limited

May 18, 2007

FILE#: 7D5-145-1
Faxed

Alan D. Gold
Professional Corporation
Barristers
Suite 210
20 Adelaide Street East
Toronto, Ontario
M5C 2T6

Attn: Mr. A. Gold.

Dear _______________:

Re: FILE #5627

At your request, a report was prepared based upon the information provided.

DATA:

1) *Physical Description:* Male, 5'9"; and 180 pounds.
2) *Ate* breakfast and lunch but *no* dinner
3) Consumed one (1) bottle of Labatt Blue Beer, one (1) or two (2) single shots of rye with ginger ale, and one (1) unidentified shooter drink between 10:00 PM and 1:00 AM
4) Stopped by the police at 2:05 AM
5) Breath Tests: Intoxilyer® 5000C

   3:46 AM – 118 mg/100 ml
   4:06 AM – 116 mg/100 ml

ASSUMPTIONS:

1) It was assumed that your client was alcohol-free prior to the stated consumption start-time
2) Bottle of Labatt Blue Beer: 341 ml (12 oz) @ 5%
3) Single shots of rye could contain 1.0 – 1.5 ounces of spirits (40%). The larger quantity was assumed for this report.
4) Shooters could contain 20-40% alcohol by volume and are usually 1.0 ounce in size. For the purposes of this report, the shooter was assumed to contain 1.0 ounce of spirits (40%).

CONVENTIONS:

1) BAC: Blood alcohol concentration.
2) Mg/100 ml. Milligrams of ethyl alcohol in 100 millilitres of blood.
3) Beverage Alcohol Concentrations: Percent by volume (v/v) unless otherwise stated.

4) Ounces: Fluid ounces.

CALCULATIONS:

1) Alcohol absorption, distribution and elimination are simultaneous processes, commencing when consumption begins.
2) Based upon empirical considerations your client, weighing 180 pounds, would have theoretical BAC elevations as reported in **Table 1**.

TABLE 1

Beverage Type	**BAC Elevations (mg/100ml)**
Per Beer (12 oz @ 5%)	23.8
Per Ounce of Spirits (40%)	15.9

BAC elevations are theoretical values since they only take into account the absorption and distribution of alcoholic beverages but do not reflect any elimination of alcohol from the body.

3) Empirical studies have shown that the elimination rates encountered in a given population will fall into the range of 10-20 mg/100 ml/hr with the vast majority of individuals having an elimination rate within the range of 13-18 mg/100 ml/hr. The average elimination rate is considered to be 15 mg/100 ml/hr. Only about 1% of the drinking population would have a BAC in the range of 10-11 mg/100 ml.

4) Based upon the consumption of one (1) beer (12 oz @ 5%), 3.0 ounces of rye (40%) and 1.0 ounce of shooter beverage (40%) between 10:00 PM and 1:00 AM, your client's BAC at 3:46 AM should have been 0-29 mg/100 ml of blood, when consideration is given to the universally accepted elimination rate range of 10-20 mg/100 ml/hr. At 2:05 AM, his BAC should *not* have exceeded 5-46 mg/100 ml of blood.

   Using the *average* elimination rate of 15 mg/100 ml/hr, your client's BAC at 3:46 AM should have been negligible. At 2:05 AM, his BAC should not have exceeded 26 mg/100 ml of blood.

   The values reported above represent the highest possible readings, since they assume the fasting state and completion of the absorption phase at the relevant times. If this had not been the case, his readings would have been lower.

5) In order to generate a reading of 118 mg/100 ml of blood at 3:46 AM, it would have been necessary for your client to consume an *additional* quantity of alcohol, equal to that listed in **Table II**. The following amounts assume that consumption commenced at 10:00 PM and that there was continuous elimination of alcohol between that time and 3:46 AM, the following morning.

TABLE II

	Elimination Rate		
	10 mg/100 ml/hr	**15 mg/100 ml/hr**	**20 mg/100 ml/hr**
Beers (12 oz @ 5%) Spirits (40%)	3.7 beers 5.6 ounces	4.9 beers 7.4 ounces	6.1 beers 9.2 ounces

6) Assuming the breath readings to be correct and that the required amount of alcohol had been consumed, your client's BAC at 2:05 AM could have been as high as 118-152 mg/100 ml of blood. This assumes that he had achieved his highest BAC by 2:05 AM and that no alcohol was consumed thereafter. The lower end of this range takes into account the possibility for a plateau, which could exist for up to 2 hours after last consumption. The higher end presumes that his BAC was decreasing at a rate of up to 20 mg/100 ml/hr between the time of first observation and the time of the first breath test. Also, if the breath readings were presumed to be correct, it would have been necessary for him to consume the additional alcohol listed in **Table II**. Without any information concerning the consumption of the extra alcohol and the exact consumption pattern one must also consider the possibility that his BAC was climbing at 2:05 AM and hence less that the above reported range at the time of driving.

COMMENTS:

1) Based upon the information provided, either the breath readings were incorrect or your client underestimated the quantity of alcohol consumed.
2) The Intoxilyzer®5000C Test Record has been reviewed. No errors or omissions were noted. Approved instruments are generally reliable and accurate devices, but they are not necessarily infallible.

This report is provided for your consideration.

Yours truly,

G.J. Kupferschmidt B.Sc., M.Sc., M.C.I.C., C.Chem.
CJK/cg

Appendix I

Driver Record Search

Ministry of Transportation / Ministère des Transports — Licensing and Control Branch / Direction des permis et de l'immatriculation
Ontario

Application for Driver Record Search
Demande de recherches au dossier d'un conducteur

Application Date / *Date de la demande* Y/A M D/J

To be picked up / *L'auteur de la demande passera prendre la réponse*

To be mailed / *À expédier par la poste*

Your File No. / *N° de votre dossier*

Telephone No. / *N° de téléphone*

Name and Address of Individual / Company
Nom et adresse de la personne / compagnie

State the reason why this information is required.
Donnez la raison pour laquelle vous désirez ces renseignements.

Head Office Use Only
Réservé au bureau principal
Name of Driver

Ministry Use Only / *Réservé au ministère*
Personal Identification Viewed (State name of document)

Report No. | Office No. | Fee Paid $

Account No.

Please provide all known information.
Veuillez fournir tous les renseignements connus .

Driver's Licence No. / *N° du permis de conduire*

Date of Birth / *Date de naissance* Y/A M D/J

Sex / *Sexe*

Age, if birthdate unknown / *Âge, si la date de naissance est inconnue*

Driver's Name / *Nom du conducteur*
Last Name, First Name and Middle Initial / *Nom de famille, prénom et initiale*

Street Number and Name or Lot, Concession and Twp. / *N° et rue ou lot, concession, canton*

Apt. No. / *App. n°*

City, Town or Village / *Ville ou village*

Postal Code / *Code postal*

Previous Address / *Adresse précédente*

Reason for Return of Application
Raison du renvoi de la demande

Request for Search / *Demande de recherches* Check appropriate box(es) / *Cochez la ou les cases appropriées*

☐ Driver (complete driving record covering a three year period)
Conducteur (Veuillez fournir un dossier du conducteur complet pour une période de trois ans)

☐ Driver (while driving Commercial Motor Vehicles only - C.V.O.R.)
Conducteur de véhicules utilitaires seulement (I.U.V.U.)

☐ Certified copy of each search for legal purposes
Copie certifiée conforme de chaque recherche à des fins juridiques

Fees / *Droits*
$ 12.00 for each search request.
$ 6.00 for copy of each document.
$ 6.00 additional for each certified copy.

12 $ pour chaque demande de recherches.
6 $ pour chaque copie d'un document.
6 $ de plus pour chaque copie certifiée.

Please make cheque or money order payable to the Minister of Finance. / *Libellez les chèques ou mandats à l'ordre du ministre des Finances.*

Remarks / *Remarques*

The Ministry may decline to supply information unless satisfied that it is required in connection with a matter involving a driver.
Le ministère peut refuser de fournir les renseignements demandés s'il estime que la demande ne se rapporte pas à une question relative au conducteur.

Applicant's Signature
Signature de l'auteur(e) de la demande

Send application with fees to:
Envoyez les demandes et les droits au :

Ministry of Transportation
Data Management, East Bldg.
2680 Keele Street
Downsview, Ontario M3M 3E6

Ministère des Transports
Gestion des données
2680, rue Keele, édifice est
Downsview (Ontario) M3M 3E6

SR-LC-34 96-11

Index

A.L.E.R.T., see APPROVED SCREENING DEVICE

ALCOHOL INFLUENCE REPORT, see APPENDIX G

APPROVED INSTRUMENT, see APPENDIX C

APPROVED SCREENING DEVICE
Conduct of test
  calibration 4.5.2
  machine, type of 4.5.1
  operation of 4.5.3
Demand
  ''forthwith'' 4.2
  ''reasonable suspicion of alcohol in body'' 4.1
Malfunction, evidence of, 7.8
Outcome of test
  fail 4.6.3
  pass 4.6.1
  warn 4.6.2
Refusal 4.4
Right to counsel 4.1.1, 4.3
Roadside questioning and testing 4.1.1
See also APPENDIX C

BILL C-2, 7.8

BLOOD ALCOHOL CONTENT REPORT, see APPENDIX H

BLOOD TESTS
Conduct of test 6.6
Demand
  proper 6.2
  ''forthwith or as soon as practicable'' 6.3
Reasonable grounds 6.1
Refusal 6.5
Warrant to obtain 6.7

BREATHALYZER TESTS
Conduct of test
  ''qualified technician'' 5.5

"approved instrument" 5.5
Demand
"forthwith or as soon as practicable" 5.2
Reasonable grounds 5.1
Refusal 5.4

CARE OR CONTROL
Proof
Admissions 10.2
General 10.1
Ownership 10.4
Witnesses 10.3

CAUSATION, 11.1

CERTIFICATES AND NOTICE OF, see APPENDIX E

CHARGES (FORMS), see APPENDIX F

CHARTER ISSUES
Arrest, unlawful, 13.6.2
Arbitrary detention, 4.5.1,13.6.3
Abuse of process, 13.6.4
Bill C-2, re, 7.8
Counsel, right to, see RIGHT TO COUNSEL
Cruel and unusual punishment, 13.6.5
Disclosure, 7.6, 13.6.1
Licence suspensions, administrative, respecting, 14.4.2
Presumptions of alcoholic content, re, 7.8
Searches, unlawful, 4.5.1, 7.6, 13.6.2
Sentences, unconstitutional, 13.6.5
Tackling Violent Crime Act, re, 7.8

CONDITIONAL SENTENCE, 14.3

COORDINATION TESTS, 4.1.1, 7.4, 7.8, Appendix C

CRIMINAL CODE, RELATED PROVISIONS, see APPENDIX C and 7.8

DEFENCE, THE, see also, ELEMENTS OF THE OFFENCE TO BE ESTABLISHED BY PROSECUTION
Charter issues
arrest, unlawful, 13.6.2

arbitrary detention, 4.5.1, 13.6.3
abuse of process, 13.6.4
counsel, right to, see RIGHT TO COUNSEL
cruel and unusual punishment, 13.6.5
disclosure, 7.6, 13.6.1
searches, unlawful, 4.5.1, 7.6, 13.6.2
sentences, unconstitutional, 13.6.5
Disproving an element of the offence
''Carter'' defence 7.8,13.1.2(b)
''last drink'' defence 13.1.2(a)
Evidence to the contrary 7.8, 13.2
Expert evidence, advance notice of, 13.5
Expert evidence in writing, practice tip, 13.5
General 13.1
Independent blood sample analysis 13.4
Post-driving consumption 13.3

DRIVER'S LICENCE, SUSPENSION OF, 14.4.2, APPENDIX D

DRIVER RECORD SEARCH, see APPENDIX I

DRIVING (OPERATION)
Proof
admissions 9.1
ownership 9.3
witnesses 9.2

DRIVING PROHIBITION ORDERS, 14.4.1

DRUG EVALUATION OFFICERS, 7.8, Appendix C

DRUG-IMPAIRED DRIVING, 4.1.1, 5.1, 7.8, Appendix C

ELEMENTS OF THE OFFENCE TO BE ESTABLISHED BY PROSECUTION 11, 13.1.1

EVALUATION OF IMPAIRED OPERATION (DRUGS AND ALCOHOL) REGULATIONS, see APPENDIX C

HIGHWAY TRAFFIC ACT (ONTARIO), see APPENDIX D

IGNITION INTERLOCK DEVICE, 14.4.3

IMPAIRMENT, PROOF OF
Accident, involvement in 7.2

Admissibility of certificate, 7.8, 7.9.1
Admission 7.1
Approved screening device, failure of 7.7
Bill C-2 and, 7.8
Blood alcohol readings 7.9
  material time 7.9.1(b)
Blood test 7.9.2
  expert testimony relating back 7.9.2(a)
  material time 7.9.2(b)
    presumption back 7.8, 7.9.2(a)(i)
Breathalyzer readings 7.9.1
  expert testimony relating back 7.9.1(a)(ii)
  material time 7.9.1(a)
  presumption back 7.8, 7.9.1(a)(i)
Driving, nature of 7.2
Drug evaluation demand, 7.8, Appendix C
General 7
Physical symptoms
  eyes 7.3.1
  face 7.3.2
  feet, unsteady 7.3.4
  odour of alcohol 7.3.3
  police evidence, 7.3.6
  speech 7.3.5
Physical tests 4.1.1, 7.4, 7.8, Appendix C
Police officer, opinion of 7.5
  disparate police evidence, 7.3.6
Regulations re Appendix C
Videotapes 7.6

INITIAL INTERVIEW
Documents 2.3
Future obligations of client 2.3
General 2.1
Information checklist 2.2
Record of information 2.2, Appendix A

MOTOR VEHICLE
Defined 12

MOTOR VEHICLE ACT (BRITISH COLUMBIA), see APPENDIX C

"OVER '80"
Proof

Blood test readings 8.2
expert testimony relating back 8.2.1.(b)
material time 8.2.1
presumption back 8.2.1(a)
Breathalyzer readings 8.1
expert testimony relating back 8.1.1(b)
material time 8.1.1
presumption back 7.8, 8.1.1(a)

POLICE
Arresting officer, conversation with 1.6, 4.1.1
Physical coordination testing by, 4.1.1, 7.4, 7.8, Appendix C
Roadside questioning by 4.1.1

PREPARATION
Accident report 3.8
Charge(s) 3.5
Disclosure 3.6
Driving record 3.7
Elements of the offence, proof of 3.10
Examine documentation 3.1
Interview
witness 3.2
counsel 3.3
Toxicologist's report 3.4

RIGHT TO COUNSEL
Admissions, and, 9.1, 10.2
Approved screening device
generally, 4.3
proper machine required, 4.5.1
Blood tests 6.4
Breathalyzer tests
counsel of choice, right to, 5.3.5
duty counsel, right to information concerning, 5.3.1
duty to hold off where counsel unavailable, 5.3.3
exclusion of evidence, 5.3.2
generally, 5.3
legal aid, right to information concerning, 5.3.1
waiver of right, 5.3.4
Roadside questioning, and 4.1.1

REFUSAL
Advice regarding 1.5.3

Breathalyzer 5.4
Blood test 6.5

SENTENCING
Factual considerations 14.1.1, 14.1.2
Curative discharge 14.2
Driving prohibition orders
Criminal Code order, 14.4.1
ignition interlock device programs, 14.4.3
provincial licence suspension, 14.4.2
Forfeiture of automobile, 14.7
Ignition interlock device programs, 14.4.3
Legislation, see Appendix D and 7.8
Penalty
conditional sentence, 14.3
driving prohibition, 14.4
Criminal Code order, 14.4.1
ignition interlock device programs, 14.4.3
provincial licence suspension, 14.4.2
fine, 14.1
forfeiture of automobile, 14.7
imprisonment, 14.1
unconstitutional, 13.6.5
Stay pending appeal 14.7
Unconstitutional, 13.6.5
Where bodily harm or death is caused, 14.1.2

SUSPENSION, DRIVER'S LICENCE, see ALBERTA TRAFFIC SAFETY ACT, BRITISH COLUMBIA MOTOR VEHICLE ACT, AND ONTARIO HIGHWAY TRAFFIC ACT, IN APPENDIX D

TACKLING VIOLENT CRIME ACT, 7.8

TELEPHONE CALL, see TELEPHONE INTERVIEW

TELEPHONE INTERVIEW, see also INITIAL INTERVIEW
Advice
intoxication, signs of, 1.5.5
medical samples, 1.5.4
reasonable and probable grounds, 1.5.2
refusal to blow, 1.5.3
release, after, 1.5.6
right to refuse 1.5.1
two hour limit 1.5.2

Information, initial 1.4
Intoxication, signs of 1.5.5
Notes
  lawyer 1.2
  client 1.5.7
Privacy, requirement of 1.3
Release, after 1.5.6
Structuring the call 1.1

TRAFFIC SAFETY ACT (ALBERTA), see APPENDIX D

VIDEOTAPE EVIDENCE
Charter, and
  consent to videotaping 7.6
  surreptitious videotaping 7.6
  videotaping as "search and seizure" 7.6
Disclosure of 3.6
use by defence 3.6, 7.6